James Joyce

JAMES JOYCE

THE YEARS OF GROWTH

1882–1915

A BIOGRAPHY BY

PETER COSTELLO

PANTHEON BOOKS • NEW YORK

All rights reserved under International and Pan-American Copyright Conventions. Published in the United States by Pantheon Books, a division of Random House, Inc., New York. Originally published in Great Britain by Kyle Cathie Ltd., Publishers, London in 1992.

Grateful acknowledgment is made to the following for permission to reprint previously published material:

Penguin Books USA Inc.: Excerpts from *Exiles* by James Joyce. Copyright 1918 by B. W. Huebsch, renewed 1946 by Nora Joyce. Notes Copyright 1951, renewed © 1979 by Viking Penguin Inc. Excerpts from *Letters of James Joyce, Volume One* by James Joyce, edited by Stuart Gilbert. Copyright © 1957, 1966 by The Viking Press, renewed © 1985 by Viking Penguin Inc. Excerpts from *The Letters of James Joyce, Volume Two* by James Joyce, edited by Richard Ellmann. Copyright © 1966 by F. Lionel Munro, as Administrator of the Estate of James Joyce. Excerpts from *Critical Writings of James Joyce* by James Joyce, edited by Ellsworth Mason and Richard Ellmann. Copyright © 1959 by Harriet Weaver and F. Lionel Munro, as Administrators c.t.a. by the Estate of James Joyce. Reprinted by permission of Viking Penguin, a division of Penguin Books USA Inc.

Random House, Inc.: Excerpts from *Ulysses* by James Joyce. Copyright 1934 and renewed 1962 by Lucia & George Joyce. Reprinted by permission of Random House, Inc.

The Society of Authors: Excerpts from *Stephen Hero* by James Joyce. Copyright 1944 by the Estate of James Joyce. Reprinted by permission of the Society of Authors as the literary representative of the Estate of James Joyce.

Library of Congress Cataloging-in-Publication Data

Costello, Peter.
James Joyce: the years of growth, 1882–1915 / Peter Costello.
p.   cm.
Includes bibliographical references and index.
ISBN 0-679-42201-3
1. Joyce, James, 1882–1941—Biography.   2. Novelists, Irish—20th century—Biography.   I. Title.
PR6019.09Z52742   1993
823'.912—dc20
[B]   92–21496

Manufactured in the United States of America

First American Edition

9 8 7 6 5 4 3 2 1

For Mary
… remembering Paris
in the summer and the winter …

The superficial inducement, the exotic, the picturesque has an effect only on the foreigner.

To portray a city, a native must have other, deeper motives – motives of one who travels into the past instead of into the distance.

A native's book about his city will always be related to memoirs: the writer has not spent his childhood there in vain.

Walter Benjamin

In the case of James Joyce we have a series of books, two of which at least are so autobiographical in appearance that further study of the man and his background seems not only suggested by our own inquisitiveness, but almost expected by the author himself.

We want to know who are the originals of his characters, and what were the origins of his episodes, so that we may unravel the web of memory and invention and discover how far and in what ways the crude material has been transformed.

Our interest extends, therefore, inevitably and justifiably, to Joyce's family, to his friends, and to every detail of the topography and the life of Dublin, the Dublin of his childhood, adolescence and young manhood.

T.S. Eliot

'O, rocks!' she said. 'Tell us in plain words.'

Ulysses

So Daedalus designed his winding maze;
And as one entered it, only a wary mind
Could find an exit to the world again –
Such was the cleverness of that strange arbour.
Ovid, *Metamorphoses* (viii)
translated by Horace Gregory
(Copyright © 1958 The Viking Press)

CONTENTS

James
Joyce

PREFACE

Anyone setting out to write about James Joyce today should in all conscience provide some explanation of his purpose. This is especially true for an Irish writer on Joyce.

There has already been an authorized biography (by Herbert Gorman), an academic biography (by Richard Ellmann), a popular life (by Stan Gébler Davies) and several short lives (by the present writer amongst others). Joyce's wife, Nora, has herself been the subject of a long biography (by the British journalist Brenda Maddox) and books by family and friends also exist. Critical and exegetical works are as the stars in heaven.

So it is generally supposed that after fifty years of diligent research, especially by American scholars, little remains to be learnt about Joyce's life. The facts are generally agreed upon; now all that is left are the congenial pleasures of critical interpretation.

This, as I hope to show, is not the case.

I do not believe that there can be such a thing as a definitive biography, especially of a writer as protean as Joyce. Each biographer merely provides a version of the writer's life, as it appears to him in the context of his own day and his view of the writer's time. Each new version provides further definition to parts of a complex picture, fresh aspects of which are revealed all the time. Nevertheless it remains true that there are things we cannot know, and this ignorance affects what we write. Biography remains essentially a form of higher fiction.

The aims of the present book are limited. Although it contains a large amount of new material which will surprise the specialist, it is intended for the ordinary reader of James Joyce who enjoys his

1

works, the common reader who is after all the true audience for literature. I believe that such a reader wishes to learn about the connections between the writer's life and his creations. In Joyce's case these connections are of paramount interest and importance, for few modern writers have so completely made over the facts of their lives to the fictions of art.

The book covers only the author's early years: it begins and ends with his arrival in Zürich in 1915. These are the years that provided most of the materials for Joyce's books, and during which the orientation of his mind and the facility of his art were established.

Joyce's life was dominated by an almost religious idea of Exile and the Kingdom, of his own flight and the matter of Ireland. Here, the emphasis is less on the Exile than on the Kingdom, on his Dublin life as against the experience in Europe. In this regard it is important to realize that his literary predilections are Irish and European. Though reared and well-read in the British literary tradition, he cannot easily be annexed to it; nor to the American tradition, of which he read very little and cared less.

Even the most devoted Joyceans will be in for a few shocks in reading this book. I have tried everywhere to supplement the patchy record of this particular period in Joyce's life with a great deal of new and varied information from archival sources in Ireland and elsewhere, some of which was not available to or was unused by earlier writers. Though inevitably based in part on materials long familiar to students of Joyce, my book is not a réchaufé of standard works.

Since the centenary of Joyce's birth in 1982, there has been a growing feeling in some circles that the biographical information available, especially relating to his early years in Dublin, is inadequate and distorted. Surprising as it may seem, much information about Joyce's life is not actually included in the biographies, though it was available when Gorman, Ellmann and others were writing. Even now, new manuscript sources are coming to light. A book such as the late Kevin Sullivan's *Joyce Among the Jesuits*, for instance, contains a great deal of interesting material which is continually overlooked. There is even more material in the four volumes of the letters, and in the memoir *My Brother's Keeper* by his younger brother, Stanislaus Joyce. Other books by Joyce's contemporaries such as Eugene Sheehy and the Colums are also invaluable, as have been more recent books by Bruce Bradley S.J., John Ryan and others. Nor should the pioneering work by the Irish writers, the late Patricia Hutchins and John Garvin, be forgotten. Unpublished research by Michael Whelan of Leitrim and others has also been of great importance, and I should add that I am very grateful to John Wyse Jackson and Bernard McGinley for their help and advice.

The result is a version of Joyce's early life at variance with the received accounts on many points. Where this new material leads to radical revisions of events in his life, it has been carefully sourced; otherwise I have been sparing of annotations. The full bibliography will provide the student with what he needs by way of reference.

Though the interpretations in this book may seem contentious to some Joyceans, the ordinary reader may rest assured that every effort has been made to authenticate the material facts and dates, though some 'traditional' facts in Joyce's life have proved impossible to authenticate.

There are places where lack of concrete evidence has led me to speculate about events or persons. However, unlike earlier writers on Joyce, these informed opinions (or what unfriendly critics will doubtless call wild guesses) are always labelled as such. The reader is warned. As yet we do not know everything we would like to know about Joyce; even another century of research may not suffice. Though the simple intention was and is to provide a straightforward account of Joyce's early years, my research has revealed that much which was accepted about this period is simply mistaken. Sometimes it is a trivial matter, perhaps a case of the exact year in which Joyce lived in a particular house. At other times it is of greater consequence, such as the misplacing by two whole years of the date on which he lost his virginity: for Joyce, at least, a matter of profound significance. I suspect that we have only really begun to learn about him as he moves into his second century.

As my main interest here is in the social, cultural and political environment in which James Joyce was reared – those aspects of his life to which T.S. Eliot refers in my epigraph, taken from his introduction to Stanislaus Joyce's memoirs – the tendency of this book is very different from earlier works, breaking radically new ground.

There is a trend in modern Irish historiography referred to as 'revisionism' by those who do not care for the results of its findings. I suspect that this book too will be regarded as 'revisionist' in

3

tendency. Certainly it is time that what we think we know about Joyce was radically reconsidered.

Joyce commends us to wipe our glasses with what we know; when what we know seems so often mistaken, our glasses will always be clouded. Can this explain the opacity of so much which passes for Joycean criticism?

The general purpose of this book is to place the young Joyce historically in his own circumstances – a child of the late nineteenth century. Born in 1882, and dead for over half a century, James Joyce has long ceased to be modern. Yet as an historical figure he still challenges our assumptions about European literature, Irish culture and human nature.

Peter Costello
Dublin

Candlemas
2 February 1992

PROLOGUE

On the last day of June 1915 James Joyce and his family arrived in Zürich, Switzerland, after what he wryly described as 'a rather adventurous journey' by train from Trieste, the Austrian port on the Adriatic coast.

They were seeking a safe haven from the hostilities of the Great War and deserting the city where they had lived (aside from eighteen weeks in Pola and seven months in Rome) for more than ten years since leaving Ireland in 1904, a prosaic migration that Joyce had translated in his imagination into a mythical flight for freedom: Daedalus escaping from the tyranny of Minoan Crete.

As the Italian army advanced with civilized caution upon Trieste, the Austro-Hungarian military authorities had decided on the partial evacuation of the city. And though his brother, Stanislaus, had been interned for the duration as an enemy alien, the Joyces had been granted a special permit to leave the Empire.

James was now 33; his companion, Nora, was 31. Their two children Giorgio and Lucia (both born in Austria) were little more than a month short of 10 and 8 respectively. Verging on Dantean middle age, Joyce was no longer the young man so familiar from his own writings in the figure of Stephen Dedalus, the artist-artificer; rather he was approaching the age and character of Leopold Bloom, his Ulyssean-wanderer in the labyrinth of the modern city.

For Joyce this was about the fortieth change of address in his short lifetime. Where he lived was less important to him now than that sense of place carried in his memory from his Dublin years. His real life was lived within his family and his imagination. Having left Dublin, one city was as good as another. Yet Zürich, to which they had now come almost by chance, was a familiar place with special, indeed secret, associations.

Joyce and Nora had paused in Zürich for a couple of weeks in their flight from Ireland in the autumn of 1904, before moving on to Austria. Here in a small hotel room they had consummated their relationship; here they had conceived their first child; here, in a scene that was partly to inspire the famous closing passages of his long story 'The Dead', in which the husband and wife find themselves separated from each other by her feeling for a lost love, Joyce had begun to learn something of his wife's emotional past; the revelations of Nora's early experiences were to profoundly affect his own future outlook on life.

As Joyce led his small platoon through the bustling Bahnhof-Platz and across the Gessner Bridge over the River Sihl to that same little hotel – the *Gasthaus Hoffnung* at 16 Reitergasse, on the corner of the Lagerstrasse, where they had lodged in 1904 – a distinct period in his life was opening, and an old one was closing.

*

In so far as the continuum of any life can be divided and subdivided, June 1915 separates Joyce's early from his later life, his years of obscurity from his years of fame, his years of growth from his years of creation.

Since it is mainly the success of the creative years after 1915 which gives those earlier years their true significance, a short résumé of Joyce's last decades is a necessary prologue to any account of his early life.

This later Joyce is the James Joyce who established himself soon after this in the public eye – little was known about the earlier Joyce. He engaged the American writer Herbert Gorman to write his biography, the British edition of which appeared by sad chance just after his death. But that book was intended by Joyce to complete a picture created in the later years rather than to provide anything like a full disclosure of his youth. He revised his biographer's text with meticulous care over details he wished to suppress, leaving alone many of Gorman's wilder allegations about Dublin life. Joyce's earlier years would long remain a biographical mystery – as they still do to a greater extent than is realized.

*

When he came to Zürich that summer, James Joyce had already published his collection of short stories *Dubliners*. His novel *A Portrait of the Artist as a Young Man* was being serialized in a London magazine and would soon be published in book form in New York. His only play *Exiles* was complete, though unperformed. *Ulysses*, his modern version of the epic, was planned and partly written. It now seems that even the intimate familial materials which provide the core of *Finnegans Wake* were latent in the writer's imagination; like light-affected silver nitrate on glass, the images needed only to be developed.

Yet in terms of pages and words, of imagination engaged with memory, of the mobilization of technique, the greater part of his life's work remained to be done – some 1,400 pages, over 600,000 words of some of the century's most complex and allusive writing. Though *Ulysses* would arouse controversy and *Finnegans Wake* deep dismay, by 1915 Joyce had already asserted his moral and artistic stature.

A few months earlier he had been unknown except to a handful of friends and enemies; now he was in receipt of a form to complete for *Who's Who 1916*. In little more than the year after the publication of *Dubliners*, he had become recognized as a writer of sufficient significance for W.B. Yeats and others to obtain for him a grant from the Royal Literary Fund in London, followed by a small subsidy from the British Society of Authors and, finally, in August 1916 a Civil List grant from the British government. Other gifts of money and of capital funds were now to come to him from Mrs McCormick, a Rockefeller heiress living in Zürich, from his London patroness, Harriet Shaw Weaver, and later from Robert McAlmon who was married to Winifred Ellerman – the British writer Bryher, heiress to a shipping line. Supported by this generosity, the Joyces (though never completely free from financial worry in their own view) would soon be able to put the hardships of real poverty behind them.

And about time too, they would have thought. In Trieste Joyce had struggled to survive as a language teacher. A period in Rome as a bank clerk had not been a success. He had failed also in efforts to obtain an Italian university post, and had gained little from periods as a cinema manager, tweed salesman and fireworks agent. Even the Berlitz School, where he taught when he first went to live in Austria, had been abandoned in favour of giving private lessons which were more convenient, if less certain, as a means of livelihood. At one time Nora had been forced to take in washing; the sight of her red, raw arms had distressed Joyce. For years he had lived off the salary and goodwill of his brother Stanislaus, assuaged landlords with false promises of payment and cadged fees 'in advance' for language lessons. But that was now over. He had been made free to write, and this financial freedom radically altered what he was now able to do with his scheme for *Ulysses*. Later, in elaborating the materials for *Finnegans Wake*, he would take some fifteen years to complete one book. Anthony Burgess has remarked that Joyce was never a professional writer – no little essays, no reviews, no introductions to art books, no radio broadcasts. He saw himself rather as the complete artist. All his energy was reserved for his creativity.

His literary position, if controversial, was now assured. While mixed, the reviews of *Dubliners* on publication in June 1914, and the initial reception of *A Portrait of the Artist* appearing in the *Egoist* magazine, had nevertheless recognized the arrival of a significant writer. In the influential pages of the *New Statesman* he was called 'a genius'. And it was as an artist of international repute that he was to be introduced, for instance, in 1918 to Frank Budgen, the English painter who was among the first of a small protective circle of friends and admirers that was to grow up around the writer both in Zürich and later in Paris. Budgen's book about the writing of *Ulysses* remains one of the most interesting of those written by Joyce's friends.

These wartime years in Zürich, then a cosmopolitan city – the city of Conrad's *Under Western Eyes*, where foreigners made up about a third of the population – were spent working on *Ulysses*. The city was full of spies and revolutionaries, including Lenin, but Joyce now had little concern for politics; his only interest was literature. To close friends such as Budgen, he explained in detail his plans and his purpose in writing the novel. This judicious self-promotion did much to create the reputation of *Ulysses* long in advance of its final publication in book form.

For his family the move to Switzerland meant a change of language from the Italian patois of Trieste to the local dialect of German. His children picked up the language in school, his wife in the shops, though they continued to speak Italian in the home. Yet these linguistic changes and the unsettled nature of their upbringing were to leave deep psychological scars on both his son, and on his daughter whose frail hold on sanity eventually slipped completely.

In Zürich Joyce was soon involved in café life and a little later in running a dramatic group, the English Players – his small contribution to the war effort in return for his government grant, though he would not have cared to have it described in this way. His long established habits of drinking into the early hours, which he had brought from Austria, were maintained, much to the despair of his wife.

It was also in Zürich that Joyce, though uxorious and domesticated to a large extent, had several 'affairs'. These relationships were of little importance for their sexual content, which may have been quite insignificant. Yet for Joyce as for the 'Pale Galilean', adultery in the mind was still adultery; it was still a sin, and therefore dangerous. In creating *Ulysses* he found that he needed to renew his own feelings about emotional situations from his past. These new women were merely a means to an end, an attempt to retrieve the sensations aroused in him by their Dublin predecessors. Perhaps he was feeling the frustrations of middle age and thinking that Nora was growing less attractive to him. He tried to get her to 'go with other men', as she put it to Frank Budgen, which she was reluctant to do – for she was no Molly Bloom.

Yet Joyce himself was attempting also to renew his creative energies – in his relations with Marthe Fleischmann in Zürich, an affair which was consummated; he told Budgen he had been exploring the hottest and coldest parts of a woman's body (this last being evidently the heart), with Dr Gertrude Kaempffer in Locarno, and with Hella Elzholz of Berlin, who had been on holiday in Locarno. But to Miss Fleischmann, who was Jewish, he claimed she resembled a girl he once glimpsed on the beach at Clontarf in 1898, and to Dr Kaempffer he related his first experience of sexual arousal. Doubtless Miss Elzholz – whose Berlin address he carefully preserved among the notes for *Ulysses* – was privy to some other now lost secret from his early sexual life. The women in themselves were of little significance to him; they were merely a means to an end: the completion of *Ulysses*.

Slow but steady progress was made with the book from 1915 to 1918. The first episode was published in the *Little Review* of New York in March 1918, continuing to September 1920. In London the *Egoist* also began serializing what had been completed of the book from January to December 1919. Even in this limited form, *Ulysses* encountered not only opposition but also immediate admiration. Though the war had been an inconvenience for Joyce – his decade-long struggle to have his stories published ended only days before Archduke Franz Ferdinand was shot in Sarajevo – *Ulysses* seemed to reflect the sense of a need of new forms for new feelings that swept Europe after the appalling disasters of 1916. From Zürich, Lenin departed in 1917 for the Finland Station: Joyce's impact on the modern world was to be equally revolutionary, posing the truth of art and life against the lies of state and society.

After the end of the Great War, the Joyces attempted to re-establish themselves in Trieste, where he taught in the commercial college while continuing his increasingly complex work on *Ulysses*. But in October 1919 conditions were unsettled in the city, for what had been the major naval base of the Austro-Hungarian Empire was becoming an obscure backwater of Italy. The region was in political turmoil: Joyce's old literary hero, the poet Gabriele d'Annunzio, was even attempting at this time to establish the Republic of Fiume further along the Adriatic, defying the new state of Yugoslavia and earning himself the contempt of history.

A meeting in Italy in June 1920 with the American poet Ezra Pound, who had played such a vital role in bringing about the publication of some of Joyce's earlier prose work, persuaded Joyce that he would be better off moving nearer to the cultural centre of European life. For Pound and Joyce this meant Paris. Only there would he be able to promote *Ulysses* in the proper manner. That very month the family removed to Paris, where Joyce had already lived for a few significant months in the winter of 1902–3. Paris, which he oddly described as a 'convenient' city, was where he and Nora had always wanted to live when they left Ireland; it would be his base for the next two decades. There he would complete *Ulysses* and commence *Finnegans Wake*.

The serialization of the novel was troubled. In Paris the authorities could afford to ignore publications in the English language, but elsewhere the increasing frankness of the *Ulysses* episodes could not be disregarded, and encountered difficulties in America. The Society for the Suppression of Vice made a complaint in New York in October 1920 against the novel, then being serialized as Joyce wrote it in the *Little Review*. The beginning of episode XIII, 'Nausicaa', and Mr Bloom's auto-eroticism proved too much for some readers. In February 1921 the editors, Margaret Anderson and Jane Heap, were convicted of publishing obscenity. These radical-minded women escaped a prison sentence only by agreeing that they would publish no more episodes of *Ulysses*. By then the novel had just reached the beginning of episode XIV, 'Oxen of the Sun'.

Margaret Anderson replied passionately to a reader who had written to her complaining in the grossest way of her dislike of the book which Miss Anderson regarded as 'the high-water mark of the literature of today'. Joyce, she wrote, 'is not writing for you. He is writing for himself and for the people who care to find out how life has offended and hurt him.' Only an exceptional man, she wrote later, 'could revenge himself on the banality, the aridity, the obscenity from which he had suffered by transcribing it so flawlessly into an epic criticism of mankind'.

Potential legal action for obscenity made the book unattractive to the conventional publishers in London and New York who had handled Joyce's earlier work. He finally accepted the offer of the American expatriate Sylvia Beach to publish it through her Paris bookshop, Shakespeare and Co., in the rue de l'Odéon. He had also recruited in advance the critical interest of Valéry Larbaud, the leading French authority on Samuel Butler, whose lecture on *Ulysses* in December 1921 set the tone for the general critical reception of the book when it appeared the following year. The promotion of his novel, in the face of reactionary prejudice, became a moral crusade for Joyce, as it did, too, for his friends.

After extraordinary efforts on the part of the writer and the printer, Maurice Darantière, a first copy of *Ulysses* (marred alas by many misprints) was placed in the author's hands on Joyce's fortieth birthday, 2nd February 1922. Soon copies were for sale in Miss Beach's shop and the book began to enjoy a tremendous reputation both as a forbidden work and a great masterpiece, not just of Irish but of world literature. Yet in the fifteen years before the unlimited editions became available in America and Britain, Joyce sold perhaps 2,000 copies a year, some 30,000 copies – the same number (as Bruce Arnold observes) that T.E. Lawrence's *Seven Pillars of Wisdom,* an equally expensive and complex book, had sold in three months of 1927. Literary fame was not yet to be equated with popular success.

Ulysses was recognized from its publication as a landmark for its method, style and content. The frankness with which Joyce described the everyday life of a modern city appalled many, though he saw this as a necessary aspect of his total vision. The method of the book, its structure and use of stream of consciousness was seized upon by others and was to become for the next quarter of a century the badge of the *avant garde*; Joyce's influence can be seen in writers as distinct as Sean O'Casey and William Faulkner. Yet few other writers could achieve anything like Joyce's stylistic mastery: in the 'Oxen of the Sun' episode he had provided pastiches of the development of English prose. His own writing often approached more nearly to the quality of music rather than mere prose.

Though the British and American Customs either burnt or seized over 1,000 copies of the novel, *Ulysses* was freely on sale in Dublin, the city of its setting: for example, P.S. O'Hegarty of the Irish Bookshop in Dawson Street imported eight copies of the first edition, sold these and ordered more of the second, which he also sold out. Desmond Fitzgerald, the Minister of Information in the government of the new Irish Free State, even wished to propose Joyce for the Nobel Prize (an idea unwelcome then and later in Stockholm). In the event the prize for 1923 went to W.B. Yeats, an award as much to the new state as to the ageing poet. Fitzgerald, a friend of Ezra Pound in his Kensington period, was like so many of his countrymen a man of wide culture, and he recognized at once Joyce's pre-eminent distinction and what his art should mean for their common country. He did not need the *nihil obstat* of a foreign court. An ineffective Irish Customs temporary-exclusion order against *Ulysses* lapsed in 1932. New books were now censored under the Censorship of Publications Act 1926. But none of Joyce's books was banned in Ireland, save *Stephen Hero* for a short period after it was published in 1944, at which date Australia was imposing a new ban on *Ulysses*. Given the acknowledged difficulty of reading, let alone understanding, Joyce's work, it is likely that in those days he was as closely read in Ireland as anywhere else – and, given the low sales, perhaps as widely read as well.

Though Joyce himself could not be induced to return to Ireland – to have done so would have been to destroy the memories on which he relied for his writing – in 1922 now that *Ulysses* was done with and Ireland supposedly 'free', his wife and children went to Dublin and Galway, only to find themselves caught up in the terrors of the Civil War in which irreconcilable Republicans attempted to overthrow the new government of Arthur Griffith and Michael Collins. However, Joyce did travel to London that year, staying in the Euston Hotel where Parnell, the hero of his youth, had once lived; it was, he confessed, the nearest he could get to Ireland without going there. He planned to spend the winter in Nice, but instead returned to Paris. Ever restless, his mind had already moved on from *Ulysses*.

On 10th March 1923 Joyce wrote the first preliminary sketches for a new work, the title of which he kept secret even from his closest associates, though not from Nora. The notes for this book, based on a review of his previous writings, had been started almost as soon as *Ulysses* was completed the year before, and indeed had grown out of material accumulated for that earlier work.

But continuous work was always to prove difficult. In 1917 he had undergone an eye operation in Switzerland; another (the first of a long series) now followed in Paris. The summer of 1923 was passed in London and at Bognor, an unfashionable seaside resort in the south of England, which left its odd traces in his new book. In 1924, enduring increasing eye troubles, he published the first fragments of this work, then known only as 'Work in Progress'.

The late 1920s and the 1930s followed the same pattern of illness, work and travel. In twenty-one years Joyce and his family stayed in nearly one hundred hotels across Europe, many of them in fashionable seaside resorts. During this period Joyce saw the seas along the coasts of Europe in so many of their aspects that it is not surprising he should have contemplated following *Finnegans Wake*, his book of the Night, with a book of the Ocean.

On a wider front his struggle to have *Ulysses* published in Britain and America came to an end in 1933 with the judgement of an American court that the novel was not obscene, which cleared the way for an American edition in 1934 and a British one in 1936. By now *Ulysses* was becoming a modern classic rather than a famously dirty publication, and furtive possession had given way to puzzled appreciation. Indeed it had been calculated by His Honour Judge Manton of the United States Court of Appeal, who wished to sustain the ban on *Ulysses*, that out of 762 pages only 30 were in any way objectionable.

*

It was thus in the special circumstances of Paris in the early 1920s that the Joyce of literary legend emerged to view, the centre of a small though devoted circle of friends, admirers and helpers, mainly British and American, who assisted him not only with his research and writing but with his literary manoeuvres, his flat-hunting, shopping, dining-out and drinking.

Yet the life of the Joyces at this time was in no way bohemian. Their various apartments (of which there would be some fourteen in Paris) were resolutely bourgeois in the old-fashioned French manner, all in expensive *quartiers* of the city, though they were decorated with the famous family portraits, pictures of Dublin and Cork, and the rug into which had been woven a flowing motif of the River Liffey. In his style of life Joyce might have been the successful Dublin medical man he had once aspired to be. He was often cool and reserved, with a famously weak handshake and little small talk, though nearly always open and friendly with Irish visitors, especially those like the young Owen Sheehy Skeffington, the son of two of Joyce's Dublin college friends, who could provide him with details of modern Dublin. Meeting him casually many admirers were disappointed, so great was the contrast between the robust qualities of the novels and the staid nature of the man.

In the spring of 1923 Margaret Anderson visited him in Paris:

> James Joyce and his wife came to see us in Ezra's studio. Joyce was like a portrait of my father as a young man – the same gentle bearing, the same kindliness, the same deprecating humour in the smile, the same quality of personal aristocracy ... He gave me the impression of having less escape from suffering about irremediable things than anyone I had ever known. It was an impression borne out by nothing that he said so much as by the turn of his head, the droop of his wrist, the quiet tension of his face, his quick half-smile.

She was impressed with Nora Joyce, who was at her ease with Margaret and with Jane Heap as often she was not with 'intellectuals'. Nora was charming:

> She is good drama. Her Irish mockery and personal challenge furnish Joyce with a continual, necessary and delightful foil. She teases and tyrannises him. There is an undercurrent in her voice that makes her mockery at once exasperating, exciting and tender ... Nora Joyce is one of those women a man loves for ever and hopes one day to take effectively by the throat. She has spirit and independence which she has been willing (one feels not without rebellion) to subordinate to her devotion to a man she considers great in spite of 'his necessity to write those books no one can understand'.

Miss Anderson, however, was quick to observe the other aspect of the household: 'The Joyce household also comprises a son and a daughter whom their parents are enthusiastically manipulating into a singer and a dancer. But the interest of the family is clearly focused on the older generation.'

Joyce apologized that he could not ask them to dinner: they were going on holiday soon and the family portraits had been taken down from the dining-room. 'He was deeply troubled by the lack of an ancestral background for dinner.' The Americans did not mind and went to dine *en famille*. Joyce confessed that he had come to feel sustained conversation was impossible – people were always offering him soup – and in his books he had had his revenge. He refused to make concessions to his readers. He had learnt Dano-Norwegian in order to read Ibsen; his readers must learn to read him. He saw no reason to make it easy for them.

To some Irish people the mystery of Joyce was not in his current eminence, but in the Dublin origins of his genius. Others, more conservative, saw him – like his father – as a bounder and a cad. Joyce was deeply offended by a wrong-headed but oddly well-informed article by the Dublin judge Michael Lennon (whom he had entertained in Paris) on his Irish and Catholic backgrounds, written for a leading American Catholic journal in March 1931, which concluded with the thought that he might have a literary future if he returned to writing critical essays, for he was clearly not a novelist. This oddly echoed an opinion of him by John M. Synge in a private letter to Lady Gregory in 1903, when Joyce was known only as a minor poet. He too thought Joyce did not have the power for larger things. Obsessed by his earthy detail, Joyce's compatriots seemed altogether obtuse about his humane qualities.

An Irish writer of the younger generation, the poet Austin Clarke – whose own private life was to be mauled by the social attitudes of Ireland, yet who chose to live and work there – observed the Joyce of this period with a cool and detached eye. He found Mrs Joyce, so often described as handsome, to be rather homely and plain, as were her son and daughter. After a supper of roast chicken and salad (a simple dish which was for long Nora's staple fare: Joyce disliked red meat and red wine), Joyce quizzed the young poet about literary Dublin: about Yeats, AE, Seumas O'Sullivan and Gogarty, all of whom had appeared in *Ulysses*:

Some weeks later as we were sitting in a cheap café in a side street under the shadow of Saint Sulpice, drinking Pernod Fils, Joyce after a long silence, mentioned Yeats again. His remark was so surprising that I keep it in Italian: 'La poesia de Mangan e de Yeats è quella di segatora di chi sela da fa solo.'

Seeing that Clarke was puzzled by this, Joyce explained that Mangan and Yeats in their love poems both wrote in a reverential, remote way: 'He emphasized their obsession with hands, quoting Mangan and pointing to the frequency with which Yeats refers to pearl-pale hands. I realized that he was only acquainted with the early twilight poems. As I glanced at the drooping figure, I wondered if he had been addicted in youth to our national vice.'

*

Despite its 'emetic' details *Ulysses* was essentially a comic novel; and among the most effective of the characters (at least as regards his swearing) was Simon Dedalus, a life-like portrait of the author's father, John Joyce.

Joyce had remained in touch with his father in Dublin, and asked friends to call upon him as often as possible. Robert McAlmon was one of these and he has left a vivid impression of the old man sitting up in his bed with his drink, his memory running back over the events of his hectic youth while bewailing his sorry present state. John Joyce died in December 1931. Although Joyce arranged for a stone to be placed over the common grave to commemorate both his father and his mother, his piety did not extend to the brothers and sister who also lie forgotten in the same grave.

Joyce's son, Giorgio, had married in 1930, though not happily, an American, Helen Fleischmann: the union ended in separation after the birth in 1932 of a grandson, Stephen James Joyce. Joyce had been deeply upset by his father's death – during a cab ride with the Irish poet Thomas MacGreevy he broke down completely and had to struggle to regain his composure before he could enter the café where he was expected. The birth of his grandson seemed then a special gift; but it was only a token of happiness for his daughter, Lucia, was showing signs of increasing mental illness. Madness had been detected so often in Joyce's work by unfriendly critics that the recognition of it in his family was frightening and long avoided. Finally Lucia had to be placed in a Paris *maison de santé* in 1934. As

Margaret Anderson had observed, the parents were the centre of the Joyce household: their children were destroyed by the father's monomania and by Nora's self-centredness and jealousy of her off-spring. Joyce would not have forgotten that the escape of Daedalus from Crete entailed the destruction of his child, the boy Icarus. Joyce's children had flown too near the sun of their little world and their wings had melted.

Worry over Giorgio's career as a singer, as well as over Lucia's ill-health, deeply affected James and Nora. Joyce claimed so much for the family that their sufferings were even more troubling. The settled couple of the 1920s became the increasingly melancholy pair of the 1930s.

Through the 1920s and 1930s Joyce had regularly published parts of 'Work in Progress' in issues of Eugene Jolas's journal *transition*, and in small booklets from other publishers. For Joyce this had the great advantage of making his complex text available in sufficiently slow measure for it to create its own audience, and as the journal was American it also introduced the book to the wider English-speaking world. Nevertheless some of his admirers, even such old friends and supporters as his British benefactor, Harriet Weaver, and the poet Ezra Pound, found they could not follow it. Yet Joyce persisted. His brother Stanislaus, who had sustained with cash and criticism so much of his early life and work, was dismayed by the new course of Joyce's creativity. Now financially insulated against the world and against personal criticism, there was nothing else Joyce could or wished to do. The artist had perforce to follow where his imagination led.

As the temper of the times became more political with the rise of Fascism and the outbreak of the Spanish Civil War, Joyce's now wholly non-political outlook showed a refreshing mental integrity for the period. But it left him marginalized, both as a man and as an artist. *Ulysses*, the culmination of an ancient humanistic tradition, had opened up literary perspectives for others to follow. His friend, the young Dublin-born writer Sam Beckett (who had succeeded Thomas MacGreevy in Joyce's inner circle), was only one of these: in 1939 Joyce received a gift from the author of the first book from Ireland which could be said to show his influence: Flann O'Brien's *At Swim-Two-Birds*. But though critics when discussing 'Work in Progress' might speak of the Book of Kells, of the secret languages of Ireland, of its night talk and its Catholic nature – even the official

Vatican paper *L'Osservatore Romano* found a few words of praise for it in 1937 – the new book did not capture the popular audience Joyce wanted. Readers who had admired *Ulysses* felt that a book which made such demands upon a reader had passed beyond the currency of civilization into the privacy of a cult. In the agony of his own sufferings, Joyce had ceased for many to address the human condition.

On 2nd February 1939 Joyce's 'Work in Progress' was completed with the printing of a first copy of *Finnegans Wake* – the name revealed at last, though the commercial edition was not published until May. The book was widely noticed and respectfully reviewed, and there was no repeat of the controversy which had surrounded *Ulysses*. Joyce was disappointed with its reception, however. Politics, which he had come to despise, was all people talked about, when they should be giving their undivided attention to his creation. He felt ill and depressed.

War came again to Europe in the autumn. Every time he published, his books heralded some disaster: the Great War, the Irish Civil War, the Second World War. It was time to leave Paris and once again a flight into exile began. The Joyces stayed first at La Baule, near where Lucia was being treated; then at St Gérand-le-Puy, near Vichy. On 14th December 1940, after lengthy negotiations with the Swiss authorities who were wary in their cautious way of Joyce's alleged Jewish connections – an echo here of the difficulties which had affected their flight in 1915 – the family finally left France for Zürich. They failed to take Lucia with them, as her papers were not in order. It was in Zürich, once again their wartime refuge, that Joyce died suddenly at 2 a.m. on 13th January 1941 at the Red Cross Hospital. He had always thought the 13th an unlucky day.

For many years Joyce had suffered from mysterious stomach pains. These can be traced back to the lack of food, nervous stress and excess drink in Paris in 1902 and Dublin in 1903. Intent upon his eyes, he had neglected medical advice to have his stomach x-rayed. Now a post-mortem revealed that he had died from peritonitis brought on by a perforated ulcer.

His Triestian friend Alessandro Francini Bruni, looking at the dead author's face, thought how young he looked, and recalled the medieval belief that in Heaven the glorified bodies of the faithful (to which Joyce had adverted in *A Portrait*) were all at the perfect age of 32. This had been Joyce's age, just, when the Great War disrupted his life in Trieste. What followed was, in this view, a slow declension from bodily perfection.

James Joyce was buried on 15th January 1941 with perfunctory ceremony in Flüntern Cemetery, while snow fell as if in imitation of the closing passage of his story 'The Dead'.

His wife Nora survived him by a decade, dying in 1951 in Zürich where she too is buried. His son died in 1976, his daughter in 1982. Of his immediate family he is survived only by his childless grandson Stephen James Joyce, who lives in Paris.

*

James Joyce had been born in Dublin in the spring of 1882 and had last seen the city in the autumn of 1912. Between these dates he gathered the impressions from which all his creative work – including the unpublished *Giacomo Joyce* – was drawn. Even *Finnegans Wake*, published so much later, drew upon his recollections of his childhood experiences in the 1880s for much of its substance.

It is these early years which are of greatest interest to his readers, for they provide the biographical background to his work as an artist. But Joyce was not only the sum of his own experiences: he was the sum of the experiences, beliefs, memories, foibles, frivolities; the lives, deaths, debts and opinions of his ancestors, family, relatives, friends and acquaintances. No biographer of Joyce can ignore the sheer density of other lives upon which he draws as an artist. The sketches are all straight from life. Often the people who interested him were socially speaking insignificant. For instance, Alfred H. Hunter, the original Dublin model of Mr Bloom, died in 1926 in a tumbling Dublin tenement, quite ignorant in his poverty of the character he had inspired. But they are now significant to us not for what they were in life, but for what they were to Joyce. They are important because they belonged to him – as he has Stephen Dedalus remark of Ireland. Their experiences were often beyond his range emotionally, physically and socially. Often they provided what life had deprived him of.

Joyce imagined Stephen Dedalus flying beyond the nets of nationality, language and religion. Yet paradoxically, the more Joyce asserted his freedom, the more dependent he became. As an artist he achieved a technical freedom unimagined by his peers, which still astonishes and delights. But his culture, the culture of his books and characters, remains that of late nineteenth-century Dublin.

Joyce never escaped from Dublin. Like all of us, he was less free than he imagined as a youth, a fact he ruefully acknowledged in later life when he doubted that he had ever left Ireland in spirit. He too was only human, and as such a creature of heredity. The struggle of heredity with environment is a theme in much of his work and he was always conscious of this. The momentary couplings of his ancestors had made him what he was: '*Give us a touch, Poldy. I'm dying for it*' – '*They did the couplers will.*' Joyce was constrained and conditioned by events and decisions long done with before he was born.

Aside from the vagaries of his own soul, Joyce had two lifelong obsessions: his family and the city of Dublin. But the Joyces were not native Dubliners, nor even Irish originally. He owed his connection with the city so central to his creative life to his mother's ancestors; and it is with these people, Dubliners of the late Georgian era, that a beginning can be made in tracing out some of the influences on the early life of James Joyce.

PART I

THE DEAD

ome time in the years before the Battle of Waterloo a Dublin merchant named Patrick Flynn opened a factory for making starch and blueing at 53 Back Lane, in the parish of St Nicholas-without-the-City-Walls.

By now Mr Flynn would have faded from all knowledge were it not that his genes contributed in part to the genetic make-up of the author of *Ulysses*; for he was James Joyce's maternal great-grandfather.

It was from the Flynn family that Joyce was to derive most of the details for his long story 'The Dead', in which he describes these ancestral Dubliners of his under the name of Morkan – that name being taken by him from a spirits and tea merchant on Arran Quay in the Dublin of his own day. The Flynns and their connections in the musical and commercial world of mid-Victorian Dublin provided Joyce with an image of a more old-fashioned urban life against which he could test the pretensions and follies of the modern city in which he grew up.

The Flynns belonged to the then strongly emerging Catholic commercial class in Georgian Dublin. Once an English and largely Protestant city, by the late eighteenth century Dublin was overwhelmingly Catholic. This was despite the anti-Catholic Penal Laws, which were in any case something of a legal fiction. By 1780 perhaps some three-quarters of the country's trade was already in Catholic hands and though Catholics were conscious of Protestant wealth, the extent of Catholic enterprise was often overlooked. The next century was to see a move from dominance in trade and industry to a control of political life. In their obscure way, the Flynns

23

were very much of their period, typical of the changing social scene in the city.

Back Lane, formerly Rochelle Street, was in the highest and oldest part of Dublin, where the original Viking settlement of the ninth century had been laid, and around which the medieval English city subsequently spread out. It was there that the Jesuits had briefly established a Catholic university in the seventeenth century, and there that many Catholic and democratic movements had met in the Taylors Hall towards the end of the eighteenth century. Some eighteenth-century buildings still line the street (one dating from 1760), but the site of the Flynn factory has long since been cleared away for the working-class houses of John Dillon Street. Even by 1815 the city had spread and this ancient district was already in decline. This was the Dublin of his childhood described by the Romantic poet James Clarence Mangan (born on nearby Fishamble Street in 1809), in whose fragmentary autobiography the young Joyce was to see a Dublin literary model for the decline into squalid poverty of his own family at the end of the century.

City directories of the period show that by 1818 Patrick Flynn was running a spirit store at the Back Lane address. The starch and blueing factory had been removed by Patrick and James Flynn (who I take to be his sons, or a son and brother) to premises at Thomas Street and Francis Street. Later they had other premises in Back Lane at numbers 50 and 51 until 1835. But as one of the Morkan sisters in 'The Dead' points out, the 'ancestral mansion' was elsewhere.

The city valuation of 1830 shows the Flynns resident at what was later number 16 Ellis Quay on the north side of the Liffey, on the river bank below Stoneybatter. The quay dated back to the reign of Charles II and, though number 16 was built only in the last part of the eighteenth century, it belonged to a quarter of Dublin that contrasted, in its quaint grey-bricked charm, with the rapidly enlarging city of the Victorian era, with its raw red-brick and sharp-cut limestone.

Patrick and James Flynn continued in the starch and blue business at various premises in Francis Street. Their products were luxury items – the starch to stiffen shirts and petticoats, the blue to heighten the colour of whites in washing. James eventually retired in the 1830s, but Patrick continued the business into the 1850s at 79 Thomas Street (on the corner with Francis Street), dying about 1854.

It was of this Patrick Flynn, James Joyce's grandfather, that family tradition related the story of Johnny the mill horse which was harnessed up to take Mr Flynn out to the Phoenix Park to observe a grand military review. The horse became mesmerized by the equestrian statue of William III in College Green and went round and round it while his master roared ineffectual orders at him, an anecdote Joyce incorporates into 'The Dead.'*

After his death, Patrick Flynn's widow Ellen kept up the firm for a time, but eventually sold out. The whole family now resided at 16 Ellis Quay, where the widow's son Patrick is listed variously in the late 1850s as a starch and blue merchant, an accountant and a book-keeper. When he died at the end of May 1896, aged 60, he had been living in a room in nearby Queen Street and was described simply as a clerk. His several sisters, the Misses Flynn, ran a small school for teaching singing and pianoforte. One of them, Miss Elizabeth Flynn, seems also to have run a school in Harcourt Street for a time. Another, Annie Flynn, born in 1845, was for a time a governess – perhaps in France at the court of the Emperor Louis Napoléon.

An elder sister Julia Clare, born about 1829, married a man named Martin Lyons, then a commercial traveller, who later set up as a paper and hide merchant and stationer, with a printing works largely for legal materials at 6 Ormond Quay and a yard for the hides at 16 Usher's Court. (The leather would have been utilized in binding ledgers.) Her children Frederick M. Lyons and James Joseph Lyons were later in business as fashionable stationers at 56 Grafton Street, dealing in the kinds of fancy heliotrope notepaper that Joyce himself preferred, though this firm seems not to have prospered. Other members of the Lyons family were clothiers in Henry Street. Martin Lyons died on 2nd February 1871 at his home, 113 Lower Gardiner Street (then a respectable address) from liver disease and dropsy.

The youngest sister Ellen Mary married a Matthew Callanan, sometime secretary of the Irish Farmers Club in Upper Sackville Street, by whom she had a daughter Mary Ellen born about 1871. For a time in the 1860s both families lived near each other on Grantham Terrace, Seville Place, in the shadow of St Laurence's

---

* Yet family tradition does not explain why Mr Flynn should have taken such an odd route out to the Phoenix Park. As the Dublin Orangemen, the stoutly anti-Catholic section of the Protestant merchant class, held an annual parade around the statue to celebrate the Battle of the Boyne in 1689, the implication is that Johnny, like some other characters in the story, is a Protestant.

25

church on the north side of the river, where one of the parish priests Father Edward O'Connell (chaplain to Lord Mayor Peter Paul McSwiney), may have been a Joyce connection.

After the early deaths of their husbands and the decline of their brother Patrick, the sisters (including those who were unmarried and also their aunts) moved back south of the Liffey at the beginning of 1882, leasing the upper stories of an eighteenth-century house overlooking the Liffey quays at 15 Ushers Island, in the same area where the late Mr Lyons had run his hide business. Here in the large gracious rooms, the sisters continued to advertise their music classes still under the style of the Misses Flynn. Here they gave the annual Christmastime parties for their pupils and musical friends which Joyce's parents attended and which inspired the setting of his story 'The Dead'.

Their friends in the Dublin musical world included Melfort d'Alton, a well-known music teacher and singer of sentimental Irish folk songs*, and Mervyn Archdall Browne (1862–1930), an amateur musician, teacher and organist (and incidental bankrupt), both of whom Joyce was to recall as personalities for 'The Dead'. The Misses Flynn had been pupils of the famous Dublin composer Michael Balfe (so Joyce claimed) and, as their great-nephew put it, 'trilled and warbled in a Dublin church up to the age of seventy'. This was in the ancient Franciscan church on the south quays popularly known as Adam and Eve's, the name of which is evoked in the opening passage of *Finnegans Wake*.

The house belonged to Roe's the distillers, and the ground floor was leased out as offices to a corn merchant and his son named Smith. There was a caretaker in the basement, named Tallon, whose daughter Elizabeth (born about 1880) stayed with the Flynns into the new century, and she is the model for the maid Lily of 'The Dead'.

In about 1856 another of the sisters, Margaret Theresa Flynn – then about 23 years old – had married in her turn a John Murray who introduced into this long line of Dubliners a new and rural strain.

*

* Barton McGuckin (born 1853), who had had a successful career to 1896 as the principal tenor of the famous Royal Carl Rosa Opera Company, seems – despite Professor Ellmann's opinion – to be an unlikely model for Bartell D'Arcy.

John Murray's family can be traced back to Co. Leitrim at the end of the eighteenth century; most of their clan were located in the barony of Mohill, but especially in the parish of Gortletteragh on the western shore of Lough Rinn and the surrounding district. John's father William, born about the turn of the nineteenth century, farmed in Tulcon on the western shore of Lough Rinn, where John was born in 1824. His mother was a Bridget Byrne.

Early in the nineteenth century some of these Murrays are said to have moved south into Longford. Though sprung from small tenant farmers, they must have become prosperous enough – not only because John Murray was involved in the corn and whiskey businesses, then thriving areas of both export and import, but also because they produced several generations of priests.

John Murray's uncle, the Reverend Patrick Murray, born in Tulcon in 1800, was ordained in June 1827, eventually becoming, by the time of his death in 1854, parish priest of Mullahoran in Cavan. There in the 1830s and 1840s he ran a classical school at which he educated his nephew (John's younger brother), another Patrick Murray born in 1830.

This Patrick Murray was ordained in his turn, in April 1857, and after several postings eventually became parish priest of Carraig Finnea, near Granard, where he died in 1912. This second Father Murray was involved in the Land War, founding the Finnea branch of the United Land League in 1879, and was well thought of locally as a patriot priest. As a child James Joyce was sufficiently familiar with Father Murray – from his rare visits to Dublin – to remember his heavy jowly appearance and to recognize the same local accent in his friend the poet Padraic Colum (whose father was master of the county workhouse in Longford in the early 1880s). Local Finnea tradition spoke of the Reverend Patrick Murray as a man of notable literary talent: he is the only one of James Joyce's numerous ancestors of whom this claim has been made. But as yet none of his writings – doubtless in the sentimental national tradition which Joyce despised – has been traced.

The eldest brother was Hugh Murray, born in 1820, who married a local girl and farmed in Gortletteragh townland itself, having been moved there from Tulcon in 1866 by the notorious Lord Leitrim, derided in the Christmas dinner scene in *A Portrait*. Hugh's descendants, Joyce's distant cousins, still live in Gortletteragh, Co. Leitrim; others live in England and America. Aside from the priests, their provincial connections do not seem to have impinged much on the Dublin Murrays or their relatives the Joyces – though family tradition has it that an aunt of James Joyce (otherwise unrecorded) is buried in the family tomb in Gortletteragh. In turn the rural Murrays have been reluctant to acknowledge their connection with the notorious author. Yet if genetics means anything, Joyce owed much of his artistic temperament to the Murray strain of priests, teachers and singers.

Though not with the same professional expertise as the Flynns, these Murrays were musical people. It was from his grandfather John Murray that James Joyce as a small child learnt the words of 'a lost song' *The Yellow Ale*, which he later told his friend, the Dublin writer James Stephens, was the most beautiful in the world, and which he was wont to sing for Parisian friends in the 1920s.

Where and when John and Margaret married is as yet unknown, though it must have been in St Paul's, Arran Quay, the Flynns' parish church. How he came to Dublin is also a mystery. A clue lies in *Ulysses* where Mr Bloom muses about a city publican: 'Where do they get the money? Coming up redheaded curates from County Leitrim, rinsing empties and old man in the cellar. Then, lo and behold, they blossom out as Adam Findlaters or Dan Tallons.' The 'redheaded curate from County Leitrim' can only have been John Murray; though he was not to rise to such heights, that seems to have been how he began: as an assistant in a public house.

In the late 1850s and early 1860s, however, he and his wife were running their own Dublin tea and wine merchant's premises – in other words a pub called *The Eagle House* – in Roundtown (now Terenure), the same district into which their grandson would be born; the house is only a step away from the church where Joyce was baptized. The pub still stands on the corner of Terenure Roads East and North, though the large ornamental eagles which gave it its name have gone. The Murrays' three surviving children were born there: two boys, William (born 1857, died 1912) and John (born 1856, died 1910), and a daughter born in May 1859 who was given the family name Mary Jane, but was known as May.

The family situation in *The Eagle House* – of a father and mother with a beautiful daughter and two quarrelling sons – is the basic situation in *Finnegans Wake*, where the central character H.C. Ear-wicker also lives in a pub with his wife, beautiful daughter and two quarrelling sons. This discovery demonstrates with some finality that all Joyce's books, even his last and most enigmatic, have an essentially autobiographical basis. I think that what he had heard from his mother about her early childhood in *The Eagle House* provided Joyce with the model for his last work, though other elements were added from different parts of the Joyces' family experiences. May Joyce at least recalled the bird-cage that during the summer months used to hang in a window of her childhood home. Though the relations of Shem and Shaun in *Finnegans Wake* are often seen as deriving from those of James and his younger brother Stanislaus, this new information suggests that the brotherly ill-feeling explored by Joyce had a remoter, though familiar source. Certainly the Murray brothers seem to have been strong personalities.

John Murray worked in the *Freeman's Journal* (he is the 'Red' Murray of *Ulysses* from the rufous colour of his hair, inherited from his father). He was 'the Cornet Player' and 'The Marquess of Lorne' to John Joyce.* 'He was led astray by books when he was a young man' and lapsed from the Church but 'only for a time'; the only one in the whole family to do so until Joyce himself, May Joyce claimed. One of his anecdotes related being taken into the back room of a second-hand bookseller's in High Street and shown his salacious stock. In 1891, he married Elizabeth Harris, the daughter of a commercial traveller; he had to marry her because his eldest child Lilla (later a nun) was – in the decorous language of Stanislaus Joyce – 'a bastard': that is to say, conceived out of wedlock. Aunt Lillie was thought a common little creature by the snobbish Joyces, and John Joyce used to call her 'Amina' and 'La Somnambula'. When married, John (35) and Lillie (16½) were living in the same lodging at 39 Lower Abbey Street and their love match gave Joyce the germ of 'The Boarding House' – in which Polly Mooney traps her humble clerk into marriage by presenting herself to him in her shift – a story which explains the significance of the 'sleepwalking'. The Murrays had four surviving children: Elizabeth Mary, Isabella Margaret, Valentine John and Gerard. Another son, Walter, died in 1897, aged 2, while they were living on Raymond Street, off the South Circular Road; he fell into a tub of hot water and the shock

---

* John Sutherland, Marquess of Lorne, born 1845, heir of the Duke of Argyll, married Queen Victoria's artist daughter Princess Louise, a contemporary model of refinement, in 1871.

killed him. Joyce's reaction to this tragedy in a family he did not care for was to give the dead boy's name to Richie Goulding's son in *Ulysses*; a cruel touch. This family later lived at 39 Drumcondra Road, and one of their annual Hallowe'en parties is recollected in Joyce's story, 'Clay'. His early lapse made the married John Murray a stern and puritanical man, given to denouncing writers such as Zola.

William, John Murray's younger brother, was a domestic tyrant whose ill-treatment of his seven-year-old son Hubert ('Bertie') while they were living at 77 Haddington Road (near Beggars Bush military barracks) inspired Joyce's story 'Counterparts'. However, he was married to the veritable saint in Joyce's immediate family, Josephine Giltrap. She was the daughter of a well-off law agent James J. Giltrap, the 'Papa Giltrap' to whom belonged the original Irish red-setter dog 'Garryowen' (whelped in 1871), which appears in the 'Cyclops' episode in company with the Citizen. (It is all too typical of Joyce's works that even the dogs in them have an immediate personal connection with his family.) William had originally worked as an accountant for James Giltrap in his Morgan Place office, and in effect married his boss's daughter. After Giltrap died in the early 1890s, William worked on his own account for a while and then joined Collis and Ward, a firm of solicitors, again as a cost accountant. Josephine Giltrap was well-educated, having been sent to a convent school at Glossop in Derbyshire, England. She seems to have been not only a sensible woman, but one with sufficient brains and reading to cope with her wayward nephew James in his rebellious 'Stephen Dedalus' period. Their first child died, but they had two other boys and four girls while living at a host of addresses, some of which (such as Ontario Terrace and Holles Street) were later used by Joyce as homes for Mr Bloom. The economic troubles which beset the Blooms may have been modelled in part on the troubled experiences of the Murrays. In his last years William Murray had a secret which was to affect profoundly Joyce's view of Dublin.

In contrast May Murray was educated in part by her aunts the Misses Flynn, and was a gentle creature who must have suffered much from her mother's lingering last illness.

Her father, John Murray, was made of sterner stuff however. Margaret Theresa died in February 1881 and in November of that year, with what even today might be considered indecent haste, John Murray remarried. His second wife was Christina Margaret O'Neill, born Margaret Christina O'Donohoe, and was the younger sister of Maria O'Donohoe – the spinster Aunt Maria of 'Clay'. Their father was William O'Donohoe, a hotel owner. His profession and manner of death may have suggested Virag Bloom's ownership of the Queen's Hotel in Ennis and his peculiar suicide, remembered by his son Leopold in *Ulysses*.

Their mother, however, was yet another of the Flynn sisters. John Murray had in fact married his late wife's niece, the child of his children's aunt, an unusual union which disgusted Jack* Joyce, who referred to him in future years as 'the old fornicator'.

At the time of his marriage, though he used an address of convenience in Blackhall Place on the marriage register, John Murray was (according to the notice he inserted in the papers) living in Church House, Chapelizod – the actual 'House by the Churchyard' which has such a curious significance for Joyce in *Finnegans Wake*, and in which he placed the lodgings of Mr Duffy in 'A Painful Case'. John Murray's career had been a mixed one. His wife ran *The Eagle House* for some time before they gave it up, suggesting that he may have been a bankrupt in the early 1860s, though I have no evidence for this beyond the fact that the pub was held under his wife's name. Exactly what he did between 1867 and 1880 is unclear. Described on his daughter's marriage certificate in 1880 as a corn agent, by 1882 he was a commercial traveller. Family tradition thought of him as an agent for wines. In fact for many years he travelled for John Power's Whiskey Distillery and later worked for T.W. Begge's, a tea and wine merchants at 28 Bachelor's Walk. His second wife – perhaps separated from him by then – died in 1891 in the Flynn household on Usher's Island, and he went to live with his son John in Drumcondra, where he died, paralysed after a stroke, in 1894.

John Murray, in the way of business either as a traveller or a corn agent, dealt with the distillery at Chapelizod, on the outskirts of Dublin, in the late 1870s. He was taken with the fine singing voice of the young man who was the Secretary of the company, and invited him to visit his home in Clanbrassil Street. There he was welcome for a time, but the Murrays were dismayed when a serious relationship sprang up between the adolescent May Murray and the handsome young man whose name was John Stanislaus Joyce.

*

* John Stanislaus Joyce was Jack to his family and cronies.

Like the Murrays, John Joyce was also a provincial, hailing from Cork. He held both his native place and his family name in great esteem, but was oddly vague about historical details.

The earliest Irish Joyce known to history was an Anglo-Norman settler of the twelfth century who came to Ireland from Wales. His language would have been Norman French, though Joyce liked to imagine that his ancestors' original language was Gaelic. In his extended voyage around Ireland he married Nora, daughter of the O'Brien of Thomond. The Joyces were granted – or rather they seized from the native Irish – a run of land on the borders of Galway and Mayo, an area that is still called today 'The Joyce Country', lying between the Maamturk Mountains and Lough Mask. But theirs was a poor kingdom in the poorest province of Ireland, a district of brown bog, grey rock and black lakes.

During the Cromwellian and Williamite wars of the seventeenth century the Joyces, like so many Catholic families, were deprived of their lands and scattered from their own fiefdom. They spread southwards into Galway and Clare, and by the eighteenth century were found in Kerry and Cork. There were also Joyces in the Connemara marble quarries, and it is said that the Joyces of Co. Cork preserve a memory of having come south as masons at the end of the eighteenth century.

And it is in Co. Cork at the end of the eighteenth century that Joyce's own ancestors are picked up. They lived then in the neighbourhood of Fermoy, a town developed by the entrepreneur John Anderson over the thirty-odd years since 1792, before which it had been only a few cabins at a cross-roads beside a ruined abbey. The town's growth as a military, stage-coaching and market centre created opportunities for many rising Catholics, among them the Joyces.

James Joyce claimed that his family had once held extensive lands in Munster; such at least is the story that his authorized biographers have been happy to record for him. It was once a common enough fantasy among Catholics in trade that they had landed ancestors, but there is no evidence to support Joyce's claim. Indeed it was only by the exercise of certain legal devices that Catholics could hold land at all before 1782. It was not unusual for the head of the family to conform to the established Anglican faith of the Church of Ireland in order to keep his estate. Again, there is no evidence of this in the case of the Joyces.

The Fermoy Joyces, like the majority of their Catholic countrymen, were small tenant farmers. John Stanislaus Joyce and his son James were much given to references to their family coat of arms; but these in fact were the arms of the Joyces of Corgary in Connaught, to which the writer's family would seem to have no claim, and it is unlikely that the Ulster King of Arms (then the appropriate heraldic authority in Ireland) would have recognized their use by a middle-class family which knew so little about their origins.*

James Joyce once remarked of Tolstoy that as a Russian noble, he would have known his great-great-grandfather's Christian name – a fact which lay at the base of the essentially feudal art of the Russians, who had a scrupulous instinct for caste. The Irish, too, have a fine sense of caste, but given the turbulent nature of the country's history many Irish people have long since lost such links with their families' past. The later Joyces, like many of their kind – the sometime serfs of Ireland – could not get back much beyond the Act of Union in 1800.

The name of Joyce's own great-great-grandfather was George Joyce of Fermoy. George had one son, James (the writer's great-grandfather), who married an Ann McCann of Ulster. Nothing seems to be known about Ann or the McCann family, though oddly Joyce's own godfather was one Philip McCann, a Dublin ships' chandler from Shortstone in Dundalk (just south of the Ulster border), who may have been a distant connection.

On a visit to Cork as a child in 1894, with his father, the writer was to hear this great-grandfather James Joyce the elder, from whom his own name came, extolled by one of the older generation of Corkonians as 'a fierce old fire-eater'. In his youth James Joyce the elder had been a Whiteboy, one of those agrarian terrorists who ravaged rural Munster from 1760 onwards.

There was a serious Whiteboy outbreak in 1822, and a special Act of Parliament had to be passed to deal with it. Much of the province was in a state of armed insurrection, and in north Cork bands of Whiteboys descended from the hills to raid towns for food and arms.

* It has been suggested to me by the local historian of Fermoy, Niall Brunicardi, that the Fermoy Joyces were in fact descended from the English Joys of Wexford and not the Norman Joyces of Connaught. That James Joyce was not a Joyce at all would indeed be an amusing irony, but no firm evidence has been adduced to support this pleasing notion.

The military were called out and many arrests were made. At a special assize in Cork city in mid-February 1823 some 300 prisoners were dealt with, of whom 36 were sentenced to death.

James Joyce the elder was among the condemned Whiteboys, but was reprieved by a government anxious to assuage the widespread civil disaffection. His radicalism and fervent anti-clericalism confirm the family's status as small tenant farmers. Catholic priests in the nineteenth century were nearly always the sons of the gentry, strong farmers or merchants: their spiritual influence owed much to their social standing in the community. In a period when there were few professions for educated men, the priesthood offered opportunities to many younger sons of better families. The Joyces were not of that class. It was from his great-grandfather that the strong, bad-tempered, anti-clerical strain passed into the culture of the Joyce family, and eventually to Joyce himself.

Yet the radical James Joyce the elder (as the old Corkonian again recalled for his grandson) was also a keen rider to hounds – but, as readers of Somerville and Ross will know, in rural Ireland following the local hunt is no real indication of superior social standing; it indicates nothing more than the means to keep a horse. Many small farmers were as keen on the chase and the kill as any scion of the 'Big House'.

The first certain date which the writer's family tradition retained was the birth in 1827 at Rose Cottage, just outside Fermoy, of James Augustine Joyce, the son of James and Ann McCann Joyce. There were no more children of this marriage: an unusual fact which suggests it was not sexually successful.

Rose Cottage, where the Joyces lived until 1830, and which still stands today, was a small single-storey farmhouse of the late eighteenth century, facing a yard surrounded by outhouses, and very typical of its kind. The lane from the house to the main road which runs between Fermoy and Mallow was known into recent times as 'Joyce's Boreen'.

Nearby are limestone quarries, and during the 1820s James Joyce the elder was in the lime-burning business; the lime was used as a fertilizer. On early maps his kiln is marked as standing in the field behind the cottage. The Joyces, however, were ambitious; they were not so attached to the land as to let it interfere with their social mobility. Though they never lost the association with Fermoy (which John Stanislaus Joyce was to revisit as late as 1910, doubtless on a last pious pilgrimage to the family cottage and the graves of his ancestors), like all ambitious Irishmen they soon broke their connection with the soil and moved to the city. Their rise can be traced through property deeds of the period.

On 16th July 1830 George Joyce (who had probably already done contract work in Fermoy) acquired his first piece of urban property in Cork, at 16 White Street, in the south-east quarter of what was then the edge of the expanding city.* The property, owned by a Charles Connell (more properly perhaps Charles O'Connell) was the first of a series of properties in and around the same district in the east end of the city which were to be the keystone of the family's prosperity for some sixty years. Here the original James Joyce and his son James Augustine Joyce re-established their lime and salt business. These were the most prosperous years in Cork's history, and the Joyces prospered with them.

The city was small, a little over 100,000 people at that date. But though small it was charming and distinctive, with an old-fashioned seventeenth-century air about it, though some grand modern buildings were being erected along the main streets. Cork Harbour was an important port on the European and American routes; brandy was smuggled from the one, emigrants sent to the other. From the agricultural hinterland it exported vast quantities of salted provisions. In the season 100,000 cattle were slaughtered, largely to fill the annual Navy contracts of Great Britain. Butter from Cork and Kerry went out through the Cork Butter Market, which was the centre of the national trade. Whiskey and porter went to the West Indies. And besides there were factories for sailcloth, coarse sheeting, woollens and glass. Culturally Cork was on a par with Dublin in its own estimation, for there were literary, artistic and musical clubs – such as the Temperance Institute founded by the famous Father Matthew – with public lectures on historical and literary subjects. There was a lively local school of musicians and poets, of whom Francis O'Mahony ('Father Prout') was the most notable: their tendency was comical and sentimental, never intimate or romantic. It was a garrulous, versifying, musical city with its own proper pride; the Joyces, however, were concerned less with culture and more with business.

---

* White Street may have been named for the architect Henry White, for whom James Joyce acted as executor after his death in 1842.

A lease of 1835 records that James Joyce and Jeremiah O'Connor purchased lands at Carraigeeny outside Cork city; they were to sell this lot in 1842 for £500. Directories of the period record James Joyce as still at 16 White Street, on the corner with South Terrace. The salt and lime business went into decline in the late 1840s, owing to the deteriorating conditions in rural Ireland after the Famine – when the corpses of the dead who had died of hunger on the streets of Cork were collected at dawn by a municipal cart. In 1852 they were advantageously bankrupted, using company law to escape from the debts and difficulties of a declining business. Undismayed, James Joyce went on to create a new and more prosperous business as a successful building contractor, returning to the trade of his ancestors, though of a grander kind than Tim Finnegan in *Finnegans Wake*. Having had a builder in the family must have added piquant associations to Ibsen's play *The Master Builder* when Joyce came to read it.

The name Joyce's Court was attached to a set of six small tenements just off White Street.* The properties that the Joyces owned were small houses, yards and out-offices, and they might unkindly be characterized as slum landlords. More properties were added, and on 7th January 1846 James Joyce purchased the lease of the rear plot of South Terrace, a set of stables, from Sir Thomas Deane, the Cork architect. These ran alongside the property of a William Pennefather; how the Joyces worsted him was for long an anecdote of John Joyce (and is duly mentioned in *A Portrait of the Artist*), but the details of the feud are not recorded.

George and James Joyce give every indication of being strong self-willed men, who made a success of their enterprises. James Augustine Joyce, in contrast, was little more than a feckless charmer; a typical man of the third generation only too happy to spend what his father and grandfather had won. A horse trainer by trade, with premises at Winthrop Street, he was also a gambler, and his reckless way with bets on his own and other peoples' horses saw him through a great deal of money. By an arrangement between the families, a marriage was made for him with a former nun, one Ellen O'Connell, born about 1816, who was a good decade older than he was.

*

---

* The name plaque above the entrance to this alley was stolen some years ago by a crazed collector.

James Joyce's grandmother Ellen and her sister Alicia O'Connell had entered the South Presentation Convent in October 1836, but Ellen left after four months.

The convent records have a curious note about this:

> It was a matter of her own choosing. She became nervously and unnecessarily anxious about her health, which was not, in reality, *bad*. She had just finished the fourth month of her Postulantship. She was a nice, amiable and good girl – *too good*, to encounter the rough seas of this world; where she can scarcely escape the meeting of many a rock and many a breaker – but, little as her religious training had been, may she have learnt from her short novitiate, to look up only to the *one eye*, that steadily and securely guides, each bark of this uncertain life.

Whether this delicate, even hysterical, personality – reminiscent perhaps of Joyce's young woman in 'Eveline', or indeed of Joyce himself – was really suited to married life must be a moot question. Her portrait, painted shortly after her marriage, certainly reveals an anxious and over-sensitive face.

She was the daughter of John O'Connell who owned a large drapery store in Cork city, at 16 Great Georges Street (now Washington Street). John Joyce and his son speak also of Charles O'Connell, who would have been John's father (John Joyce or his interviewer seem to have become confused on this point. It is significant of his interest in family legend rather than hard facts that he passed on his confusion to his sons. Charles O'Connell was also the grandfather of John Joyce's cousin John Daly, whose mother was a Mary O'Connell, an aunt perhaps of Ellen and Alicia.)

These O'Connells were related to Daniel O'Connell, 'the Liberator', who had done so much to create the democratic (as opposed to the revolutionary) tradition in Ireland. This connection was through the O'Connells of Tarmons in Co. Kerry to the original John O'Connell, the builder of Derrynane House, grandfather of the Liberator, who could trace his lineage back to the fourteenth century. The land at Tarmons was sold in 1785 – nothing is to be seen there today, I am informed by Professor Maurice O'Connell – and these O'Connells moved into business in Nile Street in Cork city and into some obscurity. They fell into trade, unlike the Joyces who rose into it. Yet this was a relationship which Daniel O'Connell was pleased to recognize: when he came to Cork to attend the annual assizes up to 1829, the year he was elected to Parliament, he would call upon his cousins. With Charles O'Connell he would walk up and down the street arm in arm, both wearing (as John Joyce's mother recalled) the knee-breeches fashionable in those days.

James Augustine Joyce and Ellen O'Connell were married in the church of SS Peter and Paul, Paul Street, Cork, on 29th January 1847. As was then common, their marriage was followed a year later by a post-nuptial settlement on 28th February 1848; this agreement was to have far-reaching consequences.

Earlier that February James Joyce senior had acquired from William Pennefather (then of Island House) property in Anglesea Street, Cork. Further property was bought on 24th February. By the terms of the settlement John O'Connell assigned James Augustine Joyce £1,000 as a marriage portion; and his father (out of the great love he bore him, according to the deed) gave him a half share in lands at Skahard (now a public park) and Goat Island in the Douglas River. For his part the newly-married James Joyce put into trust the properties around White and Anglesea Streets. The trustees were a Michael Murphy and his wife's brother William O'Connell, a draper in Castle Street. The contributions of the Joyce and O'Connell families were about equal, though the O'Connell name carried more social prestige. As the O'Connells had the real wealth, however, the writer's brother Stanislaus resented the 'large, square, low-fronted' O'Connell features found among members of his family – he refers to his father's O'Connell 'snout' – preferring what he thought of as the fairer features of the Joyce face, even though he did not share them.

These properties were now protected by the trust for the benefit of Ellen Joyce and their eventual family – a testamentary fact cryptically alluded to by Joyce in *Exiles*.

On 4th July 1849 Ellen Joyce was delivered of a son, who was baptized two days later – sponsored by his relatives William O'Connell and Ellen O'Connell – as John Stanislaus Joyce. He was to be their only son, remarkably the only son of an only son of an only son. Here again the marriage failed on the rock of sexual feeling, or the lack of it. In his own life, however, John Joyce proved to have the fecundity for which the O'Connells rather than the Joyces were famous – and Daniel O'Connell infamous.* Yet in later life he would

---

* In his own time it was said unfairly (and untruly, modern historians believe) that one could not throw a stick over a workhouse wall without striking a bastard offspring of the Liberator.

treat his own eldest surviving son James as if he too were another only son.

In 1850 John O'Connell became an Alderman for the St Patrick's Ward of Cork city. His influence secured for his son-in-law (whom family tradition credits with a double bankruptcy) a municipal sinecure as Inspector of Hackney Coaches. The belief that the world owed the Joyces a living seems to have begun with John Joyce's father, and not to have been renounced by his son and grandson.

The Joyces resided now at 6 Anglesea Street, a less than fashionable address on the south-east of Cork, overlooking the railway sidings, the gasworks and the city cattle markets.

John O'Connell died in the early 1850s, hence all that John Stanislaus Joyce knew of him came from his mother's stories. Nor are the activities of James Joyce the builder clear. What records there are deal with the buying and selling of land, and his ownership of a brickfield outside Cork. In 1852 the brickfield is noted in *Griffith's Valuation*, the official record of lands, their owners and their value, and the sale of lands at Ballinasmought on the north of the city is recorded in a deed of 1853.

In contrast to the Joyces, the O'Connells were a well-placed mercantile, clerical-minded family. Ellen Joyce had been educated by Ursuline nuns – in Cork, as elsewhere, the most fashionable educational order of the day. Thackeray in his *Irish Sketchbook* has a delighted account of his visit in 1842 to this very institution at Blackrock, just outside the city, which charmed him by its elegance amid the surrounding Irish squalor. She retained something of the gentility of the nuns, which Thackeray mentions, all her life. Emma Bovary, it will be recalled, was also educated by the Ursuline nuns: the provincial parallel is almost exact.

Ellen's sister Alicia, however, who had remained to take her final vows, eventually became superior of the South City Presentation Convent; she died in 1872 of liver disease. She had no connection with another Presentation house at Crosshaven, though the Joyces confusedly thought she had. Their brother Charles, another of a family said to have numbered some nineteen children, was ordained in 1854 and held several chaplaincies in the city. He seems to have been suspended as a priest about 1863 while a curate in the rural parish of Iniskeen, but though no longer listed among the clergy of Ireland he still styled himself the Reverend Charles O'Connell until the end of his life (his name so appears on a baptismal certificate of

1886). The suspension was said to have arisen from his refusal to accept his share of the parish dues, as he had independent means, which was interpreted as disobedience to his superiors. The air of obscure clerical scandal hovering around Charles O'Connell was to be passed on to the unfortunate priest in 'The Sisters'.*

As a child John Joyce was prepared for his First Holy Communion about 1857 by Sister Xavier (his aunt Alicia). He attended St Colman's College in Fermoy from St Patrick's Day 1859 and was said to be a favourite of the rector, the famous Dr Thomas Croke, founder of the Gaelic Athletic Association and bitter opponent of Parnell, who had opened the College in the previous September. Croke spoilt him as he was the youngest in the school, always putting the boy next to him at dinner in the refectory. Dr Croke was said to have left a permanent mark on St Colman's by inculcating among his students the 'two great College virtues – humility and obedience'. But not on John Joyce. He left on 19th February 1860, his fees unpaid, due to ill-health.

Given his intemperate language about them in later life, when discussing the future education of his son James, we may well suppose (though inquiries have failed to confirm this) that John Joyce was largely educated by the Christian Brothers, perhaps at their College ('Christians') in Cork, which ranked with Clongowes in the eyes of some. Family tradition says that frequent illness kept him from school, but he seems to have been a man of some education, able to quote the classics and to write a fair hand. For a time he certainly attended a private school in Cork city, established at 3 Grand Parade by Mr Daniel O'Sullivan, from where he went on to university in the autumn of 1865.

In order to improve his health John Joyce's father was accustomed to send him out with the Queenstown pilot boats, on which the boy collected a fine repertoire of oaths. The references to Cork Harbour that occur in the 'Eumaeus' episode of *Ulysses*, associated as they are with the rambling recollections of the sailor, may owe something to John's youthful summers at Glenbrook, a resort opposite Carrigaloe.

He admired his father, who was that excellent thing: a gentleman.

---

* Professor Ellmann's account of these (and other) matters is hopelessly confused. The priest he identified was in fact a Cornelius O'Connell born in Co. Cork and no relation of these O'Connells. Here it is clear that by relying on information from the notorious Eoin O'Mahony and a source who preferred to remain anonymous he was led astray, perhaps deliberately.

One evening in 1863 (so John Joyce related) he and his friends were smoking on the corner of South Terrace when his father passed. The next Sunday, though the boy was only 14, he was nonchalantly offered a cigar by his father while they took their weekly constitutional after dinner. From his own father John Joyce derived his determination in life always to be a gentleman – a matter he insisted upon with all the vulgar energy of the self-made. It was a worldly ambition passed on in turn to his son James. Living off the wealth made by others, this ancestral James A. Joyce was anxious to escape from the stink of the lime-kiln, the muck of the brickfield.

On 26th September 1866 James A. Joyce fell ill with fever and inflammation of the lungs. His illness was to be long, painful and terminal. When he died on Sunday, 28th October at his home, 6 Anglesea Street, he was only 39.

(It is said that as he lay dying he realized his son's anxiety to hear the great Italian tenor Mario sing in the Italian Opera season at the Theatre Royal in Dublin. When the boy returned he found his father not dead, as he liked to relate, but certainly dying. The Dublin season ended after a last night on the 5th October, with a morning concert on 6th October in the Antient Concert Rooms. There is no evidence that Mario sang that year in Cork, so John Joyce must have travelled up to the capital with a party, staying perhaps in the Gresham Hotel, one of the new directors of which since 1865 was a neighbour of the Joyces at 32 South Terrace, Francis Lyons, a merchant. Mario's Christ-like features, it will be recalled, are mentioned by Joyce in *Ulysses*.)

It must have been shortly before this time that the painting of John Joyce, now in Buffalo University, was executed. The family already owned a pair of portraits executed by John Comerford (1771–1832) – who had done portraits of the Liberator – of Charles O'Connell with his favourite spaniel, and his wife. This was the lady who made the hunting waistcoat, decorated with foxes and horns, eventually inherited by Joyce and now in the Joyce Museum in Dublin. These had been matched by another pair of portraits by William Roe (?1800–?1852) of James A. Joyce and his wife Ellen, done shortly after their marriage, perhaps about 1850. Each holds a rose, symbolic of love in the language of flowers. Now that he was head of the family, a portrait of John Stanislaus was painted to complete the set. The sensitive features of a music-loving youth, derived from his mother, are already beginning to coarsen into the more familiar features of Jack Joyce as the abusive Simon Dedalus.

The following year, 1867, John Joyce returned to Queen's College Cork in October to study medicine, the second faculty in the college. He had matriculated in 1865 to do arts but had not continued, probably because of his father's death. Initially he did well, by his own account winning one of the six junior scholarships of £20 – though the college calendar knows nothing of this. In the summer of 1868 he passed his first year medical examination. His second year was more convivial. He was not averse to a little womanizing: Cork as a seaport was famous for its 'Holy Ground', as the brothel quarter was called. In old age Jack Joyce confessed to a medical friend, F. J. Walsh, that while a student (say about 1867) he had discovered a syphilitic chancre on his penis and had treated it himself with carbolic, the usual treatment of the day. This would have cured only the symptoms, not the disease. Yet it seems most unlikely that a real syphilitic could sire some 16 or 17 reportedly unsyphilitic children and live to the age of 82. We have to look elsewhere for James Joyce's fixation with this particular social disease.

John Joyce joined the Queen's College Dramatic Society, and was one of those involved in their first public performance (in support of two local charities) at the Theatre Royal Cork on 11th March 1869. This occasion was enlivened by a political demonstration from the gallery against Mr Alfred Dan, who at Christmas had attacked the Mayor's nationalist views and was now to be barracked whenever he appeared. A local critic for the *Constitution* (a Unionist paper), however, records that Mr Joyce, 'who was exceedingly funny and intensely popular in his singing of "The Groves of Blackpool" and "Paddy McFadden",' also 'showed an amount of skill not at all to be despised'.

On 16th April in another benefit he performed in *The Mummy*, a comic play. 'This piece, though rather stupid, was made funny enough by the excellent acting of Mr Joyce who took the "Irish character". In this he displayed a considerable talent for imitation, which tickled the fancy of the audience.'

As a result of his involvement with the drama society John Joyce failed his second medical examination in the summer of 1869 and had to repeat the year, but in the summer of 1870 he failed again. It is hard to see him as a serious student. Then, as now, medicine had its social aspects; it was the most popular career for many Catholics, bringing with it both easy wealth and social status. For his degree, however, John Joyce would also have to have studied a modern Continental language and taken a course of Natural Philosophy before his medical work. Probably he would have preferred playing backgammon and billiards, coffee and cigar parties in his friends' rooms, and reading *Tristram Shandy* like his peers. Rising early to read in the library or hear lectures would have been disagreeable; it is not surprising that he failed.

However, by now he may not have cared. On 4th July 1870, on his 21st birthday, he came into £1,000 from his grandfather O'Connell's estate. I suspect that this may not have been in the form of capital he could spend, but as some kind of annuity or sum in trust – and may have been the marriage settlement sum. The O'Connells are likely to have been too cautious to pass simple cash in hand.

The following month, August 1870, war broke out between Prussia and France, an event which caused great excitement in Ireland. Both military and ambulance brigades were raised to go to the aid of Catholic France and the Emperor who had defended the Pope from armies of the new Italy. John Joyce and some of his friends ran off to join up and fight, but his mother pursued him to London and brought him back to Cork.

He failed to settle down. In 1871 there were Fenian demonstrations in Cork following the release of prisoners from the Rising of 1865, and John Joyce became mixed up with these revolutionary Republicans, again to his mother's dismay. He was a friend of the Clerkenwell prisoners Richard Burke (a Cork man) and Joseph Theobald Casey, who appears in *Ulysses* as Kevin Egan, which was why years later his son James looked Casey up in Paris: Casey thought he heard John's tone in James's voice.

The four years between 1870 and 1874 are vague in John Joyce's life. Presumably he enjoyed rowing on the River Lee and riding to hounds with the local harriers – in old age he claimed there were few fields in Cork he did not know. It seems likely that at this time he gained some experience in commerce or law, maybe in a Cork solicitor's office. He wrote a fine scrivener's hand which he may have spent some time learning, unless it was a result of his excellent education under Mr O'Sullivan. Doubtless family connections served him well: his relations the O'Connells, Dalys and McSwineys were all prominent in Cork public life. His cousin John Daly was

Lord Mayor of Cork in 1871 and again in 1872; Peter Paul McSwiney had been Lord Mayor of Dublin.

Not all the family were successful, however. In 1869 his uncle William O'Connell, who had taken over the drapery business in Great George's Street in 1854 from his father John, went bankrupt. He had not paid much attention to John Joyce after his father's death, or so John Joyce thought; though the records suggest that he had carefully attended to many matters relating to the leases of the property which he held in trust for his sister Mrs Joyce. His son eventually took his family to London, leaving a daughter behind as a nun in Cork city. May O'Connell (born 2nd February 1883) entered the Presentation convent in Crosshaven as Sister Ita.

Mrs Joyce, anxious to promote the future of her son, decided that they would move to Dublin. A farewell dinner given for the young man by his cronies to mark his departure for the capital seems to have been towards the end of 1874. In December of that year their relation, Peter Paul McSwiney, whose mother had been an O'Connell and who was part owner with George Delaney of Dublin's finest and only Catholic department store (now Clerys), was elected Lord Mayor of Dublin for the following year. (It was his second term of office; he had also been Lord Mayor in 1864.) This year marked the centenary of Daniel O'Connell's birth, in which Peter Paul McSwiney would play a leading if controversial role. As an O'Connellite and a prominent member of the clerical party (many saw him as the spokesman in Dublin affairs of Cardinal Cullen – then presiding over the creation of the modern Catholic church in Ireland), he was to be attacked by the rising party of young Home Rulers. A public dinner at the end of August would end in chaos. Yet a man with his influence would have been able to secure John Stanislaus Joyce some opening in a comfortable position. Mrs Joyce wanted to see him as Mayor's secretary, but this post was already gifted to the painter Michael Angelo Hayes, McSwiney's brother-in-law.

What did emerge was a position in a new enterprise, in which both John Daly and Peter Paul McSwiney – as well as other friends of John Joyce's late father – were involved, an enterprise which was to leave its mark on literature through the pages of *Finnegans Wake*. This was the Dublin and Chapelizod Distillery Company.

The scheme had its beginnings with a Cork wine merchant, now based in Dublin, Henry Joseph Alleyn. He acquired the site by the

River Liffey in the village of Chapelizod, on which there was a flax mill founded by the railway pioneer William Dargan, along with a Mr Hoey, in 1873. (Before Dargan bought it, the site had been until about 1860 the barracks of the Royal Irish Artillery.) In turn he leased the property to the Dublin and Chapelizod Distillery in which he also became a partner. To be near the works, he moved out from Merrion Square to a mansion in Palmerstown, from where he descended daily to inspect the progress being made by the workers, who disliked him.

The capital of the firm was to be £80,000, some £20,000 of which would be issued to Alleyn for virtually nothing. However unusual this was later to seem, the agreement was laid out clearly in the articles of association. In seeking further capital it was agreed with the young John Joyce that he would invest some £500 and be made the Company Secretary. This was apparently early in 1875. Soon work was going rapidly ahead on the site in line with a most lavish and optimistic prospectus.

John Joyce was to enjoy his time in Chapelizod. Since there was a works manager his own effort was of an agreeably limited kind, concerned more with the financial than the technical side. But he acquired a smattering of the technical jargon of the trade, and in later years James Joyce would recall (as he notes in 'The Sisters') the talk of 'worms and feints'. In old age his only regular reading was the organ of the Licensed Vintners Association. There were jovial evenings in Robert Broadbent's hotel near the bridge (the very hotel in which *Finnegans Wake* is set) where he lodged, and the entertainment of bowling matches with other Dublin teams.

At long last, however, the peculiar arrangement with Alleyn came to John Joyce's notice: perhaps the Company Secretary had at last got round to reading the articles of the firm. Trouble now arose over Alleyn's large holding, John Joyce and others maintaining that he was taking out too much from the firm. As Company Secretary, Joyce called a shareholders' meeting, the notices and resolutions of which were to be the subject of legal criticisms later from the Master of the Rolls. After a great deal of bitter discussion it was decided to buy out Alleyn's interest by means of a mortgage. This deed was signed on 31st July 1876.

By now the company was in decline, despite John Joyce's hard work. Irish whiskey had not proved as popular on the English market as once it had been, and was falling away before the rising taste for

Scotch. On 1st August 1877 a creditor of the firm obtained an order calling in the Receiver, who made a great effort to sell it, advertising it locally and in London. The whole matter was finally resolved before the Master of the Rolls in January 1878, when an order was made winding up the company. The Master of the Rolls was severe in his criticism of the directors, and by inference of the Company Secretary, and defended the character and public reputation of Henry Alleyn.

John Joyce, naturally enough, did not see it that way. For him Alleyn was a villain, and his figure duly entered the demonology of his son James. (His name was given to the unpleasant solicitor in 'Counterparts'.) Henry Alleyn, who had other interests in the city with his brother, did not (as John Joyce imagined) flee the country in disgrace; he merely retired to his property in Cork. In January 1880 he died at Menton, in the south of France, where he is buried.

As for the distillery ('the mill that was still' in *Finnegans Wake*), it was eventually bought up by the Distillers Company of Scotland for a mere £26,000. (Run as a going concern for some years, during the 1890s when James Joyce knew Chapelizod it was indeed temporarily disused, as he recalls in 'A Painful Case'.) John Joyce was to claim that under the terms of the winding-up settlement there was money due to him (his £500 investment we may suppose) from a trust fund in the Bank of Ireland, where the monies of the High Court would be held. But this sum seems to have existed only in his imagination.

For James Joyce, Chapelizod retained its fascination. It was associated in medieval tradition with the legend of Tristan and Isolde ('Iseult's Chapel'). Joyce gave Mr Duffy lodgings there in 'A Painful Case', and set the dream of H.C. Earwicker in the Mullingar Hotel, of which that estimable man (clearly English) was the proprietor in succession to the English Protestant Robert Broadbent. As John Joyce and his family were accustomed in later years to picnic at the Strawberry Beds further out along the Liffey, the curious village would have been familiar to James from childhood. It had its own literary association through the residence there of the novelist Sheridan Le Fanu, who made it the setting of *The House by the Churchyard* (1863) – this being the very house from which Mr Duffy looks out over the temporarily disused distillery and the river, and in which old John Murray too had lived for a time. That novel was one of the few books John Joyce owned.

Having lost his position in the distillery at the end of 1877, John Joyce now set himself up as an accountant with an office in a building at 13 Westland Row, directly opposite the church and the railway station familiar to readers of *Ulysses*. This was in 1879. The office was convenient for the railway line along the coast to Kingstown / Dalkey where he was then living with his mother at an address (as yet untraced) somewhere in the Monkstown district. John Joyce kept a small boat at Dalkey harbour which he sailed in Dublin Bay. As an accountant he would have been involved less in auditing (as now) than in the collection of bad debts – Mr Bloom's experiences dunning the good nuns in the Tranquilla Convent may perhaps have been transferred to him from John Joyce.

This excursion into self-employment did not last long, for in the following year (1879) John Joyce was appointed Secretary of the newly formed United Liberal Club, which had rooms at 54 Dawson Street. The Club had grown out of the Liberal Registration Association, in which Catholic politicians such as Peter Paul McSwiney were involved.

This was a political rather than a social club, its main business being the registration of Liberal voters and the fighting of elections. At that date the numbers entitled to vote were restricted to a few thousand only, the franchise being based on property qualifications. Though his son would refer to his father as 'a shouting politician', suggesting a more demotic level of political action, John Joyce was in his element at the Liberal Club. He may have obtained this post through a family connection with Peter Paul McSwiney and Father Edward O'Connell, who was involved with the Liberal Registration Association.

In the general election held in April 1880 John Joyce helped to unseat one of the Guinnesses and secured the election of Maurice Brooks (a wealthy Dublin Protestant timber merchant and builders' supplier) and Dr Robert Lyons, an eminent medical man who had come from Cork originally where his father had been Lord Mayor. But these results were part of a pattern across the country in which the old patrician politicians were swept away after a campaign organized by Charles Stewart Parnell and the Land League (founded the year before in Dublin), who took advantage of the newly extended franchise.

This election was one of the events in his life that James Joyce had his father questioned about in his old age. The post-election

47

spree in the Oval Bar was one of John Joyce's more hectic anecdotes. The thrill of winning was crowned for him by a gift from the new members of £100 each. There was talk even of his standing at the next election (but that would not be until 1885). This notion was also mooted for Bloom, we are told in *Ulysses*.

John Joyce moved in musical circles in Dublin too. He had sung at a public concert in the Antient Concert Rooms (where his son would follow him years later), and he was made aware that his voice was much admired from a distance by the famous tenor Barton McGuckin. For his friend Stuart Gilbert, Joyce provided a note on the musical culture of Dublin at this time:

> One of the most remarkable features of Dublin life in the heyday of Mr Bloom [and of John Joyce] was the boundless enthusiasm of all classes of citizens for music, especially of the vocal and operatic varieties. This passion is illustrated by their cult of the divo, carried to a degree unknown even in Italy. All the great singers came to Dublin, and the names Campanini, Joe Maas, Maria Piccolomini (creator of Violetta in *La Traviata*), Tietjens, Giuglini, Trebelli-Bettini and many others [including the original Madame Sinico, singing wife of a Triestian opera star] were household words. Their memories went back even to the legendary Lablache (the Chaliapin of his time), who was born (of an Irish mother and a French father) in the eighteenth century. Other well-known vocalists of Irish blood were Catherine Hayes, William Ludwig (né Ledwidge) and Foli (né Foley). The personalities and careers of such artists were an unfailing theme of conversation – the tragic *fianali*, for example of Giuglini and of Ilma de Murska, and the curious appearance and supposed royal descent of Mario, Cavaliere de Candida (who had flourished sixty years before [1904] and was, for the Irish 'king's sons', the *Prince of Candida.*) ... When Trebelli was singing at the Old Royal, the Dubliners were wont to unhorse her carriage and draw her in state to her hotel. The first interpreter of the roles of Basilio and Don Curzio was Michael Kelly, and many of the greatest modern singers (John Sullivan, regarded by some Italians as the most remarkable dramatic tenor since the death of Tamango, John McCormack, Margaret Sheridan, for example) are Irish.

In this passage we have the key to the culture and the mental outlook not only of John Joyce but of James Joyce himself. An obsession with *bel canto* dominates Joyce's work: what after all is *Finnegans Wake* but a species of operatic chorus? Behind all the years of Joyce's youthful development we must hear constantly the strains of music and opera.

By now John Joyce was established in Dublin and his mind turned to marriage. His son would later describe him as a lady-killer, and John himself admitted to many romances.* He had been engaged to two girls, Hannah Sullivan and Annie Lee, the sister of his two good friends John George and Paddy Lee, but each engagement had been broken off in fits of jealousy. In later years their photographs were displayed on the piano of the Joyces' house. His philandering ceased when he came to know the Murray family and, visiting their home at Clanbrassil Street, he became friendly with the daughter, May. John Murray opposed the match, as did Ellen Joyce, but the couple persisted. John Joyce took lodgings at 15 Clanbrassil Street to be near to the Murrays at number 7. The couple were married on 5th May 1880 at Rathmines Church; the witnesses were Jack Joyce's friend John George Lee and Margaretta Lyons, a cousin of May Joyce's.

John Joyce's background provides sufficient explanation of his own rude vigour, his sharp wit, and his bitter tongue in the Joyce line; his fecundity in the O'Connell tradition. But what of the girl he was marrying? May Joyce had been born in 1859, and at the time of her marriage was ten days from her 21st birthday.

John Joyce did not like his father-in-law: the Joyce blood was, he felt, superior. Yet the Murray line of priests and schoolmasters and the Flynn line of teachers and musicians contrasted with the character of the Joyces and the O'Connells. Aside from the stories of John Joyce about Dublin, the ancestral Joyces gave little literary material to the writer. They might as well not have existed. Yet countless characters and incidents were derived from the Murrays and the Flynns: they are 'his people', and not the Joyces. There is a nice irony in Joyce's literary talents and his vocational outlook coming from his mother's clerical connections. Her gentle faith, the music, the poetry and the refinement of manners of her family background would mark her son more than the raw, angry energy of her husband.

*

* I suspect that while living in Cork he had also been an admirer of a girl relative named Justice, and it was an affair of his (rather than his son's) which is alluded to in *Exiles.*

49

The couple spent their honeymoon in London and at Royal Windsor, where John Joyce had a memorable encounter on the River Thames with another boatman, who was roughly and rudely cursed – an incident which provided him with yet another rounded anecdote.

Returning to Dublin, they rented a house near Mrs Joyce's parents at 13 Ontario Terrace, Rathmines. There on Thursday, 23rd November 1880, a son was born whom they named John Augustine Joyce. The child lived only 8 days, dying on 1st December. There is no record that he was baptized, though doubtless he was – if not, his death would have had for his mother the added pain of thinking her first-born consigned to Limbo rather than ascending to Heaven. John Joyce said later that his own life died with his first-born, but John Augustine lives on in literature as Bloom's son Rudy, who haunts the pages of *Ulysses*.

(If the infant Joyce was full term, he would have been conceived in March, two months before the ceremony, suggesting that the Joyces, like the Blooms, anticipatorily consummated their marriage and conceived their first child before the banns. But the death certificate states (on the basis of information supplied by Margaret Theresa Murray) that the child was premature by some three months.) A few days later John Augustine Joyce was buried in Glasnevin in a family grave which John Joyce bought for the occasion and which he himself would occupy in time.

(Bloom, too, is given a residence in Ontario Terrace, about 1898. At J. and T. Davy's, the grocers on Charlemont Mall across the canal bridge, he puts into circulation a notched florin, to see if it will return later in his change. Was this perhaps a test made by John Joyce himself? Molly Bloom recalled this address because of Leopold's mild sexual interest in their maid.)

After this unhappy experience the Joyces moved again, this time to 30 Emorville Avenue, off the South Circular Road, where *Slater's Directory* for 1881 records John Joyce, secretary of the United Liberal Club. Here, during May 1881, a second child was conceived.

This newly-built district (Emorville Avenue dated from 1877) was then rapidly becoming the Jewish quarter of Dublin. Some Jews already lived there, and after an influx of Eastern European Jews a synagogue would be opened in St Kevin's Parade in 1883, and another in Lombard Street (into which Emorville Avenue runs, and where Bloom would live) in 1893. This house thus gave the Joyce family an initial contact with an area which would provide material for *Ulysses*. John Joyce may well have known some of the Jews mentioned by name in *Ulysses*, such as Moisel.

But the district had other and perhaps more important associations. Here they would have been neighbours not only of the Murrays, but also of the Giltraps who lived beside the Protestant church on the South Circular Road, and the Powell family who lived off it in Stamer Street. Captain Malachy Powell was to be a model for Molly Bloom's military father, his daughters were also to make their appearance as friends of the Blooms in their early married life. Also in Stamer Street lived the Tarpey family.

In February 1881 Mrs Joyce's mother died. Margaret Theresa Murray had been ill for many years, though well enough to assist her daughter at the birth of her first child. She suffered from an unspecified long-term disease of the womb, but died after only a short illness.

Mrs Ellen Joyce had returned to Cork soon after her son's marriage, of which she strongly disapproved. She died there on 27th June 1881, without sending for him. ('The Dead' suggests that she may well have been nursed for a time by the Joyces at an address in the Monkstown area.) John Joyce, for once a dutiful son, inserted a death notice in the *Freeman's Journal*, but Ellen Joyce's death was not noticed in the Cork papers nor even registered, suggesting that having fallen out with her son, she was by then not even on good terms with her own brothers. She had been unable to break the trust established by her husband in 1849 and after her death, William O'Connell (as the surviving trustee) completed his duty by making over to John Joyce on 30th July 1881 all the properties which had formed his grandfather's estate. These brought him an annual rent roll of nearly £500. A few days later, on 4th August, tragedy struck him also with the death of his wife Mary at their house in Nile Street: this O'Connell death *was* advertised.

Through the influence of Peter Paul McSwiney, of John Daly or of Dr Lyons, who had the ear of Gladstone and the new Liberal administration, John Joyce was appointed to a post in the Collector General's office, as a Collector of Rates for Dublin, which position had become vacant in January 1881. The Lord Lieutenant, Earl Cowper, wrote on 25th March to the Chief Secretary, the notorious W.E. 'Buckshot' Forster – so called from the Quaker politician having issued the police with shotgun cartridges rather than bullets to save life during Land War skirmishes – nominating Mr John

Joyce as a collector. However, it was by now necessary for every candidate for a Civil Service post to sit an examination. John Joyce sat this in April but did not do well. On 16th May the Chief Secretary wrote again re-nominating him and after another examination, Mr Joyce was pleased to confirm that he had received his notification of appointment from the Civil Service Commissioners, dated 18th July 1881.

This post was not a sinecure, work of a daily and sometimes demanding kind being required. The remuneration was £650. With over £1,000 a year, John Joyce could consider himself well established as a gentleman.

The actual job seems to have begun in January 1882. John Joyce was given the rural districts to collect, including the area around the Phoenix Park. His office hours, from 10 a.m. to 4 p.m., were light by the standards of the day, but he had to be out and about travelling the streets of his areas calling on ratepayers and assessing buildings. The offices were at 43 Fleet Street in the city centre and though they had been unfavourably reported upon by a Royal Commission some years before as unhealthy, the area was well served with pubs which furnished Joyce with congenial company.

The summer of 1881 was passed at 47 Northumberland Avenue, which may well have been the apartment of the late Mrs Joyce. From this residence in Kingstown Joyce retained the friendship of former American sea-captain Thomas Cunniam, who ran a pub on the corner of Marine Road and George's Street. (In one of the upper windows was a Virgin: Stanislaus Joyce, who thought him 'a drunken vulgarian', called him 'Captain Cunniam of the Shrine in Kingstown'. In fact Cunniam later went to live on the north side and left his son to run the pubs they owned in Kingstown and Dublin.) It was typical of John Joyce to retain such a raffish connection from such a respectable area, though as the Cunniams were prominent in local politics well into the new century the connection may have been a useful one for him. But there were other friends as well, among them Martin Kane (the Martin Cunningham of Joyce's fiction) and the Lees.

John Joyce should have been comfortably settled by now. On 2nd December 1881 a deed using the Kingstown address (which the Joyces may well have been just leaving) records a mortgage on the Cork property taken out by John Joyce from the Collector General. This was to cover the statutory security for any possible malfeasance with the funds arising from his new position as a collector which was to begin in the New Year. However, like so many of John Joyce's future mortgages, this loan was only a temporary expedient and was paid off and released in 1883.

By the end of the year the Joyces had moved to 41 Brighton Square, Rathgar. This was a small, though attractive, house built in red brick in a newly developed area – it was about ten years old and had had only one previous occupant.

It was in this house, at 6 a.m. on 2nd February 1882, that May Joyce gave birth to her second child, another boy. John Joyce was delighted. On 5th February, with their relations Philip McCann and Helen McCann as sponsors, the infant grandson of the late Patrick Flynn of Back Lane was baptized by the Reverend Father John O'Mulloy C.C. at St Joseph's Chapel of Ease, Roundtown, into the One, Holy, Roman, Catholic and Apostolic Church under the sonorous names of his paternal grandfather: James Augustine Joyce.

PART II

2

'BABY TUCKOO'

James Joyce's earliest memory (as he recalls in the opening passage of *A Portrait of the Artist*) was of his father telling him a traditional folk story from rural Ireland.

John Joyce used to take his son ('Baby Tuckoo') out into the little park in front of the house in Brighton Square, and relate to him the tale of the magic cow which came down from the mountains and carried away little boys. Though doubtless the original beast had descended that Fermoy bohereen to which the family had given their name, the infant James could only imagine that this particular cow came down along a more familiar local lane nearby, where Betty Byrne had her little sweet-shop in which she sold lemon platt. Rural Ireland would have no claim upon his totally urban imagination: the city park and Betty Byrne's shop would be his special territory.

Nearly fifty years later, in 1931, John Joyce himself was able to recall this idyll of his son's infancy only months before his death. Earlier, in 1906, the first photographs of James's own son, Giorgio, John Joyce's grandson, revived similar memories associated for John 'with all the happiest moments of my life'.

The Joyces remained at Brighton Square for two more years, but this would have been at an age when James (as we must call him at this stage of his life) would recall little of what went on around him. For Ireland, however, these were troubled and far from happy times: those rural lanes were rank with blood.

The early months of 1882 had been marked by frequent murders in parts of Ireland, as evicted tenants wreaked revenge on those who moved into their land. After Easter, Parnell was released on 9th April from Kilmainham Gaol. On Friday 5th May a huge torchlight procession through Dublin was held for Parnell, and to celebrate the new government policy following the 'Treaty of Kilmainham', which saw the resignation of W. E. ('Buckshot') Forster as Chief Secretary for Ireland, and the appointment of Earl Spenser as Viceroy. Michael Davitt, too, was released on 6th May, a Saturday. That evening, about 7 p.m., in the Phoenix Park where the Viceroy lived, a Republican terrorist group styling themselves 'The Invincibles' murdered the new Chief Secretary Lord Frederick Cavendish, and his assistant Thomas Henry Burke (a Catholic), in full view of the Viceregal Lodge. They cut them to death with surgical knives.

In the House of Commons Parnell rose before a chilly and reserved audience to denounce the murders. The feeling of the House was that

> . . . the knives of this dastardly gang had struck a heavy blow at the heart of him and his chief associates. It was a painful sight, [Parnell] this lonely man, feared and disliked by so many, almost rigid with combined fury and resentment, biting out his bitter words with not a movement of the body – pausing every now and then, with that nervous trick of his of gnawing at his slight fair moustache – (always, with him, a sign of strain and tension, and a fear of losing control).*

This brutal crime, which stunned Ireland and amazed Europe, was followed by a new Irish Crime Bill on 20th May and a wave of arrests. Repression brought only more resentment, more clashes, yet more arrests.

However, this ghastly murder was only one of the sensational crimes of the day that were to echo through Joyce's imagination, making their due appearance in *Ulysses* and *Finnegans Wake*. In this year, on the night of 17th–18th August, there also occurred near Maamtrasna in the Joyce Country, the notorious Joyce murders with which Tim Harrington (a political associate of John Joyce) was to be involved, and to which Joyce was to refer – in an article published years later in Trieste – as a specimen of the injustices of Ireland under British rule. The victims had been murdered by other members of their family in a quarrel that owed as much to spite as to politics, a view of the matter nevertheless uncongenial to Nationalists. The

---

* The murders had a close association with the Flynns, as the Invincibles had originally intended to take W. E. Forster prisoner to a house beside the Flynns in John Street and kill him there. Eventually betrayed, the Invincibles were charged in February 1883 and brought to trial that April.

trials, in which the inability of the defendants to speak English told against them, were in November 1882, and the executions in December. The trial of Hosty King in *Finnegans Wake* (as John Garvin pointed out) echoes this celebrated case.

These serious disorders explain in part the official figures issued in December which showed that during 1882 some 89,566 Irish people had emigrated. Nationalists, who saw such people as 'exiles', blamed these and other troubles on the British government, yet the guns fired through the cabin windows by Irishmen killed other Irishmen. The Land War was not just a war against English landlords but against Irish tenants; it was, in its way, a Civil War.

The Ireland of Joyce's birth, in addition to new economic difficulties, was riven with terror, murder, mayhem and bad faith. Little wonder that the emigrant ships to America and Australia were full. Many of those they left behind believed, like Parnell, that only breaking the Union with England would serve the best interests of Ireland's future. The Land War was a prelude to the struggle for Home Rule.

These events were merely background to the limited life of the child, however. His was a simple world. He recalls that he suffered as a child from enuresis, a common enough complaint among imaginative but highly-strung children. The words describing the feel of the warm urine, the queer smell of the rubber sheet which his mother put on the bed, signal an imagination already fixated not only on words but also on texture and smell, a world already experienced through blunted sight. They also reveal the child's growing sense of shame associated with the functions of his body and the need for love.

Even after the family moved away, Brighton Square retained lasting connections for the Joyce family, of later significance to the then uncomprehending infant. The houses here were newish, built in the last decade, part of the expanding Victorian suburbs that make up the real Dublin. Off Brighton Square ran other roads with larger and older houses, and here the Joyces made friends. William Murray and his family lived for a time on Brighton Road. Also on Brighton Road, in the attractive double-fronted Brighton House, lived Matthew A. Dillon – the 'Mat Dillon' of *Ulysses* – and his happy family, 'a bevy of girls' as Joyce describes them. In *Ulysses* Bloom recalls the Dillons' large lilac-filled garden and the gaiety of the girls who spilled over the summer lawns. Mat Dillon was related to Dillon the auctioneer on Batchelor's Walk – outside whose premises Dilly Dedalus waits in *Ulysses* for her father who has been raising money by selling the household furniture – and perhaps to Valentine Blake Dillon, sometime Lord Mayor of Dublin, also mentioned frequently in the novel.

The family friendship with the builder Luke Doyle and his wife Caroline (mentioned in *Ulysses* as attending the Blooms' wedding along with Alderman Hooper), was also, it seems, a friendship of John and May Joyce. The Doyles lived in Camac Place in Kimmage, then on the attractive rural side of the Grand Canal at Dolphin's Barn. Later they moved to Mount Brown in Kilmainham. Much of the convincing background to the life of the Blooms was thus ready to hand for Joyce's eventual use.

While they lived on Brighton Square the Joyces had sung in the fashionable new Church of the Three Patrons on Rathgar Road – a circumstance recalled in *Ulysses*. Mrs Joyce seems also to have sung betimes in Mount Argus Church, and Joyce, while working on *Finnegans Wake*, was to inquire of his father what recollections he had, of any kind, of the Retreat House and of the famous Father Charles, widely regarded in the Dublin of the day as a genuine saint, to whom many miraculous cures were credited even in his lifetime. (He has now been beatified.) John Joyce remembered this saintly figure, but the only personal detail he could recall was his heavy smoking; mere sanctity meant little to him. Another prominent member of the same Passionist Community was Father Sebastian, a famous preacher much admired in the better social circles of Dublin; in *Ulysses* he is comically numbered among the 'lovers' supposedly empassioned with Molly Bloom.

Also in Harold's Cross was Our Lady's Hospice for the Dying, where Joyce was to place the death of old Mrs Dante Riordan in *Ulysses*. In fact it was there that several of his own relatives were to pass away.

The Joyces stayed just over two years on Brighton Square. Here a second child, Margaret, their first daughter, was born on 18th January 1884. Her godparents, when she was baptized in St Joseph's church, were John Murray junior and his sister-in-law Josephine Murray (Catherine O'Donnell standing in as her proxy). Though John Joyce often asserted his dislike of the Murrays, they stood at baptism for some five of his children between 1884 and 1891.

Josephine Murray was to be an important person in the lives of those children in later years, taking her role as godmother seriously.

John Joyce was anxious to move up in the world. On 13th December 1883 he took out another mortgage with Joseph Carroll on his Cork property, value unknown. This was followed in March 1884 by a third mortgage, though in September of that year he was able to obtain a deed of release for the mortgage on his Cork properties to Edward Byrne, the Collector General (dating from 1881), which had covered his initial security in his new post. The autumn saw yet another mortgage, from the National Bank in Cork, and in November from Stanley Carr Joyce of the Irish Discount House, a notorious figure in the shady financial world of the day. Carr Joyce provided another loan in August 1884.

These loans represent a large outlay in a very limited period, though the exact sums involved are not known. His son Stanislaus believed that John Joyce was having to make up borrowings from his collecting-bag, though at this date it seems unlikely given the accounting system at the office; indeed such borrowings (if discovered) would have been criminal and would have led to his dismissal. At this date there is no record of such trouble at his work. He was simply living beyond his means, perhaps investing in dubious business ventures – the latter idea is more likely. But the mortgages may have been no more burdensome than the overdrafts of today, and (as my investigation of them has shown) were in due course paid off in 1887.

In the course of 1884, probably about April (Lady Day on 25th March was one of the Quarter Days, fixed dates from which leases were dated), the Joyces moved from Brighton Square to 23 Castlewood Avenue, Rathmines. This was a large double-fronted, three-storey house which still stands, beside Belgrave Square, and in real terms was a superior address in a respectable, indeed Unionist district.

Mrs Joyce was now expecting a fourth child, which was born on 17th December 1884. John Stanislaus Joyce – who preferred in later life to call himself plain Stanislaus to avoid confusion with his odious father* – was baptized a few days later with William O'Connell as

---

* A French dictionary which he used at school, now in the Joyce Tower, Sandycove, is signed 'John Stanislaus Joyce'.

godfather and Elizabeth Conway as his godmother: these are the 'Uncle Charles' and 'Dante' of Joyce's fiction.

By now these relatives from John Joyce's side of the family formed part of the Joyce household. 'Bill' O'Connell, then in his sixties, was an old-fashioned gentleman of benign outlook, indifferent to the bankruptcy which had befallen his draper's business in Cork. Though his son William Desmond and his family were now settled in Dublin – they eventually moved to London – he came to live with the Joyces some time after his own wife died on 4th August 1881. With John Joyce he could recall the pleasant and more carefree days in the city of Cork. He was a pleasant and congenial old man, always willing and calm.

Not so Mrs Conway. The daughter of an Edmund Hearn of Cork city, she was apparently a connection of John Joyce on his mother's side. The family tradition was that she had entered a convent in America, but left when her brother died leaving her a £30,000 fortune which he had made in the West African coastal trade. In fact it now seems she was a Sister of Mercy teaching in a convent school in western Pennsylvania. Her two brothers had died in the summer of 1862, Michael at Bonny on the Nigerian Coast on 1st May, John at Fernando Po on 26th June. Between them they left some £48,000. Their will is lost, but the executors were their brother, Thomas Edmund Hearn of Cork, and sister, a Mrs Maria Elizabeth Justice of Mount Justice, Millstreet, Co. Cork. The family name Justice was to be used by Joyce for an important character, Beatrice Justice, in his play *Exiles*, which suggests some complicated family connection dating back to his father's early years, which carried for Joyce or his father some intense emotional burden.*

In 1875 Elizabeth Hearn had married Patrick Henry Conway, the son of a Dublin solicitor, who worked as a clerk in the Bank of Ireland. After a few years of marriage Mr Conway had gone out to South America – perhaps to Buenos Aires like Frank in Joyce's story 'Eveline' – taking his wife's fortune with him, doubtless with the intention of investing it. After an intermittent correspondence she ceased to hear from him. This was about 1882, soon after Joyce's birth, as Mrs Conway and her wandering husband called each other 'Alice' and 'Jumbo' in their letters, after the contemporary music-

---

* But not, it is now clear, the sort of weight beloved of Joycean symbol-hunters and Ph.D. students.

hall song of that year about the famous pachyderms of London Zoo, one of which was sold away to America at this time: the elephants' love is mentioned in passing in 'Cyclops'. Her fortune gone, Mrs Conway fell back on the kindness of friends and relations, though her hold over John Joyce seems curious in the circumstances.

She came to the Joyces as a governess for the increasing number of children they now had. James Joyce's first teacher, she had an immense, deep and lasting influence on his imagination. Her role as a fount of knowledge is mentioned early on in *A Portrait of the Artist*. Indeed she seems at this date to have mattered more to him than his own mother, whose almost annual confinements may have made her a rather distant figure at times to the ever-accumulating infants in the Joyce nursery.

Mrs Conway taught James to fear thunder as the wrath of God. Embittered with a millenarian outlook, she often took the young Joyce children (at a later date than this, perhaps in 1890) all the way into the National Gallery on Merrion Square in the centre of Dublin, to show them Francis Danby's extraordinary painting 'The Opening of the Sixth Seal' (1828), which had been bought by the Dublin gallery in 1871. Stanislaus Joyce failed to recall the painter's name and his recollection of the painting was wrong in detail, but I found no difficulty in identifying what in its day was a famous picture.

This immense painting, largely in red and black, and dominated by a flash of lightning, illustrated that terrible passage in the Apocalypse (VI 12–17) which describes the end of the world and the mountains falling on the sinful, accompanied by flashes of lightning and rolls of thunder. St John writes:

And I saw, when he opened the sixth seal; and, behold, there was a great earthquake, and the sun became black as sackcloth of hair; and the whole moon became as blood; and the stars from heaven fell upon the earth, as the fig-tree casteth its green figs when it is shaken by a great wind. And the heaven departed as a book folded up; and every mountain, and the islands were moved out of their places. And the kings of the earth, and the princes, and tribunes, and the rich and the strong and every bondman and every freeman hid themselves in the dens and in the rocks of mountains; and they say to the mountains and the rocks: Fall upon us and hide us from the face of him that sitteth upon the throne and from the wrath of the Lamb. For the great day of their wrath is come. And who shall be able to stand?

This terrifying vision of the end of creation and the dissolution of the living made an indelible impression on the active, yet still childish, imagination of the young Joyce. He never recovered from this early experience. The thunder that rolls through *Finnegans Wake* had its remote origin here in the fevered visions of both Mrs Conway and Francis Danby. About 1899, when he was a university student, Joyce was to write out by hand a copy of passages from Revelations in the Anglican King James Version of the Bible, doubtless to compare with the more familiar Douay version of his childhood. This curious manuscript survives in the Cornell University Joyce collection.

For Joyce, God seems always to have worn the visage of anger rather than the face of love. To the end of his life thunder announced the imminence of the end of the world, and the voice of Mrs Conway reading aloud the words of St John the Divine. In later years his Continental friends in Trieste, Zürich and Paris were amazed at what seemed to them Joyce's seemingly irrational fears of thunder and lightning: he would close the shutters and hide in his bed. As he explained, *they* had not been brought up in Catholic Ireland. But Danby was a Protestant, and Mrs Conway's millennial fears owed more to the hectic fevers of the Evangelical Protestant tradition than to anything particular to Catholicism as a whole or to its peculiar Irish form.

Mrs Conway, however, also took them at Christmas (again perhaps at a later date than this) to see the crib at the Oblate Fathers church at Inchicore, one of the first of its kind in the city, a marvellous set piece of wax sculptures.* Here was the warmer, more homely side of religion: the love of the Holy Family, in which he might have seen reflected a little of the spirit of his own gentle mother. This aspect was for Joyce always a minor key in the composition of the Catholic faith.

Mrs Conway was, however, an educated woman and taught James and the others the rudiments of reading, writing and geography. Her teaching experiences in America served her well. As her brothers had been connected with Africa the features of that continent, too, such as the Mozambique Channel, were pointed out to James. A nationalist in politics, she was an enthusiast for both Parnell and for

---

* Though Molly Bloom (in her down-to-earth way) would wonder about the size of the new-born Infant held by the Madonna, feeling no woman could bear a child that size.

Michael Davitt since the founding of the Land League in 1879. But for her the Church came before the Nation, Eternal Salvation before the benefits of Home Rule.

There was also a more shadowy figure associated with the Joyces at this time: the real Uncle Charles. In October 1885 Mrs Joyce conceived again, and when another boy was born on 24th July 1886 he was called Charles Patrick after his godfather the Reverend Charles O'Connell. John Joyce's uncle, 'Father O'Connell', had not been listed among the Irish Catholic clergy since 1863, and must have died soon after this ceremony, perhaps in the early 1890s – though I have not been able to trace the exact date. Possibly he was the real-life model for the strange priest in 'The Sisters' – who had been deprived of his parish and whose wits had wandered as a consequence of a series of strokes – to whom Joyce gave his mother's mother's family name of Flynn.

The godmother of Charles Joyce was an Emma Tarpey, though what connection she had in Joyce's mind with the mysterious Luke Tarpey, one of the Four Old Men of *Finnegans Wake*, is not clear. She was a relation of Hugh Tarpey, a city hotel owner who had been Lord Mayor of Dublin in 1878 and 1879 and High Sheriff in 1880. As mentioned earlier the Tarpey family lived on Stamer Street, off the South Circular Road, near the Murrays and the Giltraps, and were neighbours of the Powells, another family of importance to Joyce – old Malachy Powell, an ex-army man, was to model for Molly Bloom's father Major Tweedy. John Joyce was still involved with politics, though he had now moved on from being an O'Connellite Liberal towards supporting Parnell and Home Rule, and would have known Hugh Tarpey well as a prominent local politician.

In the General Election of 1880, in which the Irish Party did well, Charles Stewart Parnell had been returned for the City of Cork, along with John Joyce's cousin and business associate John Daly (sometime Lord Mayor of Cork) – circumstance enough to confirm the trend of John Joyce's change of politics. On 11th December 1883 at the Rotunda in Dublin he watched Parnell receive a National Tribute, a collection of £38,000 made by his party, with unsmiling indifference. Parnell's stern resolve, which verged on contempt, was much admired by John Joyce, and the admiration remembered by James.

Gladstone had won that election in which John Joyce had been directly involved in 1880. However, in June 1885 Salisbury and the

Conservatives came to power. This administration did not last long, and Gladstone and the Liberals returned in February 1886, remaining in power until 1892 when he ventured on his last term in office. In March 1894 the Liberals again won the election, and stayed in power for a further eight years until defeated by Balfour and the Tories in 1902.

Ownership of the land was the central question in Ireland in the 1880s. Most felt that only an Irish government in Ireland could solve it and the Liberals had come to agree with this view, but Gladstone's Home Rule Bill was defeated in June 1886; and it was the controversy over this which led to the return of Lord Salisbury in July. Yet another election was called and this time the question of Home Rule was to the fore. The extension of the franchise from 222,000 to 740,000 by the Third Reform Act in 1885 meant that the Nationalist vote in Ireland swept the country except for Ulster. (It was this election that effectively partitioned Ireland, though Irish Nationalists were loath to admit it.) Though the settlement of the Land Question remained unresolved, Irish politics was becoming more democratic and so moving further down the social scale. These elections saw the emergence of the modern Irish political system.

In Dublin John Joyce was involved with Alderman Hooper, an M.P. from East Cork, Valentine Blake Dillon and John Henry Menton in the elections of 1885 and 1886. In 1886 the Plan of Campaign, which was to overthrow the landlords of Ireland as a class, was published in the Irish Party's paper *United Ireland* on 21st October, initiating a new phase of the struggle. The hidden influence of the revolutionary Fenian movement, the Irish Republican Brotherhood, in the person of John Devoy, lay behind this new departure. The Unionist reaction was unsurprising. Between 7th March and 17th April 1887, *The Times* in London published a series of articles dealing with 'Parnellism and Crime', partly written by an Irish journalist named Woulfe Flanagan, in which telling use was made of facsimiles of letters from Parnell which seemed to lend support to the violence then endemic in the country.

Despite the passions of politics that moved the country, daily life went on much as usual for the Joyces. Though imposing enough, the house in Castlewood Avenue was not as large as it seemed. Yet here John Joyce now proudly displayed on the drawing-room walls his series of family portraits, by which he set immense store, though some of his friends thought they were a job lot he had put together to pass off as his ancestors. When the Joyces gave a party for his musical acquaintances and political associates, John Joyce would engage a uniformed footman, and this too-grand gesture was thought risible by some of his friends. At one dance he was asked who was the young lady on the other side of the room. 'The young lady,' he replied, 'is the mother of three children.' Touchily jealous of his beautiful young wife, he was not amused when the tale was repeated.

On 21st April 1887 John Joyce took out his sixth mortgage on his property, an additional one from the National Bank, which refers to him as then living in Bray. But this year also saw him pay off three earlier mortgages including a debt to the National Bank and take another from Walter Morragh. That he paid his previous debts is more significant than his contracting of more. John Joyce was still stable financially.

Earlier in the year the Joyces had moved out of Dublin to Bray, twelve miles away on the Wicklow sea-coast, where he had leased a house on the sea-front, 1 Martello Terrace. Though less imposing than the Castlewood Avenue house, it had some thirteen rooms, including a nursery which saw the arrival of another boy, George Alfred, on 4th July, a pretty baby much admired when he was taken out in his pram along the sea-front. The infant was baptized on 14th July in the Church of the Holy Redeemer, Bray, with his uncle John Murray and his cousin Mary Ellen Callanan standing for him, this latter lady being the young music teacher Mary Ellen of 'The Dead'.

The Joyces remained in touch with friends in Dublin such as the Dillons: in *Ulysses* Joyce places a meeting between Stephen and his mother and the Blooms at a game of bowls (John Joyce's game) at the Dillons in the spring of 1887. Another of the guests was John Joyce's political friend John Henry Menton, a prominent Dublin solicitor, as well as Alderman Hooper and Val Dillon. Here again the bevy of Dillon girls was in attendance: Tiny, Floey, Atty, Sara, Nannie and Mammie, the eldest of whom would have then been in their late teens, the youngest about James's age.

On 1st February 1888 Mrs Joyce sang in a concert at Mount Argus, the monastery near their former home in Dublin, along with the Misses Dillon (daughters of Mat Dillon) and the Misses Bloom.

These Bloom girls were the teenage daughters of Max (Mark) James Bloom, a well-known dentist – he was dentist to Maynooth College for many years. Max's father had been a Joseph Blum [sic], one of two Jewish brothers who ran a toy-shop at 12 Nassau Street in the middle decades of the century. Max adopted the Catholic faith on his marriage to a Miss Catherine Brown; as she was born about 1830, it is likely that Max was born somewhere in Europe before his father came to Ireland.

Mark Bloom's daughters Florence and Beatrice, the youngest of his family, were well-known music teachers at the Royal Irish Academy of Music (and contemporaries of Mary Ellen Callanan). After completing *Ulysses* Joyce specially asked of A.J. Leventhal, the Trinity academic – himself a member of the Dublin Hebrew community, who was a tutor and friend of Samuel Beckett's – about the Blooms, particularly the musical Blooms whom he associated with the South Circular Road, and was relieved to hear they were now a thing of the past.

Mark Bloom's son Marcus Joseph was a prominent dentist in Clark Street – a fact mentioned in *Ulysses* – and inherited from his father the position as Maynooth's dentist. But his son Joseph Bloom lived between 1891 and 1906 at 38 Lombard Street, off the South Circular Road, an address given to Leopold Bloom in *Ulysses*. In the years before the Great War he lived with his mother and musical sisters in Sandymount, at 10 Tritonville Road.

These were the only Blooms in Dublin for a long time until the great influx of Eastern European Jews in the last decades of the century. That they were associated with Joyce's family in the musical circles of the city suggests that these must have been the Blooms who lent their name to Joyce's wandering Jew, and that Leopold Bloom was modelled on the mysterious ne'er-do-well of the family, young Joseph Bloom. Like Leopold he had a Gentile mother and was therefore not a true Jew, who should strictly speaking be born of a Jewish mother, paternity in Hebrew tradition being regarded as an unverifiable thing. As they had taken the Christian faith, their own interest in Jewish custom may have been small. Both were of an age, Joseph being born about 1861, Leopold (in Joyce's scheme for the novel) in 1866. It is not without the bounds of possibility that the meetings recalled in *Ulysses* between Leopold Bloom and Stephen Dedalus in the Dillons' house and in Breslin's Hotel in Bray were in fact meetings between Joseph Bloom and the young James Joyce. That the Bloom connection in Joyce's life can now be traced back to his childhood years suggests that carried for him a significance which as yet remains unknown.

*

It was in Bray that James Joyce begins to emerge from the years of his infancy as a distinct personality.

Here he attended his first school, a dame school (as an infants' school was known at that date) run by a Miss Raynor and her mother

Cecilian Intelligence.

ST. PAUL'S RETREAT, MOUNT ARGUS.

THERE was a solemn High Mass (Haller's Requiem) for the repose of the soul of the late Mrs. Murphy, Harcourt-street, on the 1st Feb., in the church of St. Paul of the Cross, Mount Argus. The music was magnificently rendered by a large choir, many of whom had formerly assisted Mrs. Murphy in her works of charity. The principal singers were :— *Soprani*—Miss Connell, Mrs. Joyce, Miss Dillon, Miss Geale, and Miss Grandy. *Contralti*—Miss Boylan, the Misses Bloom, Miss Smith, Mrs. Kearney, Miss Gordon, and Miss A. Dillon. *Tenori*—Mr. Alcorn, Mr. Farrell, Mr. Gleeson, Mr. O'Gorman, Mr. Cameron, and Mr. W. Sheridan. *Bassi*—Mr. M'Dermott, Mr. S. Smyth, Mr. G. White, and Mr. Beardwood. Mr. F. Manly presided at the organ, and Mr. C. K. Irwin conducted. The following clergymen officiated at the High Mass—Rev. Father Cassimir, celebrant ; Rev. Father Gabriel, deacon ; Rev. Father Constantine, sub-deacon. Chanters— Rev. Dr. Burke, St. Kevin's, and Rev. Father Victory, Marlborough-street. Amongst the clergy (which included the Community of Mount Argus) were the Rev. Dr. Murphy, secretary to his Grace the Archbishop ; the Rev. Father Donegan, O.C.C., chaplain to the Lord Mayor ; Rev. Father Baxter, Rev. D. Heffernan, Rev. M. Doyle, Very Rev. Dr. Murphy, P.P., V.G. Kildare, &c.

ST. ANDREW'S, WESTLAND ROW.
(ORGANIST—MR. J. SEYMOUR).

ORDER of the Sacred music performed during the Forty Hours' Exposition of the Blessed Sacrament, February, 19-21.

Quadragesima Sunday—(Organ silent).
Ordinary of the Mass "Jesu Redemptor," *A. Kaim.*
Introit, "Invocabit," and Communion, "Scapulis suis."
Plain Chant.
Gradual & Tract "Angelis suis," *F. Witt.*
Offertory "Scapulis suis," *F. Witt.*
"Pange lingua" (Laudes Eucharisticæ) *M. Haller.*

on Seapoint Road. He went there with a neighbour's child, the daughter of James Noy Vance, a chemist. Eleanor Vance had been called after her mother, but her family preferred to use the form Eileen, which was perhaps more Irish. The Vances were Church of Ireland, Protestants in the crude Roman Catholic parlance of the day, and Mrs Conway did not approve of the friendship between the children; anyone who consorted with Protestants would go to Hell. Perhaps inspired by Mrs Conway's preoccupations, James and the children played a game of Hell in which he took the part of the Devil. His Satanic Majesty's victims were placed under an inverted wheelbarrow, while James spun the wheel (representing the bellows) crying 'Hotter, hotter, hotter.' He also took the part of Satan in a tableau of the Garden of Eden, in which his sister Margaret played Eve and Stanislaus Adam. In *Finnegans Wake* he would find parts for these and other members of his family in a more elaborate creation myth.

John Joyce, meantime, was still travelling up to Dublin by train for his work. In 1887 he had taken out a further loan from the National Bank in April, and another in May from Walter Morragh, a moneylender. The interest on these loans must have taken much of his income from the actual properties, yet there seems to have been no financial crisis; the loans were still not large, the interest was covered, and often enough releases were soon obtained. Three earlier loans were paid off during 1887. Though he contracted new debts, at this stage he was still able to pay them off, and appears to have felt unencumbered by what must have seemed to him paltry debts.

It must have been about this time while crossing Phoenix Park with his collector's bag that John Joyce was attacked by a robber – an incident which took place outside the Viceregal Lodge very near where the Phoenix Park Murders had been committed in 1882. This incident also entered into his repertoire of stories, to be endlessly repeated over the years until it at last became embroidered into the fabric of *Finnegans Wake*, along with so much more of his Dublin arcane lore. Indeed, much of what we know about John Joyce consists of tales retold. Yet the office where he worked is of interest, not just for the fun it gave him but for those who worked with him. Among them was Frederick Buckley, about whom the tale of the Russian general – which would play an even more significant part in *Finnegans Wake* – grew up; and W.A. Weatherup (retired in 1887), who also makes a cryptic appearance in Joyce's work, in the 'Aeolus' section of *Ulysses*.

In 1888 John Joyce was moved into the city proper as collector for the North Dock Ward, the poorer area between Sackville Street and the port of Dublin. He was soon to be on good terms with various shipping gentry based here. This year brought complaints against his colleague in the Mountjoy Ward, Mr E.G. Cotter (doubtless the 'Old Cotter' of 'The Sisters') and against John Joyce, whose work was so unsatisfactory that it was even proposed in 1889 that he be dismissed from the service. This did not happen, but again he was placed on probation for a period, and certificates of his behaviour had to be furnished on a monthly basis. His conduct improved, however, and in 1890 he was retained.

Life for John Joyce was not all work. On 26th June 1888 the Bray Boat Club, of which he was an active member, gave a summer concert in Edward Breslin's Hotel on the Quinnsborough Road, at which James Joyce sang with his parents. This was his first public performance, and the applause of an appreciative audience must have been gratifying to his parents' pride and the infant's vanity.

However, a great change was under way. His father, wishing his clever eldest boy to have the best education the country could provide, had decided to send him to the Jesuits at Clongowes Wood College in Kildare. Though the French College of the Holy Ghost Fathers in Blackrock was (so many thought) academically better and more nationalist in outlook, the choice of the Jesuits was not surprising.

A main reason was the O'Connell connection. Daniel O'Connell had sent his sons there, and they had been followed in the mid-1840s by John and Charles O'Connell and other relatives. His cousin John Daly had also gone to Clongowes, as had others with whom he had been involved in business. The Jesuits, even if they were considered less nationalist in outlook, were at least gentlemen ... and that was a matter of moment with John Joyce.

After a delightful few weeks of buying new clothes and a fine trunk to hold them, which meant several agreeable visits to Dublin, James and his parents set out from Kingsbridge Station on 1st September for Clongowes Wood.

CLONGOWES WOOD

SEPTEMBER 1888—JUNE 1891

On the morning of that last day in August, 1888, James and his parents had been to a photographer in Dublin to have their portraits taken along with his maternal grandfather, old John Murray. One picture was of the boy by himself, perhaps for his mother to keep by her on her dressing-table in Bray. The other was of the family group, doubtless for James to have at school.

Small and vulnerable, dressed in the then newly-fashionable man-o'-war suit, the boy lies at his mother's knee, engrossed in a book on her lap in which she is pointing out some passage to him. The two men look on, with bland indifference. The Book and the Family: for Joyce this was a symbolic picture, one he describes explicitly in 'The Dead'.

The train of the Great Southern Railway Company carried the family along the valley of the River Liffey to Sallins, a journey of about 54 minutes. The carriages would have been crowded with boys, most of them old hands, some new and a few in tears at their first separation from home. At Sallins station a long line of jaunting cars was waiting, ready to take the returning students the remaining couple of miles through fields and woods to Clane village, beyond which lay the 500-acre demesne of Clongowes Wood College. In the fields could be seen fat cattle and conical heaps of hay, for this was rich farming country at the end of summer.

From first sight Clongowes, seen from the machiolated main gate through the long rows of ancient elms lining the drive, was impress-ive. The castle had four towers, ivy creeping up the walls, and was as ancient as it was romantic. It had been built by the Eustace family in the late Middle Ages as one of a series of strongholds along the

Pale, the border dividing the English holdings from the lands of the Irish to the west. During Ormond's war with Parliament in 1642 it had been blown up by Colonel Monck. In 1667 the lands passed into the hands of Richard Reynell, Chief Justice of the Common Pleas under Cromwell, who sold them almost immediately to a Dublin merchant named Thomas Browne, who changed the name to Castle Browne. The castle was rebuilt by Stephen Fitzwilliam Browne in 1718; and remodelled by Thomas Wogan Browne in its present style after 1788, the remnants of the old ruin being incorporated in the new baronial edifice. But in 1814 the last heir, wishing to continue his military career in the army of Saxony – he had marched with Napoleon to the battle of Moscow – sold the house and estate to the Jesuit, Father Peter Kenny, who planned to establish a college for the sons of the Catholic gentry in Ireland. This school was opened just before the Pope lifted his ban on the Jesuit order, which had been suppressed for political reasons in the previous century.

The history of the school, its curious ghost stories and the legends of Wolfe Tone and Hamilton Rowan, doubtless fascinated the young Joyce, finding their due place in *A Portrait of the Artist*. Inevitably doubt has been cast on some Clongowes folk tales, not on the ghost of Marshal Browne, to which Joyce refers, but on Hamilton Rowan throwing his hat out onto the ha-ha to mislead the British troops. This, almost certainly, never happened, though the tale survives through the pages of Joyce's book.

In the seven decades since the college was founded developments had extended the older buildings. Alongside were newer buildings, dating from 1870 and 1886, a quadrangle, a study hall, and a separate infirmary, in which the school proper was housed. There was a chapel, dating from 1819, in front of the castle; and a flagstaff from which the Union flag, the banner of Empire, was flown on the annual sports day. The temper of the school was on the whole both Catholic and mildly nationalist (but not Nationalist). Whereas the boys had once come from the ranks of the Catholic gentry, by now the pupils were the sons of professional men, civil servants and merchants, a class with an interest in maintaining the status quo. British army bands and cricket teams from the Curragh Camp were welcomed to play on those same sports days.

On the gravel before the castle door the cars among which the Joyces arrived dropped their passengers and their trunks.

This was a crucial point in James's life. As he had Gorman observe:

'The life of James Joyce may properly be said to begin here in the Castle at Clongowes Wood when the Rector, a bland and courtly humanist, turned him over to a black-soutaned father who guided him through the corridors to his [quarters].' This was an over-statement, but one which may reflect Joyce's own view, for the school was nevertheless a new stage in the boy's growth to manhood.

The rector was Father John Stanislaus Conmee, a figure who weaves in and out of Joyce's life and fiction, eventually becoming a significant figure in the cast of *Ulysses*, where he is characterized as 'the decentest rector that was ever in Clongowes'. In August 1904 he became Provincial of the Order in Ireland, and was among the most distinguished Jesuits of the day – quick-witted, eloquent, and forceful in his convictions, but mild and gracious in manner. He died in 1910.

Herbert Gorman signals the significance of this moment for Joyce, and the phrase 'a bland and courtly humanist' was Joyce's own, added by him to Gorman's proofs. Conmee, 'whose reign was mild', was himself an author, having written a little brochure on rural life a generation before in the country north of Athlone called *Old Times in the Barony*. This nostalgic review of an uncomplicated way of life around his native Athlone is a true reflection of the writer, and though a small thing in itself reflected also the intensively literary outlook of the Jesuits.

Joyce's tearful mother hugged him. His father gave him money, called on him to be brave and not to tell tales, and to remember that his O'Connell great-uncle had presented an address to the Liberator at Clongowes in the early 1840s, not long before the great patriot's death. Clongowes was a place where a Joyce should feel at home.

This O'Connell connection with Clongowes – as a lawyer Daniel O'Connell had assisted Father Peter Kenny with the difficulties over the purchase of the castle in 1814 – mattered greatly to John Joyce. Clongowes might not have been an obvious first choice for a family living in Bray – the French College in Blackcock would have done almost as well – but he had decided on Clongowes for its reputation in some circles as the leading school in Ireland. Aside from his O'Connell relatives, there from 1841 to 1849, many other relations and friends had gone there: John Dunbar, M.P. for New Ross, from 1840-44; John Daly, M.P. for Cork, from 1844-45 – his grand-children were contemporaries of Joyce's in the early 1890s; and others. John Joyce was convinced that his son would receive a fine education and mix with the sons of other gentlemen. Influential social connections would result. The school possessed an air of assured social confidence; the fees were £25 per annum (half the full rate), to include everything: a sum that John Joyce could then easily afford.

The Clongowes at which James arrived that afternoon was significantly different from the school commended to his father, however. The old school had been a smaller institution, with under 150 boys, and retained many of the customs brought by Peter Kenny from Sicily in 1814, some of which dated back further to Douai. This was the school described in *Schoolboys Three* (1895) by W.P. Kelly, an almost unique account of life in a nineteenth-century Catholic boarding school – that novel dealt with Clongowes in the benign 1860s. Though Clongowes had the higher social distinction, the academic palm went to Tullabeg, its sister school in Offaly. But the better school ran into financial difficulties and in the autumn of 1886, almost overnight, the two schools had been combined, with some 500 boys. This size could not be sustained. There then followed a sharp fall in numbers due to graduation and withdrawals; the new Clongowes now numbered 218 students (according to the return made by the rector to the Intermediate Board in 1891) – though Joyce seems to have thought there were 300 the year he arrived. The life of the school was regulated by the needs of the new 'Intermediate', the government examination of the day, from which schools derived a financial benefit depending on their academic results. These exams were presided over with ruthless determination by the Prefect of Studies, Father James Daly – the infamous and tyrannical 'Father Dolan' of Joyce's novel.

Father Daly is presented by Joyce, or rather by his biographers, as a crude and uncultured man: 'Dolan: it was like the name of a woman who washed clothes.' Joyce's observations on his victims must be received with caution, however. In fact James Daly came of a distinguished landed family in the west of Ireland, the Dalys of Castle Daly (neighbours of Lady Gregory at Gort), who had a long connection with Clongowes going back to 1821. But if distinguished, Father Daly, as even his family had to admit, was 'eccentric'. He had come to Clongowes from Belvedere in 1887 after the amalgamation with Tullabeg, largely to elevate the academic standards of the school, which he did with effective vigour. Within Joyce's time it reached the top of the list of schools, as judged by the

75

official results of the Intermediate exams. For all his achievements at Clongowes* he has gained more notoriety in the wider world by his association with Joyce – Gorman refers to him as a clerical martinet who should have been a Christian Brother – a Joycean form of insult, which is foolish nonsense. Whatever his faults, Father Daly was something of a hero for the Irish Jesuits.

Yet by all accounts, Clongowes under Father Daly in these decades before the Great War was a place of high pressure and psychological drama. It left its mark on many of its pupils, as Edward Boyd Barrett testifies in his vivid memoirs, which describe a Clongowes only slightly later than Joyce's – he came to the school in 1895. Boyd Barrett is explicit about the homosexual element at the school, as is Francis Hackett in his novel *The Green Lion*, which also deals with this period. Joyce was to retain a contempt for the British public school system which he always associated with homosexuality; and he confessed that he was grateful he had not been exposed, by reason of his age and the nature of Clongowes, to much of it. In any case the traditions of Clongowes went back to sixteenth-century Europe and owed little to any British institutions.

James was very young to have been sent away to school. He was to live for his first year in the Infirmary under the benign eye of Nanny Galvin, the school matron, which would have made his initial transition from home to school easier. Yet the loss of maternal attachment (so vital in the early development of every child) must have been felt, and probably did much to create the detached and often cold personality reflected both in his later life and in his writings. For James Joyce, a forlorn infant standing that first afternoon in the cold stone-flagged hall of Clongowes, hung with portraits of Jesuit saints such as Ignatius Loyola, the impulse to love, as opposed to the power of sex, almost – but not quite – died. Only later would it have its renewal.

The next day, the 1st September, he was placed by the Prefect of Studies in Elements, the lowest class of the Lower Line, where he was to stay for all his time in Clongowes. The school was divided into three Lines (a division based on the disposition of the boys in the playground at Douai in Elizabethan times). There were some 37 boys in this class, enough for a small child to feel lost in. Asked his

* Described in my history of the school.

age, he is said to have replied, 'Half-past Six', and this became his school nickname.

It was not, however, until 14th September that full classes began, by which time all the students had returned to the school. James was to take a little simple English, Maths, Latin, and Religious Knowledge. He probably found his teachers mild and friendly enough, the work easy and interesting.

Though the majority of the boys were from Ireland and England, a few came from remoter and more exotic parts of the world to which Irish Catholics had penetrated: India, Canada, the West Indies and Argentina. There were also foreign Catholics from such places as Portugal, who fascinated the young James.

However, James was the smallest and youngest in what must have seemed at first a strange and noisy world of large, burly youths. In a school photograph of the day 'Half-past Six' sits crosslegged at the feet of Father Power, the contrast between his small frame and the older and bigger boy behind him revealing just what divided him from the rest of the school. But in Clongowes there was no fagging – an iniquitous system, the Jesuits thought – little corporal punishment, and no pupil prefects with authority over other boys.

That first term in the Infirmary, Joyce had the company of a boy from South America named Eugene Kenny. Though they were looked after by Miss Galvin, the nurse was under the supervision of a Jesuit lay brother, John Hanly, the actual Infirmarian. The model for Brother Michael in *A Portrait of the Artist*, he had 'a different look' from the other Jesuits in the school. In the Jesuit houses of those days the brothers were something of an underclass. But though he was not a priest, Brother Hanly was a kind man, and Joyce suitably rewarded his kindness. Before entering the Jesuits he had been a pharmaceutical chemist, hence his employment at Clongowes.

Among the teachers the scholastic William Gleeson – Mr Gleeson in *A Portrait* – made an initial impression as a cricketer rather than as a master. Joyce's actual masters were two other Jesuits, Father William Power and Mr James Jeffcoat, a scholastic – the Father Arnall and Mr Harford of the novel. There was also Andrew Macardle, who may have been Joyce's first teacher – Mr McGlade, the Prefect of the Lower Line in the novel.

It is likely that it was during his first term in 1888 that James was knocked over by a cyclist on the cinder track that ran around the field at the back of the college, and had his glasses broken. For this some exemplary, though unrecorded, punishment was meted out to him by Father Daly, and he took his grievance to the rector Father John Conmee, much in the way he describes in his novel. Justice (it seemed to the child) had triumphed over arbitrary authority, though as Joyce suggests the matter may not have been like that at all, for in his novel it becomes a pleasant joke between the two priests. Gorman was to claim that this daring feat (which he had been told of by Joyce) remained a part of the school folklore, but alas this was merely wishful thinking. Joyce was effectively forgotten at Clongowes for many years, and his time there is therefore difficult to reconstruct.

On Thursday 20th December 1888, James went home for Christmas to the house in Bray which would have been full of talk about the Parnell Commission which had been sitting in London since September, hearing evidence from a stream of witnesses about the fearful terrorism that had stalked the Irish countryside during the Land War; his father's friend Tim Harrington was appearing for Henry Asquith M.P. Politics, however, belonged more to his home life than the life of school; and thus belongs more properly in the following chapter. As usual his mother was pregnant with her annual infant: a daughter Eileen was born on 22nd January 1889.

On 10th January James returned to Clongowes, where he celebrated his seventh birthday in February. In the eyes of the Church he was now come of an age to tell right from wrong. That same month it was recorded that he was punished for not bringing his books to class – these would have been kept in his desk in the Study Hall, where the boys did their preparation in the evenings after tea.

Meanwhile, at the Parnell Commission Richard Pigott, a ne'er-do-well editor and journalist, entered the witness box to give evidence on 20th February. On the examination of Charles Russell, counsel for Parnell, he was trapped. His mis-spelling of the word 'hesitancy' at the start of his cross-examination by Charles Russell had revealed him as the forger of the letters supposedly written by Parnell himself, for in them the same error occurred. The exposure of Pigott saved Parnell, and the horrors described by many of the other 400 or so witnesses who had testified before the Commission could be conveniently forgotten by Irish nationalists. Pigott confessed to two journalists and then fled London for Madrid. There, on 1st March, police officers arrested him on a charge of perjury. Stepping back into his hotel room for a moment, he shot himself in the mouth.

This sordid end to an extraordinary affair had its echo in Clongowes, where Pigott's sons, Joseph and Francis, were students. When the dreadful news came from Madrid one of the Jesuit fathers went from class to class warning the boys to be silent. But one blurted out the truth to the Pigotts, who were withdrawn shortly after. James, however, was not to forget Pigott and his mis-spellings, and they duly appeared in *Finnegans Wake*.

The punishment book records a further offence of 'vulgar language' on 14th March 1889, an appropriate crime for Joyce to be charged with, many may still think. But on the whole he was a model student.

That Easter, on 21st April, he made his First Holy Communion. He was told by one of the Jesuits – perhaps Father Arnall, who was the boys' Confessor – that the great Napoleon (that arch-enemy of Albion) said that his first communion was the happiest day of his life. (The Napoleonic connections of General Browne would have been enough to explain this enthusiasm for Buonaparte, otherwise revered then only by political radicals.) James was now able to become an altar boy, serving mass and assisting at Benediction and other rites. This gave him a special status in the school and in his own eyes, for he got to carry the incense boat. An older boy, often the tall teenager George Redington Roche, bore the thurifer from which came the scented smoke which for all cradle Catholics has a special nostalgia for the days of wide-eyed and contented belief. James and the other altar boys were deployed by Brother Hanly, who was also the sacristan in charge of making the preparations for all the school's religious ceremonies.

With the summer term the school turned to the only sports that interested Joyce: cricket and running. Cricket was the one sport in which he retained any interest as an adult; his books are scattered with references to famous names of the day. In an Irish context, however, cricket would increasingly be seen as a 'West-British' and snobbish sport rather than a game of imaginative skill. On the annual sports day he won several cups – either this year or those that followed, as his brother recalls – which went to decorate the family sideboard in Bray when he returned home for the summer holidays.

Though Parnell had been vindicated by the outcome of the Parnell Commision in the autumn of 1889, a suit for divorce was entered on the day before Christmas by Captain O'Shea naming Parnell as co-respondent. Though the growing disquiet about Parnell's affairs (not yet a full public scandal) was doubtless discussed after Christmas in the Joyce home, it may not have made much impact on the young James. Domestic matters were of more interest. Mrs Joyce was in the last weeks of yet another pregnancy: her daughter Mary Cathleen would be born on 18th January 1890.

Back at Clongowes, that March there was great excitement when some boys ran off to the woods, and on 4th March 1890 a boy was actually expelled, for an unrecorded reason. In *A Portrait* this incident is transformed to suggest some unsavoury episode, but the official school records know nothing of that. 'Smugging', the word whispered among the small boys of the school, was actually contemporary slang for stealing – perhaps the altar wine mentioned by one of the boys. In the eyes of young Catholics this would have been a strange enough crime. Yet the incident is referred to in *A Portrait* in such a way as to suggest obscure sexual secrets which the young Stephen could not fathom. Certainly there was a certain amount of romance among the boys, and hushed-up offences are always thought to be sexual in nature, as a vague Clongowes tradition about this episode insists.

School life, rather than home life, may by now have been coming to seem like his 'real life', for James was well settled in. Indeed home may almost have been forgotten, and his mother had to write to the rector, who reassured her (3rd March 1890) that James would write, that he had a dirty face, and that he was taking the cod-liver oil. Many years later Joyce would write in 'Ithaca' that Stephen Dedalus, too, was a hydrophobe.

If James's washing was neglected, his culture was not: in the autumn of 1890 he began piano lessons with a Mr Edward Haughton, a well-known Dublin musician and organist, brought down from Dublin by the Jesuits to teach the boys. Though Joyce became an accomplished pianist, he never learnt, then or later, to read music at sight. Music, begun early, remained all his life a source of joy and solace to Joyce. These lessons, for which his father paid an extra 11/6d, continued in 1891. His abilities did not go unrecognized: he also sang (Gorman says) in a school concert.

A summer in Bray passed and James returned to school, his father paying his fees promptly by cheque on 20th October 1890 – £23/17/0, a moiety of the full annual rate of fifty guineas which he now had to pay. But storm clouds were gathering both for the Joyces and for the country, though James would not have fully realized this in the security of the school's daily round.

The passage of the Dublin Corporation Act in 1890 presaged changes in John Joyce's job. And even in Clongowes there would have been talk about the O'Shea divorce case and the row in the Irish Party in November and December. On Saturday 6th December Parnell was defeated by 55 votes to 33 and the Irish Parliamentary Party split apart.

Only echoes of this controversy reached the boys at school. They were more concerned then with the sudden death of one of their number, Stanislaus Little, of a lung disease, and his burial in the community graveyard beside the gates on 10th December. This cypress-shaded glade impressed Joyce sufficiently for him to dream about it.

Later that month, shortly before the end of term, Joyce and his fellows had to sit (as he would every year until the end of his schooldays) for the 'Bishops' Exam', a test set by the Irish hierarchy to test the religious knowledge of school-children. The matter was not difficult: some parts of the Maynooth Catechism, some 150 pages of Bible history and over 200 pages from Deharbe's Catechism. These materials were set all over Ireland; they produced good Catholics, and many priests; yet the traditions of Catholic Ireland (many only dating half a century to the advent of Cardinal Cullen and his Italian ideas) were as effective in sustaining the faith. Mere education would not be enough, but it gave James that essential grounding in the matter of Catholicism which would never leave him, even though his belief eventually failed.

James returned to Clongowes and his father paid the second moiety of his fees promptly enough on 25th February 1891: £25/17/9. As yet no real financial difficulties beset John Joyce. The future, if uncertain, held no threat.

Now in his tenth year, that spring (probably in March), James was confirmed, becoming in the eyes of the Church a fully assenting adult Christian. He took the name of the Jesuit saint Aloysius Gonzaga* as an additional name, but it was one he never used. That spring too James was sufficiently ill for a doctor to be called in to

* The arms of the college – four quartered eagles – were derived from the arms of the Gonzagas, Renaissance Lords of Mantua, the princely family to which St Aloysius belonged.

treat him – the bill for the visit was 3/6d. He was transferred back to the Infirmary, a separate block from the main school, and so was provided with the inspiration for part of Stephen's sickness in his novel. What had affected him was unknown. A touch of 'the colly-wobbles', referred to in his novel, could have meant anything from a fever to mere diarrhoea. Whatever it was, it passed with the return of fine weather.

At the Easter holiday (spent at the school) James had his first dramatic role. These annual plays were (at that date at least) mostly farces, musicals and operettas. In this play *Aladdin*, he played an imp. There was also a musical section of the programme which gave the boys of all ages an opportunity to show their talent with selections from the lighter and more accessible composers. These included some operatic pieces – Rummell's variations on *Don Giovanni*, Oesten's fantasia on *Martha*, and Althaus's on *Il Trovatore* – and these may have been James's introduction (outside his home) to the art to which he was so passionately devoted in later years.

Easter 1891 also brought round the cricket-playing again. That term closed, much as does the end of *A Portrait*, with the evocation of the summer glory of Clongowes Wood College at its finest season. James Joyce – like Gerard Manley Hopkins a few years before – had known peace here. Easter and Whitsun passed and another sports day meant more cups for athletics. There were to be changes at Clongowes: Father Conmee was to be replaced by Father Devitt. For James too there would be changes. After this summer the season of peace would be past.

*

There is no doubt that Clongowes greatly affected the development of James Joyce as an artist. He himself testifies to this, not only in his own writings but also through his biographer Herbert Gorman, who wrote nothing that had not Joyce's approval.

Gorman emphasizes what the school – and the stirring events in its history – meant to Joyce. 'They speak again of the layer upon layer of conflicting cultures, always with the dark mythos as foundation, that is the Island of today and the old mother of James Joyce. Even those far-away Brownes were important links in the long chain of Time that was to wind itself so unmistakably about the artist's mind.'

And again Gorman writes: 'This college was a particularly apposite selection for an imaginative boy. Within the broad limits of its green-grassed demesne lingered vestiges of all the varying layers of civilisation, perceptible hints and reminders of the historical progression that had evolved the modern Ireland, this Parnell-dominated land, of young James Joyce.'

North-east of the school, towards Mainham, was an ancient tumulus known as 'Queen Buan's Grave'. She was the consort of Mesgedra, King of Leinster, who had died there when the Ulster champion Conal Cearnach boasted to her that he carried in his chariot her slain husband's head. The two champions had met and fought at the ford of Clane nearby.

Sir Samuel Ferguson, the great Irish poet of the previous generation, wrote about this incident in his long poem 'Mesgedra', which was included with notes about the legendary background in T. W. Lyster's anthology of school poems prepared for the Intermediate. If Joyce did not hear of the poem at Clongowes, he certainly read it a year or so later, for Mr Bloom recalls lines from 'Mesgedra' while lunching in Davy Byrne's which he says are 'in the schoolbook'.

The poem's connection with Clongowes had another aspect. Ferguson concludes with a long lyrical passage which describes the 'murmuring Liffey and the banks of Clane' past which the river flows down from the Wicklow mountains along the valley where Clongowes lies, through Dublin city and out into the Irish Sea. The poet also refers – along with the Duke of Ormond, Henry de Londres, and Henry Grattan – to Sir Almeric de Tristram and the unhappy Isolde, both evoked in opening passages of *Finnegans Wake*. Lyster's footnotes duly provide further information on all of them.

> For others these. I, from the twilight waste
>   Where pale Tradition sits by Memory's grave,
> Gather this wreath, and ere the nightfall, haste,
>   To fling my votive garland on thy wave.
>
> Wave, waft it softly! and when lovers stray
>   At summer eve by stream and dimpling pool,
> Gather thy murmurs into voice and say,
>   With liquid utterance passionate and full,
>
> 'Scorn not sweet maiden, scorn not, vigorous youth,
>   The lay, though breathing of an Irish home,
> That tells of woman-love and warrior-ruth
>   And old expectancy of Christ to come.'

Here, in these closing stanzas of the poem, we can readily detect the remote source of the images that lie behind the famous closing passages of *Finnegans Wake*. That Joyce's last writing should have its origins in his earliest childhood reading is only to be expected.

The River Liffey lay a short walk away to the south: at Wogan's Hole the boys from Clongowes swam and boated in the summer term. Already known to him as the river from whose clear crystal waters his father had made whiskey, the Liffey now refreshed in recreation James's own particular spirit – the play on words would be his own. Its beauty, even if not supported by poetry, would have impressed itself early on his memory and so on his writing.

But the legendary past was not all that James took away from Clongowes. The essential nature of Jesuit education, aside from its system, was its literary nature; it depended on reading and translation from Latin and Greek into English and vice versa. From his earliest days literature became for Joyce the basis of everything. And though his education was still only in its early stages when he left Clongowes – and probably had barely touched upon the elementary grammar of English and Latin – nevertheless the foundations of an attitude of mind had been laid. One of the more eccentric figures in the early days of the school was Francis Sylvester Mahony, about whom many wild tales were told, though the Cork writer was a teacher there for only a short time and left under a cloud after getting a party of boys drunk on an outing. His literary fame rested on his verbal and linguistic skill in writing poems in Latin, Greek and other languages, notably in his versions of Moore's poems, which he claimed the Dublin-born poet had plagiarized from various classical originals which he provided. Language as play was a lesson to be learnt early by some at Clongowes.

Joyce's studies at Clongowes were of a simple though essential kind. It was not perhaps until September 1890 that he entered upon a full course of studies at Clongowes – hence the increased fees paid by John Joyce during his son's last terms. This involved going to classes in the morning, and again after midday dinner. Recreation in the afternoon was followed by tea, free time and some hours of preparation for the next day in the Great Study Hall.

And what did he study? Maths (which he did not care for), Spelling, Writing practice (which he liked), Geography, Latin and some History. He mentions some of his books: Dr Corwall's Spelling Book; Richmal Mangall's *Historical and Miscellaneous Questions*;

Peter Parley's *Tales of Ancient and Modern Greece* and *Tales of Ancient Rome* – in which he would have been first introduced to Troy, Ulysses and Aeneas, those classical stories of cities and wanderers.

Central to the whole scheme of Jesuit education was the preparation of an educated Catholic, a man to take his place with other men in the real world. Religion was not a peripheral subject but the one around which all others had their due place, according to the scheme of the old (though by then updated) *Ratio Studiorum* of 1599. This was not only a matter of class-room learning, the catechism, simple stories from the Bible, traditions of the faith. It was a matter of the daily round: from private prayers and mass in the morning, through various devotions such as the rosary round to night prayers before bed. James's day was shaped by religious devotions.

It is perhaps significant that James carried away no friendships from Clongowes, though some students such as the Hackett brothers, Francis and Byrne, were accustomed in later years to claim one with him on the basis of sharing a school. He himself created the image of an isolated child, living very much in his own mind. Yet others around him at that time had the impression of a lively, contented child. There is, of course, no essential contradiction between these two views.

He does mention some boys by name, but without knowing them at all well, seeming to have had no real pal to go around with. Rody Kickham, Cecil Thunder, Jack Lawton, Jimmy Magee – these and nine others were real enough. Fictional names were given to those involved in the smuggling incident: Simon Moonan, Athy, Tusker Boyle and Corrigan. One boy named Wells would appear again in Joyce's fiction; he it was who threw James into the ditch in front of the castle. For James, Clongowes was important not for those he met but for what he learnt there; at this school, he was introduced to books and to poetry, to the past as living in the landscape of the present, to the eruptions of passion into the placid everydayness of life.

His brother Stanislaus (only 3 when James went to Clongowes, 6 when he left) speaks of his precocity. Yet the impression left with the Jesuits was not of precocity but of a boy 'more delicate than brilliant', about whom there was little to remark intellectually. His days at Clongowes were (in Kevin Sullivan's phrase) 'serene and uneventful'. For all that he may have had some unhappy moments at the hands of Father Daly, for all that he may at times have been lonely, his time at Clongowes was a happy one. Here he acquired a taste for athletics and a love of cricket, and a positive dislike of rugby and boxing.

The settled contentment of much of his time in the school is conveyed by the closing passage in *A Portrait* where the boys are playing cricket in the summer evening, while life itself, like an ornamental urn filling up, goes on accumulating its momentary, passing impressions. The concluding passage of the first chapter of Joyce's novel evokes a summer evening at Clongowes, reflecting all that Joyce felt about the school:

> The air was soft and grey and mild and evening was coming. There was a smell of evening in the air, the smell of the fields in the country where they digged up turnips to peel them and eat them when they went out for a walk to Major Barton's, the smell there was in the little wood beyond the pavilion where the gallnuts were.
>
> The fellows were practising long shies and bowling lobs and slow twisters. In the soft grey silence he could hear the bump of the balls: and from here and from there through the quiet air the sound of the cricket bats; pick, pack, puck: like drops of water in a fountain falling softly in the brimming bowl.

4

Bray and Eileen

Home Life from 1887 to 1891

I t was to the family home in Bray that James returned, almost from exile in Clongowes, for the summer holidays of 1891, as he had returned for all his previous holidays from the school.

Home life was a great contrast to school life. His parents may have come to mean much less to him emotionally than his masters and friends at school, the Jesuit Fathers and Mother Church. He had become a child of Mary and of the Church, rather than simply the infant of May Joyce and her husband. *Amor matris*, however, as Stephen remarks in *Ulysses*, 'may be the only true thing in life'. Paternity might be a fiction, but the presence of his father in the home was real enough. Whatever the world might offer, the family was an institution from which James Joyce would never be free.

If Clongowes had its life and associations which entranced the small child, Bray too had its peculiar attractions. His life there provides a domestic counterpoint to his school experiences. Though he left it at the age of 9, Bray exerted its own special influence on the growing boy. 'Unreasoning infancy,' writes Gorman, again echoing his master's voice, 'was left behind at Bray.' A large part of that maturity was James's growing sense of the political life of the country.

Life at home was eventful. It had been about Easter 1887 that John Joyce had moved his family from the city to Bray in Co. Wicklow, leasing a house on the sea-front at 1 Martello Terrace from Mrs Kelly, the widow of Joseph Kelly, the man who had built the terrace in the early 1860s.

This house was at the end of the newly improved Esplanade, and looked south towards the looming mass of Bray Head, which was a scenic advantage. Only the bath buildings next door separated the Joyces from the ocean. To the end of his life James retained a sensible dread of sea-waves, caused by unhappy experiences in the winters of Bray. In winter the seas sometimes dashed over the sea-wall, sending spume flying over the house and flooding over the open area in front of the terrace until the water almost washed into the hall.

It was the building of the Dublin and South-Eastern Railway along the sea coast to Wexford in 1851 that had created Bray, until then little more than a fishing village on the sandy shore. But by 1887 it had become a proper town by Act of Parliament, a sea-front had been created, and long avenues of large distinguished houses ran back from it to the main street, with its churches and town hall. At this date Bray, with some 6,000 residents and some fine hotels along the sea-front, was at the height of its distinction as a resort, much favoured by visitors from Scotland and the North of England, and was spoken of as 'the Brighton of Ireland'. In later life Joyce had a distinct taste for British seaside resorts of a similar kind, from Bognor to Torquay; perhaps from a simple wish to recapture something of the unforced gaiety he had known as a child.

A more distinguished visitor while the Joyces lived there was Queen Elizabeth of Roumania, better known at that time as the writer Carmen Sylva; her husband had been crowned King of his newly independent country in 1881 with a crown forged from cannon captured at Plevna – a siege whose name echoes so curiously in *Ulysses*: Molly Bloom's father, Major Tweedy, claimed to have fought there. Local gossip about Her Majesty had doubtless lodged in the young boy's imagination. Royal vistors apart, Bray to some nationalists had a very British air. Mrs Conway was to cause a scene on the esplanade by hitting a gentleman over the head with her umbrella because he chose to stand for 'God Save the Queen' when it was played by a military band. Carmen Sylva might be appreciated; but not Queen Victoria.

The Joyce house was large enough, for it had some thirteen rooms. Off the large entrance hall was a parlour where casual visitors were received – the scene of Joyce's earliest surviving epiphany incorporated into the opening of *A Portrait*. Behind this was the dining-room, which Joyce imagined as the setting for the fictional Christmas dinner in 1891 at which Mr Casey weeps for his dead king, his lost leader Charles Stewart Parnell; the row was real enough but the actual dinner took place elsewhere. Upstairs was a large sitting-room extending along the entire front of the house, from which the views were very fine, but this seems to have been a room for the adults and not the children. Here frequent visitors from Dublin would be entertained with music and singing. Aside from this there were five bedrooms into which were crowded the Joyces, Mrs Conway, Uncle Bill and the Joyce children, boys and girls in separate rooms. But despite its fine view it could not have been thought of as one of the better houses in Bray; these all lay further inland on quieter roads. John Joyce – Jack as he was to these convivial friends – enjoyed both the swimming and the rowing available in Bray.

Behind the houses of Martello Terrace at that date were fishermen's cottages and another long stretch of strand running north to Killiney and Dalkey. In later years the young Joyces and their friends would war upon the boys from the cottages, as the young James was not the weakling he makes himself out to be in *A Portrait*.

As mentioned earlier, it was in Bray that another son, George Alfred, was born on 4th July 1887. He was christened for his remote Joyce ancestor on 14th July in Holy Redeemer Church, with John Murray and Mary Ellen Callanan, a Flynn cousin (the Mary Ellen of 'The Dead'), standing as godparents.

John Joyce was eager enough to have visitors, but the frequent visits of one guest in particular were a feature of these years in Bray. This was John Kelly, a Fenian much involved in the Land War as an organizer for the Land League and a close associate of John Joyce's friend Tim Harrington, the Parnellite lawyer and journalist. On 19th July 1887 a new Crimes Act was passed for Ireland which was to affect John Kelly, for between December and January 1888 there were to be many arrests under the Act, and he was one of those summarily incarcerated for their political activities. The events of the Land War were scrutinized by the Parnell-*Times* Commission of Inquiry, which began to sit in London on 17th September 1888, ending its deliberations over a year later in November 1889, at about the time that the Land League's 'Plan of Campaign' failed.

The Joyces had not lost their contact with Dublin, Mrs Joyce singing in Mount Argus in February 1888. At the Rates Office, that month also saw the 'Case of Mr Joyce' receive official attention, a serious enough matter which after much discussion almost led to his dismissal. He was now moved to the North Dock Ward, which was more commercial than residential, but this move made him known to various shipping companies. However, as we shall later see, by

1889 John Joyce was fully reinstated in the confidence of his employers.

The earliest recollections of Stanislaus belonged to this period. The children put on a small play of the Garden of Eden for their parents and for their nursemaid Cranly. Stanislaus was Adam, Margaret was Eve, and James reserved for himself the role of Satan. His brother recalled the energetic manner in which James wriggled across the floor 'with a long tail probably made of a rolled-up sheet or towel'.

James was now wearing glasses for his poor sight, but this did not deter him much. In the few months of 1887 and 1888 when he had attended Miss Raynor's school, he had made a special friend. Another pupil at the school was Eileen Vance, the daughter of their neighbour in Martello Terrace, the local chemist James Noy Vance, who with his brother William owned premises at 92 Main Street, Bray.

Vance hailed from Cork, and had originally studied for a medical degree before becoming a chemist. He was, however, 'as good as a doctor'. In *Ulysses* Vance is given the post of science teacher in the High School, Harcourt Street, and lectures the young Bloom, then a schoolboy, on the elements of physics. The Vance family were connected with the High School – some cousins went there though Vance himself never taught there. However, Joyce may well have heard the mnemonic 'Roygbiv' for the colours of the spectrum which Bloom remembers from Vance.

James was bitten by an Irish terrier on the esplanade and his wound was treated by Mr Vance. Joyce's lifelong reverence for cats and fear of dogs dated from this time. The Vance family lived at two different houses on Martello Terrace, first at number 2 until 1888 and then at number 4 until 1890. Their grandmother lived for a time in 1889 at number 8. They soon became friends with the Joyces. Vance was a cheerful, hard-working man, whose wife Eleanor Augusta suffered from heart disease and spent the greater part of the day on the sofa reading novels. Mrs Vance (formerly Atkinson) had lived in Harold's Cross before her marriage in 1879 at the age of 20, her groom being then 45. She died at 5 Loreto Villas (their new home) on 13th May 1894, aged 35, after two weeks' illness with typhoid. His devotion to her was often the the subject of comment amongst his friends, most of whom habitually neglected their wives (according to Stanislaus Joyce); but the comment was not altogether hostile because he was too clever and vivacious in company to incur contempt, being full of amusing stories of his domestic life and his troubles with servants.

The earliest of Joyce's epiphanies to survive recalls an incident in the front parlour of the house in Martello Terrace, when Vance comes in with a stick demanding that James apologize, his mother's insistence being followed by Vance turning the matter into a joke: the eagles would come and pull out his eyes. Under the table Joyce recited to himself:

> Pull out his eyes,
> Apologise,
> Apologise,
> Pull out his eyes . . .

It was an incident of childhood that would eventually provide him with material for the opening passages of his novel. The disasters of life were already being transmuted into the triumphs of art.

His friendship with Eileen Vance meant a great deal to James. (She had been christened Eleanor after her mother – the Gaelicization of her name was a romantic touch, suggesting that Vance's views verged towards Irish Ireland rather than West Britain.) Another sister, Norah, was called 'Boodie', which Joyce adopted in the novel for one of Stephen's sisters. The third girl was named Violet. Eileen seems by all accounts to have been an attractive girl with a lively sense of fun. Stanislaus recalls that she was 'a pale, oval-faced girl with long dark hair, which she often wore in plaits over each shoulder in front, framing her face'. Though seeming cold and distant, she was not. She wrote to him at Clongowes for St Valentine's Day 1889, including a verse which her father may have composed:

> Oh, Jimmy Joyce, you are my darlin',
> You are my looking-glass night and mornin',
> I'd rather have you without a farthin',
> Than Johnny Jones, with his ass and garden.*

It was assumed by the parents, if only in a jocular way, that the pair would marry. Indeed in Eileen commenting on a young man, in her

---

* Thus Stanislaus Joyce; Ellmann gives a different version, naming Harry Newall, a local cripple, as the owner of the ass.

teens, her sister Norah exclaimed, 'Oh you can't look at him, you're going to marry Jimmie Joyce.'

In his imagination Joyce associated Eileen and her physical beauty with the Catholic Litany of the Virgin: *Tower of Ivory, House of Gold*, and recalled how he had admired her skin, her fine hair and lovely laugh, as they looked up the lawn of Breslin's hotel through the railings at the fashionable visitors.

Her tales of James, however, had odd flourishes to them. As an old woman she recalled his claim that he was punished at home by having his head thrust down the toilet bowl and the flush pulled – a bizarre but not unlikely thing. This was a common but cruel punishment of the day, though more likely to have been enforced by Mrs Conway or their nurse Cranly than by the gentler Mrs Joyce. Yet already the pain of love was being confused with the delights of punishment. The Vances moved to Loreto Terrace at the end of 1890, so would have missed the rows in the Joyce household at the time of the Parnell crisis.

James Noy Vance was an Anglican who had a great admiration for James and shared John Joyce's high hopes for him. He died in the late 1890s while James was triumphing in the Intermediate Exams, seemingly fulfilling those very hopes. Indeed in the summer of 1897 or 1898 Margaret ('Poppie') Joyce went down to spend the summer with the Vances in Bray. One afternoon James and his father came too, and he sat (as Eileen thought) appraising him.

In the scheme which Joyce drew up for his novel *Stephen Hero* in 1904, Eileen in Bray is associated with Wells, a school at Belvedere acquaintance who summers in Bray; later, in *A Portrait*, we learn that he has become a secular priest. Here perhaps was an early instance of that sense of betrayal Joyce was to feel all his life. As is so often the case, the young man's feelings for the girl were very different from hers for the boy. Eileen assumed a role in the artistic scheme of Joyce's life greater than she would have guessed.

The casual talk in the happy Bray years of James and Eileen being united in marriage was a pleasantry which disgusted Mrs Conway: to marry a Protestant was to go to Hell. But, as his brother thought later, the diet of admiration provided by Vance and others which surrounded Joyce from early childhood had a profound effect on his belief in his own abilities.

Other beliefs affected him too. A sombre occasion was an encounter while on a walk through the nearby village of Little Bray, across the bridge over the Dargle. From one of the little houses there a funeral was starting out and the Joyce children stopped with their nurse Cranly to watch. A distraught woman tried to throw herself from an upper window as the coffin of an infant was carried away. Later Cranly explained that she was the child's mother and that she was in despair because the infant had not been baptized. Mrs Conway added that the child would pass its eternal life in Limbo: 'So now you see what happens. The child will never go to Heaven. Now you see what comes of not baptizing immediately.'

The effect on James and Stanislaus was profound. In a family where some five or six siblings miscarried, or died at birth without benefit of baptism, this may have been a point of controversy with the Joyces. There is no record, for instance, that John Augustine, the child who died in December 1880, was baptized.

But Mrs Conway had her tender points, exchanging small cashew-nut sweetmeats (which she used to sweeten her breath) for the tissue paper which in those days came wrapped around parcels. James observed her religious rites with interest: her little red lamp of Colza oil before the Statue of Our Lady as the Immaculate Conception, among his first experiences of a taste for a devotion to the Virgin Mary. He was also engaged by her pair of hair-brushes with their maroon and green baize backs for Michael Davitt and Charles Stewart Parnell. When the lightning flashed she taught him to say: 'Jesus of Nazareth, the King of the Jews, from a sudden and unprovided for death deliver us, O Lord.' 'Dante', as the boys called her (from the southern Cork pronunciation of 'the Auntie' as 'de Auntie') would sit upright in a cushioned chair, complaining (as in *Finnegans Wake*) of her 'back by back by back'. She wore a heavy velvet skirt, jewelled slippers and a black lace cap.

In February 1888 James reached his sixth birthday. The concert in Bray Boat Club on 26th June, at which he sang with his parents in the club premises at 8 Martello Terrace, was not the only musical occasion in his young life. Mrs Joyce was now a member of the choir in Little Bray Church, where the parish priest was the famous Father James Healy, a notable wit and character in the social life of the day. This church was among that small group – including the Three Patrons and Haddington Road – that did much at this time to encourage musical religious services in the Dublin region.

Mrs Conway had added to his education by teaching him the elements of English history and geography. Her preparation during the summer had allowed him – entrance tests being of a simple kind at the time – to enter Clongowes in the autumn of 1888.

James's brief break from school at Christmas and his long summers were spent in Bray. In the spring and summer of 1889, John Kelly seems to have been with them. Every morning before Mass he had a cold tub. Stanislaus recalls how Kelly lost hold of the donkey which Stanislaus was riding, allowing the beast to escape up the Main Street, causing a great diversion. John Joyce would invite him to stay after his prison sentences, of which there were some three or four at this date. There was a bustle one night when a police sergeant (also named Joyce) called to say that a warrant had arrived for Kelly's arrest but he was delaying the execution of it. Kelly got away up the Cabinteely Road. (The incident is mentioned in *A Portrait*.) This was John Kelly's last visit to Bray, but not to the Joyces.

At this date it is unlikely that James fully comprehended Kelly's political life; understanding of that only came later. At this time he was more like an entertaining uncle. He would be pressed into reciting 'The Auld Plaid Shawl', 'Sheamus O'Brien' or 'The Goat', and to Mrs Joyce's accompaniment he would sing 'The Diver' or 'In Cellar Cool'. John Kelly had a pleasant bass voice against John Joyce's tenor. Once after a visit to Dublin to hear the Royal Carl Rosa Opera at the Gaiety he remarked: 'Do you mind what I am telling you, John. If you got three months in jail, you'd sing any of those fellows off the stage.'

Guests were entertained in that long drawing-room on the second floor with its views of the mountains. Here James learnt to enjoy the airs of Moore's Irish melodies and the other arias, songs and ballads which are such an integral part of his writings, especially *Finnegans Wake*.

That summer of 1889, James's first summer home from school, was enlivened by a comic incident. Short of a ball, the boys and their friends played football with Bill O'Connell's best hat, which had to be sent for repairs without their irascible father hearing of it. The hat was returned and Bill O'Connell wore it on a picnic to Bray Head, but was dismayed to find that whatever the hatter had used on it was attractive to bees, who swarmed around it. John Joyce remarked on this in astonishment. 'Ah, they're only having their tea,' Bill O'Connell exclaimed.

John Joyce may have found it more convenient in the winter to keep a room in Dublin. On 13th October 1889 he acquired the

freehold of a piece of property in Cork, using an address in Dublin –
26 Sandford Road, Ranelagh. As no connection with this address is
otherwise known it adds yet another small mystery to his activities,
though there is no evidence that under the name of Browne (the
householder's name) he was keeping a second family there. Stanislaus
recalls an episode in which James cycled at the age of 7 from the
outskirts of Dublin to visit Cranly, their nurse in Bray, leaving his
distraught parents to search for him among their relatives. But
this Ulyssean attempt to visit Cranly may have been made from
Ranelagh. Even as a boy James, though not yet old enough to 'be
about his father's business', was not afraid to leave home. A daring
sense of adventure came early to him – or was he merely searching
for unquestioning affection?

That autumn the Parnell Commission concluded in November
with what Nationalists saw as a vindication of Parnell. His counsel
Charles Russell had destroyed the credibility of Pigott in the witness
box and the letters which had connected Parnell directly with the
violence of rural Ireland. In the excitement it was all too easy to
overlook the mass of evidence from over 400 witnesses about the
brutal activities of the Land League which had presented an appalling picture of murder and coercion during the Land War.

This victory, however, was followed on 24th December (as indicated earlier) by the application from Captain William O'Shea for a
divorce from his wife Katherine, which named C.S. Parnell as co-
respondent. The couple had been living together for some time, but
in secrecy. Mrs O'Shea had borne Parnell a child, which died but
had been registered and buried under O'Shea's name. O'Shea had
winked at the relationship since an inheritance from Mrs O'Shea's
wealthy aged aunt stood to be gained by avoiding scandal; but the
aunt had died, the money was in dispute, and he was no longer
inclined to connive at his wife's infidelity with the leader of his
party (who incidentally had gained O'Shea his Parliamentary seat in
Galway). He wished to end the pretence. The first bitter ripples
of the great controversy flowed over the Joyce household that
Christmas, but as yet no one was clear about the matter. Nationalists
in and out of Parliament knew that Parnell would have some explanation.

1890 came and, as we have seen, a daughter Mary Cathleen was
born to the Joyces on 18th January; she was baptized on James's
birthday, 2nd February, with William Murray and a Flynn relative

Maria O'Donohoe (the Maria of 'Clay') as witnesses. These new children may well have been resented by James as the eldest, for each one challenged his place in his mother's affections and his father's devotion. His sense of isolation in school may well have been reinforced by his changing position at home.

A large family was an expensive matter, even then. Quite what John Joyce's expenses were is a mystery, and research has not fully exposed them, but from time to time he needed more money than his income provided. On 9th April 1890, for instance, he took out a mortgage with Margaret Bridgeman, a moneylender who was married to a civil engineer, and who is mentioned in *Ulysses* as the late Patrick Dignam's creditor – yet another instance of the deeply personal nature of some of the merely passing references in Joyce's works.

This summer, too, James would have spent at Bray. Living beside the sea in a resort town, there seems to have been no question of the Joyces taking a holiday elsewhere. There were outings, however, to Bray Head or into the lovely countryside of nearby Wicklow, like one to Powerscourt Demesne to see the famous waterfall, a picnic marked by the odd incident of John Joyce and the petticoat. When the party reached the glade below the falls where they planned to eat, it was found that the rug had been left behind. Christina Murray, John Murray's second wife, took off her voluminous white petticoat and the food was spread out on this. John Joyce was obscurely but permanently offended by what she had done – perhaps because like his son James he considered women's underclothes to be 'secret, secret, secret'. His disgust at the Murrays was epitomized in his application to John Murray, then in his late sixties, of the vulgar epithets. John Joyce's attitudes to sexual matters seem to have been peculiar. The father of a numerous brood, he would joke over selecting for his share of the Christmas turkey the Pope's (or Parson's) Nose – the bird's sexual organ – which was believed to renew a man's sexual vitality. Yet in other ways, such as at this picnic, he could show himself to be a prude.

In the autumn of 1890 the great Parnell scandal broke. On 1st November Parnell issued a sessional whip to the members of the Irish Parliamentary Party at Westminster to meet as customary to plan their tactics for the new parliament. That day the trial of the divorce of Mrs and Captain O'Shea began in the London High Court. Uncontested, it ended on the 17th with the granting of a decree nisi to Captain O'Shea. But the evidence given was of a sensational and comic kind – with allegations of Parnell using a false name, 'Mr Fox', and escaping from Mrs O'Shea's house at Eltham down a fire-escape. Whatever may have been the moral considerations of the case, Parnell's dignity certainly took a fall and it may have been at this time that Mrs Conway, horrified by the revelations in court, ripped off the green cover from her brush and told James that Parnell was 'a bad man.' Sex had become involved with politics: but quite how the hero of his father and John Kelly could be wicked must have puzzled the boy.

Now began the divisions in the Irish Party. In Dublin a meeting of the National League in the Leinster hall voted its support for Parnell on 20th November, the same day that an editorial appeared in the British *Methodist Times* (an influential nonconformist paper) referring to the 'obscene race' that Parnell led – the nonconformists also confusing sex and politics. A meeting of the English National Liberals in Sheffield on 21st November was to be influenced by this rising groundswell of outraged English nonconformist opinion against Parnell. Yet his Irish support was still wide, and on 25th November he was re-elected Chairman of the Irish Party. The next day, however, a letter from Gladstone to John Morley was published, criticizing Parnell and suggesting he should step aside, and a second meeting of the Irish Party was put off until 1st December. The interim saw the issuing of a manifesto by Parnell, followed by Gladstone's reply. Though Parnell had the support of many Irish-Americans, mostly active Fenians, already doubts were current among his followers at home. His attack on Gladstone put the Irish Party in the hands of the Tories if they were to achieve anything in the way of the new legislation they sought, and the Tories were the avowed opponents of Home Rule. The political considerations were now as crucial as anything moral or personal.

On 1st to 6th December took place the debates in 'Committee Room 15' which concluded with the splitting of the Party and Parnell's defiant espousal of a rump faction. The Irish bishops had issued their own manifesto on 3rd December, but there were other considerations for members of the Party based on Parnell's attitude and his political actions. The influence of their graces on Parnell's fall was only one of many other considerations on the day.

On Saturday 6th December the Party split, 53–33, on Parnell's leadership. This was seen by some as betrayal by Tim Healy, who now emerged as the leader of the larger wing nominally commanded by Justin McCarthy. Much was made of Healy's retort to Parnell's query about who would be master of the Party, as to 'who would its mistress be'. No gentleman, the Parnellites claimed, would have mentioned a lady's name in such a place. But, for the Healyites, Kitty O'Shea (a name she never used) was not a lady but a trollop. A further meeting (which Parnell and his supporters did not attend) was held on 8th December, after which the new whip of the Irish Party moved in the House the writ for a by-election in Kilkenny: this was an appeal to the people, a test of which faction really had the nation's support. The next day, 9th December, the new Land Act (Parnell's greatest achievement so far) received the Royal Assent and became law.

Parnell departed for Ireland to rouse support for his position among the rank and file of the Party throughout Ireland, and on 10th December he arrived in Dublin. His first act was to capture the offices of *United Ireland*, expelling the editor Mathias McDonnell Bodkin. He also spoke at the Rotunda against the issue of a manifesto by the Patriots. The next day, the *United Irishman* having been retaken, he again stormed the offices – an incident featured in *Ulysses*, when Mr Bloom remembers picking up Parnell's hat and handing it back to him. Perhaps John Joyce was present at this fracas, certainly there was no doubt where he now stood. A test of feeling among the ordinary voters in the country as a whole was provided by the by-election at Kilkenny on 22nd December, when the Parnellite candidate, the Corkman John Pope-Hennessy, was soundly defeated. Parnell's paper *The Insuppressible*, in which he waged verbal war on his enemies, appeared at this time (from 24th December to 24th January).

Because so many of the Irish Party were journalists, Ireland roared with controversy, as did the Joyce household. That autumn the excitement of the fall of Parnell heralded a heated Christmas at the Joyce house. The famous dinner scene in his novel is based on these three Christmases: 1889 had seen Parnell vindicated and the issue of the divorce writ; the Christmas of 1890 was particularly exciting, after the Party split. What 1891 would bring, no one yet foresaw. The divisions carried over into that year. On 11th February Parnell refused to compromise by resigning the leadership of his wing in a

meeting at Boulogne with William O'Brien and John Dillon: this
closed off any hope of reuniting the former comrades. (The Joyces'
dislike of John Dillon carried over into the next generation, for in
Paris in the 1920s Joyce upbraided Padraic Colum for talking to
John Dillon's son, the eminent Celtic scholar Myles Dillon.)

The controversy surrounding Parnell was to colour Joyce's
outlook on matters of sexual morality and politics for the rest of his
life. Though he would later call himself a Socialist for a brief time,
he remained at heart a Fenian Parnellite, and in his own life would
refuse to recognize the conventions of society that had destroyed the
Member for Cork City.

The season of Parnell's fall saw also the passage of the Corporation
of Dublin Act 1890, which allowed for the Corporation to collect its
own rates. It was likely that this would mean changes in John Joyce's
office, but as yet it was unclear what they were. His affairs were still
stable enough for him to be able to pay James's school fees by cheque
on 5th February 1891. However, it was the last payment the school
would receive.

*

After leaving Clongowes at the end of the cricket season, Joyce
passed the summer of 1891 at Bray. On 25th June Parnell married
Katherine O'Shea in a civil ceremony in Brighton, where they had
now gone to live, an event which caused further controversy between
his enemies and his followers. In the eyes of some, marriage only
made his sin worse. With flagging energy Parnell continued to fight
for his position.

On 20th August Joyce's step-grandmother, Christina Murray –
she of the infamous petticoat – died in the quaint old house on
Usher's Island attended by her aunts, the Misses Flynn. At about
this time John Joyce decided to move his family and home yet again,
having chosen a house nearer the city, on Carysfort Avenue in the
township of Blackrock. Though he was to leave the final Clongowes
account for that autumn unpaid, his finances seem still to have been
solid. Possibly he decided against paying the bill because James was
back at school for only a short time. At this date it does not seem to
have been lack of money that caused the move, or left the debt with
the Jesuits. The family moved for the perhaps too mundane reason
that life in Martello Terrace must have become unbearable. Work
had begun on building a new pier and harbour directly behind

the houses; the noise of the pile-drivers, as well as the dirt and inconvenience, must have been appalling and have proved too much even for John Joyce. The seaside had lost its appeal. So, late in the autumn of 1891, the Joyces left Bray and moved closer to Dublin.

5

THE SHADOW OF PARNELL

BLACKROCK: SUMMER 1891– NOVEMBER 1892

James certainly returned to the Jesuits at Clongowes in the autumn of 1891, but this was to prove his last term at the college. His name was included by the new rector, Father Matthew Devitt, in the official return made to the Intermediate Education Board on 15th November, which included those boys who were there on 1st November, or perhaps merely those who had been enrolled for that term. The accuracy of this return is confirmed by the fact that the last address that the Jesuit bursar at Clongowes had in the college records for James Joyce was not 1 Martello Terrace, Bray but 'Leoville House', Blackrock, the house to which the family had moved that autumn.

Though he returned to Clongowes, Joyce did not remain for long. *A Portrait* suggests that Stephen may have fallen ill from a fever – possibly amoebic dysentery – contracted after he was pushed into the square ditch in front of the castle. In the novel Stephen lies restless and feverish in the Infirmary on the night of 5th to 6th October (76 days from the end of term, as he has just carefully recorded on the calendar in his desk in the Study Hall) while Parnell himself, after ruining his health in energetic campaigning throughout Ireland, is dying at his Brighton home in the south of England. Stephen lives. Parnell dies.

Stanislaus Joyce claimed that his brother was always well, but this contradicts the evidence of the Clongowes accounts, and it does seem that some kind of ill-health, resulting in a few months' debility, brought about James's removal from Clongowes, as typhoid had brought about his father's departure from St Colman's. His removal was not due to lack of money on his father's part. It is clear from the school records that many boys at Clongowes were retained there free or almost free of charge, if their family circumstances warranted it. Any hardship at home would have received the kindest consideration from the rector, especially because James Joyce was a bright child who would prove an asset to the school in the all-important Intermediate exams. John Joyce, perhaps because his son was there for only a part of the term, was to leave the final account he received from Clongowes unpaid, as his own father had left his final college bill from St Colman's unpaid a generation before.

*

Whatever the exact reason, James came home from Clongowes in late October or early November 1891 at a tormented time for Ireland.

Against good advice, Parnell spoke at Creggs in Mayo on 27th September. It was a cold, wet day and he caught a chill. On the night of Wednesday, 30th September, he left Ireland on the Mail Boat from Kingstown for the last time. He was already very ill, his friends realized. 'I shall be all right,' he told them. 'I shall be back next Saturday week.' He never returned; he died at Brighton close to midnight on 6th October 1891.

From England Parnell's remains were brought home, his coffin being landed at Kingstown. On 11th October, a day of pelting rain, he was buried in Glasnevin, followed to the grave by a huge, mourning crowd. If he was still at Clongowes, James was only able to dream about the funeral, and how the leader's body was landed in Ireland.

But if James *was* still at Clongowes then, as he suggests in his novel, he was certainly in Bray in November. His sister Eva was born there on 26th November, and baptized the same day. James (young as he was) and his aunt, Josephine Murray, stood as the infant's godparents.

Was the mother, or the child, in danger of death? Or were the family members already making final urgent preparations to move to Blackrock? Certainly they were at the new house on the edge of the city by the end of 1891, because the city directory for the following year lists them at that address on the basis of information compiled by the end of October. This suggests that the house was leased from the Quarter Day of Michaelmas (29th September) or even from Martinmas (11th November), but that because Mrs Joyce was in the final days of her pregnancy the move was postponed. In any case, it may be safely said that James returned to Clongowes for only a few weeks, and that by Christmas 1891 the Joyces were living in Blackrock.

Parnell's death left a vacancy in one of the Cork City seats. A by-election was called soon after and held on 6th November. For a hectic fortnight the streets which John Joyce so fondly recalled from his youth suffered from electioneering, as Parnellites and Anti-Parnellites clashed in public and private. Timothy Harrington, friend of John Joyce and John Kelly, was to the fore in the cause of Parnell. Other politicians who spoke, for and against, included Davitt, Tim Healy and William O'Brien, all of whom made speeches to large and over-excited crowds. John Redmond, a famous old Clongownian, was standing in the Parnellite interest; but he was defeated by Martin Flavin, a local butter merchant and man of influence who had the support of the local Catholic clergy.

The other seat in Cork City was held by Maurice Healy, a lawyer and journalist, brother of the by-then-infamous Tim Healy. James by this time had written his poem 'Et Tu, Healy', which his brother always associated with Blackrock though it may have been started at Bray. John Joyce was intensely proud of this effort by his eldest son and was later to take steps to share his pride, and his hatred of the Healys, with the world.

November passed into December and family life resumed. The smaller Joyces had been sent to Sion Hill, the nearby Dominican convent.* James, who was still recovering his health, stayed at home to study under his mother's supervision. This he did with great diligence, coming to her every hour or so to have her hear his lessons.

Mrs Conway (as Stanislaus recalls) was still one of the household, and gave the Joyce home its religious tone. Every evening she would lead the children in the recital of the Mysteries of the Rosary, in the conservatory at the back of the house. The nearness to the city may have meant that it was at this date she took the Joyce children on those visits to see Danby's 'Opening of the Sixth Seal', and at Christmas season to see the wonderful crib at Inchichore.

For Christmas Day dinner during the holiday season of 1891, John Joyce invited his Fenian friend John Kelly, newly released from a final period of incarceration in Tullamore Gaol. Kelly had been deeply affected by the recent political events. He and a friend

---

* So Stanislaus claimed; but no junior school records survive from this period.

had met Parnell at Westland Row Station that evening in September when the Chief was making his final journey home to Brighton, and they had gone out with him to the Mail Boat at Kingstown. John Kelly was almost the last man in Ireland to have shaken Parnell's hand. The thoughts and conversation of John Kelly and Jack Joyce that holiday ran on Parnell and his achievements. Returning from mass filled with indignation at political remarks from some of the clergy on the current crisis, they settled to the dinner which Joyce has described so vividly in his novel (though in the book he transposes it for structural reasons to Bray.) It was the first dinner which he had been allowed to come down to from the nursery. The genial graciousness of John Joyce's old-fashioned courtesy soon collapsed into a rancour more suited to the bar-room; but this was a scene – one of the most powerful in Irish literature, with its dynamic clash of politics and religion, the nation's two great passions – that was being echoed all across the deeply divided country.

A few days after this fearful row, which left the already dying Kelly weeping over the table for his lost leader, Mrs Conway left the house.

Though Margaret Joyce (then aged ten) went with her for a short time as a companion, Mrs Conway never returned to the Joyces. After staying here and there in Dublin with other friends, she died on 16th November 1896 in the home of Charles Butler at 4 Pemroke Villas, Merrion Road. She left an estate of £40 – all that remained of her inherited fortune – which her mysterious husband Patrick Conway emerged from the obscurity of a central Dublin address to claim. Thus passed out of Joyce's life the opinionated woman who had been one of the most baleful of the formative influences on his developing imagination.

*

The spring of 1892 came, but still James did not return to school. The strange limbo life that he lived at this time is well suggested in *A Portrait*.

The new house at 23 Carysfort Avenue – a long quiet road lined with respectable middle-class homes – was largish, rambling but comfortable, convenient both to the shops and to the railway station. Socially it was a distinct step up from Bray.

There was a pillared portico, above which reclined the large stone lion which gave 'Leoville' its name. The panels of the front door were filled by two leaded panels of coloured glass which showed Dante and, opposite, his beloved Beatrice. This was perhaps James's first introduction to the Florentine poet, who was to later mean so much to him, and to the theme of his chaste and hopeless love which was to echo so long in his own work, especially in *Giacomo Joyce*.

The Joyces' house stood on a bend beside the local Anglican church, Christ Church. Next door, at 25 Carysfort Avenue, lived a Church of Ireland family named Raynold, Mr William Elford Raynold being then the manager of a wholesale wine and tea merchants. James became friendly with Aubrey Raynold, the youngest of the Raynold children, who was ten months younger than him. They formed a gang among the other boys of their age along the Avenue.

It was with Aubrey Raynold that James began to write his first novel. This *urschrift* too is now lost, but as young Stephen Dedalus is deeply absorbed with the romances of Dumas *père* we may imagine that their schoolboy efforts were influenced by the French author, especially the grim but exciting tale of the Count of Monte Cristo's revenge. James dreamed of the young Mercedes as an image of womanhood. In his imagination he took himself among the sunny white homes of Marseilles – in the illustrations to the novel, the heroine's plaits would have recalled those of Eileen Vance. Aubrey, however, grew up to become a prosaic bank clerk and seems never to have written anything as an adult. The family eventually left Ireland, along with many others of their persuasion, at the time of the Troubles.

Yet this period in Blackrock was crucial in Joyce's development. From Clongowes he had brought an established taste for reading which he was now at leisure to develop on his own. Reading Dumas provided an escape, but was also a pointer to the future: that Joyce would work (like the Count of Monte Cristo) to gain his way by silence, exile and cunning, in life as in literature.

This year in Blackrock of working on his own and reading freely had a vital effect on Joyce's development. The sense of isolation he had a felt at Clongowes now became more emphatic. With much time on his hands and without many companions of his own age, a habit of life was established. He became the shaper of his own mind, giving it a direction towards the literary which would never be displaced. Here he began to write.

*

Bill O'Connell remained with the family after the departure of Mrs Conway. He was banned from smoking his terrible tobacco and banished to the shed at the end of the garden, but with James he would go around the village, visiting his acquaintances, and shopping for Mrs Joyce much as he had done in Bray. A prayer in the Catholic parish church, St John the Baptist, completed the pair's daily round. He also oversaw James as he ran his laps in the local park, down by the railway near the sea. These athletics were an attempt to build up the child through exercises after his illness. Of Mike Flynn, the trainer who was to die soon after, no trace has been found, though he must have existed under that or another name.

John Joyce made friends with William Field, the local butcher and Member of Parliament. Field was long to remain a connection of the Joyces and to feature in *Ulysses*. James himself was still in touch with him in 1912. Was John Joyce, like Bloom, to gain a job through this connection? Field had begun life as an advanced Nationalist, with radical ideas on both the land question and the problem of town labour, but though he later modified his views he was at this date still a Parnellite. (He had been one of those who met the Chief's coffin at Kingstown.) He had made his money as a butcher in Kingstown and from a chain of still-remembered meat shops throughout Dublin; police supply contracts had added to his wealth and the papers referred to him as 'a merchant prince'. He was the author of several small publications on economic and labour affairs, and remained in Parliament until 1918. He sent his son, the Jimmy of Joyce's story 'After the Race', to an English school and then on to Cambridge University. But having money, Jimmy fell into bad ways. Popular, he divided his time between musical and motoring circles, and so provided Joyce with the germ of his story.

*

During that long and often lonely summer in Blackrock, James became aware of difficulties facing his father. The servants whispered together in the hall, while his father stood before the fireplace in the dining-room, denouncing his enemies to Bill O'Connell, who would urge him to sit down and take his dinner.

John Joyce talked vaguely to his family of 'business difficulties', and indeed there may well have been some fall in whatever investments he then had (a fate shared by many others about this time). He is usually represented as a hopeless spendthrift – Stanislaus recounts his embarrassment on seeing his father weaving his way home up the Main Street of Blackrock, like some fallen drunkard out of Dickens. But the case was not so simple.

Aside from his rents, John Joyce earned an average of £431/14s/10d over these years, though in 1892 his income was only £396/7s/0d. He was not given an actual salary, but was paid on a poundage rate, in relation to the amount of rates he secured, plus a bonus. That year he had £300 in poundage, and £128/16s/6d in emoluments for extra work performed 'under Acts of Parliament' in relation to franchise investigation claims, and attendance on Poor Law, Parliamentary and Jurors Revision Courts – some of which inconveniently met at the same time. He was by any standards very well-off at a period when the average industrial wage was £150, since he earned something in the region of £25,000 in terms of today's money. However, there may be more to his downfall than has been appreciated.

John Joyce was never made a bankrupt – his name cannot be found in the court returns published in the *Dublin Gazette* over these years. Yet Stanislaus claims that he was. And James (who has Stephen Dedalus say explicitly that his father was a bankrupt) refers in his notes for his novel to those 'business difficulties' without elaboration, just as elsewhere he numbers among his father's avocations that of 'small investor'. Were there (as I suppose) investments that went wrong at this time? Certainly there was a great deal of share activity at this date in Ireland, with many new companies being formed, and consequent crashes among the over-extended. Owing to lack of real interest on the part of his elder sons, John Joyce's finances remain a small mystery.

My research has now cast a little more light on what happened. John Joyce's troubles began on 22nd June 1892, when he lost an action taken against him in the Queen's Bench Division (as the Civil Courts were then styled) by James Reuben Dodd, for the sum of £22/15s/0d, with an award of £5/6s/0d in costs. We will hear of Mr Dodd again. On 18th October Richard Dawson, a corn and potato merchant at 46 Bolton Street, won an action for £30/0s/0d and £5/11s/0d costs. Yet another action was taken by Francis H. Caulfield, a moneylender in Fownes Street, settled on 1st February 1893 for £13/0s/0d and £2/4s/0d costs. These were small sums perhaps, but coming together the three actions might have been characterized as a plot.

The crunch came, however, when John Joyce's name appeared in *Stubbs Weekly Gazette* and *Perry's Gazette*, both of which listed bankrupts and debtors, on 2nd November. He had passed John Lawler – a financial agent at 110 Middle Abbey Street – a Bill of Sale on the furniture in his Blackrock house for a loan of £130/10s/0d – a serious sum of money, the equivalent of nearly £8,000 today. The next day he was suspended by the Collector-General as his financial probity was (rightly) under doubt. So, though he was not actually made bankrupt, John Joyce had suffered a serious public disgrace. But the main immediate problem facing him in 1892 was his increasingly doubtful position in the Rates Office. Here, too, he might well have suspected enemies at work.

In February 1891 the Corporation appointed Charles Dawson, well-known as a city baker, to take charge of the collection of municipal rates from the Collector-General's Office. At the beginning of 1892, however, the death of the Collector-General brought the matter of a separate department back to the notice of the Corporation, who suggested that a temporary appointment should be made. Then on 9th May 1892 the Corporation acted, accepting a recommendation of a sub-committee which had met on 4th May, resolving to take over the collecting of the city rates starting on 1st January 1893. The government appointed a new Collector-General on 29th July, and an inquiry was launched into the manner of collecting the city rates. Since this inquiry would not report until 22nd August, what this meant in practice was as yet not clear. John Joyce's position as a government employee might still be safe, despite his other troubles.

Meanwhile, there was the country-wide excitement of the General Election in July, after the resignation of Salisbury's administration, which pitched Parnellites and Anti-Parnellites against each other across the country.

In Cork City, in which John Joyce retained the intense interest of a property-owner, the seat once held by Parnell was taken by the Anti-Parnellite William O'Brien (as Martin Flavin, who had secured it at the November by-election, did not stand again). At this point John Joyce, pleading illness, took time out from the office to travel down to Cork to urge his tenants to vote for the Parnellite candidate. When his real purpose came to the notice of his employers – who had paid another official to undertake his duties while he was 'ill' – a serious view was taken by his superiors in the Rates Office of this lying dereliction, and the matter was officially noted in his file.

It was perhaps in this connection that John Joyce had his son's poem on Parnell printed on yellow paper as a small flyer or pamphlet; Stanislaus recalls their father bringing them home, rolled up under his arm, from Alley and O'Reilly of Ryder's Row in the city centre (an address near enough to Bolton Street). The poem was probably given its title 'Et Tu, Healy' by John Joyce in a spirit of partisanship, for it seems to have borne no title originally and the present one does not fit the style of the surviving fragments. The interests of the Healy family were strong in Cork. He may have intended to distribute the poem in a city where James's verses would have been much appreciated by the anti-Healy Parnellites. He claimed to have even sent the Pope a copy, though the Vatican Library is unable to confirm this. I suspect that it was this real political purpose and not mere fatherly whim which brought about the publication – albeit in an ephemeral and now vanished form of Joyce's first work. The few lines recalled by his brother, and recorded in the tortured text of *Finnegans Wake*, suggest that the poem was a drearily sentimental one. Some lines from it ran:

> My cot alas that dear old shady home
> Where oft in youthful sport I played
> Upon thy verdant grassy fields all day
> Or lingered for a moment in thy bosom shade . . .

In the final results the Parnellites won only 9 seats in Ireland, as against 72 for their enemies. The Irish people as a whole did not seem to support the late leader of the Irish Party as passionately as legend would suggest, and had spoken against the memory of Parnell. Whatever the politics and the personalities of the matter, for James Joyce Parnell was to remain a hero, a man of nobility who had defied the forces of convention and of the Church. For his father, he had also the special merit of representing Cork.

The Parnellites were fighting very much a rearguard action. Many of those with Irish Republican Brotherhood connections were under police observation by the Special Branch. John Kelly, for instance, and Andrew Kettle, both friends of the Joyces, were photographed surreptitiously by the secret police in August 1892. This photograph is, it seems, the only existing one of John Kelly.

Mrs Conway was not the only one to abandon the Joyce household at this time. On 28th August Bill O'Connell returned to Cork, where he died suddenly on the last day of the month from the heart condition that had been troubling him for some time, at the house of his friend J.F. Callaghan in Montenotte. His funeral was held on 3rd September to St Joseph's Cemetery at 8.30 a.m. from St Patrick's Church. There is no evidence that John Joyce attended, but it is hard to imagine that he did not go from a sense of family loyalty.

He returned to work in Dublin to discover that the staff in the Collector-General's office were now expressing their concern about the future of their jobs. The inquiry into the running of the office had reported at the end of August, and a conference was held in the City Hall on 19th September. The staff made a formal protest at the end of September about their security. Throughout October there were further contacts between the government and the Corporation. It was only at the end of that month that the government pointed out more difficulties over retiring staff to the Corporation, but as yet nothing final had been settled.

With the return of the Carysfort Avenue children to their schools in September, James found himself alone again. He was not to go back to Clongowes – his father's financial difficulties precluded that. Mike Flynn had gone into hospital and died soon after. Aubrey Raynold had little time to spend with him now that he had homework to do, and their gang fell apart. James would go out with the local milkman to the fields where the cows were kept at Stradbrook, and ride around with him while he delivered the loose fresh milk. This was so pleasant a memory (initially) that he gave the same activity to the young Roman-born Archie Rowan in *Exiles*. (Brigid, the elderly housekeeper with the iron-grey hair in that play, must also be modelled on the cook engaged by Mrs Joyce to assist her after the departure of Mrs Conway.) His mother was now in the last months of yet another pregnancy and may have had little time for him. He wandered the autumnal streets in an odd mood which he describes in his novel.

> The ambition which he felt astir at times in the darkness of his soul sought no outlet ... He returned to Mercedes and, as he brooded upon her image, a strange unrest crept into his blood. Sometimes a fever gathered within him and led him to rove alone in the evening along the quiet avenue. The peace of the gardens and the kindly lights in the windows poured a tender influence into his restless heart. The noise of children at play annoyed him and their silly voices made him feel, even

more keenly than he had felt at Clongowes, that he was different from others. He did not want to play. He wanted to meet in the world the unsubstantial image which his soul so constantly beheld. He did not know where to seek it or how: but a premonition which led him on told him that this image would, without any overt act of his, encounter him. They would meet quietly as if they had known each other and had made their tryst, perhaps at one of the gates or in some more secret place. They would be alone, surrounded by darkness and silence: and in that moment of supreme tenderness he would be transfigured. He would fade into something impalpable under her eyes and then in a moment, he would be transfigured. Weakness and timidity and inexperience would fall from him in that magic moment.

John Joyce, too, felt that he was different from others. A man who always felt himself hard done by, the plots which he raged against were not (as some have thought) imaginary ones. Aside from the enemies dragging him through the courts and disgracing his family's good name in *Stubbs*, he had no friends at the office.

The first moves to close the office coincided with these new troubles. As the staff were to be reduced at the end of the year and he was destined to be pensioned off on one-third of his salary from the first day of January, this was a grim prelude to a new life.

Not only was he suspended at the beginning of November, but his future – portentously dealt with in a file labelled 'The Case of Mr Joyce' – was receiving little sympathy. On 10th November it was recommended that in view of his previous conduct he should now be informed that his services were being dispensed with.

On 10th November the Corporation committee finally put forward the proposal which was accepted by the city council that the city establish their own rates collection office. As there would now be less work in the Collector-General's Office, John Joyce's retirement by the end of the year, along with the other senior collectors, had been made an official certainty. What had seemed in 1880 a lifetime sinecure was now abruptly terminated. Indeed, an official minute on 28th December suggested that he should have no pension at all. It being no longer possible for the Joyces to remain in Blackrock, cheaper accommodation was sought.

Meantime, on 8th November while John Joyce was toiling with the consequences of his suspension and the closure of the office, May Joyce was delivered of another daughter, Florence Elizabeth. This seems to have been a family name in Mrs Joyce's family, as one of the Murray girls was also called Florence. On the registration form John Joyce is still correctly said to be in the Rates Office. Yet oddly the child was not baptized in Blackrock until 2nd December, with John Kelly, the agitator, and Elizabeth Flynn, one of Mrs Joyce's aunts, standing for her. It may be that the family had to return to St John's for this ceremony, for by that date it is likely that the Joyces had already moved.

It seems that the moneylender John Lawler closed on the Bill of Sale and took the household furniture. The Joyces had to leave Blackrock, and arrived in their new home with nothing to furnish it: *A Portrait* refers to 'the half-furnished and uncarpeted' parlour. The years of settled comfort were now left behind, a thing of memory and remorse.

6

THE CITY

It was late in November 1892 that the Joyces moved across the city to a new home on the north side of the Liffey. On the hall floor of the echoing house in Blackrock lay the last surviving copies of 'Et Tu, Healy', soiled by the removal men's boots. The yellow vans moving through the city fogs impressed the young Joyce as he sat with his mother in the train carrying the family northwards. His mother's tears also saddened him. (The move must have occurred after the end of October, for John Joyce is still listed at 'Leoville' in the Thom's city directory for 1893.)*

From now on the Joyces were to be committed to life on the north side of the city. In the view of many Dubliners, then and now, this had distinct social implications, for the city middle-class life was already moving south of the river. On the north, large areas of once respectable property were falling into tenements. As a result, however, the new township of Drumcondra, largely developed by James Fitzgerald Lombard in league with his son-in-law William Martin Murphy, provided a Catholic Nationalist stronghold to balance the mainly Unionist atmosphere of Rathmines and Pembroke on the south of the city. One of those involved in these developments was a Patrick Murray, a connection of the Murray family, whose son Joyce was later to employ as his solicitor. The Joyces were to be associated with this area of Dublin until the death of John Joyce in 1931.

* Stanislaus mentions lodgings in 29 Hardwicke Street at this time, a matter Ellmann believes, but it is hard to imagine that all the Joyces crowded into a boarding-house. There is no confirmatory evidence of their living at this address.

Dublin then meant the older and mixed city bounded by the canals built at the end of the eighteenth century, yet for most Dubliners the city mentally included the greater urban area. It was impossible to generalize about such a wide and varied area, for this greater Dublin was largely Victorian, largely red-brick and largely Catholic. Even the city centre had a great deal of new building in it: the banks, the hotels, the business houses, the clubs, the theatres and music halls, most of the public buildings and the churches all belonged to the nineteenth century, many to the last fifty years. This being so, it was appropriate that however others lived, the Joyces were still able to live in some style.

Their new home was a Georgian house, 14 Fitzgibbon Street, on the right at the top of the street, just off Mountjoy Square, which at that time was still a good address. (This is more or less where Father Conmee meets the three schoolboys in *Ulysses*.) Their neighbours would have included lawyers, solicitors, journalists and Members of Parliament. The house still stands (though renumbered as 34) tall and gloomy, much as Joyce describes it in *A Portrait*, in which he tells of moving in and the efforts to heat the then cold and cheerless rooms.

In contrast to earlier Christmases, that of 1892 was marked in James's increasingly retentive memory by visits to the many relatives of whom he probably saw little in earlier years. There was a visit to his aunt Josephine, William's vivacious and homely wife, who had just moved from Brighton Avenue to 25 Lower Hatch Street – they did not arrive at North Strand until 1902 – where he observed his small cousin Alice dreaming over the picture of beautiful Mabel Hunter, 'the exquisite creature' then appearing in the seasonal pantomime at the Gaiety Theatre; and also the rougher behaviour of his cousin Jim mauling the paper with his coal-blackened hands.

The holiday season with its gaily-lit shops angered the child:

> The causes of his embitterment were many, remote and near. He was angry with himself for being young and the prey of restless foolish impulses, angry also with the change of fortune which was reshaping the world about him into a vision of squalor and insincerity. Yet his anger lent nothing to the vision. He chronicled with patience what he saw, detaching himself from it and tasting its mortifying flavour in secret.

The kindness of his aunt Josephine did not detract from the fact that the Joyces'new life was a declension of quality from their old ways.

There was also a visit to the queer old house on Usher's Island, where his mother's relatives the Flynns lived. His aunt Annie was ill and dying at this time, which caused them all concern but provided Joyce with one of those curious vignettes of life which he was later to call epiphanies. He and his mother were offered tea in the narrow room looking out over the river from which the Flynns could see, directly opposite, their earlier family home on Ellis Quay. Aunt Julia (then nearly 70) made tea for James and his mother and told them what the priest and doctor had said. James listened, while he watched the radiant caverns of the glowing coals and through his imagination followed his own adventures. He gathered that there had been changes in the old woman of late:

> Suddenly he became aware of something in the doorway. A skull appeared suspended in the gloom of the doorway. A feeble creature like a monkey was there, drawn thither by the sound of the voices at the fire.

The feeble laughter of the confused old woman scared the child. Sharing the house were his aunts Julia Lyons and Ellen Callanan, Ellen's daughter Mary Ellen and the unmarried sisters Annie and Eliza. Here (as his parents doubtless recalled) the Misses Flynn had been accustomed to hold an annual party at Christmas time. It is unlikely that there was one this year, what with the age and ill-health of the old ladies. But the happy recollections of better days, and of talk about the singers and musical life of Victorian Dublin, entered into the child's imagination – its echoes of a more gracious way of life contrasting with the present-day squalor, illness and death. (This scene, like so much of Joyce's novel, drew upon a 'snapshot' epiphany of the day.)

That Christmas must have been one of the last the ladies spent on Usher's Island. James was to make the parties for which they were famous the centre-piece of 'The Dead'. In the old days his parents had come in from Bray or Blackrock to attend these, staying over-night in the Gresham (where the Cork management doubtless gave John Joyce a special rate). Now they could take James with them, a witness to the fading away of the old attractive culture of mid-Victorian Dublin.

Of even more memorable importance and imaginative conse-quence was a children's Christmas party held in the Dillons' big house in Harold's Cross. This provided Joyce with the materials for a notable scene in which the girl he admires comes out with him wrapped in her shawl to walk with him to the horse-drawn tram which was standing at the terminus, then on the corner of Brighton Square, a step away from the actual house where he had been born. The last tram left the terminus at 8·45 and took 45 minutes to reach the Pillar: he would not be home till nearly ten o'clock.

This girl was the youngest of the Dillons, the dark Mamie. In later years she spent some time in Spain and also smoked, both suggesting that she was more advanced and adventurous than other girls of her age. For Joyce she was to be one of the models not only for Emma Clery, but also for Molly Bloom.

At the party he represents himself as adopting a silent, watchful manner and taking little part in the games: 'He felt himself a gloomy figure amid the gay cocked hats and sunbonnets.' He duly sang his party song, as he had sung his party song since infancy. Yet he felt a feverish agitation: 'Amid the music and laughter her glance travelled to his corner, flattering, taunting, searching, exciting his heart.' This was something more than the feelings he had for Eileen in Bray; the hormones were stirring in his bloodstream.

When she put on her shawl to walk to the tram she brought back the image of Eileen Vance in Bray. Mamie wished, he thought, that he would take hold of her and kiss her, paying proper tribute to her feminine vanities. 'But he did neither: and, when he was sitting alone in the deserted tram, he tore his ticket into shreds and stared gloomily at the corrugated footboard.'

The next day Joyce tried to submerge his feelings in composing a poem. At the head of the paper he wrote – as had generations of Jesuit students – A.M.D.G. Significantly the resulting poem sounds very like the lyrics later to emerge in *Chamber Music*, most of the poems in which belonged to his adolescence and early manhood. Like so many young men he then retired to brood in his mother's mirror on his changing features.

*

Though James may not have been aware of it, concern was mounting in the house. On 24th December John Joyce took out a charge on his Cork property with Reuben Dodd, a solicitor and insurance agent who also lent money. Money-lending does not seem to have been a major matter with him, however, as John Joyce's is one of only a few deeds in his name which are on record for this period. Dodd had been a Parnellite – his sons recalled the Chief calling at their house on the South Circular Road – and initially may have been sympathetic to John Joyce.

On Stephen's Day the Joyces went, like so many families of their class, to the Gaiety Theatre in South King Street near St Stephen's Green, to see the annual pantomime. That year the show was *Sinbad the Sailor* with Edward Royce, of whom his mother had happy memories from the Christmas of 1873. This was probably James's first visit to the theatre.

On 1st January 1893 the collection of rates was formally taken over by the Corporation, under Charles Dawson. The old office in which John Joyce worked would not close until 30th September 1899, but from this date in 1893 he was pensioned off with £132/2s/10d annually. There was discussion in the Rates Office that he should be paid a pension of £280/12s/8d (based on his average pay over the last three years). This would have been £264/4s/8d if calculated on his pay for 1892. If he was pensioned on his term of service, he would have received only £77/3s/5d. At one stage it was even proposed that he should be given no pension at all. As it was, the rest of the redundant staff were given three-quarters of their average salaries, but John Joyce was deliberately punished by being granted only a third. His pension rights were secured by legislation, and though he may have resented the sum, there is no doubt that he was fully entitled to it, and the story that he only got it because his wife pleaded his case has no support that I can find in the official files.

Indeed, he was entitled to more. In May 1909 he consulted a solicitor, J.J Clancy, about the matter of his pension rights, and the opinion of a Queen's Counsel was to be sought. As no more was heard of the matter, the barrister's opinion must have been unfavourable. John Joyce was in his own eyes, and on the evidence long concealed in the confidential Civil Service records, the victim of high-handed government bureaucrats.

Investigation of his case had disclosed that a cheque which had been paid to him was unaccounted for, and another receipt which was not correct. The day after his pension was granted, on 13th January, it was suspended. The new officials took a dim view of John Joyce, and thought that he had been treated too lightly by an over-considerate Collector-General in 1889. Though there had been monthly reports on him since then, and there had been no *serious* complaints about him, his conduct did not compare well with others in the office. The dispute over these matters dragged on until 30th May, when it was finally agreed that the pension would be paid to him after all. The cheque and the receipt had been explained away; it was a close-run thing.

There is little doubt that though John Joyce had held the position for twelve years, rate collecting had small appeal for him. When he retired he was collecting over the North Dock area, which was now combined with South Dock and Mountjoy and collected by Mr Mayne. The report of the Chief of the Rates Department for the new year was blunt about the improved collection rates. The collection in Mountjoy and North Dock Wards was impeded by the vast accumulation of arrears from previous years. 'They amounted on these two wards to the sum of £6,862. In the great number of cases this Department got no particulars of liable parties; and in many instances when their names had been ascertained the people were either dead or untraceable.' Whatever difficulties may have arisen for John Joyce with regard to dock sheds, his other work was sloppy. Yet from a passing remark made in *A Portrait*, he may have hoped to secure a job from the Corporation. Another sinecure would have been agreeable, but he was to be disappointed in this. His politics were not such as to recommend him to either the government or the newly influential.

John Joyce may indeed have suffered because of his public support of Parnell. In the public field, 1893 was marked by the defeat of the Second Home Rule Bill, which Gladstone introduced on 13th February and got through the Commons only to have it rejected by the Lords. This was a matter of great consequence for Ireland's political future, since a divided Irish Party would be unable to gain any concessions from the British government for some years. But for James there was meanwhile the excitement of discovering the city of Dublin for the first time.

Until now his life had been passed in pleasant suburbs or in rural seclusion. 'Dublin city was a new and complex sensation.' Fitzgibbon Street was a fine enough quarter, but behind it in Great Charles Street – with its Free Anglican church – and further on the city was already falling into decay. He could now strike out and follow the roads where they led down to the river and the ships, or out on the North Circular Road along which the cattle herds were driven after market day in Cabra. Years later he commented to his brother Stanislaus that he had done little to describe the actual physical beauty of Dublin. It was, he thought, more beautiful than many other cities he had seen. The charm of the older Dublin in which he now lived was matched in the streets of the city centre by a Victorian exuberance of style and decor. These too caught his imagination.

His sight was not good. What he absorbed he took in mostly through the sensations of smell and sound – all his books are filled with these sensations rather than actual visions. The small corner of a shop window he could see and appreciate; the wide vista of the encircling mountains glimpsed at the end of so many Dublin streets passes unmentioned. He was building up in his mind a mental map of Dublin, which year by year extended to include districts and streets as remote as Malahide and Dolphin's Barn. This is the mental map that lies beneath the streets of his work, a map which bears but little relation to the Ordnance Survey for it simply leaves out large areas of the city. Joyce's Dublin is in many ways an astonishingly small place, small-scale as it must have appeared to the youthful observer in the early months of 1893.

At this time his mother must have got to know the Misses Monahan who ran the little drapers at 109 Great Britain, now Parnell Street. This is the shop where he places 'The Sisters'. If the priest with the curious past owed something to his uncle Father Charles O'Connell, the emphasis on paralysis in this story came from somewhere else.

From January to March 1893 James and Stanislaus are said (by Stanislaus) to have attended the Christian Brothers at Richmond Street, though the school records provide no confirmation of this. Stanislaus may have been mistaken, and the boys may have been sent for a short time to a local National School – perhaps St Francis Xavier's run by the Jesuits on Dorset Street. Joyce chose in any case not to recall this episode, as he did many other matters in his early life. He could countenance poverty while remaining something of a snob.

On 30th January 1893 John Joyce converted the charge on his Cork property into a statutory mortgage with Reuben Dodd. A few days later James celebrated his eleventh birthday and entered his twelfth year. That February was especially cold – so much so that Joyce later asked his aunt about the canal being frozen over near Clanbrassil Street, and made it one of the memory points for Mr Bloom. This was the time, too, when the Joyces attended the banquet in Glencree (also introduced into *Ulysses*); Valentine Blake Dillon and others were there, and afterwards their party returned over the Featherbed Mountain. Considering the attention given to it by Joyce, this seems to have been the very last social event the family attended before their social circle contracted as John Joyce fell into financial difficulties.

John Joyce was moving slowly towards more difficult times, but as yet the crisis had not been reached. February and March saw dramatic falls in Bank and Railway shares, the two prime areas of safe investment in those days. If his own investments and rents were falling, he could have been affected in a general or perhaps even in a specific way.

It was about this time that he had a chance meeting on the corner of Fitzgibbon Street and Mountjoy Square with Father Conmee, who was now based in Belvedere College – again the spot where the priest meets the schoolboys in *Ulysses*. Appraised of the troubled times facing John Joyce on his small pension, he offered to arrange that James and Stanislaus should be taken into Belvedere, the Jesuit day school on Great Denmark Street, for nothing. John returned home in high fettle to announce this coup to his wife and to pass on the news to the children. James's period of freedom was ending as Easter Sunday came.

In his novel *Stephen Hero*, Joyce made this moment the end of the eighth chapter. In his own life, however, it meant the opening of a new chapter, the seventh part of his early life as he was to lay it out in *A Portrait of the Artist*.

7

BELVEDERE

In 1893 Easter Sunday fell on 2nd April. The following Thursday, 6th April, when the new term opened, James (then 11) and Stanislaus (aged 8) were sent off from Fitzgibbon Street across Mountjoy Square and through Gardiner's Place to Great Denmark Street, where they were duly enrolled in Belvedere College by the Prefect of Studies, James's old friend the Reverend Father John Conmee. Stanislaus was placed in Elements, the second lowest class; James in IIIrd of Grammar.

This was the first real school that Stanislaus had attended, apart from his vague recollection that he and James had gone to another school nearby for a time. But for James much would have been both familiar and strange after Clongowes, and not only because of the special consideration they received from Father Conmee: familiar because the course of Jesuit studies on which he was now entered was much the same as at Clongowes, as was the style of teaching and the attitudes of the masters; strange because this was a day school and the afternoons and evenings would be his own to make use of as he wished, either to study or to roam about the neighbouring streets of the city.

The boys too were different. At Clongowes there were many sons of the Catholic gentry, magistrates and army men; at Belvedere they were the sons of businessmen and lower middle-class Catholics. Yet this difference was not too extreme; at Clongowes Joyce had been above his station, while at Belvedere his friends' families were much more like his own father.

In his original draft of *Stephen Hero* this new departure marked the end of Chapter VII – in *A Portrait*, the end of Chapter III. As only a third of the school year remained – about ten weeks or so – it was unusual but not uncommon for boys to be enrolled at this time. It seems the Joyce boys were taken on free of charge by the school – though no financial records survive to confirm this fact, and the fees were still just within John Joyce's reach. This too was not unusual. A bright boy was valuable to a school – more valuable than what his fees would bring – in the way of Intermediate prizes.

Joyce's notes for his book and the eventual account of these years in *A Portrait* depart from the scheme of real life in many ways. The events were, however, merely displaced rather than invented. They were given new meaning and arranged less in accordance with the author's life than with the developing needs of art, they became a key to events which had their own particular significance and did not depend on their being dealt with in chronological order.

In his notes, for instance, Joyce places the Whitsun play in which Stephen appears at Whitsun 1893 rather than 1898. The play he saw in May 1893 was the first of six which he could draw upon for the details of his novel. In the notes, too, he associates this term with 'Emma again' and 'Letter from Eileen Dixon', though in the novel the date would seem to be 1895. In any case these first weeks were taken up in coming to know the school. The contrast between Eileen and Emma (that is, between Eileen Vance and the Dillon girl) belonged, we may suppose, to real life.

Belvedere had been founded by the Jesuits in 1841, to continue a very old tradition of Jesuit education in the city. The community lived in a large mansion facing down North Great George's Street, while the school proper was in buildings across the garden, the side of which was bordered with the shed referred to in the novel. The chapel was in this second building, and a door from it gave into the gym-cum-theatre which filled the fourth side of the square. Killeen House (the town house of Lord Fingal) had been acquired by the school also. Belvedere House was associated with the strange tale of the Rochfort family, but though the houses were decorated with wonderful plaster work, the actual classrooms were small, modest and undecorated. As in all schools romance was a thing of memory, real life one of day-to-day work.

The most stimulating part of James's work was his weekly essay, prepared for Mr George Dempsey, which increased its challenge as the years went on. He was also stimulated by rivalry with Albrecht Connolly, a model for Heron in the novel. This relationship had its beginning in the last term of 1893, but would only develop fully later.

*

The end of the school term in June 1893 meant a return to more domestic matters, even for young James. John Joyce was being pressed by Reuben Dodd; the sum owing was a mere £400, but what annoyed Dodd was not Joyce's inability to repay the loan but his attempt to escape it by trying to get his deeds back in an underhand manner. This verged on criminal behaviour, though Joyce may have seen it only as a cute stroke. Dodd was implacable. There seemed to be only one solution to these pressing debts: a sale of part or all of Joyce's inherited property in Cork.

That summer John Joyce took James down to Cork with him (the visit is described in *A Portrait*). The boy was to recall the cricketers playing in the summer sun.*

Trailing James behind him, his father rambled around the city, looking up his old friends and drinking in his old student haunts around Cork University. They went into the College itself, now empty of students during the summer break, and his father talked to the College porter with ribald freedom about the antics of his young days. Joyce retained the striking image of the word 'foetus' cut on one of the desks of the University medical school. His father's tales and the shame of bodily functions confused his emerging sexuality.

John Joyce also tried to have two of his daughters taken into the Presentation convent at Crosshaven, where there was an O'Connell relative. Father and son were unimpressed by her singing; the Reverend Mother in her turn was unimpressed with John Joyce and refused his request. William O'Connell's grand-daughter was now a nun in the Order in Cork. Father and son also visited Youghal, with its hectic summer beach, old houses and the traditions about Walter Raleigh. James liked Youghal 'very much'.

On the way home they encountered James's god-father Philip McCann on the same train, and the look of reproach in his eyes when he heard of the state of John Joyce's affairs lingered in the boy's memory.

---

* There is a possibility that a trip had also been made in the summer of 1892 for William O'Connell's funeral, which seems to fit with Gorman's vague dating.

Ireland as a whole was concerned at this time with the Second Home Rule Bill, which was rejected by the House of Lords on 5th September. John Joyce, however, was more concerned with having a home of his own to rule. On 6th September – by which time James was back at school – he wrote (*see* pp. 126–7) from 14 Fitzgibbon Street to the Chief Secretary (then John Morley, the British historian and future biographer of Gladstone) to inquire if he could commute his pension, explaining that he wished to use the money to pay off what was outstanding on a small property he had in Cork. His request was duly passed on to the Collector-General and then to the Solicitor-General, who was of the opinion that there was no way in which the law would allow them to meet the request. When he received this news towards the end of December, John Joyce's last chance of raising money to pay off Reuben Dodd was gone.

This was a worrying time for Joyce's wife, who was as usual expecting a child. On 27th November 1893, at the Fitzgibbon Street house, another daughter was born; she was to be named Mabel – perhaps for the beautiful Mabel Hunter, the actress so much admired in Dublin. On the registration form John Joyce gave his profession as 'Accountant', though this was perhaps only valid in the sense that he was being held to account for monies. On 21st December Mabel was baptized in the Pro-Cathedral, St Mary's in Marlborough Street, with Richard John Thornton ('Mr Kernan' of 'Grace', whose brother was the model for the narrator of 'Cyclops', according to Stanislaus, though Joyce met him only once) and Anne Flynn (one of Mrs Joyce's relatives) standing as godparents. Thornton is yet another of those cloudy personalities in the Joyce background whose full significance is now lost to us. It seems there was an epiphany of Thornton connected in Joyce's mind with Stephen's increasing irreligion, and it is possible that Thornton's loutish anti-clericalism impressed the growing boy in some shocking way.*

The plans to sell the Cork property had been forced ahead; the auction was held in Cork on 14th December, and the houses sold off

---

* The Thorntons, along with the Gallahers (the family of Patrick Frederick Gallaher, died 1865, a famous ventriloquist, whose son John edited the *Freeman's Journal*), are emerging from the shadows. Lydia Thornton (née Crossley), born about 1850, an English Catholic, married Richard Thornton in 1869. Their daughter Eveline, born in 1884, lent her name, but not her personality, to Joyce's character. They had two sons: John, born 1887, and Richard, born 1873, an artist who died in October 1895. With the Dillons, Powells and Tarpeys, they will be the subject of another study, *Joyce's Families*.

in three lots. John Joyce does not seem to have attended this sad occasion. Doubtless he had been foolish and feckless, but at this time others beside himself were also in trouble. The price of corn, for instance, was half what it had been in the 1870s, and at 22s 10d the lowest it would reach until 1914. Such a fall in prices may well have seriously affected the rents he was able to take from the leases, and so explain his growing difficulties.

On 8th February 1894 the purchasers of the properties, Mullins and Murphy, signed the deed of sale in Dublin, paying £475 and £1,400 respectively. On 14th February Dodd, having been paid, signed a release from his mortgage. And on 16th February McMullen, the third buyer, signed his deed of sale, which was for the 1830 property, the first piece bought by George Joyce. So the last of John Joyce's inheritance passed out of his hands. All the legal work involved in calling in the other mortgages and obtaining releases for them was undertaken by Dodd. One has an image of the pathetic Joyces being browbeaten by a man who became in John Joyce's demonology an arch figure of hate, a hatred he communicated to his son James and which is duly reproduced in *Ulysses*: 'May the devil break the hasp of your back', Simon Dedalus remarks as Dodd vanishes from the sight of the funeral party crossing the city.

*

Joyce's first stories are drawn from the experiences of these early years, but often in ways which have not been fully appreciated before this. In 'The Sisters', the first of the *Dubliners*, the child is fascinated by the talk he has heard from the gossip of his elders about the illness of the old priest, lying in a coma paralysed after his third stroke:

> I said softly to myself the word paralysis. It had always sounded strangely in my ears, like the word gnomon in the Euclid and the word simony in the Catechism. But now it sounded to me like the name of some maleficent and sinful being. It filled me with fear, and yet I longed to be near to it and to look upon its deadly work.

The natural fear of a child consciously facing death for the first time is reflected here. But on 3rd March 1894 old John Murray, James's maternal grandfather, died (in a coma induced by a paralytic stroke) at 8 Lismore Road, where he was living with his son John and his family. The paralysis which works its evil way in 'The Sisters' was

14 FitzGibbon Street
Mountjoy Square
Dublin 6th Sept 1893

The Under Secretary
Dublin Castle
Dame Street

Sir.

I beg leave to inform you that I was formerly a Rate Collector in the Collectr Generals office in this City. On the 1st of January last I was retired on a pension of £132.. 2. 10 per annum

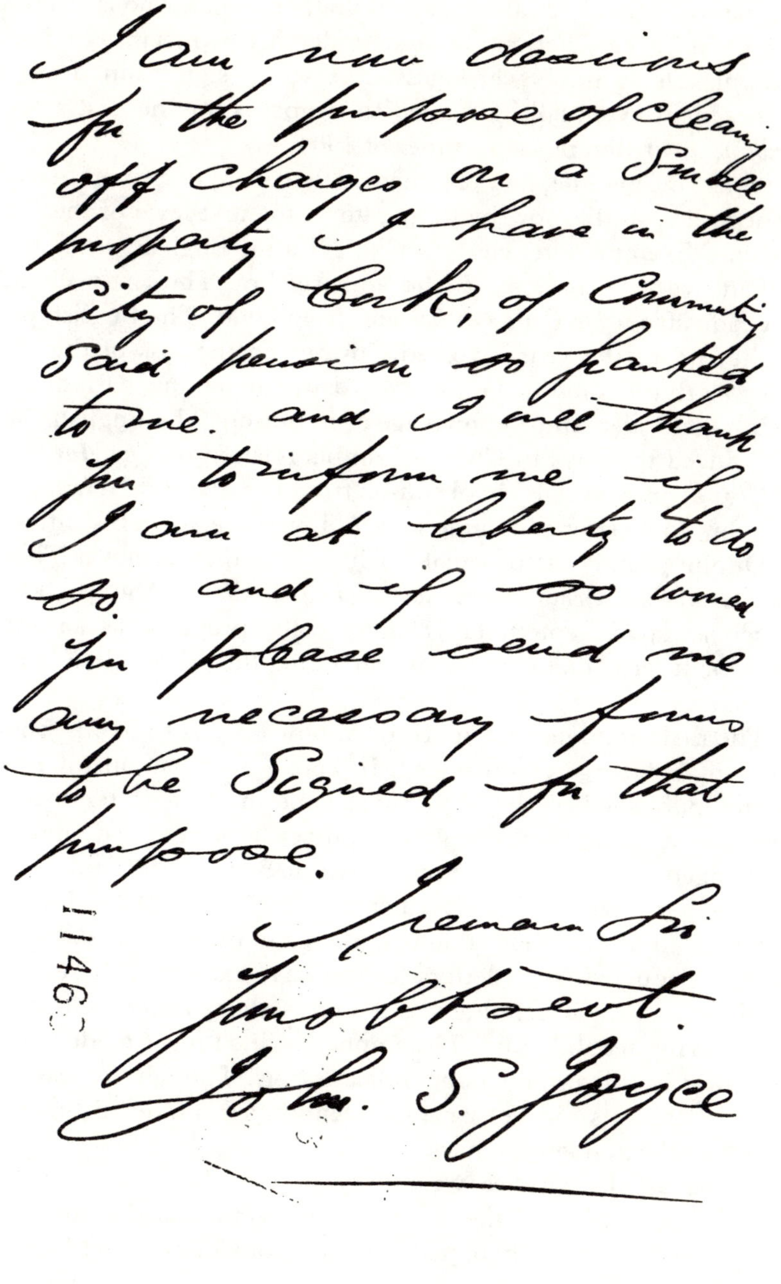

I am now desirous
for the purpose of clean
off charges on a Small
property I have in the
City of Cork, of Commuting
Said pension so granted
to me. and I will thank
you to inform me if
I am at liberty to do
so. and if so When
you please send me
any necessary forms
to be Signed for that
purpose.

I remain Sir

Yr mo. obt. sert.

John. S. Joyce

1146

the paralysis that had killed his grandfather, a man who is strikingly absent in Joyce's fiction, at least under his own name or in any recognizable form. Nevertheless, this was a significant death for Joyce, for it eventually provided the impetus for the first story of *Dubliners*, written in the summer of 1904.

James, meanwhile, had returned to Belvedere in September 1893 to begin his studies for the Preparatory, the first level of the Intermediate Examination. He was taking Latin, English, French and Italian, with Arithmetic, Euclid and Algebra. The Latin included selections from *De Bello Gallico* and from Ovid. The English paper at the end of the year involved Cowper on the loss of the *Royal George*, Byron on the Goths, Wordsworth on the daffodils, Sir Ralph the Rover, and a knowledge of Ferguson. The English course introduced the boys to Charles Lamb's relation of *The Adventures of Ulysses*, in a special school edition from Browne and Nolan, edited by John Cook (later to include some of Joyce's verses in his anthology of Dublin poetry). Also available a little later that term was Thomas W. Lyster's *Select Poetry for Young Students,* the preface to which is dated September 1893, specially prepared as an anthology for Intermediate pupils and including the poems already mentioned.

The main influence on Joyce from now on was to be his English master Mr George Dempsey – 'Mr Tate' – who had one of Joyce's poems published in the school magazine in 1907. After the publication of *A Portrait* in 1916 contact was renewed and they exchanged Christmas greetings between Switzerland and Dublin. In the last years of his life, between 1922 and 1924, Dempsey supplied Joyce with books, information and materials for *Finnegans Wake*. Though Joyce's letters to him have vanished, there is little doubt that this was an influential as well as a long-lasting relationship between master and pupil. The emphasis which Joyce made Gorman give it in his biography alone indicates this. Though the less-than-frank Stanislaus did not care for Dempsey, his older brother did, and the affection left its mark.

These secular studies were only part of James's curriculum. Religious studies, and the annual retreat which all the boys in the senior classes of the school had to attend, took place towards the end of this term. The retreats took the same form every year, their effect varying with the personal circumstances of each student. Though presented in the novel with every quality of searing novelty, such retreats were in reality a commonplace feature of Jesuit schoolboy life, only feared by those deeply in sin.

On 2nd February 1894 James celebrated his twelfth birthday. About this time he was advised by the school medical officer, Dr Thomas O'Connell Redmond, to leave off the glasses which had been prescribed for him at Clongowes. Since he did not wear them again for another ten years, much of his impressionable youth was passed with restricted sight. The printed word may well have been more real to him than the physical world around him. For the young Joyce, the world was not visual but aural and literary.

If the annual retreat was a feature of the autumn term, the annual play highlighted the summer term. Belvedere was very proud of its theatre, photographs of which appeared among those featured in an article on the school in a city journal in July. This production was at Whitsun on 12th May; James did not have a part.

A disturbing drama of an emotional kind was however being played out in his schoolboy's mind. On 19th May he attended the last night of the 'Araby' Bazaar, a gala fund-raising event for Jervis Street Hospital at the Royal Dublin Society in Ballsbridge. This meant leaving Fitzgibbon Street (not North Richmond Street, as in his story) and catching a train on the loop line across the city to Pembroke. We know he went because he was seen by a school friend W.G. Fallon, who thought him discomposed and unhappy. The turmoil of his story, though largely changed from his own experience, was real enough. But who 'Mangan's sister' was – in whom the young boy has such an interest – no record now exists to suggest.

This summer too (or that of 1893) included whatever was the germ of another of those childhood incidents that contributed to 'The Sisters'. His mother had apparently come to know the two ladies, the Misses Monahan, who ran a small drapers shop at 109 Great Britain Street (now Parnell Street), just at the bottom of the street leading up to the school. This was the last summer they spent at this address. They had been there for some twenty years and it is easy to imagine the shabby nature of the little shop. Though their brother was indeed named James he was not a priest, and there is no evidence that they had a sick priest as a lodger – he may well have been suggested by the curious name of their tenant in real life, Francis Morron. The priest was, as I indicated earlier, probably suggested to Joyce by Father Charles O'Connell, James's father's relative to whom he gave his mother's family name.

Also belonging to this summer apparently was the germ of 'An Encounter', when James and Stanislaus went miching; they avoided a day's school in the first week of June 1894, shortly before the end of term, and crossed the river to explore the unknown and mysterious streets of Ringsend and Irishtown. There in a field by the Dodder (which can still be identified by the slope rising to the river bank) they met the homosexual whom Stanislaus nicknamed 'The Captain of Fifty'. He spoke to them not only of girls but also of Walter Scott, and in Joyce's mind an admiration for Scott was equated with the perverting influences of an English public school education – the kind of thing to which he had been only briefly exposed in Clongowes. The admirer of Scott was to make his appearance again in Joyce's life, as the Captain who is a regular reader in the National Library. Their strange josser may well have been a figure then familiar to at least a few of his early readers. Joyce's homophobia lasted well into his later life: in Zürich he is recorded as teasing an inverted artist by advancing a pair of miniature drawers (from Nora's doll which he carried in his pocket) across the table on his stiffened fingers. His prejudice was of course partly a personal fear, and partly a less crude version of the common Catholic view of the day. (The preliminaries to the Wilde *affaire* belong to this year, as the adult Joyce would have known.) If his mind brooded upon the religious mysteries of the paralysed priest, this adventure showed that the city contained other dangers to the spirit – sexual mysteries which the child failed to grasp, lacking as they did the physicality of the word 'foetus' or the romance of chivalry.

This adventure seems to have happened in the first week of June 1894. On 12th June James sat the first of his Intermediate examinations. A photograph of the school taken at this time shows him lolling on the end of a front row, straining his eyes to glare at the camera. That summer the Joyces moved from the mansion in Fitzgibbon Street (at £25 a year) to a small recently-built villa in Drumcondra (at £17 a year). John Murray had left them little or nothing. This move was a long way down the social scale; John Joyce – bereft of his property, with only his pension and a small annuity to keep him going – had fallen over the cliff from the middle classes into the upper working-classes. The family would never again recover the station in life into which James had been born.

At the time, this district was nearly rural: the fields began just beyond the house and reached out to woods and low hills. It was

there, according to Stanislaus, that two Dominicans called on John
Joyce after his son's success in the examinations was announced in
September, suggesting that he might go to one of their schools in
the country. As one of the Powell family, Father Jordan Francis
('Frank') Powell, was a member of the Dominican community at St
Saviour's in Dominick Street and an old friend of the Joyces, it is
more than likely that he was one of these priests who wanted Joyce
to go to Newbridge College in Kildare. But young James announced
that as he had begun with the Jesuits he would finish with them, and
his father was pleased enough to pander to him on the point. Placed
103 out of 271, he had won an exhibition worth £20, £2 for Latin
composition and a 3rd class prize, worth £1 of books. Though he
was an outstanding student in Belvedere, this is not to say that he
was among the leading students in Ireland overall. His academic
achievements should not be exaggerated.

*

In September 1894 Belvedere found that it had a new rector: Father
Wheeler had gone, and Father Henry had come. A convert, Father
Henry had some of the keenness for the faith lacking in cradle
Catholics, and though Gorman speaks ill of him, Joyce seems to
have liked and respected him. He was in charge of teaching Latin,
and Joyce stood out at once as one of the leading students in the
school. Father Henry was to be an influential person in Joyce's life,
for he was also director of the Sodality of Our Lady.

Joyce's time was consumed now by his studies for the Junior grade
of the Intermediate. He sat these examinations as usual on 17th June
1895 and subsequent days, and won an exhibition of £20 for three
years; he also sat tests in physics and chemistry, in which he did not
do well, being placed 164 out of 202. In this year, too, he was reading
Robinson Crusoe in his English course, the plain vigour of whose
prose was to retain his admiration. He may also have encountered
Lockhart's *Life of Napoleon*, as the source of the Napoleonic lore
that is scattered in his works. In French he was reading Xavier de
Maistre, Lamartine and Florian; in Italian Metastasio. His total
marks, at 2,699, were an improvement on his previous performance.

The summer holidays had come again. On 18th July another child,
Frederick, was born to the fecund Mrs Joyce. Though careless about
registering the birth, John Joyce placed an announcement in *The
Freeman's Journal*. The infant was baptized on 28th July (a Sunday,

oddly enough) in the local church. But he was sickly, and three days later died at Hollywell Villas, but as the death was not registered the cause remains unknown. So yet another of Mrs Joyce's infants was consigned by her to the keeping of God in the family plot in Glasnevin. It was soon after this (as Stanislaus records) that John Joyce in a fit of drunken rage attempted to kill his wife. She fled next door to the McKernans, a policeman called and John was restrained, but the sordid doom so long expected now hung over the house.

To the early autumn of this year probably belongs the celebrated fight between Joyce and his peers over the status of Byron. Schoolboys do not usually fight over literature, but this incident would have arisen naturally out of current talk in school and home.

On 1st January 1896 it became known that the new Conservative Prime Minister Lord Salisbury had appointed Alfred Austin, a leader writer on *The Standard*, to be Poet Laureate. The post had been vacant since the death of Tennyson in 1892, and was given by Salisbury to Austin simply because no one else applied for it. Austin (who was known in Ireland through an appreciative account of an Irish trip in 1894) was not only a Catholic – a point which would have drawn comment from such a teacher as George Dempsey – but had also been educated at Stonyhurst, which in the eyes of the Jesuits made him 'one of ours'. Austin's own poetry was not of much account (as his effusion on the Jameson raid of 12th January 1896 was to show), but he was an admirer of Scott and Byron, and had defended Byron against the attacks of Mrs Stowe in 1869. In 1870 he had attacked Tennyson, Morris and some other poets of the day as being 'feminine'. This then is the forgotten background to the row between Joyce and his school-friends: Byron was in their Lyster anthology; Tennyson was not. Heron in forwarding Tennyson was commending the modern; Stephen in defending Byron was echoing the taste of the establishment, of the school books and the Poet Laureate. This is an irony lost on many admirers of Joyce.

It is not clear when the Joyces left Drumcondra, for though they are not listed in the directory for that address after October, John Joyce paid the rates in 1896 on the Millbourne Avenue villa. I suspect from this that they did not move until the early summer of 1896.

James was elected a member of the Sodality of Our Lady on 7th December 1895. This was a signal honour indeed, an indication of the esteem in which he was held by both the boys and the Jesuits. As he celebrated his fourteenth birthday the following February, this would have been an appropriate time for the priests to plant in his mind the idea of a vocation. The scene in *A Portrait* takes place in summer soon after the Easter holiday, shortly after term has been resumed – that is, in May 1895, the month dedicated to Our Lady and to which Joyce had a special attachment. The director (Father Henry) speaks seriously to him about the matter of a vocation; his head filled with the glowing thoughts of high devotion, the boy walks back through the streets to the villa on the edge of town. There he is plunged again into the sordid details of family life; he learns that his parents, threatened with eviction, are out searching for a house. The sounds of childish song cheer him only a little, recalling as he does the words of Cardinal Newman on Virgil: 'his single words and phrases, his pathetic half-lines, giving utterance, as the voice of Nature herself, to that pain and weariness, yet hope of better things, which is the experience of her children in every time.' Between Joyce and a true vocation there lay not only all those hardships of his family, but now in this his fourteenth year the first stirrings of his body's rebellion. Within his budding glands the hormones were flowing.

8

SIN AND SALVATION

1896–1898

Some time early in 1896, then, the Joyces left the villa in Millbourne Avenue where they had been rusticating for nearly two years and moved back into the city proper. Their new residence was 13 North Richmond Street, a blind road off the North Circular Road.* As the valuation of the Drumcondra house had been only £17 and that of Richmond Street £22, this might imply a rise in John Joyce's fortunes, but it seems not to have been the case.

This old-fashioned house in a respectable street must have been at a cheap rent, for it had been left vacant after the death of a local curate in St Agatha's, Father Edward Quaid (his name is recalled by Joyce in *A Portrait* as one of the Christian Brothers crossing the bridge to Bull Island). He had died in the house on 2nd March 1895. As described in 'An Encounter', when the Joyces moved in the house was scattered with the old priest's possessions: a rusted bicycle lamp, mouldering yellow-back novels, even the *Memoirs of Vidocq* – racy reading for a priest. The Joyces were to stay here only a few months, until the autumn of 1896 when yet another move took them on to 29 Windsor Avenue.

---

* By an odd coincidence there was another John Joyce living at 17 Richmond North Street; he died in 1898, leaving over £20,000 to his widow. His long residence there has deceived Joyce's earlier biographers into thinking that the writer's family lived on Richmond North Street for several years, but this is not the case: in fact their stay was so short that it left no trace in the usual records. Joyce himself suggests in *Finnegans Wake* that the Joyces lived at number 12 – '12 Norse Richmound' – but this house was occupied from the 1870s to 1898 by a doctor's widow, the Hon. Juliana Michell, a sister of the 3rd Lord Mountmorris, murdered in 1881 at Clonbur in the Joyce Country, during the Land War. She died in 1898 and her son George and his wife moved to Mountjoy Square.

This change of residence marked another transition in James's personal life. He admitted to his brother that his first sexual experiences dated from his fourteenth year. But these experiences must be understood in their context. What was involved here was not intercourse, but merely auto-eroticism.

Details of the experience were recounted by Joyce in 1917 to the Swiss woman, Dr Gertrude Kaempffer, with whom he was attempting to ingratiate himself for some obscure sexual purpose. It must also be remembered that James as a child was not well-nourished; he was slight and often awkward, and though in his fifteenth year he probably appeared to be much younger.

He was out in the country walking with the girl who looked after the younger Joyce children for his mother when she retired behind a bush to relieve herself. Aroused by the mere flowing sounds of micturition, he had an erection which he relieved.

There was more to the matter: for this same servant girl featured in inquiries made by the Jesuits after Stanislaus had mentioned a passing incident of rough-and-tumble between her and his brother James. Mrs Joyce told Mrs Joe Gallaher that 'some woman' had attempted to seduce her son. The poor girl was dismissed, and no more heard about the matter. I suspect (largely because it is Joyce's typical method) that this girl was called Mary Driscoll – the name given to the young servant of the Blooms in Ontario Terrace whose large bottom excited Leopold Bloom to make a direct assault upon her in the rear premises, only to be beaten off by a scouring brush. She was from the lower strata of society and they paid her £4 a year.

A side-light upon all of this is the odd fact that the Joyces, despite their decline, still had servants of some kind, if only a girl to look after the smaller children, at this late date. But Mary Driscoll – if that was her name – seems to have no successors. Joyce himself, however, remained enamoured of large bottoms and servant girls – as a student he and his friend Vincent Cosgrave would follow them round the streets.

The notes for the original version of his novel suggest that 'Mr Casey' was to play a telling role in Joyce's account of these Dublin years. John Kelly's admiration for James was confirmed by Stanislaus, but with little detail. Kelly had gone to America for some years in order to regain his health, unsuccessfully. Formerly he had lived in the National Club on Rutland Square, but on his return from America he went to live in the home of Daniel J. Hishon (presumably Jewish), an insurance agent with strong Parnellite leanings, at 16 Belvidere Road, just off Lower Dorset Street, within walking distance of the Joyce home.

For years Kelly had been suffering from the tuberculosis contracted as a result of his prison terms and hard life, and shortly after Easter 1896 he went into the Mater Hospital on Eccles Street. He died in hospital on 13th April; he was only in his mid forties, but years of imprisonment had wrecked his health.

It is clear from Joyce's own notes and from the comments by Stanislaus that John Kelly was an impressive figure in the years of Joyce's adolescence. He was, for instance, one of John Joyce's closest friends. Kelly's almost saintly dedication to the National cause was, in the eyes of his friends, entirely admirable. He was a man of great moral stature – outside of the Jesuits, perhaps the finest man that James knew at this time. The lost chapters of *Stephen Hero* contained a much longer treatment of 'Mr Casey' in these years after the Joyces moved to the north side. There, it is likely, he was shown as a counterweight to the school influence of Mr Dempsey. Kelly's influence on young James's social attitudes was important. Politically Joyce was a Fenian, and something of the Fenian outlook on life remained with him into his later years – in *Ulysses* Mr Deasy (albeit a stout Unionist) characterizes Stephen Dedalus as 'a Fenian'.

There was also another aspect of John Kelly. As a youth it had been intended that he should study for the priesthood along with his friend William Sheehan; but when the day came to leave for the diocesan college, Kelly's trousers were not ready. He stayed at home and went into the drapery business; his friend rose to be Bishop of Waterford. This lost vocation – or rather change of vocation – may well have impressed Joyce.

Born in Tralee, Co. Kerry, in about 1848, he had owned a prosperous drapery shop in that town until the outbreak of the Land War. A friend of Tim Harrington and his brother, who edited various newspapers in Kerry and later in Dublin, Kelly gave up his shop, followed them to the capital and became an organizer for the Land League. He took part in most of the major boycotts and campaigns over the next couple of years, and as a consequence was committed to prison many times for terms of six months hard labour: he had to pick oakum, hence the reference in *A Portrait* to making a present for Queen Victoria. His health was ruined by the hardness of this

136

campaigning life, but to the end he retained the affection of a wide circle of friends.

The Jewish connection provided by John Kelly's last years spent in Daniel Hishon's house may also have been influential. Though John Joyce may well have had some contact with the Dublin Jewish community, it was through Hishon that James is likely to have met some of the more radical-minded of them.

John Kelly's funeral was held from the Mater to Glasnevin on 16th April. It was attended by John Joyce and John Henry Menton, the solicitor who features in *Ulysses*, and many other Parnellites. Kelly's death was widely noticed (see overleaf), and the Parnellite paper *United Ireland* even published a memorial poem. On the first anniversary of John Kelly's death John Joyce was one of those involved in erecting and unveiling the Celtic cross that marks the grave, a step away from Parnell's in Glasnevin. John Kelly's integrity, in the face of appalling odds, left its mark on Joyce: in later life he too resisted pain and illness to preserve his chosen vocation.

*

Another play was presented at Belvedere at Whitsun on 24th May and was thought well enough of to be reviewed in the papers. As he was under age for the Junior level, Joyce had no Intermediate examination to sit and this free year, if it can be so described, like the year at Blackrock had its special effect. At this time James began to make use of the City of Dublin Public Library at Capel Street, less than a mile away from his home by foot, to explore widely the ranges of English literature.

The public library was opened in 1884 and was the twenty-fourth such library in the British Isles. Though overseen by a committee of city councillors and clergymen, it was run by a librarian. The man appointed (who was to remain in the post until the Great War) was Patrick Grogan, who had formerly worked in the library at Maynooth College where he had catalogued the books of Dr Charles Russell: clearly a safe pair of hands, a man who could be relied upon to choose the books wisely. These included not only the novels of Conan Doyle – one of which Mr Bloom has out on loan in 1904 – then an immediate vogue, but more sensational books. Stanislaus Joyce was dispatched by James one day to bring back a copy of Hardy's novel *Jude the Obscure*, which had created great controversy on its publication in 1895. Confused about the title, the boy asked Grogan for

FUNERAL OF MR. JOHN KELLY.

Yesterday morning the remains of the late Mr John Kelly were removed from the Mater Misericordiæ Hospital to their last resting place in Glasnevin Cemetery, where as brave and true an Irishman as ever breathed his native air now sleeps his last sleep, in a grave close to the Parnell circle. After a short life, into which too much of hardship entered, earned because of love of country, Mr John Kelly has gone down into his grave deserving the grateful remembrance and gratitude of every man having a drop of Irish blood in his veins. His life in youthful as well as in mature years was spent for Ireland's sake. He was called upon to bear a heavy burden in the days when to work for the rights of the people got as its immediate reward the penalty of the prison cell. Quietly and uncomplainingly he took his chances, and as quietly he has passed away, leaving behind him a remembrance of heroism and steadfastness of principle which centuries will not blot out. The funeral cortege was a large one, and the coffin was covered with a large number of wreaths sent by, amongst others—Mr Henry Harrison, ex-M P; Mr J H Menton, Messrs Walter and Louis Dalton, Tipperary; and Mr E W O'Reilly.

The members of the Catholic Club also forwarded a beautiful floral harp and a handsome wreath.

Amongst those who attended the funeral were:—Messrs J J Clancy, M P; E Byrne, F J I; John O'Connor, B L, ex-M P; Dr J E Kenny, ex-M P; Henry Harrison, ex-M P; John Wyse Power, John Clancy, sub-sheriff; W E Clancy, City Marshal; D J Hishon, J P Quinn, E Haviland Burke, D Harrington, Valentine Kilbride, solicitor; P Gregan, T C; J Hennessy, F Crosbie, F Doyle, "Independent"; P D Hughes, Ignatius Hughes, W J M'Dermott, W O'Brien, Drumcondra; Jno M'Grath, "United Ireland"; P J Nagle, John Nagle, J B Harrington, M Ginnane, Eugene O'Sullivan, W B Barry, J J Moore, F Murnane, T Dixon, H L Carr, P Glennon, Wm B O'Brien, Angus M'Kay, Alderman Burke, J H Menton, solicitor; Thos Sherlock, T C; T J O'Reilly, Thos Grehan, Captain Hall, R Thompson, Thomas Cahill, J J Grehan, J G Nagle, James Darcy, P L G; T J O'Neill, P L G; Edward Cussen, M J Cooke, Dr R D Kenny, Laurence Keogh, P L G; Peter Hynes, T C, Kingstown; George Triston, J J Joyce, T J Brennan, James T Cousins, J J M'Hale, Louisburgh; W Ryan, Frank Murnane, J J Moore, R Russell, J J Nagle, J Thompson, Master, Rathdrum Union; J J O'Meara, solicitor; E A Ennis, B L; Michael Cross, John J O'Connor, J F M'Carthy, J P; P Ryan, P S Smith, H E Thornton, E W O'Reilly, Michael Lambert, James Derwin, Jas Derwin, Jun; George Washington, P Fagan, John Murphy, Clontarf; Alderman Downey, Drogheda; P Connolly, Town Clerk, Drogheda; P Lyons, T C, do; John M'Guinness, T C, do; Luke J Elcock, T C, do; Owen Fox, do; Gerald Daly, T C, do; M J Nugent, T C, do; P M'Namara, do; Joseph Johnston, Dundalk; T Maxwell, do; Joseph Finnegan, do; Thos Doyle, T C; Patrick Butler, James Hopper, R J Maher, T M O'Reilly, Dr T S Rice, John G Joyce, John O'Connell, superintendent, Glasnevin Cemetery; John Lenehan, B L; J Clinch, T C; J O'Sullivan, P J Gleeson, M J Keating, M J Higgins, John Gore, Patk

Jude the Obscene; but even if he had had the title right he would have been disappointed, for the library did not stock it. The library did stock Rabelais, but no Flaubert, one Balzac (*Old Goriot*) and two Zolas (*The Downfall* and *The Dream*). Now or a little later Joyce was quizzed by his uncle John about reading Zola – perhaps even these very books from Capel Street – but his father said that the boy could read what he liked. His taste in books was also questioned by Grogan himself, who was an acquaintance of his father's. John Joyce called into the library to gossip rather than read.

Joyce used Capel Street and later the newer branch at Charleville Mall, where he was friends with the librarian P.J. Hoey (fired by the Corporation in 1907), who met the Joyces by arrangement in Ostend in 1926. In a house with little money for new books, a public library played an essential role; nor were these libraries badly stocked, as the surviving catalogues show. Padraic Colum recalls that he first encountered the plays of Ibsen on the shelves of a public library; and Joyce too would have found others besides Ibsen to attract him – certainly the widest ranges of the English classics, if not the latest works of Continental fiction. As is so often the case, access to free books at this critical age was the making of the writer, and during this year of grace James Joyce made full use of his opportunity.

*

On his return to school in the autumn of 1896 he was singled out for a special honour, on 25th September being elected Prefect of the Sodality of Our Lady. The first assistant was Albrecht Connolly ('Heron'); the second assistant was Leo Wilkins (mentioned in 'An Encounter'); and the secretary was Michael Cassidy. In the special Catholic context of Belvedere College, this elevation made James virtually Head Boy of the school, though that over-British title was not used by the Jesuits.

The death of Mrs Conway in November no doubt brought to his mind the early religious fervour she had instilled in him, something to be reinforced by his annual retreat in December and his involvement in the reception of new members of the Sodality on 6th December. Whatever the sexual sins he had fallen into, there is little doubt that they were followed by a period of religious fervour which can be placed in 1897. Joyce's special devotion to the Virgin Mary was one aspect of this. Another was the gross mortification of the body which he mentions, such as sniffing urine – this was not religion, but sexual deviance. For all Joyce's devotion and application, there was always something a little extreme in his religion, which would in turn bring an extreme reaction. Most of the boys in Belvedere, as in Irish life generally, happily followed a middle way. Religious enthusiasts were not trusted. The boy Joyce saying his rosary openly on the way to school (as his sister recalls) was an extremist. But it would be wrong to see him at this date as independent-minded, that would suggest a contemptible level of hypocrisy. The simple truth was that in his middle teens James Joyce was a devout Catholic. As yet the artist had not usurped the priest.

*

In late September or thereabouts the Joyces moved from North Richmond Street. Certainly they were gone by October, for at that date number 13 was listed as 'vacant' in the city directory. They went to 29 Windsor Avenue, which belonged to Mrs Love (mother of Hugh C. Love, a civil servant who features under the odd guise of an Anglican clergyman in *Ulysses*.) This house was just built and was valued at £17 a year, the same as the villa in Drumcondra. They remained there until the early summer of 1899, during which time John Joyce paid only a quarter's rent; through a legal fault in the lease, he was able to hang on until proceedings were taken to evict him. (Here Joyce would place Bob Cowley, Simon Dedalus's friend, against whom similar proceedings are being taken, the legal niceties of which are discussed in *Ulysses*.)

James was now engaged on his studies for the Middle Year of the Intermediate, which he sat in June 1897, but he was not so deeply engaged as to be without entertainment. The friendship with the Sheehy family belongs to these last years of his Belvedere period. David Sheehy was an M.P. at Westminster and the father of a lively and gregarious brood of children, all of remarkable qualities. Although he was a sober Redmondite, politics did not stand in the way of this friendship. James and his mother, and sometimes Stanislaus, came to the house in Belvedere Place for music and dramatics. James needed bringing out of himself, and compared with the others was considered serious-minded and withdrawn.

From this period dates his earliest surviving piece of writing, a school theme on 'Trust not in appearances', an essay very typical of the normal work expected from students at Belvedere, with the caveat that Joyce wrote at a higher level of achievement than his peers. Nevertheless, no glimpse of future genius is to be found in the sententious sentiments suitable for his teachers.

On 16th November 1896 Mrs Conway died: with her death the last of the three great figures in James's childhood passed away. He was by now entered upon his adolescence with all the troubles of mind and body against which Mrs Conway had warned him so long ago in Bray, bursting upon him.

There is no doubt that James Joyce was a devout schoolboy. He would not have been selected by the Jesuits and his peers to be Prefect of the Sodality had it been thought that he was anything less than an orthodox Catholic. The original of the famous retreat in *Portrait of an Artist* is usually placed at the end of November in this year, and it is thought that the priest who was in charge was Father Cullen. It was followed on 6th December by a Sodality reception. But it was no one specific retreat that Joyce had in mind, for he made use of his brother's experience of a later retreat and of other Jesuit sources in writing the Hellfire Sermons.

To these adolescent years, on the basis of a reading of *A Portrait*, has been assigned the first of Joyce's sexual adventures with prostitutes. This is not the case. What did trouble Joyce, as it troubles the young Bloom, was 'self-abuse' and the tortuous dreams and longings that it engendered. James's juvenile sins were restricted to masturbation. During the course of the nineteenth century medical and religious opinion had elevated auto-eroticism into a pervasive sin. Joyce may have committed the sins which are held up against Bloom, but indeed for a young Catholic of his generation that was enough. He was polluting the Temple of the Holy Spirit.

Not all Joyce's interests were secret, however. To this period belong the Irish activities of the Commission on Irish Taxation chaired by H.C.E. Childers from whom HCE – 'Here Comes Everybody' in *Finnegans Wake* – was derived. Exactly what role Childers played in the mythology of John Joyce is not yet clear. Also at this time 'A Royal Divorce', the drama which features in *Finnegans Wake*, was played in the Gaiety Theatre, perhaps with the Joyces among the appreciative audience.

In February 1897 Joyce celebrated his fifteenth birthday. Easter was on 18th April; May saw the annual Sodality reception, and June the familiar round of Intermediate exams. The Joyces were still living in 29 Windsor Avenue in the autumn of 1897, where some time earlier in the year Mrs Joyce had lost a child – the last she would bear her husband, as she was now 38. Whatever distress she felt, her husband lamented this dead morsel of humanity with the wild claim that 'by God he's not dead yet'. Was it at this time too that James (as he mentions in his 1904 essay 'A Portrait of the Artist') was surprised praying in a wood at Malahide, where he had ridden on a borrowed bicycle? This fervour was doubtless associated with his fears for his mother.

Back in Belvedere on 17th September Richard (Dick) Sheehy was elected second assistant and James O'Neill secretary of the Sodality. James remained Prefect. The return to school brought with it the announcement of the Intermediate results as usual. He won an exhibition (£30 for two years) and £3 for an essay. Doubtless some of this was spent on a dinner and on his mother (saddened by the loss of two babies in a row), as suggested in *A Portrait*, but little difference did it make to the poverty in which the family lived all the year round. James demonstrated his Fenian sympathies on Ivy Day, 6th October, by wearing an ivy leaf to school, in memory of Parnell's passing. Though the Jesuits (whatever their own feelings) cannot have cared for overt politics in the classroom, his views were doubtless shared by many in the schoolyard and also by their parents.

On 26th October 1897 Joyce used some of his prize money to buy a copy of Thomas à Kempis's *Imitation of Christ*, which he inscribed with his own name, the date and 'A.M.D.G.' – a sure indication (along with his tenure of the Sodality prefectship) of a depth of religious fervour. The *Imitation* was a constant resource of Catholics, especially on retreats, though it contained a disparagement of philosophy and creation of which modern theologians cannot approve. But these aspects appealed to Irish Catholics, just as they were eventually to appal Joyce.

In the autumn, probably at the beginning of November, it is likely that James took his *Imitation* to his last school retreat. In his novel he dates this to the following year (when Stanislaus would have taken his place and perhaps provided him with notes, for it was an event they certainly discussed). This final school retreat may well have induced in him once again those feelings of shame and contempt for the body which his style of religious upbringing had given him.

At the end of term there was the annual reception for members of the Sodality of Our Lady, over which Joyce again presided as Prefect. This was a serious matter which he took seriously, for he cannot readily be accused of hypocrisy. When he believed he believed, and at the end of his school life he still believed. On 12th January 1898 Joyce's shadowy godfather, Philip McCann, died in the Regent Hotel, D'Olier St, where he had lived since giving up Fairfield, his big house in Sandymount, after the death of his wife. He was only 52, but had been ill for a long time with tuberculosis. Though his will was destroyed during the Republican revolt, it is likely that having no children of his own he remembered his talented and impoverished godson in its provisions. Belvedere at that date offered no games, beyond the gym of which James was secretary. But at Clongowes he had enjoyed athletics, and about this time Pat Harding*, a young solicitor, offered to train James for hurdles. But James, now past his sixteenth birthday, was no longer interested in such boyish pursuits.

To this year belongs another piece of early work, a fluent translation of the Horatian ode 'O fons Bandusiae' (Ode III.13), where the skill which a Jesuit education had imparted to him in handling languages is evident, and where the image of the overflowing bowl with which he had closed his account of happiness at Clongowes is repeated.

> Brighter than glass Bandusian spring
>   For mellow wine and flowers meet,
> The morrow thee a kid shall bring
>   Boding of rivalry and sweet
> Love in his swelling forms. In vain
> He, wanton offspring, deep shall stain
> Thy clear cold streams with crimson rain.
>
> The raging dog star's season thou,
>   Still safe from in the heat of day,
> When oxen weary of the plough
>   Yieldst thankful cool for herds that stray
> Be of the noble founts! I sing
> The oak tree o'er thine echoing
> Crags, thy waters murmuring.

Here we can see the end to which his classical education had tended, the production of pleasant and charming versions from the Latin. The talent was there, but still dormant; the translation work imposed

* Pat Harding had an accident in 1909 which Joyce reported to Stanislaus; he died in 1911.

discipline and was an effective training in handling language.

Easter is the most significant part of the liturgical year. This year it was on 10th April; on 7th May (Our Lady's month), Joyce signed Patrick Dwyer's Sodality membership certificate as one of his final acts as *Praeces* of the Sodality of Our Lady at his last Sodality reception. Perhaps at this time the matter of a vocation was raised again – what else can those visits to the rector's study at lunch-time have meant, except earnest talk about Joyce's future? But by now the moment when he might have taken up the call of the Catholic priesthood was past; the lure of the secular was too strong.

On 19th May Gladstone finally died. The one-time champion of the Irish race was now hated for his stand over Parnell, and Joyce reflected this Nationalist view with his contempt for the audience in the Rotunda who were moved by the film of Gladstone's funeral (held in Westminster Abbey on 28th May) accompanied by 'Willie We Have Missed You'. The Irish people, in his view, were all too often a craven horde of cringers. He had no time himself for such sentimentality in others.

On the last Saturday in May, the 28th, there was a performance in Belvedere of an adaptation of Anstey's book *Vice Versa*, in which Joyce had a part. The evening's entertainment was in two sections. Part one was a mixture of musical and gymnastic events, then after an interval came the play. Joyce played Dr Grimstone, the headmaster 'of Crichton House, Rodwell Regis, who enjoys the the sweets of life himself but does not approve of them either figuratively or otherwise for anyone else.' He brought to the part the all-too-recognizable mannerisms of his own rector, Father Henry (who was English). The rector had the good sense to laugh heartily at the parody.

There were two girls' parts: the cook was played by John Morgan, and Joseph Duggan played Dr Grimstone's daughter, pretty Dulcie – an echo of the green room ragging arises in *Ulysses* when Bloom recalls another play with female impersonation. Joyce seems also to associate this transvestite tendency with the eldest of the Gallaher boys, Gerard.

Joyce makes this play the occasion for the reappearance of Emma Clery in Stephen's life. Possibly, however, neither the Dillon girls nor Eileen Vance attended the play. Such is Stephen's shameful despair that what might have been a triumph finishes with him roaming through the streets, ending his wandering under the street sign for Lotts – a mixture of urine and horse-manure, Stephen observes. Romance, for Joyce, was always quickly soiled by the realities of life.

On 14th June 1898 there was the final religious examination, for the Irish bishops. James and three of his friends – all there was in the upper class – refused to sit this as it would prevent them preparing for the more important public examination. This was not irreverence, but the hard practicality of middle-class Dublin. These exams tested a basic level of Catholic doctrine, an area in which James was already proficient.

The next day he began to sit his final Intermediate examinations, in which he did not do as well as in previous years, though he held his place in the Belvedere ranks. Already perhaps he was feeling no longer a schoolboy, but a student.

Among the books which James studied for the Intermediate that year was Machiavelli's *History of Florence* in the original Italian. The significance of this should not be overlooked. The theme of Machiavelli was the greatness of Florence, the city of Dante and Bruno, of Savonarola and the Medicis. For him the unit of history, life and culture was the city state of Renaissance Italy. This theme obviously impressed Joyce, for he would owe all his own loyalties not to that novel and ill-contrived idea of the nineteenth century, the Irish nation (a diffuse and largely imaginary thing), but to Dublin, which for him was indeed a city state, the unit of his history, his life, his culture. From Machiavelli he took the justification of the central fact of his life: the city of Dublin as it had entered his imagination since the dank autumn of 1893. What he had intuited then could now be justified. The setting of his future work as an artist was complete.

In the early summer of 1898 James Joyce left school, though this was not the end of his education at the hands of the Jesuits. With the coming of autumn it had been decided that he was to go on to University College, the Catholic University on St Stephen's Green, on the south side of the city. But there was a long summer season to pass before then, and by the autumn the schoolboy would have become a young man.

PART III

9

The Summer of 1898

J ames Joyce left Belvedere in June 1898, his future career having
been the subject of discussion both in school and at home. The
Jesuits in their sensible way suggested a Guinness clerkship,
which involved sitting one of the stiffest examinations in the city.
At home, his father talked of James going in for the Law, his own
experiences doubtless suggesting this to be among the most profitable
of professions. But because of the money presumably left for James
in the will of his godfather Philip McCann it was settled that he
would go on to University College in the autumn.

The summer of 1898 was a transition for Joyce between adolescence and youth. Writing to his brother, he explained the sense
of the passage now placed at the end of *A Portrait of the Artist* where
Stephen is summoned by the spell of arms: the white arms of roads,
'with their promise of close embraces'; the black arms of ships, 'their
tales of distant nations'. Voices urge him on to escape with them.
'The air is thick with their company as they call me their kinsman,
making ready to go, shaking the wings of their exultant and terrible
youth.'

This 'was to mark the precise point between boyhood (pueritia)
and adolescence (adulescentia) – 17 years.' The passage, which had
been an epiphany, was used by Joyce to the end of Stephen's schooldays in *Stephen Hero* and a call to manhood.* Joyce had now reached
this stage in his own life – he was in his seventeenth year after

* It was later removed to the conclusion of *A Portrait*, where it marks instead
Stephen's departure for Paris.

February 1898 – and he would have wished to observe the classical proprieties.

He describes in the novel a scene closely observed from life. Stephen is waiting for his father to emerge from the pub on Fairview Strand where he is talking to the university tutor. Significantly, the boy is not invited into their company. Despairing of waiting, he walks out along the sea-front to the Bull Island, where he meets Patrick Dwyer, his fellow Sodality member from school, and other local friends at the swimming place at the end of the harbour wall. Here, in a spot isolated in the middle of Dublin Bay, the magical presence of the sea and the mountains is overwhelming, even today. Then, the scene before him would have been thronged with the masts of ships moored all along the quays of the Liffey.

Bored with the childish chaffing of his now former classmates, from whom the tides of life are cutting him off, he turns away and walks through the sand dunes towards the beach of the inner lagoon. There he encounters a young girl, her skirts tucked up, wading through the shallows like a crane. What might for others have been a merely passing moment, was elevated in Joyce's now heightened sensitivity as an adolescent into one of the mystical experiences (which Traherne, Blake, and Richard Jefferies among others also experienced) and which seem at the time to provide an insight into the true meaning of life.

In the draft of *Stephen Hero* the girl is called Lucy – the name Joyce would give his own daughter. Lucy was a third-century saint of Syracuse, who was the special patron of those with weak sight. She was also the messenger of Beatrice to Virgil in *The Inferno* (Canto ii, 97ff): '*Or ha bisogno il tuo fedele di te, ed io a te lo raccomando*' – 'Now thy faithful one has need of thee; and I commend him to thee.' Years later, of course, he was reminded of this girl by Marthe Fleischmann in Zürich. The girl on the beach seemed to him a herald from what the novel calls 'the fair courts of life'. These courts he was now about to enter.

*

This encounter, occurring towards the end of July 1898, marked for Joyce that transition from childhood to manhood – to live, to err, to fall, to triumph, to create life out of life. He was not a sentimentalist; he was in search of a deeper reality. In the second week of August,

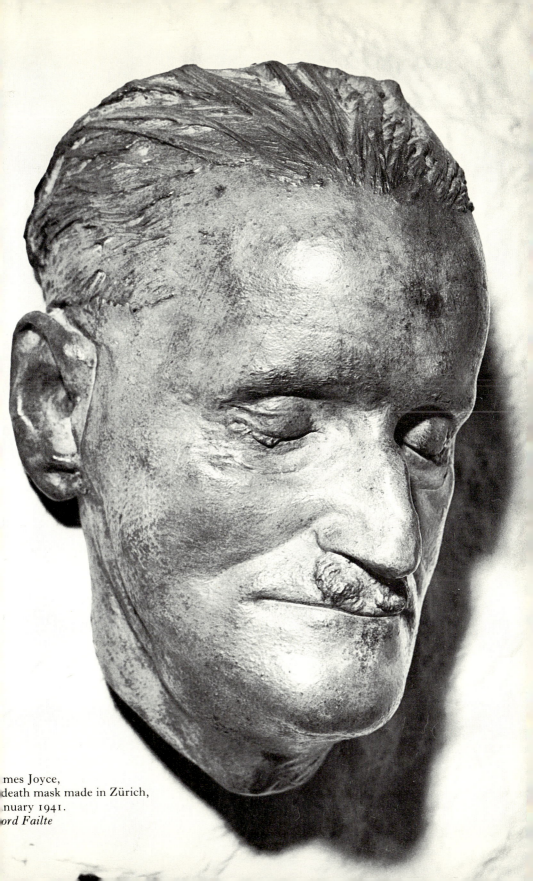

James Joyce,
death mask made in Zürich,
January 1941.
Cead Mile Failte

James A. Joyce, grandfather of the writer, from a painting by William Roe, circa 1849. *The Poetry Room, Lockwood Memorial Library, State University of New York at Buffalo*

Ellen O'Connell, Mrs James Joyce grandmother of the writer, from a portrai by William Roe, circa 1849. *The Poetr Room, Lockwood Memorial Library, Stat University of New York at Buffalo*

John Stanislaus Joyce, the writer's father, aged about 16, from a painting by an unknown artist, circa 1865. *The Poetry Room, Lockwood Memorial Library, State University of New York at Buffalo*

Mary Jane Murray, Mrs John Stanislaus Joyce, the writer's mother. *Nationa Library of Ireland*

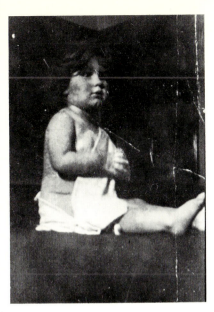

'Baby Tuckoo': James Joyce as an infant. *Southern Illinois University Library*

'Half-Past Six': James Joyce, aged $6\frac{1}{2}$, photographed on the day he entered Clongowes, September 1888. *National Library of Ireland*

Dante Conway's vision of the world's end: 'The Opening of the Sixth Seal', painting by Francis Danby. *National Gallery of Ireland*

Gravel Football, the unique Clongowes game, described by Joyce.
Clongowes Archives, courtesy of Father Roland Burke-Savage S.J.

A typical Clongowes classroom of Joyce's time, with AMDG at
the head of the blackboard work. *Author's collection*

The Small Boys' Dormitory, with the curtains which Joyce
mentions. *Author's collection*

The College Infirmary, in which Joyce stayed first and where
Stephen Dedalus dreams of Parnell's death. *Author's collection*

Funeral of Charles Stewart Parnell, 11th October 1891. *Illustrated London News*

Charles Stewart Parnell at the height of his powers. *Illustrated London News*

John Kelly ('Mr Casey'), photographed on a Dublin street by the secret police in August 1892. *National Archives of Ireland*

'The night we missed the boat at Algeciras' (*Ulysses*): Algeciras (The Galway Stall) at the Araby Bazaar, May 1894. *The Illustrograph*

The Lower School in Belvedere (with James Joyce seated first row, far left), June 1894, possibly the month of 'An Encounter'. *The Illustrograph*

The hall at Belvedere, with the scene set for the 1894 play. *The Illustrograph*

The Belvedere Sodality, with James Joyce as Prefect (seated, third from left), photographed in 1898, from a photograph originally in the possession of Patrick O'Dwyer. *University College Dublin (Curran Papers, Special Collections)*

between the 8th and the 13th, he passed the next crucial stage in his life.

One evening that week he attended a performance of *Sweet Brier* at the Gaiety Theatre in South King Street. Walking back across the city afterwards to his home to Clontarf, he encountered a prostitute. He was now ready to experiment, and did so. But this encounter – like Bloom's with Bridie Kelly – may well have been cheap, brief and ineffectual, and by its fumbling inadequacy left him disgusted with the appetites of the flesh.*

Entering the house at 29 Windsor Drive, he found his father in conversation with young Alfred Bergan, then a youth of 18. They, too, had been to the play. Joyce listened to their comments, but kept his own thoughts to himself.

This encounter had at last freed him to pursue the sensations of experience. Now in the autumn of 1898 he made the first of his visits to the red-light district in Monto. The scene in *A Portrait*, where he transfers these experiences to his last years at school (though still leaving them in 1898) may well preserve a sense of his feeling on this occasion. The description of the room in the brothel, with the large doll perched open-legged on the fireside chair, is doubtless drawn from a lost epiphany written about this date. Stephen's tears of relief make a curious reaction, however. Joyce implies that he has at last shuffled off the tiresome constraint of his virginity.

Remorse duly followed on sin, and the walk across the city to find absolution at the hands of the Carmelite Franciscans in the gothic chapel in Church Street. Joyce had still lost neither his faith nor his sense of sin. He naturally preferred the poorer (and less familiar) districts for his confessional outpourings than either the local priests of Fairview parish or the clever Jesuits at Gardiner Street.

*

On Monday 15th August, Joyce and his father were present at the unveiling of a slab set into the roadway, marking the site for the Wolfe Tone centenary memorial at the top of Grafton Street. This may well have disgusted him too – the outpourings of Nationalist rhetoric followed by a failure to erect anything, wild declarations of

---

* Richard Ellmann places this episode in 1896. However, Joyce mentioned the name of the play to his brother: and *Sweet Brier* was only licensed by the Lord Chamberlain in 1898, and first staged in Dublin between the above dates. Joseph Holloway gives details of the play and its cast in his diary.

love followed by impotence. The will and imagination of the Irish people seemed to be paralysed. Seeking a sexual reason for this, he suspected that the city as a whole was infected with syphilitic paralysis, the G.P.I (General Paralysis of the Insane) of the medical students he was soon to know so well.

The results of the last Intermediate exam he had sat were announced on 3rd September: Joyce had won £30 for a second year, and £4 for the best essay, together with a 3rd class prize of £1 in books. He anticipated the money on 9th September by buying a copy of the fourth edition (published in 1894) of John Ruskin's *Mornings in Florence*. The spell of this great Victorian sage was still strong, but for Joyce to choose this handbook on Christian art is an indication perhaps that as yet his faith had not waned, that religion would justify itself in art. The book was written in 1874, soon after Ruskin himself had recovered his faith through a visit to Assisi and the shrine of St Francis. For Ruskin art, religion, morality and right living were all one. In form the book was a guide to the monuments of Florence, a city which the impoverished Joyce was then unlikely to see. Ruskin expounds his well-known views on the relations of faith to art, but Joyce may well have been impressed by his account of the meaning of the decorated ceiling of St Mary's Cathedral and the figures surrounding St Thomas Aquinas. On the text from Wisdom (vii.7), 'I willed and sense was given me', Ruskin comments:

> You must begin your education with the distinct resolution to know what is true, and choice of the strait and rough road to such knowledge. The choice is offered to every youth and maid at some moment of their life; choice between the easy downward road, so broad that we can dance down it in companies, and the steep narrow way, which we must enter alone. Then, and for many a day afterwards, they need that form of persistent Option, and Will: but day by day, the 'sense' of rightness of what they have deepens in them, not in consequence of the effort, but by the gift granted in reward of it. And the Sense of difference between right and wrong, and between beautiful and unbeautiful things, is confirmed in the heroic, and fulfilled in the industrious, soul.

By now Joyce had made his choice, and was about to begin his real education, but other literary work was not neglected. Towards the end of September he completed, doubtless as a pre-university exercise, an essay on force which still survives but is little more than the accomplishment of a clever schoolboy.

With his entrance into the university in October, his youth had its beginings, but not yet his manhood. As he himself writes, he was at this date still 'soothed by devotional exercises', as he relates in an essay on his early years written in January 1904. The Catholic faith in which his mother, Mrs Conway, and the Jesuits had reared him had not yet ebbed away completely; but the currents of his mind and body were already flowing away from the Church, towards that other life which the bird girl on the beach and the writings of Ruskin had intimated to him – a life of the spirit in which he could redeem the still sordid claims of the body. Such a redemption would be a transmutation of his religious impulse.

*

And so the Joyce who entered University College in the autumn of 1898 was not the Joyce who had left Belvedere in June. During the summer of 1898 the schoolboy had become a young man. It now remained for the young man to become an artist.

PART IV

ON ST STEPHEN'S GREEN

1898–1900

It was at University College at the age of 16 that James Joyce began to emerge as the more familiar figure of later years.

At the opening of the college year in 1899, when he had already been a student for a year, he first came to the notice of his friend Constantine Curran, a freshman. Curran was immediately struck by Joyce's distinctive character, the ever-so-slightly-bored way in which he would admit his acquaintance not only with the latest literature, but with a wide range of classics. Later he came to realize, in analysing the situation, that Joyce had deliberately adopted a literary pose, what Curran thought of as his D'Annunzian mask. He had appropriated the public styles of that poet's characters, standing aloof from the crowd in the pride of his own self-possession.

This remaking of Joyce was the work of his first years at college.

*

So it was in the autumn of 1898, feeling himself a man among boys, that Joyce came to University College at 86 St Stephen's Green, an elegant eighteenth-century town house of shabby distinction. Here in his first two years he would make his mark as a personality, while in his last two years he would emerge as potentially one of the college's most distinguished students. The turning point would be in 1900 with his paper on 'Drama and Life' and the publication of his essay on Ibsen in a London review. The essay on force, which had been completed on 27th September, would have given his professors little intimation of the nature of his own profound and forceful character.

At this date, when on his own admission he was still 'soothed by devotional exercises', he had not reached the critical stage of rejecting the faith in which he had been reared; it would take his years at college to undo the work his schools had done.

There remains some mystery about the practical matter of the payment of Joyce's college fees. That the Jesuits may have continued to educate him for nothing is a possibility, but they were not entirely free in this matter as some fees would still have been due to the Royal University for examinations and for Joyce to receive his degree. Stephen Dedalus had his fees paid by his godfather, so (as indicated earlier) it is more than likely that some money was left in the will of Philip McCann for Joyce's education to continue, but as his will has been destroyed this cannot be proved. Finally, it may be that John Joyce paid the fees and that meeting them explains part of the purpose of the new mortgages which he took out in 1902 just before Joyce graduated.

University College traced its history back to the Catholic university founded in 1854 by John Henry Newman for the Irish Catholic hierarchy. Despite the fine flourish of its beginnings, and the open ambition of the bishops that an institution to rival the Protestant Trinity College would be erected in Drumcondra, the scheme came to nothing. The foundations were laid, but as so often in Ireland nothing was built. The truth was that without a Royal charter the college could not grant degrees, and no wise Catholic parent (whatever the bishops might feel or say) would wish to waste his son's time with no prospect of a final qualification. Hence most Catholics desiring a university education went to Trinity, or to England.

The failing college was placed in the hands of the Jesuits in the early 1880s, but it was not until the foundation of the Royal University – which established a degree-granting body – and the establishment of the Intermediate Education exams that the student numbers began to rise. In Joyce's day there were nearly 300 students at the college, including the medical students, to Trinity's 1,100. Already agitation on 'the University Question' was in course, with a view to establishing the National University of Ireland (of which University College would be a constituent part), which went all the way to meeting the demands of the hierarchy and the Irish Nationalists, achieved in 1908. Joyce entered a college heady with ambition and rising nationalist fervour in which the arts and literature came second to the practical affairs of man and nation.

At college Joyce was to make and maintain some significant friendships with John Francis Byrne (a bluff Wicklow man), Constantine Curran (a civilized Dubliner), George Clancy (an uncomplicated Limerick nationalist), Thomas Kettle (a Catholic intellectual) and Francis Skeffington (a feminist and socialist) among others. But for his first year he was largely feeling his way, converting his schoolboy image into an adult ideal. These friends made their way into his books (with the exception of Curran, who it seems was to have a place in the lost pages of *Stephen Hero*). Cranly (Jeff Byrne), Davin (George Clancy) and McCann (Skeffington) were transformations of real people that stayed close to the features of the originals.

What is significant is what Joyce leaves out. Of nearly 800 students who would have passed through the college in his time, only a handful – the handful he knew well – are recreated in his fiction. At 16 he was still young and found easy social intercourse difficult. In 1901, the year in which the first Gaelic versions of names appear in the college register, there are also the names of three Jews: Isaac Sieve, Louis Cohen and Solomon Levy. Their presence seems to have passed unnoticed in the recollections of their Christian contemporaries, but possibly they provided Joyce with a further contact with Dublin's small Hebrew community.

Joyce's first college session may have been largely occupied with settling into a new position. Domestic matters, however, still engaged him. At the beginning of December (Thursday 1st to Saturday 3rd) his brother Stanislaus made his annual retreat at school – the date of the retreat in Joyce's novel. This retreat is discussed in *Stephen Hero*, and Maurice (modelled on Stanislaus) grimly defines it as: 'The usual thing. Stink in the morning and pain of loss in the afternoon.' Doubtless his notes and recollections of this event, seemingly presided over by Father James Cullen, would have served to refresh Joyce's own memory in due course. The changing and fluctuating relationship with his brother that he developed at this time would last them through many later years of trial. Discussion with Stanislaus enabled Joyce to survive the developing horror he felt for Irish family life.

Joyce was following the Modern Languages Course, which was seen by most of the students (who were planning professional careers in law and medicine) as 'the Ladies' Course'. Having already read his way through much of English literature, he now commenced on a wider survey of modern European writing. Some of the books he owned later passed into the hands of C.P. Curran and carry dates. Maurice Maeterlinck's *Allodine and Palomides*, in an 1890 edition, was read in 1899, as was *Melisande and Pelleas*. But later in 1900 he would be reading Ibsen's *Little Eyolf* and *The Wild Duck* and D'Annunzio's *La Gioconda*; in 1901 Huysmans *La Bas* and Ibsen's *Bygmyster Solness* in the original Dano-Norwegian; and in 1902 Paul Verlaine, *Les Poètes Maudits*, and Fogazzaro's *Picollo*. In January 1898 he completed an essay (which survives) on the study of language, which was to be his significant pursuit during his college years. Already it is likely that he was realizing the limitations of the course he was following at the college and the need to educate himself. This he would do as much through extra-curricular activities as through reading.

The main interest he had among the thirty or so societies and clubs in the college was the debating society, the Literary and Historical Society, which traced its beginnings back to Newman's day. In January 1899 he spoke for the first time at the L. and H., and was to be a regular attender and contributor from the house at meetings up to his last year in college. If his academic standing fell over this period, he made his mark in the annals of a society in which future public figures were training themselves.

In February 1899 he celebrated his seventeenth birthday. A few weeks later, on 18th February he was elected a member of the Executive Committee of the L. and H. A month later, on 21st March, he vied with Ulsterman Louis J. Walsh (already becoming the strenuous Sinn Fein politician) for the post of treasurer, losing by 5 votes to 2. This in itself was a small indication not only of the place he already held in college, but also of his rising personal ambitions.

In the second week of March 1899 Mrs Patrick Campbell and her company presented her sensational production of *Magda* in Dublin. James and his parents went to see this one evening and on returning home there was a general conversation on the play. To his astonished parents he remarked that they had not really needed to go to it; the theme of the play was genius breaking out in the home, which they would soon see in their own house. His family, if not the world, was warned. It was altogether a suitable ending to his first year at college. The problem was, what form would his genius take?

*

The steady round of college life was splendidly disrupted at the beginning of May by another theatrical event. On 8th May the Abbey Theatre Company opened in the Antient Concert Rooms in Brunswick Street with their production of Yeats's poetic play *The Countess Kathleen*. Though Yeats had obtained from his friend the Jesuit Father Thomas Finlay an opinion that there was nothing blasphemous about his drama, that did not satisfy the Nationalist students who protested from the gallery on the opening night, which Joyce attended. (The incident duly found its way into *A Portrait of the Artist*.) On 10th May a letter was published in the *Freeman's Journal* protesting again against the play; this was signed by some 23 students from University College. There were 64 students in Joyce's year alone, some 400-odd in the student body as a whole, which means that perhaps one out of every sixteen students signed. An editorial in the student magazine was later to accuse Joyce of being alone in standing aloof from the protest. This was simply not so: he was merely a part of the great majority indifferent to a student rag. (According to Joseph Holloway the protesters were 'an organized claque of about twenty brainless, beardless, idiotic-youths [who] did all they knew to interfere with the progress of the play by their meaningless automatic hissing and senseless comments, and only succeeded in showing what poor things mortals can become when the seat of reason is knocked awry by animus, spite and bigotry.' They had been annoyed by previous references made by Yeats in a talk on Thomas Davis, poetic idol of Nation-minded people, 'but their poor spite was completely frustrated by enthusiastic applause which drowned their empty-headed expressions of dissent'.) The following night Edward Martyn's play *The Heather Field*, an Ibsenesque drama of failed idealism and potentially a far more disturbing play in its critique of the Irish psyche, went unbooed.

Joyce's lone stand against the tide of ignorance has passed into legend; alas, he merely seems to have stood among the multitude that did not care one way or another what Yeats thought.

In his examinations Joyce took Honours in Latin. At Belvedere Stanislaus was admitted on 27th May into the Sodality of Our Lady by Father Charles Farley, who is mentioned in *Ulysses* in connection with Molly Bloom (for whom we may perhaps read Mrs Joyce) singing in the choir of the Jesuit church at Gardiner Street. The devotion of mother and son would be rewarded by Stanislaus eventually becoming, like his brother James, *Praeceps* of the Sodality. This is one of the many facts of their early life that conveniently fail to find a place in Stanislaus's memoirs.

The Joyces were once again on the move. Mrs Love finally forced them out, and John Joyce had to set about finding a new abode of some kind. This he managed without too much strain to himself, and they passed that summer at a house in Convent Avenue (actually 225 Richmond Road). This was only a temporary refuge, but in any case home was a matter of decreasing interest to Joyce, for he was not much there, having fallen into the habit of reading in the National Library and then walking about the city with his friends or his brother, deep in conversation. To the month of July belongs the incident he records in *Stephen Hero* of his friend J.F. Byrne reading a large scientific volume, *Disease of the Ox*, while he tries to tempt him out for a walk.

It was not college work that Joyce was doing. By September he had completed an essay on the exhibition of the painting by the Hungarian Mihaly Munkacsy 'Ecce Homo' (then on a European tour) at the Royal Hibernian Academy. This showed the tortured person of Christ being offered by Pilate to a raving crowd in the courtyard below the balcony on which stand the figures symbolic of state and church. The painter saw Christ as a human protagonist in a drama, and in this respect succeeded. 'Belief in the divinity of Christ is not a salient feature of secular Christendom,' Joyce concluded. 'But occasional sympathy with the eternal conflict of truth and error, right and wrong, as exemplified in the drama at Golgotha is not beyond its approval.'

Joyce was not much interested in art, though he owned a well-marked copy of the catalogue to the National Gallery which he and Stanislaus still visited from time to time. The essay was a step in his own developing ideas not only of religion but also of drama. This finished piece of work may have been intended for publication in the *New Ireland Review*, a serious-minded monthly edited from University College by Father Thomas Finlay. There is no direct evidence of this, but Joyce's mind was certainly turning in the direction of magazine publication.

At the beginning of October (just as the new university session was beginning) he was in touch with the editor of the *Fortnightly Review*. His friend Eugene Sheehy later believed that this contact was made for him by George Dempsey, his former Belvedere teacher, who himself wrote for the newspapers. Further evidence of his ambition came at a meeting of the L. and H. at which Joyce seconded the new members and himself offered to read a paper. Two weeks later his subject, 'Drama and Life', was posted in the society's programme.

That autumn also saw the beginning of the Boer War in South Africa, which was to prove both controversial and tragic. Starting with the Boer ultimatum on 9th October, it was to form the rumbling background to Irish life for the next two years, and is seen by some as the remote origin of the Easter Rising, Ireland's attack on the Empire.

That autumn the Joyces moved yet again, this time to a house at 13 Richmond Avenue (now demolished), a large rambling mansion which they shared with an Ulsterman named Richard Hughes and his young family. John Joyce enjoyed Hughes' company and spent many evenings arguing politics with him, Hughes doubt-less stimulating him by his exposition of a Northern Unionist's views.

All his life Joyce took an interest in murder cases (Arthur Power in Paris recalls discussing with him the Bywaters and Thompson case). The end of October 1899 was enlivened for north-siders by the trial of Samuel Childs for murdering his brother. Joyce attended the trial not only out of criminal curiosity, but also for family reasons. His aunt Josephine's mother, Mrs Giltrap, was a neighbour of the brothers on Bengal Terrace and must have taken a horrid delight in the details of the crime. In the event Childs was acquitted, but the case passed into Dublin folklore among associates of the Joyces, and the house on Bengal Terrace is remarked upon during the drive to the cemetary in *Ulysses*.

The feast of Hallowe'en, the Eve of All Saints' Day, with its traditional events and games was for all Dublin families of this period a significant one. This year the Joyces may have been among the party who celebrated the evening in John Murray's home in nearby Drumcondra. Among the other guests was little Maria O'Donohoe, who in June had been diagnosed as having an inoperable internal tumour. On 8th December 1899 she died in the Hospice at Harold's Cross, where she had gone from the Flynns' home at 15 Usher's Island. Her death following so soon upon Hallowe'en, when by old European tradition the dead are said to walk abroad from their graves, provided Joyce at a later date with the theme and the cir-cumstance for his story 'Clay', in which Maria the spinster relation has intimations of death at a family Hallowe'en party when she places her hand in the bowl of clay during a game.

On 13th November a paper by Arthur Clery (later to write for the college magazine and *The Leader*, an outspoken and anti-intellectual nationalist paper, under the pen-name of Chanel) proved an outstanding success and urged Joyce on to emulation. On 23rd November he attended a committee meeting of the L. and H. remaining among the small number of culturally active students.

On 16th December Joseph Chamberlain, the Empire-minded Colonial Secretary and trenchant opponent of Home Rule, visited Dublin to be presented with an honorary degree by Trinity College. This was made the occasion of a vulgar display by Trinity students in which the Irish national flag was thrown down on the floor for him to walk over. News of this spread and ugly crowds gathered on College Green at day's end, forcing Chamberlain to flee the college by a back door and escape to a boat on the Liffey. The following St Patrick's Day the same Trinity students were to pelt the Lord Mayor of Dublin, Joyce's friend Tim Harrington, with oranges; an unsubtle way of making a political point against Irish nationalists. Joyce's view of Trinity College as 'dull stone set in the ring of the city' arose from these events, as much as from his family's outlook.

Over that Christmas Joyce worked on his paper for the L. and H., which he completed on 10th January. He had composed and polished it with the critical aid of Stanislaus and knew it to be an effective piece of writing. He had also been engaged on an article dealing with Ibsen's new play *When We Dead Awaken*. Stanislaus recalled that Joyce had stayed up all night to read the drama when it arrived by post. On 19th January he heard from W.L. Courtney, the editor of the *Fortnightly Review*, that he could not take it.

Disappointment did not cloud the reading of his paper on 20th January 1900, however. 'Drama and Life' proved to be a great success, adding once again to the laurels of the L. and H. This was a signal achievement for a young man then approaching his eighteenth birthday. But another triumph soon followed. For his birthday Joyce seems to have spent some money on books: certainly there exists a copy of Hauptmann's *The Coming of Peace* dated 'February 1900'. As this month saw the relief of Kimberley and Ladysmith and the surrender of Cronje at Paadeberg, the play's title was appropriate enough to the period. A day or two after his birthday he heard again from Courtney that he would publish the article after all. Joyce, however, who had been using a French version, had to make his quotations suit the new English edition. After further correspondence between Courtney and William Archer, Ibsen's translator, and Joyce and Courtney, his article was sent to the printer.

With the article out of the way, Joyce was now involved with a student production of a comedy *Cupid's Confidant* in which he played a villain. This was performed publicly and received a favourable review from J.B. Hall in the *Freeman's Journal*. (Hall was an acquaintance of the Joyces and James was to make use of his memoirs in writing *Finnegans Wake*.)

At the end of March the *Fortnightly Review* appeared with Joyce's article. A librarian at the National Library recalled him approaching the desk with diffidence to ask for the new issue. Among his contemporaries and his professors the impression was wonderful: here clearly was a real achievement. For all his eccentricities Joyce (who had earned the college nickname of 'The Hatter' after the Mad Hatter in *Alice*) was already recognized as an exceptional individual. Now he was a person of actual achievement.

Perhaps as pleasurable for Joyce was the fact that he was paid 12 guineas for the article, and the cheque arrived a week later. With money in hand and the Easter holiday coming up, a trip to London suggested itself to James and his father. This would enable them to be out of the city for a large part of the time when Queen Victoria was visiting it. She had come to thank Dublin for its support of the British cause in the Boer War and despite the occasional nationalist protest she was warmly welcomed. In London the Joyces found a warm welcome from Mr Courtney and this was an opportunity for James to make some useful contacts. His father, however, proved less popular as he was inclined, like most Irishmen of his kind, to make pro-Boer statements. This would have been the weekend of 15th April.

On 18th April Ibsen wrote in person to thank Archer for the article which he had just tried to read. A week later Archer wrote to Joyce passing on the playwright's thanks; this letter Joyce received by first delivery on 25th April 1900, while he was sitting on a swing in the garden of 13 Richmond Avenue. He had just returned from a dance and was sitting with Susan McKernan, the 10-year-old daughter of their old neighbour. She was to be one of his models for Gertie McDowell, with whom Leopold Bloom is enchanted on Sandymount Strand in *Ulysses*.

Joyce opened Archer's letter at once, and this remained a memorable moment for him. Here, beyond the dreams of any young man, was recognition from one of the great masters of modern literature. His efforts were rewarded, his ambition sustained. With solemn courtesy Joyce replied briefly and respectfully to the sage of Christiania. *When We Dead Awaken* would be Ibsen's last play: he died in 1906. One age was passing, in Joyce's view; another, his own, was arriving.

That was at the end of April, while the family were still living at 13 Richmond Avenue. In May they moved with the Hughes family to another house, 8 Royal Terrace, where again they shared the premises. The Joyce brothers nowhere refer to this fact, but Census returns for 1901 are quite clear about the matter. Among their neighbours was Mervyn Archdall Browne, whose conversation about the dead bodies in Glasnevin recalled by Bloom in *Ulysses* may belong to this time.

In May Joyce was elected to the L. and H. committee, but lost out to Hugh Kennedy who became auditor. That month Mafeking was relieved, and the occasion was marked by an extraordinary demonstration in London. In Dublin, however, Joyce and his friend Jeff Byrne were attending (along with other faculty members and students of the college) a public meeting in the Antient Concert Rooms on 'School and the Nation', which dealt largely with the role of the Irish language in modern education. Joyce's attendance in an audience of committed Gaelic enthusiasts was duly reported in *An Claidheamh Soluis*, the Gaelic League paper edited by Patrick Pearse (later the leader of the 1916 Rising), with whom he was slightly acquainted.

Joyce, however, was already feeling that his future lay more abroad. At the end of May he went again to London, this time without his father. He wrote to William Archer, and went off to see Eleanora Duse at the Lyceum in *La Gioconda*, of which he had just bought a copy. Oddly enough Archer had forgotten who 'Mr Joyce' was, and replied asking rather brusquely what business he had with him. Reminded about the identity of the young man, he hastily asked him to lunch at his club. This was an attempt on Joyce's part to reinforce the effect of his article and of Ibsen's letter on a man whose influence in literary London was considerable.

College over, for a rarity Joyce had a summer holiday when he and his brother went with their father to the town of Mullingar in

Co. Westmeath. John Joyce had been engaged by a Dublin solicitor who acted for the county council to assist in the revision of the electoral lists. The Joyces probably did not stay in the Greville Hotel, but lodged with a photographer named Shaw who took in visitors. This man employed a young girl from Bray as a photographic assistant. Mullingar was to provide Joyce with one of the few settings of his fiction outside Dublin in *Stephen Hero*, and would be where Milly Bloom was sent by her father Leopold to work as an assistant for a photographer.

Here Joyce, in the intervals of reading D'Annunzio's *The Child of Pleasure*, set to work to write his first play. He called it, significantly, *My Brilliant Career*.

The diffident young man who had entered college in the autumn of 1898 had become by this date – the summer of 1900 – a person of some real and recognized achievement. Now with his play he would demonstrate, he hoped, the genius of which he had told his parents the autumn before. But nothing in life was ever to prove as simple as that for James Joyce.

11

The Drama of Life

1900–1902

*M*y *Brilliant Career*, written in the summer months of 1900, was the first considerable work which Joyce undertook. It no longer survives, but the plot dealt with the experiences of a young doctor in a disease-ridden town much like Mullingar. The play must have been a cross between Ibsen's *An Enemy of the People* and Edward Martyn's recent Irish drama *The Heather Field*. It was inspired by a contemporary epidemic, oddly enough, in Glasgow, that city with which the Joyces had some as yet unascertained connections, and which James and his father had visited. Joyce dedicated the play to 'My Own Soul'. Given it to read as he sat up in bed, John Joyce exclaimed on seeing the dedication: 'Holy Paul!'

On his return to Dublin at the end of August Joyce sent the play to William Archer in London. Archer read it, taking a note of the dedication, but sent it back with his critical regrets. Despite Joyce's theories, the play would not work on the stage. He had still to learn that there was more to life and to drama than he had as yet experienced, or could express. His grasp on real life was not likely to be improved by D'Annunzio's *La Gloria* and *Sogno da Tramonto Autumno*, which he was reading through in September.

He passed on to reading the plays and novels of Gerhart Hauptmann, that grim German whose views of humanity were more in accord with the events of Dublin life with which he now engaged himself. On 23rd August the body of a housemaid named Brigid Gannon was found in the Dodder at Newbridge Road, from where the funeral starts in *Ulysses*. Between 24th August and 4th September inquests were held on the body, during which a strange tale began to emerge. The maid's corpse had been found and identified by policemen from Donnybrook station, one of whom had actually been with her on the night she died. Tim Harrington was involved in the case as counsel for one of the policemen, on whose behalf he made vigorous legal representations. The policeman was called Henry Flower – the pen-name adopted by Leopold Bloom for his illicit correspondence in *Ulysses*. Henry Flower quickly became a figure of Dublin folklore; as a child, my mother taught me a rhyme from her own childhood about the case:

> He took her to the Dodder
> to teach her how to swim;
> He stuffed her nose with cotton wool,
> and then he threw her in.

On 5th September a judge quashed the inquest's original verdict of accidental death, and on 11th September Henry Flower was arrested. On 14th September Sergeant Hanily, Flower's friend who had first recognized the body after it was discovered, cut his own throat and died in Irishtown police barracks. Flower's trial dragged on into October, when on the 16th the Grand Jury returned 'No True Bill' against him. The next day he resigned from the police and left the country (for Australia according to my mother's recollection of gossip at the time, but this is not known for certain).

This was yet another murder case which left its traces through Joyce's work. It is clear from the records of the day that the whole truth about the murder was not uncovered.* The life of Dublin's ill-paid and hard-worked servants which the case revealed, their courtships undertaken walking round the streets and river banks of the city, are utilized in Joyce's story 'Two Gallants', in which Corley takes his slavey (it seems) to these same fields and inveigles a gold sovereign out of her. Like Brigid Gannon, she worked in a house in Lower Baggot Street. The real life of the city was slowly seeping into Joyce's still over-literary imagination.

Archer's rejection of his play (in a letter dated 15th September) may well have been a disappointment to Joyce, for his developing interest had little welcome at home either. In Dublin *Diarmuid and Grainne*, a typical piece of the Irish Revival's dramatic movement,

---

* In the 1940s another maidservant, the companion of Brigid Gannon that night, confessed on her deathbed that she had drowned her.

opened at this time. It was not the kind of drama that appealed to him, however, having no reference to real life, only to the romance of a facile kind of heroic folklore.

Of far more interest to Joyce's father than his son's play was the General Election in November, in which the now reunited Irish Party renewed its strength and began the long slow struggle to achieve Home Rule, secured by 1914. New political figures were emerging. By his lingering admiration of Parnell John Joyce had placed himself beyond friendly political influences which might have found him a post in Dublin Corporation. Like his son, he had been rejected, but – unlike his son – he planned to do nothing about it.

Back at college, Joyce pursued his studies in a desultory way; he was reading English, French, Italian and Logic for his B.A. Honours degree. He retained his membership of the Literary and Historical Society and at a November meeting Hugh Kennedy read a paper on 'The University Question', that burning topic of the hour for the new Catholic professional class into which his father still hoped Jim might climb. A Royal Commission was then sitting, whose report would again fail to meet the ever-rising demands of Irish Nationalists. At a committee meeting of the L. and H. on 16th November his friend Jeff Byrne was elected a member, and its meetings and discussions provided much entertainment for Joyce and his contemporaries during the winter.

Joyce now began to collect his poems under the title of *Shine and Dark*, a reflection of the contrary moods they evoked. This manuscript was lent to his friend George Clancy to read. Joyce used to visit Clancy in his rooms in Grantham Street, one of the streets in the quarter off the South Circular Road where the Jewish community was then living, and with which his family had old attachments. Though a simple and uncomplicated person in many ways, George Clancy was an active and responsible young man; in later life he was murdered during the Troubles while serving as Mayor of Limerick. His straightforward manly qualities appealed to the more complex Joyce, perhaps in the same way that the personality of his future wife Nora Barnacle would. Through Clancy he came in contact with the true feelings of that greater Ireland beyond the city limits of his imagination. As he became a popular politician in later years, we can be sure that what Clancy thought, the majority thought. Joyce records, as from his character Davin in *A Portrait*, one of Clancy's tales: about how on a long walk over the wild hills near his home, a young wife in a cottage where he paused made an ambiguous proposal, a story of rustic temptation which might have found its way eventually into a series of stories on rural life which Joyce once contemplated. The tale suggested that beneath the surface the countryside had a ripe, but hidden, sexual sense. The hidden Ireland of Joyce's imagination was a sexual one. In a sense he feared the life of rural Ireland, but it was a fear of the unknown. He would listen to Clancy talking of life in Limerick, and in exchange would relate tales of his own experience that his friend found shocking as a reflection of city life. In the free Ireland of his imagination there would be no sin.

In *Stephen Hero*, one of the great scenes is the collection of signatures for the Czar's Peace Pledge Campaign – widely promoted throughout the British Isles by W.T. Stead and the *Review of Reviews* in 1901. Joyce represents Stephen as standing aloof from this as he had in life. Such political action did not engage his sympathies. They lay elsewhere. That he was engaged on reading Huysmans' *La Bas* and Horton's *Book of Images* – both redolent of the *fin de siècle* decadence that appeals to many young imaginations – is indication enough that his interests were diverging from those of his fellow students. The peace campaign was promoted in the college by Frank Skeffington, known as 'Knickerbockers' from his characteristic dress.

Skeffington was a socialist, and more congenial to Joyce than many others to be found around Newman House. Politics of the conservative nationalist kind possessed the active minded in the college, and for them Joyce felt little tenderness. The attitude was reciprocated. A typical venture of the day was the paper on 26th January by William Dawson at L. and H. on 'Ireland and Imperialism', which condemned with all the appropriate invective of an Irishman who could not recognize how he had benefited from the same Imperialism – he was the son of the Dawson appointed in 1891 to collect the city rates.

James's nineteenth birthday still found the Joyces living at 8 Royal Terrace. This was the house in which he begins the description of Stephen's walk across the city into college. The various sights along the route bring associations to his mind, largely literary: the trees at Fairview bring thoughts of the girls in Hauptmann's, Baird's stoneyard the thought of Ibsen's *Master Builder*, and so on. He refers also (in that oblique passing manner he so often uses for the most personal of details) to the dusty ships' chandler on Burgh Quay. In the text this evokes no association, but this had been the store owned by his godfather Philip McCann – his share of the profits from which was perhaps paying his college fees of 10 guineas a year.

For Joyce Dublin was not so much a series of sights and buildings, but a series of associations, both literary and deeply personal. He was creating a literary method which would result in *Ulysses* and *Finnegans Wake*, in both of which the literary associations are more easily detected than the underlying personal ones.

In March of 1901, in his most solemn mood, he wrote to Henrik Ibsen on his eightieth birthday, reminding him of their earlier association. This was an intentional act of homage from one of the rising generation to the idol of his youth, a dramatist whose influence would pervade Joyce's work for another ten years. This time there was no reply from the already dying dramatist.

This was also the month when he may have read the new edition of George Moore's novel *Vain Fortune*, still a widely read book, from which he was to lift the confessional scene between the couple for the conclusion of his own story 'The Dead'. Moore, who represented the realistic side of the Revival, was an important but largely unacknowledged influence on Joyce. Unacknowledged influences (as Samuel Butler remarks) are often the most important ones. One of Moore's titles even, *Confessions of a Young Man*, reissued in 1904, influenced Joyce's choice of title for his own autobiographical work.

On 9th March a general meeting of the L. and H. dealt with the always contentious matter of women members: it was generally thought unsuitable, even dangerous, for them to attend debates. Joyce doubtless agreed. As he found that women praying in church put him off his own devotions, he is unlikely to have desired their presence at the discussion of intellectual matters. He still preferred male company.

By now Joyce was pursuing a more intensive course of reading. We know for certain that he was reading Ibsen's *Bygmyster Solness* (*The Master Builder*) – as mentioned earlier – and *Nar Vi Dode Vagnar* (*When We Dead Awaken*), in their original Dano-Norwegian; also Tolstoy's *The Fruits of Enlightenment*, and that on 7th May he bought Colonel Olcott's *Theosophical Studies*. This indeed seems to have been his year for occult and Buddhist inquiries, but again these topics (we must recall) were interests widely shared in Dublin intellectual life of the period, dominated as it was by Yeats and

George Russell and others with transcendental and arcane connections. Joyce had still not strayed far from the milieu of Dublin thought.

Further fruits of a different kind of enlightenment appeared on 1st June in the form of the first issue of *St Stephen's*, a new college paper which was to have a brief career of great distinction. This was edited by a group of students, but the classics professor, Father Henry Browne, as Dean of Residence, acted as a censor to the copy.

On 16th June Joyce attended a meeting of the Literary Conference, an offshoot of the Sodality in University College. The matter under discussion was Canon Patrick Sheehan's novel *My New Curate* (1899), an important and admired novel, but not one which Joyce would have found congenial in its espousal of rural virtues and nationalist values, even though it was set in the area from which his own ancestors came in Co. Cork. Yet Sheehan had at that date an international reputation (this novel alone was translated into at least nine foreign languages), and was indisputably the most popular Irish novelist of the day. If Joyce rejected Sheehan, he would still have had to come to terms with his work. The book saw the rural parish it described as a centre of paralysis, or at the very least inertia, with which the young, modern-minded priest of the title has little patience. The meeting was chaired by Father Henry Browne.

That summer Joyce had further experiences of the rural Ireland the Cork Canon described so well, when he passed July and August with his father in Mullingar for a second year. While John Joyce applied himself to the voters' lists – doubtless a congenial task, requiring many visits to public houses and drinks in front parlours – his son worked. This time Joyce devoted himself to translating Gerhart Hauptmann's play *Vor Sonnenaufgang* under the title of *Before Sunrise*. He completed his version (in a school copybook on which one of his little sisters later scrawled a huge chicken and a lopsided kangaroo) on 23rd July. He also translated Hauptmann's most recent drama *Michael Kramer* in August. An ambition to have these presented by Yeats's new theatre group was in due course frustrated by the poet's indifference to the excitements of contemporary European theatre.

These visits to Mullingar provided Joyce with experiences which he was later to use in *Stephen Hero*. Here he placed the home of Stephen's godfather Mr Fulham, who knows Mr Tate, the English master at Belvedere, and who is paying Stephen's college fees. Here

Stephen encounters Miss Howard, another of those Joycean young women who attract yet dismiss the admiration of men, but the account of these visits is largely lost and the pages that survive provide only a glimpse of what must have been (for Joyce) a social chapter of importance. The small town, with its landed gentry, Catholic and Protestant, its clergy and shopkeepers, its doctors and British officers, its frustrated journalists and deranged peasants, was all fresh and novel to the young man's eye. But the mature artist, seeking to unify the novel, ruthlessly removed them. Mere local colour had to give to the growth of the poet's soul. What remains provides a glimpse of Joyce under Hauptmann's influence as a social critic of intolerable conditions. The myths about Ireland provided by the Revival and by Canon Sheehan did not stand up to scrutiny on the spot.

*

The results of Joyce's Second University Examination, which he had sat in the third week of June, were disappointing. Latin (1,200 marks), 353; English (900 marks), 313; French (900 marks), 489; Italian (900 marks), 295; Logic (900 marks), 240. His marks in Italian and Logic were below standard, but he was awarded a pass for his answering as a whole. These results must have been humiliating for Joyce, and *Stephen Hero* describes a domestic row over the matter, with the father raving at the son's idleness. Stephen (like Joyce) had spent the year 'thinking'. It was to be hoped that the coming year would provide better results. As it stood, James Joyce was a far from distinguished student.

In October 1901 Joyce began his last year at college, taking English, French and Italian for the B.A. Honours course. The English course was long enough, with some sixteen texts of various periods from Sweet's Anglo-Saxon primer to Byron in Matthew Arnold's selection. The French course was a mere ten texts, though the Italian with Dante's *Purgatio* and Tasso's *Gerusalemme Liberata* must have seemed more interesting. It was not a heavy work-load, but Joyce seems not to have overburdened himself with it.

In September he had sent his collection of poems to William Archer for his appraisal. Archer, kindly critic as ever, suggested that he should not think of publishing them. This was at the end of September, but by then Joyce had entered into a great college contro-versy. He had written a paper attacking the Irish Theatre movement,

'The Day of the Rabblement', which was too outspoken and was refused publication in *St Stephen's* by the censor Father Henry Browne. He also refused to sanction a paper by Frank Skeffington on the question of women at the University, for that young feminist 'A Forgotten Aspect of the University Question'. Joyce and Skeffington, finding the Rector refused to aid them by revoking the edict of censorship, decided to publish the papers themselves, and they appeared in a pink wrapped pamphlet on 21st October. This enterprise cost them 10 guineas (a year's fees) at Gerrard's, the printers on the other side of the Green. The costs suggest that some 1,200 copies may have been printed, more than enough to go round the student body, but this is uncertain as the price recalled years later by one of the partners in the firm seems exaggerated. For the first time Joyce's name appeared on a formal publication: for both the authors it was a landmark in their lives. Joyce was paying attention to such pamphlet works and would have read one by John F. Taylor defending the Irish language, a record of an address given to the law students of the university, which is mentioned in *Ulysses* and which came out on 24th October 1901.

That autumn the Joyces moved to 32 Glengarriff Parade, one of a set of small working-class streets off the North Circular Road, in the shadow of Mountjoy Gaol. The significance of this address is that it is the one which appears after Joyce's name in the manuscript records of the College Sodality. This body had had a chequered history but was now on a sounder footing. Joyce seems to have been a member of it since he entered University College, and remained one up to 1902. He had, of course, been a member of the same Sodality in Belvedere, as had his brothers Stanislaus and Charles; indeed Stanislaus was president in his turn at this period. What level of spiritual devotion this implies on Joyce's part is difficult to say, as habit often plays a large part in the religious life of Irishmen; and Joyce's own versions of his college years suggest that his unbelief was well established. Yet the College Sodality was a voluntary body, only a small number of students were members and not all of those attended constantly.

Joyce also attended several more meetings of the Sodality's Literary Conference, speaking to the paper. In the autumn of 1901 yet another college group was created with the inauguration of the Academy of St Thomas Aquinas on 27th November. This was a purely philosophical group, and again Joyce attended and contributed to several discussions, all of which were of a serious and academic nature.

Despite the tendencies of his mind and imagination at this date, it seems that James Joyce was still more or less a practising Catholic. His reading was continuing to take him in another direction, however: W.M. Adams, *The House of the Hidden Places*, about esoteric Egyptian religion; the essays and poems of James Clarence Mangan; *John Sherman* by Yeats, and (as indicated earlier) Paul Verlaine's *Les Poètes Maudits*, and finally Fogazzaro's *Piccolo Mondo Antico* (though this was on his Italian course).

The drug-addicted Romantic Mangan was the main interest. On 1st February he read a long-prepared paper to the L. and H.; George Moore had been invited to preside on this occasion, but refused. Though received with interest and respect, Joyce's paper aroused Hugh Kennedy to a fierce rebuttal of some of Joyce's ideas, for Mangan was one of the few Irish poets widely read by those who had little deep interest in literature. For Joyce, Mangan was a poet who addressed the deepest of human feelings, he was not merely the author of Nationalist sentiments about forsaken Ireland. John Joyce was a witness to this, and Jim's cool handling of the opposition must have made him think that his son had the making of a lawyer. Kennedy himself rose to be Chief Justice of Ireland.

The next day was Joyce's twentieth birthday. He chose to go and hear his friend Byrne give a talk on Thomas à Kempis to the Literary Conference – here again is an anomaly. Byrne was later to claim that he had been a free-thinker since the age of 14; Joyce too was to suggest that his own lapse from faith had occurred at the end of his schooldays. But the evidence indicates otherwise. For all intents and purposes (as the lawyers would say) both were still Catholics.

During March there was a paper read before the L. and H. by Father Sutton on his theories about Sir Francis Bacon (part of whose *Advancement of Learning* Joyce was reading for his course) being the author of the plays ascribed to 'William Shakespear'. These theories were duly to find their own small place in *Ulysses*, though at the time Joyce crowed with delight at what he thought were the good Jesuit's absurdities.

However, there were few other occasions for laughter in the coming months. On 13th March his young brother George fell ill with enteric fever, or typhoid, doubtless contracted from the impoverished conditions in which the family was living. His sickness was long-drawn-out, though at first it was thought all would be well.

That year Easter Sunday fell on 30th March. *A Portrait* suggests that Joyce refused to make his Easter duty, an annual obligation of Catholics on pain of mortal sin, despite a row with his mother; a more detailed account is given in *Stephen Hero*. Joyce would no longer imitate Christ as he had in his youth. His mother may have hoped for a change of heart in a son now much altered from the one she had reared.

Coming to the end of his studies in April, he signed on at the medical school to begin a medical course in the autumn. But already in his mother's eyes he was something of a doctor. On 25th April George grew worse: his mother came running in to Joyce incoherent with fear, speaking of something coming away from the boy's bowels. He had been improving, but the doctor had foolishly allowed his mother to give him solid food (quite contrary to accepted practice), and he suffered an intestinal perforation. This led to peritonitis, and on 3rd May George died at Glengarriff Parade. He was 14 years old.

The child was buried in the family grave at Glasnevin on 5th May; as was customary then, his mother and sisters did not attend. Returning from the funeral the party turned into one of the pubs on the Finglas Road, where Joyce asked his uncle William for stout. His father was shocked and surprised: 'Who taught you to drink stout?' he asked querulously.

Until now it is likely that Joyce drank little, if at all; from now on, however, alcohol would never be completely absent from his life. His brother's death profoundly affected him. The death of an infant or a miscarriage, those could be explained. But the death of a charming and clever young man seemed to question all that the Church taught of God's goodness and love of His creation. Whatever the priests might say, a life of great promise had been crushed by a chance of nature.

One of Joyce's rare epiphanies described his death: 'They are all asleep. I will go up now. . . . He lies on my bed where I lay last night: they have covered his eyes with pennies. . . . Poor little fellow! We have often laughed together – he bore his body very lightly . . . I am sorry he died. I cannot pray for him as the others do. . . . Poor little fellow! Everything else is so uncertain.'

The publication of his essay 'James Clarence Mangan' in *St Stephen's* in May and the interest it aroused cannot have completely assuaged the real grief Joyce felt. What Mangan had written of his own family's decline into poverty would have made it all the worse, for the same fate was overwhelming the Joyces. He quoted Mangan's phrase at the top of his paper, 'Memorial would I have . . . a constant presence with those that love me.' Joyce would always have a memory for the dead.

Whitsun passed and Trinity Sunday, 25th May 1902, was the last day on which a Catholic could canonically make his Easter duty. Failing to do so, James Joyce ceased to be a Catholic in the full sense. His brother's dismal death had, I suspect, been the last straw. His mother was naturally dismayed, as was his aunt Josephine Murray who later argued with him about his unbelief. Once he sat quaking in her kitchen while thunder rolled. Why was he afraid, if he didn't believe in God? On another occasion she asked him if he believed in a Supreme Being. He said he did and she was satisfied. But the nature of the Supreme Being was never queried. In his childhood his religious devotion had been centred on the Virgin Mary, rather than God the Father. He was not for Joyce a God of Love, but the God of Wrath, the God of Francis Danby's apocalyptic painting to which Mrs Conway had introduced him so many years ago. Now all that he felt for God was a mixture of fear and anger, and deep personal resentment.

*

That summer Joyce left University College. There remained only the examination for the Honours Degree in the autumn and the presentation of degrees in October. He now set out to explore literary Dublin and on Monday 18th August went out to see George Russell, the poet AE, in his house in Garville Avenue in distant Rathgar, arriving at nearly midnight. Their encounter, which began uneasily, soon became a topic of Dublin gossip. For Joyce told Russell that he would never be a real poet as he had not enough chaos in him. He spoke then, as he would later, in disparaging terms of Yeats – whom he believed was past developing; it was a pity they had not met early enough for Joyce to be of help to him. These stories entered the literary folklore of Dublin – as Joyce must have hoped they would – and Russell was still relating them in 1919 to Joseph Holloway, who thought on hearing them that 'Joyce at the time was the studied essence of conceit'.

(Russell's road led into Brighton Square and it would have been unlike Joyce even past midnight not to have looked again at his natal place even as he started out on his literary career. Birth and rebirth: all things, all places were symbolic for Joyce.)

But literature demanded some matter from life; that autumn John Joyce was inveigled by some of his friends into attending a triduum at the Jesuit church in Gardiner Street which was for businessmen, men of the world like themselves. This rare religious observance by his father was to provide Joyce with the germ of his story 'Grace' in *Dubliners*. Here were the elements of real life which he would eventually be able to make use of, but which now seemed only to provide his brother and himself with ribald amusement.

On 2nd October Joyce signed up to begin his actual classes at St Cecilia's, the Catholic medical school affiliated to University College, along with Seamus O'Kelly and J.F. Byrne. Many of his friends from college were now pursuing medical studies, and Joyce on the whole preferred their ready irreverence to the ponderous solemnity of more literary circles. He also remained in contact with Father Charles Ghezzi, the young Italian Jesuit at University with whom he had studied Italian. His interest in Italian culture remained a dominant one in his reading.

That autumn, the Joyces moved to 7 St Peter's Terrace (now 5 St Peter's Road), a newish set of houses off the Cabra Road, beyond the cattle markets. This must have been during September, for on the form he completed and filed on 30th August to sit his finals in October, his old address is heavily crossed out and University College written below as a temporary postal address. This small red-brick house was not rented, for John Joyce had bought it. His pension from the government amounted to £132/2s/4d a year. To buy the house he insured his life with Eagle Star Insurance for £650, and against that he borrowed £550 from the same company. To cover both the premiums on the insurance, and the interest payments on the loan, his pension of £12/6s/3d a month was paid directly to the Eagle Star, who deducted what was due to them and paid him £8 a month by cheque through David Drimmie, an insurance agent in Dublin. The arrival of this cheque would eventually become a day of horror in the Joyce household as it enabled John Joyce to go on a monthly binge from which he would return home deliriously drunk.

On the house itself he now took out another mortgage with a Mr Sheridan, initially for £100 on 24th October, but then for two further sums of £50. Eventually, for what seems to have been non-payment of interest, he was forced to sell the house in 1905. (When he died

179

the insurance money from Eagle Star Insurance fell due, but after his debts had been paid John Joyce left his son James, his only legatee, a mere £32.)

Joyce, free of college and as heedless of his future as his father was of his, was pursuing his literary interests. Early in October he met W. B. Yeats in Nassau Street, and they had several ineffectual conversations. Yeats had already heard about the advent of this new literary personality from Russell. However friendly Yeats would be, Joyce was by instinct and necessity outside his movement

In Yeats's story 'The Tables of the Law', which had been recently reissued and which Joyce greatly admired, he had read of Joachim Abbas. On 22nd October and the following day he went to Marsh's Library, founded in 1702, then a quaint and neglected place in the slum quarter around St Patrick's Cathedral, to read their copy of Joachim's prophecies, or at least those attributed to him. Here the millennial concerns which had darkened his childhood were renewed: indeed, given his imagination it is even believable that he may have thought the world was due to end soon. In one of the dusty bays of the old library, he conned the texts.

Joachim was a visionary Franciscan, who taught that there were three ages in history: the Age of the Father, which related to the Old Testament; the Age of the Son, which related to the New Testament; and the Age of the Holy Spirit, in which the Church as an institution would pass away, and a period of universal love would ensue. It would seem that Joyce, having abandoned the Church as an institution himself, was searching to retrieve something from his old faith. For in this third age there would be no Catholics, only loving, enlightened souls. And doubtless a time of universal love would have appealed to the imagination of a young man.*

*

Joyce began sitting his last college exams on 6th October, and received his degree on 30th October 1902. This was an event of tumult, in which Joyce took a leading part, speaking from the back of a cart. The rudeness of the Nationalist students to the Chancellor of the University was widely reported in the press, with the sort of

* That young artist would not have failed to have noticed on 24th October the release of the Maamtrasna murderers of Joyce family, a case with which Tim Harrington was connected (see p. 58).

sub-headlines that are used in the 'Aeolus' episode of *Ulysses*. Joyce defended the right of the students to make as much noise as they liked.

Conspicuous in public, Joyce must have had private regrets. His degree was only a Pass, though he had sat for the Honours B.A. Each of his subjects was worth 800 marks, but he got only 465 in French, 417 in Italian, and a mere 344 in English. He failed to make the Honours grade, but was granted the Pass, as his marks nearly approached the standard at which Honours were awarded. By now he was already started upon his course of medical studies at the Catholic medical school, but early in November he threw them over. The studious schoolboy who had carried all before him in exams had developed into the 'brilliant student' who now aspired to something higher than mere academic excellence.

The young man who had entered University College in the autumn of 1898 had self-consciously made himself into an artist, but as his attempts at poetry and drama had showed him only too clearly, the artist had yet to find his true subject. Joyce's determination to think what he needed to think, to experience what he needed to experience, to write what he needed to write, was now paramount to any wise advice about a sound profession, or a good position, or a secure future.

His ambition would be best served by leaving Dublin completely. That decision had complicated origins. One reason was the state of life at home; another his feeling of being ill-sorted with his male contemporaries: he felt he was drifting out of touch with them. Yet a third was apparent at the degree ceremony where Joyce, dressed in his black gown and hood lined with rabbit fur, received his Bachelor of Arts degree from the Chancellor of the Royal University, the Marquess of Dufferin and Ava. On that afternoon a degree was also conferred on a Miss M.E. Cleary – the 'Emma Clery' of Joyce's fiction, the missing person of his college years.

PART V

Stephen wished to avenge himself on Irish women who, he says, are the cause of all the moral suicide in the island.

Marginal note on the mss of Stephen Hero

12

Interlude: 'Emma Clery'

Across the pages of Joyce's early fiction there flits the figure of a young lady, in both *A Portrait of the Artist*, where she appears only under the cryptic initials E.C., and in *Stephen Hero*, where her full name is spelled out as Emma Clery.

In the finished novel she is a mere evanescent trace, a slight perfume on the autumn air about the coigns of Kildare Street. In the surviving pages of the draft, however, she is a more substantial person. Indeed, the crucial scene (which led to the book being banned in Ireland for a period) where Stephen Dedalus attempts to seduce Emma, was, so Joyce himself thought in the summer of 1905, 'a remarkable piece of writing'. Like so many scenes in his fiction, it was taken essentially from life.

'One raw misty morning after Christmas', a little after half-past ten, Stephen is taking his Italian class, Machiavelli's *History of Florence* with Father Artifoni, when he sees Emma pass along the path beside Stephen's Green. Leaving his tutor of a sudden, he runs after her, catching up with her outside the Royal University in Earlsfort Terrace. She explains that she is making her way to Leeson Park (which for Joyce seems to epitomize the acme of bourgeois respectability), and he walks with her.

He begins by explaining himself. He lives such a strange life – without help or sympathy from anyone. Sometimes he was afraid of himself – elsewhere he has told Cranly of a moment when he nearly threw himself from Howth Head on to the sea-washed rocks below. Having avoided real suicide, he was now about to commit moral suicide. The people in University College he called not men but vegetables. He had been delighted to see her, striding through the decaying city in the pride of her flesh, proud of being young and being a woman:

> There was no use in her essaying indifference now. Her cheeks were covered with a persistent flush and her eyes shone like gems. She gazed straight before her and her breath began to be agitated. They stood together in the deserted street and he continued speaking, a certain ingenuous disattachment guiding his excited passion.
>
> – I felt that I longed to hold you in my arms – your body. That's all ... Then I thought I would run after you and say that to you ... Just to live one night together, Emma, and then to say goodbye in the morning and never see each other again! There is no such thing as love in the world: only people [who] are young ...

Emma exclaims that he must be mad and breaks away from him. He has directly expressed his real feelings, not what convention dictates he should say, and she is shocked. She does not understand this new language and he explains again:

> Tonight when you are going to bed remember me and go to your window. I will be in the garden. Open the window and call my name and ask me to come in. Then come down and let me in. We will live together and in the morning we will say goodbye.

As Joyce said, it is a remarkable piece of writing, given the place and the time, a passage designed deliberately to shock. Stephen refuses to acknowledge the custom of state and nation with regard to marriage. He sees it as simony, the selling of holy things for money, to which he would not conform.

Emma Clery is very different from other women in Joyce's work. And just as Nora Joyce has been taken (in a somewhat simplistic way) to be Molly Bloom, so inevitably the real-life identity of Emma Clery has been sought. Since so many of Joyce's characters were in fact drawn from life, it was not unreasonable to assume that she too was drawn from a girl in Dublin whom Joyce had known in his college years. Patricia Hutchins – in her pioneering explorations of Joyce's world in the early 1950s – wondered if the original might not even then have been alive in Dublin.

Richard Ellmann, following a suggestion made by Stanislaus Joyce, identified her with Mary, one of the Sheehy sisters, later the wife of Thomas Kettle. But he had to admit that 'in later life Mrs Kettle was surprised to learn that Joyce had a liking for her, and she [could] remember no signs of it'; she 'declined the honour' of the identification he proposed. Ellmann had to conclude that 'Joyce invented most of the romantic episodes in his novels'.

This does not seem to be the case, for there should have been little mystery about Emma Clery. We know she is a student at University College, entered for a degree of the Royal University, that she reads in the National Library, and that she is a person of both handsome features and refined manner. Her Catholic sense of propriety is easily shocked, she is a nationalist and a Gaelic enthusiast; in her way, she is what Joyce intended her to be – a lady representative of the new Catholic middle class which was to take over the running of the country, both before and after the establishment of the Free State.

Who then *was* Emma Clery?

In the autumn of 1901 women students (many already well advanced in their studies) were first admitted to University College as members of the college proper. The Royal University, as the examining body, was already admitting women to its degrees. Special arrangements had to be made by the Jesuits for these young ladies, including lectures at which they did not have to mix with the male students. But they shared many facilities, including the National Library.

Many of these girls had already been attending university courses at convents in the city, so some were already in their final year. Among the students who took their degrees with Joyce on 30th October 1902 was a small group of ladies, the very first from University College to whom degrees were granted – the pioneer Catholic women graduates. One of them, who took a better degree than Joyce (a 2nd class Honours in Modern Languages) was a Miss M.E. Cleary.

Given Joyce's habits of mind it is easy to see that her initials – which stood for Mary Elizabeth – Emm Eeh, suggested the name Emma; the surname followed the spelling of the name familiar to him from the great Dublin store; or perhaps the form used by his college contemporary Arthur Clery ...

Who was *this* Miss Cleary? And what was her connection with James Joyce?

The only student of that name among Joyce's immediate contemporaries, her name appears not only in the college and university calendars and records, but also in the newspaper reports of the conferring. She is also listed in the register of college students appended to *A Page of Irish History*, the compilation about the troubled history of University College published by the Irish Jesuits in 1930 – long used as an essential source of information about Joyce's college years. Yet till now she has eluded his biographers.

Mary Elizabeth Cleary was born at Gubacrock, Wheathill, near Enniskillen in the Ulster county of Fermanagh, on 5th February 1882. Her father, Francis Cleary, was a Catholic small farmer. The neighbourbood being largely Protestant, the family may possibly have felt the pressure of their neighbours' discrimination; but for impoverished Catholics a way out had been created: education. Her descendants cannot now say where Mary was educated, but presumably it was with the nuns in some Ulster convent. An intelligent girl, her achievements led to her gaining admission to the Loreto College on St Stephen's Green nearby, run by the nuns to take girls through the examinations set by the Royal University. The Intermediate Education and the establishment of the Royal were two moves of great importance not only in the creation of an educated middle class in Ireland, but also in the liberation of Irish women.

Mary Cleary came to Dublin in 1898, and took her Matriculation the following year. She was thus an exact college contemporary of Joyce's. Her academic results during her college years were superior to his: in her Matriculation she won an exhibition with 1st Class Honours in Latin, and 2nd Class Honours in English and French. She achieved similar results in her First and Second University Examinations, and even a 1st class Pass in Physics in the Science and Art Examinations set by the South Kensington Examinations Board. Then in her final B.A. examination in Modern Languages she gained a 2nd Class Honours.

Mary Cleary was not merely a clever lady. She was one of a generation – not only with Joyce but with John Marcus O'Sullivan, Louis J. Walsh, Thomas Kettle, C.P. Curran, Felix Hackett and the Sheehys – whose names are distinguished in the political and academic life of modern Ireland. Mary herself was active along with Curran, Patrick Pearse, William Magennis and other friends in the Catholic Graduates and Undergraduates Association, one of the pressure groups that brought about the eventual establishment of the National University of Ireland in 1909.

She seems to have had early literary ambitions and contributed several pieces to her Loreto College magazine, including articles about the pilgrimage to Lough Derg, and a visit to the Aran islands in 1901. This last piece is illustrated with photographs, showing her wearing a smart, up-to-the-minute outfit as she stands outside an island cottage.

But there were few openings for women graduates in those days, and after leaving college Mary had to fall back on teaching. She went to work in Wales, an experience she disliked, but eventually returned to Dublin. On 16th February 1909 she was married, in the University Church beside Newman House on St Stephen's Green, to James Nahor Meenan.

Her husband was a very distinguished physician, and their family is still prominent in the Dublin medical world. One of their sons, James Meenan, was Professor of National Economics at UCD (in succession to Thomas Kettle and George O'Brien) and sometime President of the Royal Dublin Society. Mary Meenan remained a member of the Women Graduates Association of the National University until her death.* As Mrs J. N. Meenan, Mary Elizabeth Cleary did not vanish from public view.

Her son Professor James Meenan told me that when *Stephen Hero* was published in 1944 he was struck by the name of Emma Clery, and wondered about a possible connection with his mother. By then, however, Mrs Meenan had grown reluctant to talk about the past. So much of the idealism of her generation of Irish nationalists had been wasted in the bitterness of the Civil War which followed on the brief War of Independence that she could no longer associate herself with the enthusiasms of her younger self, not even with the Irish language. University College at the turn of the century was a subject she avoided.

She admitted she had known James Joyce, of course, but had found him to be a common, vulgar person. In conversation with her daughter-in-law she went further; Joyce, she admitted, 'had been keen on her'. Asked why, if that was the case, they had not married, she said she could not have married James Joyce. Not merely was he vulgar, he also told dirty stories and picked his nose.

In these comments we can recognize the pained reactions of a young woman of the period to the excessive, deliberate desire to shock so typical of the young Joyce and his *alter ego* Stephen Dedalus; also the reaction of his generation in Ireland to his literary work as it began to appear. We can also recognize, perhaps, the response

---

* She died in 1962, her husband having predeceased her in 1950.

of Emma Clery to Stephen Dedalus in that scene in *Stephen Hero.*

Mary Cleary is recalled now by her family and friends as a person of taste and refinement. That she was also conservative and puritanical in her outlook should not surprise us; she was at one with her generation and her class. James Joyce had been born and educated in more or less the same class, and could (like Richard Rowan, the returned poet in *Exiles*) have claimed the chair of Romance Languages in the National University. But he broke with his generation, and something of the emotions he felt in exile against his contemporaries – then busily advancing themselves in the new emerging Ireland – went into his portrayal of Emma Clery in his novels. By the time he completed *A Portrait* in 1916, he had mellowed; hence Emma at the end of that novel is seen in a different, almost nostalgic light. The parallels between the model and the finished portrait are clear. Already many echoes may well have struck the minds of those familiar with the details of the novels.

In *Stephen Hero* Dedalus is drawn to membership of the Gaelic League in 1900 by his interest in Emma Clery. Mary Cleary was a member of the Central branch of the League, whose headquarters in O'Connell Street are described in the novel with the minuteness of personal observation. His biographers have always written of his association with the League's college branch, asserting that his involvement was short-lived. However, the official Census form for 1901 which John Joyce completed in his own hand (another official document which Richard Ellmann overlooked), he notes that James and Stanislaus both spoke and wrote Irish – which they did not learn at school, but in the Gaelic League. Moreover, *An Claidheamh Soluis*, the paper of the language movement edited by Patrick Pearse, reported in its issue for 2nd June 1900 a meeting in Dublin on 17th May to support the League's demand for recognition of 'Irish nationality' in all grades of Irish education. The article mentions the presence of James Joyce and his friend John Francis Byrne, among other university people. Father Darlington, the Dean of Studies, was also there. This fact alone would suggest an element of interest in the activities of the Gaelic League on Joyce's part far beyond what has been previously accepted.

When Emma Clery emerges from the National Library she had been studying ancient Irish; a surviving book review by Mary Elizabeth Cleary deals with a version in modern Irish of the *Three Sorrows of Storytelling*, one of the ancient Irish classics. Emma, like Mary Cleary, writes for her convent magazine and knows the young people who write for *St Stephen's*. Mary, like Miss Ivors in 'The Dead', had visited the Aran islands and heartily recommends them to others; Emma in *Stephen Hero* is reported as having just gone there. It was details like these which led C.P. Curran, friend of both James Joyce and the Meenans, to note in his Joyce manuscript notebook (as I discovered after talking to Professor Meenan) the equation between Emma and 'M.E.C.', under which initials he too was hiding the identity of his and Joyce's friend.

In the surviving photos of Mary Cleary on Aran, her companion has been identified for me as Maire de Paor, otherwise Mary Wyse Power, the daughter of John Wyse Power. As John Wyse Nolan he appears in *Ulysses*, in which his wife's shop in Henry Street is also mentioned. Joyce was on very friendly terms with her father; in *Gas from a Burner* he recalls himself on his last visit to Dublin.

> Spouting Italian by the hour
> With O'Leary Curtis and John Wyse Power.

John Wyse Power receives only fleeting notice (one passing reference) in Professor Ellmann's biography. He was another member of that web of friends, of which little record now survives, who surrounded the young Joyce.

To return to an earlier point – Stanislaus Joyce's notion that Emma Clery was based on Mary Sheehy – this theory has little to support it. As his own writings show, Stanislaus did not share his brother's college life and knew very little about what went on around Newman House. I surmise that he knew that James was interested in a girl named Mary, and casting about in the special circle they did share, on the north side of the city, he picked upon Mary Sheehy, whom he knew from many visits to the Sheehy home in Belvedere Place. Moreover, to explain Emma Clery's (and Miss Ivor's) Gaelic enthusiasms, something of Kathleen Sheehy* was added to the mix. This is all too complicated to be convincing, though Joyce undoubtedly picked points from many people to make up the complete characters he was creating. How reliable in any case is Stanislaus Joyce? It is certainly odd that among the many brisk revelations he

---

* Later to become Mrs Francis Cruise O'Brien, mother of the diplomat and writer Conor Cruise O'Brien.

makes about himself, we hear nothing of his interest in Gaelic, just as we hear nothing of his being prefect of the Sodality at Belvedere. Stephen specifically does not tell his brother Maurice about his contretemps with Emma, 'because he had still the elder brother's wish to appear successful'.

The total character of Emma Clery also drew in part on Eileen Vance and on one of the daughters of Mat Dillon for her apparitions. And though the persona of Mary Elizabeth Cleary was the main armature around which the character was created, yet others also may be wound into the final form.

A long walk which Emma and Stephen take one evening, through the city from the Gaelic League quarters in O'Connell Street, ends on Portobello Bridge in Rathmines. We are told that the girl entered 'the fourth house in the terrace'. Then living at 48 Grove Terrace, the fourth house, was Thomas H. Justice, a commercial traveller from Co. Cork, and his family: the only people of their name in Dublin then. They had come from Cork in 1898 and were related to the Justices of Millstreet, and so a connection of the Joyces'. The family was small for that time, four boys and two girls; the youngest girl was Elizabeth, 18 in 1901. Joyce's use of the family name for Beatrice Justice, yet another of his virginal figures, shows that he was aware of the connection. Here too is another example of relationships known to Joyce which have remained unknown to us until now. Among the daughters of the Justice family he may have had in mind Elizabeth, who died in 1912.

The eldest Justice girl, Catherine, married in 1905 a well-known Dublin tenor Augustine C. Boylan, known as Gus Boylan, who worked as a master cooper in the Guinness brewery. He had won the tenor prize at the Feis Ceoil in 1901, and in 1904 the Marchant medal at the Royal Irish Academy of Music. He was associated with the Palestrina Choir at the Pro-Cathedral and, like Joyce, had sung with John McCormack. Joyce certainly must have known him, and perhaps he contributed something to the character of Blazes Boylan in *Ulysses*.

*

In the autumn of 1902 Joyce signed on as a medical student at the Catholic medical school in Cecilia Street. This development was duly reported to the wider student body in 'Notes from the Medical School' in the college magazine *St Stephen's*:

Much pleasure was occasioned at the medical school when it became known (for how could it have been unknown when it was a secret) that Messers J.F. Byrne, Seamus O'Kelly and Joyce intend to join the ranks of Cecilia Street. The veterans who are now in the last lap of their courses, look forward to their keeping the old flag flying during their time at the school.

The article was signed with the initials of James Nahor Meenan.

*

By that remarkable piece of writing in *Stephen Hero* Joyce was attempting no mere literary *tour de force*. The purpose of the scene is to show the attempted seduction by the Artist (with his amoral values) of a Virgin daughter reared in the strict conventions of the society whose moral values he has rejected. Emma and that same society, in turn, reject him with finality. Stephen's seduction of innocence fails:

—You are mad, I think, she said, brushing past him swiftly without taking any notice of his salute. She did not go quickly enough, however, to hide the tears that were in her eyes and he, surprised to see them and wondering at their cause, forgot to say the goodbye that was on his lips. As he watched her walk onward swiftly with her head slightly bowed he seemed to feel her soul and his falling asunder swiftly and for ever after an instant of all but union.

Stephen Dedalus was now placed, symbolically at least, without the pale of respectable Dublin life. And there too, by the autumn of 1902, was Joyce himself.

PART VI

'A te convien tenere altro viaggio,'
ripose, poi che lagrimar mi vide,
'se vuoi campar d'esto loco selvaggio ...'

Dante, *Inferno* (Canto I, 91–93)

13

FAUBOURG ST PATRICE

aris was a crucial experience in Joyce's development. Across the manuscript of *Stephen Hero* he would eventually write in red crayon, 'Departure for Paris', to provide him with a new conclusion for his revision of the novel. When he came to rewrite the book he incorporated here an earlier epiphany of flight, the spell of arms and of voices calling him to leave Ireland, and ended the novel with Stephen's going into exile, leaving what remained of the earlier book in abeyance.

Life was, as always, different. After only a few lectures, Joyce decided in October 1902 to abandon his medical studies at St Cecilia's in Dublin. In any case he had no money to pay the fees. He told Lady Gregory that the college authorities would not provide him with the tutoring work which would have enabled him to pay his way. As his brother claimed he had rejected advances from the university to lecture because he feared the consequences of such an entanglement, Joyce seems anxious to detect a plot against him where there may have been only a natural reaction to a difficult-to-please personality. The Jesuits provided George Clancy, for example, with a post in Clongowes, and Francis Skeffington (already a controversial personality in Dublin) with a position in the college. Many of those whom he had joined in St Cecilia's were old friends, and succeeded in doing what he planned to do – establishing themselves as successful doctors in Dublin and in the country. But Joyce could not stay the course.

Instead he decided he would go abroad, to Paris. There he would study medicine and write, in greater freedom than at home. Or so he hoped. He wrote to the Faculty of Medicine in Paris and was informed that applications from foreigners to study were dealt with by the Ministry of Education. To settle the matter it would be easier to be in Paris.

To go abroad he would have to raise his fare and he appealed first to George Russell, who thought that Yeats and Lady Gregory might be able to help. George Moore – in one of his bad moods – refused to assist, so Russell told Joyce: his friends in Paris would only wonder why he had sent them a writer and not a painter*. Maud Gonne – then married to Major John MacBride and living in Paris – would be a better friend, Russell thought. She had many connections in right-wing circles in Paris, and ought to have been able to provide Joyce with some useful openings.

Towards the end of November, only weeks after he had received his degree, Joyce wrote to Lady Gregory asking her aid in going to Paris:

I want to achieve a degree in medicine, for then I can build up my work securely. I want to achieve myself – little or great as I may be – for I know that there is no heresy or no philosophy which is so abhorrent to my church as a human being.

His nature chafed against the social and religious conventions of Dublin. He was uncertain about his future in Paris, but it could hardly be worse than it was in Dublin:

I am not despondent however because I know that even if I fail to make my way such failure proves very little. I shall try myself against the powers of the world. All things are inconstant except the faith of the soul, which changes all things and fills their inconstancy with light. And though I seem to have been driven out of my country here as an unbeliever I have found no man with a faith like mine.

Lady Gregory did more than provide him with money: she was prepared to help him, though she wondered why he did not try Trinity College. She failed to realize that Joyce fully shared the disdain of many national-minded Catholics for Trinity – that 'dull stone set in the ring of the city': he was not without his irrational prejudices. Through her he contacted Colonel Longworth of the

* Joyce retained a resentment against Moore for this – the same Moore who had thought his Ibsen essay 'preposterously clever', while admiring and learning from his books.

Dublin *Daily Express*, who offered him regular reviewing. She also contacted Yeats and arranged with him to feed and cosset Joyce on his way through London, and her London friend Dr Maclagan provided a letter to a Parisian medical man, Dr Rivière.

Also she introduced him to J.M. Synge. Synge had decided he would give up Paris, for he was following Yeats's advice and returning to the peasant life of the west of Ireland for his themes. However, he had advice for Joyce. When in Paris first he had lived in the Hotel Corneille, where generations of students have found lodgings; this he recommended to Joyce as cheap and convenient.

Joyce also wrote to William Archer in London. He, too, thought that Joyce was making a mistake, that his idea of living by teaching English was almost certainly futile and could not be combined with medical studies. From that old friend of John Kelly, Timothy Harrington – who was Lord Mayor of Dublin that year – he obtained a letter of introduction on the letterhead of the Mansion House, which was impressive but largely useless.

On 1st December he wrote again to Lady Gregory, who sent him £5. With money and support from other friends, he departed for Paris by way of London on 2nd December. He was met at the station at 6.30 by Yeats, who gave him breakfast and a couch to sleep off the effects of the journey.

The hope was that with some journalism to do Joyce might be able to pay his way in Paris. They had no luck at the editorial offices they visited, but Yeats promised introductions to C. Lewis Hind of *The Academy* and said, too, that he would speak later to the Parnellite R. Barry O'Brien, the editor of *The Speaker*. Joyce also called on his father's O'Connell cousin, Bill O'Connell's son William, who was away.

In the evening Yeats took Joyce to visit Arthur Symons, then living in a flat at Lauderdale Mansions in Maida Vale. This was not where he had once entertained Verlaine, but there was a piano (a Broadwood grand designed by Burne-Jones) and on this the poet played while Joyce and Yeats sat and listened. Symons later said that Joyce at this time 'seemed to me a curious mixture of sinister genius and uncertain talent'. Joyce may not have cared for what Symons stood for, for the *Yellow Book* period, so many of whose poets had cleaved to the Catholicism he was rejecting. Yet Joyce had with him the poems of *Chamber Music* which Symons was to help him have published.

Before departure he obtained from Yeats a letter introducing him to Maud Gonne. He then left Victoria for Paris by way of Newhaven and Dieppe. The train from the port passed through Rouen, the countryside of which was familiar to him from the bleak pages of *Madame Bovary* and 'A Simple Heart'.

On 3rd December Joyce arrived at the Gare St Lazaire in Paris, and as Synge had advised, he crossed the city to the Left Bank and took a small room at the Grand Hotel Corneille,* which was near the Odéon at 5 rue Corneille, on the corner with the rue Vaugirard. He arranged on the meagre shelves his 'new second-hand clothes' and collection of notebooks. Here would be his home for the months to come.

That night he dined (seven courses, he reported to his father for the benefit of his mother) with Dr Jacques Rivière, taking up the introduction provided by Dr Maclagan. The food was worth the trouble he had in effectively parrying the doctor's inquiries about his London friend whom Joyce had not met.

The next day, 4th December, he had to attend to the matter of his medical studies. He wrote to the Minister of Education to obtain a dispensation as a foreigner not having the essential *baccalauréate* (the French leaving certificate). Calling at the Ministry, he was told on 6th December that he would obtain this easily in a few days. He saw Dr Brouadel at the faculty, who gave him a provisional card to attend lectures in physics, chemistry and biology at the medical school. These he only attended once. He had understood that fees were not payable in advance and made preparations to catch up on the work – even buying an alarm clock to get him up in the mornings. But as in Dublin, he soon abandoned his medical studies, for the French authorities would not recognize his Dublin degree. This now left him the option of surviving in Paris on what he could earn by his writings.

His expenses were not high. He could breakfast, in the French style, for the equivalent of 3d; lunch at midday for 8d or 9d (three courses and coffee); and dine (four courses and coffee) for 1/-. As the weather was cold he found he had to drink coffee (again in the French style, black with sugar) during the day.

* In 1840 Thackeray had observed in his *Paris Sketch-Book*, 'If you are a poor student come to study the humanities, or the pleasant art of amputation, cross the river forthwith, and proceed to the Hotel Corneille, near the Odéon.' The hotel then cost only 4 francs a day.

The mainstay of his finances were the reviews he was doing for the *Daily Express* in Dublin. On 11th December his first review, dealing with George Meredith and William Rooney, appeared. Meredith he had admired; Rooney he could raise no enthusiasm for, considering that he represented mere nationalism in poetry. He wrote postcards on 15th December to his friends Jeff Byrne and Vincent Cosgrave; these were suited to the audiences – one literary, the other scabrous.

Paris was totally different from Dublin in every way:

Paris rawly waking, crude sunlight on her lemon streets. Moist pith of farls of bread, the frog green wormwood, her matin incense, caught the air. Belluomo rises from the bed of his wife's lover's wife, the kerchiefed housewife is astir, a saucer of acetic acid in her hands. In Rodot's Yvonne and Madelaine newmake their tumbled beauties, shattering with gold teeth *chaussons* of pastry, their mouths yellowed with the *pus* of *flan breton*. Faces of Paris men go by, their well-pleased pleasers, curled conquistadores.

Joyce had one real contact in Paris aside from the specious ones garnered by letters of introduction. His father's association with John Kelly's old I.R.B. connections put him in touch with the once notorious Patrick Casey who lived at the foot of Montmartre in rue Goutte-d'Or. Casey appears in *Ulysses* as Kevin Egan, adapted from the name of another old Fenian. He had taken part in the rescue of the Manchester Martyrs in which a policeman was killed, and on 13th December 1867 had been involved with Colonel Burke in the Clerkenwell explosion, when other Fenians (with reckless disregard for life) blew up the walls of the prison in an unsuccessful bid to rescue their comrades.

Like so many of his countrymen Joyce overlooks the consequences of the explosion:

Six persons were killed outright, six more died from its effects. according to the coroner's inquest: five in addition owed their deaths indirectly to this means; one young woman is in a madhouse, 40 mothers were prematurely confined, and 20 of their babies died from the effects of the explosion on the women; others of the children are dwarfed and unhealthy. One mother is now a raving maniac; 120 persons were wounded; 50 went to St Bartholomew's, Gray's Inn lane, and King's College Hospitals, 15 are permanently injured with loss of eyes, legs, arms, &t; besides £20,000 worth of damage to person and property. (*The Times*, 29 April 1868.)

Having fled to Paris, Casey had married a French woman and had a son Patrick. He worked as a typesetter on the *Herald Tribune*, then in offices near the Louvre; and mused on the great days of the Fenians, of their Paris Congress in 1889, from which they had sent a manifesto to Gladstone himself, a brash act which resulted in their leader James Stephens being expelled from France.

Joyce found Casey, as he had found John Kelly, congenial company and they often lunched together, Casey dressed in a sanguine flowered Spanish-style shirt with tassels:

> Noon slumbers. Kevin Egan rolls gunpowder cigarettes through fingers smeared with printer's ink, sipping his green fairy as Patrice his white. About us gobblers fork spiced beans down their gullets. *Un demi setier!* A jet of coffee steam from the burnished caldron. She serves me at his beck. *Il est irlandaise. Hollandaise? Non fromage. Deux Irlandais, nous, Irelande, vous savez? Ah, oui!* She thought you wanted a cheese *hollandaise*. Your postprandial, do you know that word? Postprandial. There was a fellow I knew once in Barcelona, queer fellow, used to call it his postprandial.

They talked too of Scandinavia: Casey had been shocked by the young woman who rubs male nakedness in the bath at Uppsala. She did this for all the men, she said. Not for him. It was a most licentious custom, a bath was a private thing – why, he would not even let his own brother see him in the bath.

Maud Gonne was also discussed, and her former lover the Boulangist journalist Millevoye (the father of her 'niece' Iseult); and Felix Faure whose death had been so disgraceful. They spoke of what Drumont the journalist had called Queen Victoria, the old hag with the yellow teeth. Casey's talk was largely of conspiracies: of the Fenians in the past (his main tale being how James Stephens, the Fenian Head centre, was carried away from Malahide disguised as a bride) and of Arthur Griffith now. 'To yoke me as his yokefellow, our crimes our common cause.' Casey was some time out of Ireland, yet, 'You're your father's son. I know the voice.'

Now another generation had forgotten the Fenian Casey. Only Joyce sought him out. His daily round of the printing case, the three taverns, his lair in Monmartre 'damascened with flyblown faces of the gone'. Joyce had called first on Mrs Casey, now separated from her husband, who kept a lodging-house in rue Git-le-Cour.

He also met Casey's son, who ate his spiced beans and said nothing. Patrice (a rabbit-faced vegetarian) who was a socialist, introduced Joyce to the writings of Leo Texil, a notorious anti-clerical. He would meet Patrice home on leave from the army in the Bar Mac-Mahon, where they drank warm milk. (Black tea with lemon in the Paris style he also liked – a Paris fad, Gogarty thought.) Patrice said his father hoped to win the Grand Lots, the lottery. They talked about sex, for Patrice had read about the nature of women in Michelet. Patrice was a free-thinker, but his father was a believer. Patrice talked too of his studies: at P.C.N. (Physiques, Chimiques et Naturelle). 'Eating your groatsworth of mou en civet, fleshpots of Egypt, elbowed by belching cabmen.' In a tight time, both Caseys would lend Joyce small sums of money.

Joyce's mother was concerned about his life away from home, even to the extent of warning him against not drinking the water. It was mainly to her that he wrote, justifying his attitudes. He was hoping to publish more in the London journals, but meanwhile was investigating teaching at the Berlitz School, and the possibility of giving private lessons. Nothing came of the Berlitz as that was a full-time post, but he found one pupil, Monsieur Douce, and later another. His finances were such that he urged his mother to get a set of false teeth at his expense. She was being troubled by ill-health and put it down to her teeth. Her eyes too troubled her.

He wondered if he should come home for Christmas and his mother, worried about his health, urged him to do so. He felt she failed to understand him.

> My dear Jim etc.
> If you are disappointed in my letter and if as usual I fail to understand what you wish to explain believe me it is not from any want of a longing desire to do so and speak the words you want as you so often said I am stupid and cannot grasp the great thoughts which are yours much as I desire to do so. Do not wear your soul out with tears but be as usually brave and look hopefully to the future ...

There was little enough at home. On 18th December John Joyce took out a mortgage on the house for £50 – some of this was telegraphed to Paris to pay Joyce's fare to Dublin. There he arrived on Christmas Eve. Passing through London on his way home on 23rd December he saw Yeats again.

Arriving at St Peter's Terrace on Christmas Eve, he spent the actual holiday at home, meeting Gogarty and John Eglinton the next day. That season was spent seeing friends, among them Richard Best at the National Library. He only set out to return to Paris on 17th January.

Even then he spent some five days in London (Sunday 18th to Thursday 22nd). He saw C. Lewis Hind, editor of *The Academy*, for books to review and was asked to produce some sample copy. The editor not being satisfied with his work, Joyce prepared to depart. Hind argued with him, but did not like his attitude: after all, he had only to put his head out of the window and find a dozen people to review it. 'What, your head,' said Joyce, in the punch-line to what he would work up as a comic story to disguise his failure to secure Hind's approbation. Yeats was angry with this foolishness. After all, for a young writer it cost little trouble to secure a pittance by such writing, and he had found such money valuable (and still did).

Joyce also saw Dunlop, of a new paper *Men and Women* (which the journalist George R. Sims was editing) and was offered the post of 'writer of literary and dramatic notes in Paris'. He was to send in his copy as soon as possible. (He planned to glean practical and historical details from Grant Allen's *Paris*, his copy of which he had sent from Dublin.) Payment was two guineas a thousand words, far better than *The Academy*.

It was at this time that he stayed in Kennington (on the other side of the river from Victoria station), tasting some London low life with a lady named Eve Leslie who spoke of the client who had come ten times in one night, and of her sister Maude, and Fred ('he's a white-arsed bastard') who were on the stage. Joyce (like many Irishmen) always found the English vulgar.

In further pursuit of low life, he attended a race meeting near London, impressed by the Cockney crowds and the cries of the bookies. This provided him with a rare epiphany of English life, some almost Dickensian images.

Aside from this he also managed to see Lady Gregory, and his O'Connell relation, but failed to find his father's friend Jimmy Tuohy, who, John Joyce thought, might be able to help his son.

On 23rd January he got to Paris. There he wrote his review of

Stephen Gwynn's *Ireland Today and Tomorrow*, which appeared on
29th January. On the afternoon of 24th January, a Saturday, he took
out a six-month reader's ticket at the Bibliothèque Nationale. There
he used to read in the afternoons, while in the evenings he went
instead to the Bibliothèque Geneviève. In one he read Ben Johnson,
in the other Aristotle.

> Aristotle's phrase formed itself within the gabbled verses and floated out
> into the studious silence of the library of Sainte Geneviève where he had
> read, sheltered from the sin of Paris, night by night. By his elbow a
> delicate Siamese conned a handbook of strategy. Fed and feeding brains
> about me: under the glowlamps, impaled with faintly beating feelers: and
> in my mind's darkness a sloth of the underworld, reluctant, shy of
> brightness, shifting her dragon scaly folds. Thought is the thought of
> port. Tranquil brightness. The soul is in a manner all that is: the soul
> is the form of forms. Tranquillity sudden, vast, candescent: form of
> forms.

To reach the Bibliothèque Nationale he had to pass the Paris Bourse:
'On the steps of the Paris Stock Exchange the goldskinned men
quoting prices on their gemmed fingers. Gabbles of geese. They
swarmed loud, uncouth about the temple, their heads thickplotting
under maladroit silk hats.' Joyce was young enough to despise the
appearances of capitalism in action, and even these Jewish businessmen. He thought their efforts to amount a fortune vain: 'Their
eyes knew the years of wandering and, patient, knew the dishonours
of the flesh.'

Other pleasures he merely sampled, having no money to spend in
brothels. Street-walkers ('Punks of the bankside, a penny a time,' as
Ulysses says) had to suffice: '*Cours-la-Reine. Encore vingt sous. Nous
ferons de petites cochoneries. Minette? Tu veux?*' This was the parked
area around the Grand and Petit Palais, then an area of street-
walkers.

But there was also Esther Osvalt. 'But you were delighted when
Esther Osvalt's shoe went on you: girl I knew in Paris. *Tiens, quel
petit pied!*' Her name occurs in the notes for *Stephen Hero*, and we
may suspect that in his original plan, Miss Osvalt was intended to
play a larger part in Joyce's fiction. What her role in his Parisian life
might have been, we may never know.

In Paris on 2nd February Joyce celebrated his twenty-first birthday. He received cards from various members of his family and presents from some of them, with a letter from his father, lamenting his inability to pass on to his son any patrimony other than the specious standards of an Irish gentleman which his own father had given him. That day he took the train to St Cloud; here he enjoyed himself in the park, where as Augustus Hare had observed, middle-class Paris liked nothing better than to enjoy the water playing in the grand cascade. Then he took the river steamer home to the quay beside the Louvre at a cost of 50 centimes. In the evening he went to the theatre. The pleasures of Paris met with his approval more than those of London.

This was a special day, the cost of which would have come out of his pay for the reviews which appeared a few days later in the *Daily Express*. On 8th February he enjoyed a Sarah Bernhardt première, sending an account of it to the *Express* (which did not publish it). Doubtless this was managed on a press pass, perhaps from *Men and Women* (the first issue of which appeared on 14th February.)

His daily routine was now established. Breakfast and the day reading in the Geneviève, dinner and the evening reading in the Bibliothèque. *Ulysses*, however, suggests the other way round. He was reading Ben Jonson, and on 13th February began his first series of aesthetic notes.

All of this would seem cheap enough, but he soon found that he was spending too much and would have to cut back on expenses. In March he writes a long complaint about lack of money, but as usual survives by borrowing from friends.

John Synge arrived in Paris on 6th March, having come over from Dublin to close down his Seine-side flat. He and Joyce were to meet together 'seven or eight times' for lunch during the week he was in the city. Joyce looked up Synge on 8th March – perhaps with the intention of taking him to the carnival at St Cloud. Synge might even buy him dinner. They had many fierce arguments and Joyce read the script of his play, *Riders to the Sea*, which he felt abused the ancient properties of drama. 'Harsh gargoyle face that warred against me over our mess of hash of lights in rue Saint-André-des-Arts. In words of words for words, palabras. Oisin with Patrick.' A meal in this bistro cost 1 franc 10 centimes for five courses, though light must have been the cheapest item on the menu.

Rue Monsieur le Prince through which he walked to his studies brought him thoughts of the meaning of fatherhood and sonhood, of paternity being a legal fiction: 'The unborn mars beauty: born, he brings pain, divides affection, increases care. He is male: his growth is his father's decline, his youth his father's envy, his friend his father's enemy.'

Every Sunday Joyce tried to get out of Paris into the country, and on 15th March he took another trip to Clamart. There Synge had met a drunk with a bottle one Good Friday; Joyce watched only the lizards in the early spring sun. Each had met their image. From there he walked a long way across to Sèvres and took the steamer back into Paris.

He also made several trips to Charenton, and walked in the Bois de Vincennes, where he sat above the confluence of the Seine and the Marne, watching the waters of the rivers mingle. This was a more working-class outing than his other destinations. His most fortunate trip was one he made to Tours, however. He went with Chown, the delicate Siamese student he had met at the Bibliothèque Geneviève, where he was studying manuals of military strategy in preparation for a political career in the Far East. (Chown lent him money, the large sum of 10 francs, perhaps to cover this very trip.) Their purpose was to hear an eminent opera singer perform at the Cathedral. In the railway station at Tours Joyce picked up a copy of a novel, *Les lauriers sont coupées*, by Emile Dujardin. From this then almost forgotten work he gleaned the technique of interior monologue which he was to utilize in *Ulysses*. This was an ironical discovery to make while staying over in a town dominated by a public bronze of Balzac.

Further reviews, of Ibsen and of Lady Gregory, one favourable and one unfavourable, followed. He wrote to Lady Gregory at the end of the month, expecting her to be unaffected. On the day the review appeared, she had heard from Synge, however, about Joyce's condition of life in Paris.

March was devoted to the elaboration of further notes on aesthetics. The time was moving towards Easter and he wrote home for a small devotional booklet in which he could follow the service of Tenebrae on Good Friday in Paris. Holy Week began the next day. On 7th April his interview appeared in the *Irish Times*, for he received the sum of 13/9d on 8th April.

On Good Friday he went to Notre Dame Cathedral to attend the services from midday on, during which the church is draped in purple mourning. The services on Good Friday are the most sombre in the liturgical year, yet for Joyce Tenebrae was the most moving ceremony in the Western Church. This ended at nine in the evening and having no money, he wandered about the city streets until long after lighting-up time, reciting to himself his own poems and epiphanies. He returned to the Grand Hotel Corneille at 11 o'clock; already the streets off the Place de l'Odéon were empty. On entering the hotel, he found a telegram awaiting him. With fear and suspicion he tore it open and read the blue slip on which were pasted down the words of the message: 'MOTHER DYING COME HOME FATHER'.

He was almost at a loss about what he should do. He had no money, none had been sent – but he must find the fare. He had borrowed before from old Patrick Casey, but even if he walked over to rue de la Goutte-d'Or, Casey was unlikely (poor as he was) to have enough cash to cover a ticket to Dublin.

There remained only Joseph Douce, the socialist-minded champagne maker to whom he was giving English lessons. He hurried out of the hotel and made his way to Douce's mansion, but the building was dark, the doors locked. He rang and knocked and at last roused the concierge. Douce came down from bed and came out to Joyce in his nightshirt, his hair tossed from sleep, his blond beard stirring in the evening breeze. He read the telegram, he listened to the young man's urgent pleas – then he produced 75 francs (about £3).

The next morning Joyce bought his ticket at the Gare St Lazaire and left Paris, after telegraphing his father: 'Arrive morning Jim.'

He heard the news of his mother's illness on Good Friday, and on the boat as it left Dieppe on Saturday afternoon he recorded his impression in an ephiphany. As the ferry passed out between the arms of the harbour, he lay on the deck, against the hot engine-house wall from which the smell of lukewarm grease exaled. 'Gigantic mists are marching under the French cliff, enveloping the coast from headland to headland. The sea moves with the sound of many scales . . .' From the cliff above, in the dark cathedral of Notre Dame de Bon Secours, he heard the bright, even voices of boys singing vespers before the altar on this one massless day of the year.

At Newhaven he pretended to be French to avoid tipping the porter as he dragged his single case from the ship to the train. (In the valise he had the blue French telegram, *Le Tutu* and five tattered numbers of *Pantalon Blanc et Culotte Rouge*.) On Sunday morning he landed in Dublin, as the Easter bells rang out along the city streets rejoicing for life renewed by Christ. But for Joyce Bohemia in Paris was over, the last days of careless youth were behind him.

A BOWL OF GREEN BILE

Joyce was met on the quay by his father, who was full of the details about his mother's illness. 'Hurrying to her squalid deathlair from gay Paris on the quayside I touched his hand. The voice, new warmth speaking. Dr Bob Kenny is attending her. The eyes that wish me well. But do not know me.' Dr Kenny, who lived on Rutland Square, was the younger brother of the famous medical M.P. and associate of Parnell, and City Coroner to his death in 1900, Dr Joseph E. Kenny. He was an old friend of John Joyce's and of John Kelly.

Dr Kenny had diagnosed cirrhosis of the liver (though some of the family were left with the impression that the disease was cancer) which is what appears on the death certificate. The disease was well advanced and the good doctor did not give her long. She was amused by the small, smartly turned out man, whom she nicknamed Sir Peter Teazle, from the Sheridan character.

It was some days before Joyce adjusted to the new circumstances, which had come as a severe shock. A second opinion was sought from a Trinity medical man, but he concurred. It was not until the following Saturday, for instance, that he wrote proposing a meeting in Princess Street for 1 o'clock the next day to Jeff Byrne.

Mrs Joyce's illness did not make the financial state of the family any better. To meet the costs of her care John Joyce took out a further £50 mortgage on the house on 24th April. James sent some £3 of this to Monsieur Douce in Paris, accompanied by one of his well-penned letters.

During this trying time, Joyce returned to his literary interests: perhaps reading Samuel Butler's corrosive novel on the Victorian

210

family, *The Way of All Flesh*, which was published in May 1903, the year after the satirist's death. The publisher was Grant Richards, to whom Joyce would in due course turn himself to seek publication. Slowly he picked up the threads of his Dublin friendship with Oliver St John Gogarty, for instance, and made a new one with Colum.

At the beginning of July the city was absorbed in the thrills of the Gordon Bennet motor race which was run on the second of the month. The event (and the hectic social life that surrounded it) provided Joyce with the germ of his short story 'After the Race' into which he introduced some of the characters he had known in Paris. Their feckless idleness reflected his own state of mind, for he was no longer reviewing or even writing much.

On 3rd July the Corporation meeting broke up in disorder after an argument between the Nationalist and Unionist members over the official reception of King Edward on his state visit later that month. This incident was part of the background to another short story, 'Ivy Day in the Committee Room', which drew on his brother's account of the work he and John Joyce had done in the municipal elections earlier in the year while James was in Paris. The Royal visitors were in Dublin between 21st July and 2nd August. Such Royal visits, with their outpourings of loyalist sympathies, may have entertained the mass of Dubliners, but not the Joyces.

Mrs Joyce's life was waning now, although her illness had had a slight remission, and she had been able to get up again for a short time. By her bedside on the table was a china bowl filled with the green bile torn from her rotting liver. James played the piano so that she could hear it, a setting of Yeats's poem, 'Who Goes with Fergus'. Her last days were marked by some grotesque scenes. John Joyce, drunkenly urging her to die, had to be removed by his sons. Then when she passed into a coma their uncle John Murray noticed that neither James nor Stanislaus was kneeling. Ordering them to do so, he was rebuffed. It was not the wish of their dying mother that they should do so, however, she was now beyond consciousness. Such scenes were distressing. It was then that his aunt Josephine Murray asked Joyce whether, if he did not believe in the Church and its claims, did he at least believe in a Supreme Being. He said that he did and she was content with that, but wisely did not press him on his thoughts about that distant and casually vengeful deity.

On 13th August 1903 Mary Jane Joyce died in the front bedroom of 7 St Peter's Terrace. She was buried some days later in Glasnevin in the same grave as her dead children. Years of marriage had removed her from the comfort into which she had been born. An almost annual child had worn her down: of 23 years of marriage, she had spent twelve pregnant. The last decade, since her husband's fall from grace, had destroyed her health.

The mirror in the room was covered at once, not so much out of respect for the dead but from fear: it was thought that the soul, projected out of the living into the mirror, might be carried away by the ghost of the dead, said to linger about the house until the funeral. Joyce and his sister Margaret stayed up that night to see if her ghost returned at midnight. Margaret was convinced that it did. A little later Joyce would consult the newly published book by F. J. Myers, *Human Personality and its Survival of Bodily Death*, when it came into the National Library early in October. The Catholic Church might have lost him, its teachings on the afterlife discarded, but in his own mind he was still uncertain about death and the soul. He would never achieve the easy liberalism about religion characteristic of agnostics: he carried the fear of Hell with him wherever he went. *Ulysses* would eventually be well haunted by the ghosts of Bloom's dead son and Stephen's dead mother. Joyce now had nightmares about his own mother, coming to him wrapped in her grave-clothes.

For Joyce his mother's death was a traumatic event. He tried to comfort his small sisters, distraught at the loss of their mother: Mabel and Florence were not even in their teens yet. He found his parents' love letters and read through them before burning them, telling Stanislaus there was nothing in them. The fragile affections of the past did not, it seems, meet with his sturdy contempt for sentiment. But the death exposed the futility of life. What was left of that kind, even noble woman, except a few gewgaws? It was unsettling.

Fergus song; I sang it alone in the house, holding down the long dark chords. Her door was open: she wanted to hear my music. Silent with awe and pity I went to her bedside. She was crying in her wretched bed. For those words Stephen: love's bitter mystery.

Where now?

Her secrets: old feather fans, tasselled dancecards, powdered with musk, a gaud of amber beads in her locked drawer. A birdcage hung in the sunny window of her house when she was a girl. She heard old Royce sing in the pantomime of Turcko the Terrible and laughed with others when he sang:

> I am the boy
> That can enjoy
> Invisibility.

Phantasmal mirth, folded away: muskperfumed.

> And no more turn aside and brood

Folded away in the memory of nature with her toys. Memories beset his brooding brain. Her glass of water from the kitchen tap when she had approached the sacrament. A cored apple, filled with brown sugar, roasting for her at the hob on a dark autumn evening. Her shapely fingernails reddened by the blood of squashed lice from her children's shirts.

In a dream she had come to him, her wasted body within its loose graveclothes giving off an odour of wax and rosewood, her breath bent over him with mute secret words, a faint odour of wetted ashes.

Her glazing eyes, staring out of death, to shake and bend my soul. On me alone. The ghostcandle to light her agony. Ghostly light on the tortured face. her hoarse loud breath rattling in horror, while all prayed on their knees. Her eyes on me to strike me down. Liliata rutilantium te confessorum turma circumdet: iubilantium te virginum chorus excipiat.

Ghoul! Chewer of corpses!

No mother. Let me be and let me live.

To live was now the true problem facing Joyce. John Joyce was continually drunk; the arrival of the monthly cheque from David Drimmie's only made the state of his temper worse. He was violent and abusive, and the younger girls had to be protected from him. Worse one can imagine: a man of his excessive sexual drive may have tried to comfort himself with his own children, as was so often the case in rural Ireland and the poorer quarters of the city. His younger daughters later recoiled from him, as he himself admitted. Those who have detected a theme of incest in *Finnegans Wake* need look no further than the household of John Stanislaus Joyce in the winter of 1903.

There was no home here for Joyce. Having given up Paris to return to Dublin, he would have to yet again begin his attempt on living his own life at last.

15

STEPHEN DEDALUS

1903–1904

Now that his mother was dead and the house in St Peter's Terrace was no longer a home for him, Joyce may well have moved away, to escape for a time from the Dickensian squalor into which his family was descending. Gorman suggests that he took a series of rooms at this period, on one occasion being observed by a friend carrying his dismantled iron bed to a new letting. And it may have been during this autumn of 1903 that he lodged for a period in 'The Waverly House', the private hotel at 4 Hardwicke Street which was the model for the one he describes with such detailed vividness in his short story 'The Boarding House'.* This seems likely, but there is no exact evidence, and in any case by the beginning of 1904 he had returned to 'Bleak House', as Stanislaus had nicknamed the terraced red-bricked tomb of their family's hopes.

The rent for those rooms would have been managed from the small sums he received for his reviews in the Dublin *Daily Express* through to November. The *Express* was a Conservative paper, widely seen as a mouthpiece for Unionism – as Miss Ivors, the Gaelic-speaking Nationalist, remarks in 'The Dead'. Joyce could defend himself for writing in it – all artists need money – but his own developing political opinions were very different.

Indeed, he told his brother that he was not an artist at that moment. He was interesting himself in politics because it was an area 'in which he says [he has] original ideas'. He was involved in the affairs of a

---

* Stanislaus had a recollection of an earlier stay by the Joyce family at 29 Hardwicke Street, a tenement now demolished, but there is no evidence extant to support this.

small Socialist group that met in rooms above 6 Liffey Street, on the corner with The Lotts, between Abbey Street and the Quays.

This was the Irish Republican Socialist Party, which had been founded in 1896 by James Connolly (in 1913 the creator of the Irish Citizens Army and one of the executed leaders of the Easter Rising in 1916). Joyce never met him, however, as Connolly had just departed for America at the end of August, leaving the Party badly split. The original cause of the dissension had been a bar which the Party had been running on the premises which lost money – perhaps only Socialists could achieve such a feat in Ireland. Funds which Connolly had collected abroad were used to pay off the debts incurred by this detour into capitalism. The appearance of the Party's paper, *Worker's Republic*, was interrupted.

As Joyce suggests in 'A Painful Case', in which Mr Duffy frequents just such a group, he felt himself a unique figure amidst a score of sober workmen in a garret lit by an inefficient oil-lamp (this may have been in their later rooms at 67 Middle Abbey Street). Like Mr Duffy, he must have been dismayed that the question of wages dominated their talk, rather than his 'unique ideas'. The members of the Party (never more than 50, with a hard core of 15 or so) were hard-faced realists and resented (perhaps rightly) his exactitude of mind which was the product of leisure beyond their reach. No social revolution, Joyce thought, would strike Dublin for some centuries; but he was only partly right, for the revolution did come but not in the form he then looked for.

The I.R.S.P., however, fragmented, and the fragments fragmented further. Nevertheless, these working-class activities were the essential core from which the Irish Socialist movement would later rise. From the break-up emerged after March 1904 the Irish Socialist Party, the ancestor of today's Labour Party (founded in 1912). William O'Brien, for instance, a leading figure of the Irish left until recent times, was one of the group. But Joyce, like Mr Duffy, found little in common with men who worked hard to earn their daily bread. Yet in a city divided between the Nationalists (now reunited after the Parnell split) and the Unionists, who actually controlled most of the surrounding townships – both essentially conservative movements – there was a certain quaint novelty in claiming to be a Socialist. Joyce was interested enough to sample (in much the same way that he was then sampling liqueurs) several Socialist thinkers, but never went further than the first page of a borrowed copy of *Das Kapital*. His socialism was lukewarm, his reading superficial, and his enthusiasm short-lived. He could never be the kind of writer whose work conformed directly to a party line on literature; that would merely have been to substitute the central committee for the church. Having fought hard for his freedom he was disinclined to surrender it; the promises of socialism and national liberation would, as with all political promises, prove of more value to those who seized power than to those they governed.

That Joyce was interested in other journalistic outlets is indicated by a piece on Jacques Lebaudy, the infamous French adventurer then attempting to establish a personal fief in North Africa. Such a piece has the appearance not of a letter to the press, but, perhaps, of a second leader for the *Evening Telegraph*.

During September, October and November a series of reviews (all of which have been collected into the volume of his *Critical Writings*) were published, the most pertinent being of a volume on Giordano Bruno, the Florentine philosopher whose fate under the Inquisition had long been one of Joyce's examples of the inevitable excesses of Church power. Joyce admired (as well he might) Bruno's courage, and took from him the philosophical notion of the co-incidence of contraries which underlies *Finnegans Wake*.

His developing interests contrasted with those of his fellow citizens, who held a procession in honour of the centenary of the death of Robert Emmet, yet another ineffectual Irish revolutionary, yet another example that made Joyce think of Dublin as a 'centre of paralysis'. There would be no co-incidence of contraries here.

The expectations of continuing his journalism made him decline an offer from his old friend Frank Skeffington (now Registrar of University College) on 29th September that he might give a few classes in French as temporary lecturer. It was only for three or four days, but Joyce felt that the Jesuits were trying to ensnare him again. Yet Skeffington in his college post was in no way compromised in his far more radical and unpopular ideas. Indeed, his public courage was closer to the admired Bruno's than Joyce's would ever be. Joyce's own character Gabriel Conroy (in 'The Dead') combines college work with journalism, just as Skeffington did. But Joyce refused the college offers, and the reviews for the *Express* soon came to an end.

On 15th October Joyce received a postcard from his old teacher George Dempsey, asking him to call that evening. Joyce went to his home at 13 Dunville Avenue in Ranelagh (the district in which he would set the second act of his play *Exiles*). Dempsey must have had many friends who might have been in a position to help Joyce, but here again is a relationship of importance to Joyce which is still shrouded in mystery, even at this critical point in his life. Dempsey lived above the store which his wife ran, a wine and tea merchant-cum-post-office – much the same sort of establishment as The Eagle House had been. The substance of their talk is not known, but it may well have been a suggestion on Dempsey's part that Joyce with his degree should look around for a teaching post – one which would not compromise him. In Dublin this could only have been in a Protestant school.

Joyce's last review appeared on 19th November. A post as assistant editor of *The Irish Bee Keeper* lasted less than a day, and plans of his own to start a comic paper called *The Goblin* (a rival to the then current *Lepracaun*) came to nothing.

Joyce remained alive to currents of thought in the city. I have discovered one stream that connects his college days with the events of 1904 and the inception of *Ulysses* ten years later, which has been overlooked until now.

At University College, Joyce's Dean of Residence had been Father Henry Browne S.J. As we have seen, Father Browne is now remembered in the Joycean context only as the college censor who rejected his article on the Irish theatre movement. But Browne, I now think, was of far more significance to Joyce than that; it seems to me that he had a profound creative effect.

Professor of Greek at University College (in succession to Gerard Manley Hopkins), Father Browne was a leading authority on Homer. During these years he was at work on a long book which was eventually published in 1905 by the Dublin publisher Browne and Nolan,[*] entitled *Handbook of Homeric Study* – the preface is dated 2nd February, Joyce's birthday. Much of this book had been given as talks and public lectures over the previous three or four years. One in the spring of 1903, for instance, dealt with the theory of Sir William Ridgeway about the Celtic identity of the Homeric Achaeans. This idea (as Stuart Gilbert discloses) was an important one for Joyce's conception of *Ulysses*, by connecting Celtic Dublin with the

---

[*] Browne and Nolan are much referred to in the *Wake*, and were not only the publishers, but also the classical dons at University College, Father Henry Browne and Father T.P. O'Nowlan, as well as being Giordano Bruno of Nola.

Homeric heroes. But there was more. Browne's religious ideas as expressed in his treatment of Greek religion were as advanced as his ideas in other areas. His use of archaeology to illuminate the classical texts is still a controversial approach. If he had applied the same ideas to the Bible or to St Patrick he would have incurred official censure – the fate which befell his Dublin contemporary Father Tyrrell.

More significantly, Father Browne was an early enthusiast for the theories of the French writer Victor Bérard, which held that the origins of the *Odyssey* were basically Semitic and that Phoenician voyages through the Mediterranean provided the context and texture of the epic.

This was an idea he also discussed in and out of University College, a theme with which many students were made familiar. His book, moreover, was illustrated with a large fold-out map showing 'Bérard's Theory of the Wanderings of Odysseus' through the Eastern Mediterranean, on which the titles of the places – Lotus Eaters, Cyclops, Aeolus, Circe's Island, Entrance to Hades, Land of Sirens, Scylla and Charybdis, Calypso, Ithaca – echo those of Joyce's episodes in *Ulysses*. When he arrived in Zürich in 1915 one of Joyce's first acts was to study Bérard's two volumes in detail in the public library there. A reference in Walter Leaf's study of Troy would have reminded him of his earlier encounter with the Frenchman's theories. The impulse in 1915 was not to seek new information, but to renew a pursuit which he had begun in Dublin in 1904. He wished to give his Dubliners the stature of myth, while perhaps reducing figures of myth to the mundane dimensions of his own city's daily round.

So a key book for the inception of *Ulysses* was introduced to Joyce at University College, for it cannot be mere coincidence that the only eminent classical scholar that he knew in 1904 should have been an extreme enthusiast for Bérard's 'brilliant work'.

'The Phoenicians,' Browne also writes, 'were the Semites of the West'; but to discuss their early activities 'is to enter upon the question of the debt that we Aryans owe to a people we are naturally inclined to hate.' *In peto* here we have an important motif of *Ulysses* itself, the clash of Bloom the Wandering Jew with the intolerant Cylopii of Irish Nationalism.

The country had been roused by an outbreak of virulent anti-semitism in Limerick in February, which led to the Catholic

Association (which lay behind it) being denounced from the pulpit by Archbishop Walsh. Rare in some ways in Ireland, anti-semitism existed as a persistent bias, and Joyce would have known this. The troubles had begun the year before when the Royal Irish Constabulary were asked by the Chief Secretary's office to inquire into the truth of rumours that Jews were seizing Irish land from debtor peasants, and that they were collecting tea-leaves from hotels, drying them out, adding chemicals and selling them to poor people. Police inquiries found that there was no foundation to the rumours, and indeed that the Jewish population had fallen nearly everywhere – but not in Limerick. Hatred of Jews lingered. The International Exhibition of 1907 was seen by Sinn Fein as an opportunity to allow foreign Jews into the country to make money from an Irish enterprise, and the party's year book for 1908 carried an advertisement for Cash's Tailor's of Capel Street proudly announcing that there were 'NO JEWS Connected with our Business: Only IRISH Tailors employed'. Such was the background to riots and demonstrations in Limerick which caused international concern – the Chief Secretary received letters from abroad about the matter.

This conjunction lay in the future: meanwhile, the New Year started in a different direction. On 7th January Joyce wrote, at one sitting, a long essay called 'A Portrait of the Artist', an account in veiled terms of his own spiritual and mental development.

This was offered to the editors of *Dana*, a new intellectual review run by his friends Con Curran and Fred Ryan. Curran returned it with a jocular letter, but had been dismayed at the sexuality of its content. Joyce may have intended to publish this under his adopted pen-name Stephen (from the first Christian martyr) Daedelus (from the ancient artificer of Minos – whose reality like that of Troy and Ithaca had been confirmed by yet more classical research: Joyce had been following in the magazines of the day the contemporary excavations by Arthur Evans on Crete).

Undeterred, Joyce sat down at the kitchen table in St Peter's Terrace and embarked on sketching out the scheme of a long satirical novel – 'a lying autobiography' his brother Stanislaus called it in his contemporary diary. They amused themselves assigning names to the characters, all drawn from their family and the life around them. Their father was to be 'sighing Simon', Stanislaus 'Morose Maurice', Aunt Josephine 'Aunt Bridget – Blundering Biddy' and her husband Uncle William 'Jealous Jim'; John Murray was Uncle John and his wife Aunt Essie.* He even found room for the Hon. Juliana Michell under the name of the Hon. Mrs Ambrose. Joyce's alter-ego being called Stephen Daedelus, the book was to be entitled *Stephen Hero*, which had it been completed would have run to some 50 chapters and 600,000 words, a novel of close to 1,000 printed pages. He began it with great enthusiasm, an engagement with the past that lasted until August 1905, by which time he had written some 914 pages and 25 chapters. What remains of the book is interesting for the incidents it reveals, rather than for its style or treatment, which is curiously old-fashioned and Victorian. The initial inspiration to write a novel may have come from the publication of Samuel Butler's posthumous novel *The Way of All Flesh* in 1903. Butler, too, had Homeric interests and was among the few writers Joyce read and admired.

His friends such as Oliver St John Gogarty (himself a a poet) thought of Joyce as a poet, and it was as a poet that he posed. The lyrics of *Chamber Music*, with their detached Elizabethan delicacy, were in the making at this period, their charm contrasting greatly with the conditions in which he wrote them – some lyrics being scribbled out on the back of sugar-bags, for instance, in his aunt's kitchen. The poems have a strict formality which hides the original emotions that inspired them. They suggest well the lovelorn nature of Joyce's own state, but provide little remedy beyond the brief relief of song. A letter from Arthur Symons in May encouraged him to send a selection of the poems to London, and Symons, impressed with their quality, offered to try to place them with a publisher. But by the end of the year it would be clear to him that his real talents were as a prose artist.

1904 was a crucial year for Irish culture. An aspect of this was the presentation of Synge's *Riders to the Sea* (the early script of which Joyce had read in Paris) on 25th February and the opening of the Abbey Theatre itself in December. *Dana* began in May, and eventually published one of Joyce's poems. But there also appeared an anthology of younger Irish poets, *New Songs*, from which Joyce was excluded by the editor George Russell – a significant rebuff. Arthur Griffith published *The Resurrection of Hungary*, in which he

* These fictional names of Jim and John for his uncles William and John seem to confirm their connection with the characters of Shem and Shaun in *Finnegans Wake*. Shaun is of course the Gaelic for John; and his uncle William's profession as a legal clerk was a suitable one for Shem the Penman.

outlined his scheme for a devolved government in Ireland along the lines of the relationship of Hungary to the Austrian Emperor: this marked the appearance of a significant figure for Ireland and for Joyce – 'a coming man' in Leopold Bloom's view, and Joyce too was to see in the then non-violent Sinn Fein the future hope of Ireland. Father Peter O'Leary published *Seadna*, a Gaelic classic, which made clear the distance now separating the culture of modern urbanized Ireland from the dying Gaelic culture of its rural past. George Moore published *The Lake*, in which the flight of sensitive temperament from that rural Ireland is depicted. There was also an important exhibition of paintings by George Russell and Count and Countess Markievicz in September of that year, for the other arts were also quickened at this time. Irish culture was on the ascendant, and the literary revival which had begun in 1882 had reached a critical mass.

Co-incident with Joyce's birth, 1882 is the date for the beginning of the revival which W.P. Ryan, its first historian, selected: it was the year in which the Southwark Literary Club in London had its start. In his book *The Irish Literary Revival*, published as early as 1894, Ryan mentions a score of now forgotten names, among whom only Douglas Hyde and Yeats stand out.

Many of these writers were amateurs, journalists or barristers by profession, often politicians, who wrote verse as a pastime. Journalists are a crucial element not only in *Ulysses* but also in the growth of modern Irish culture. Newspaper editors, authors and reporters (the Irish literati, in effect) numbered a mere 259 persons in the Census of 1861; and 388 in 1881. Numbers rose sharply during the Parnell era (when so many journalists, Tim Harrington and T.P. O'Connor for instance, were parliamentary members for the Irish Party) to 651 by 1891, 807 by 1901, and 1,108 by 1911. These rising numbers (in a country with a falling population) are paralleled by a rise in the circulation of Irish and British newspapers and magazines (references to which abound in Joyce's texts) and an increase in the number of Irish books being written. Many of these were popular and religious works, printed and published in Glasgow, London, New York, Boston and other centres where there were large Irish populations. Only a few would now be known to academic readers, but in their day they formed the bulk of Irish reading.

In terms of output, Irish writing was far from paralytic: it was in a vigorous state, alive with strong opinions, deep feelings, engaged passions and frustrated emotions. The moment had arrived when mere writing would explode into literature. That strain of literature associated with Yeats was idealistic and romantic in tendency (as described in detail in my book *The Heart Grown Brutal*). The emergence of a realistic antithesis to Yeats's thesis was marked by the return to Dublin of George Moore (at that date the most distinguished living novelist), and his espousal of the new literary cause by writing a series of short stories which appeared first in Gaelic translation, and in 1903 as *The Untilled Field*.

Joyce's moment had come with the co-incidence of his own maturity with that of the Irish Literary Revival. He was to Moore much what Synge was to Yeats, the younger man with the fiercer views who would dismay the new Irish audience. The events of this year would conspire to drive Joyce away from Ireland, but leave him with all the materials for his masterpieces.

At home desperation continued, however. John Joyce had taken out a mortgage with a money-lender named Sheridan on 4th November for £150 – £165 to be paid back in April 1904. Where the money to achieve that would come from was a problem he never solved. Debts accumulated, and the following year he would lose the house in a forced sale.

However, some money was still needed, and for this Joyce sang in a music festival on 24th March. Thoughts of a career as a professional singer, even at the humble level of a strolling entertainer in the English seaside resorts, was mooted. Things were so depressed that Stanislaus found occasional comfort in entertainments outside the home as well: at a concert in the Rotunda he met a lady whose conversation eventually suggests to his brother the situation in 'A Painful Case'. To some extent John Joyce also had activities outside the house that his children cared little about: in March Andrew Kettle, the Nationalist politician, called to see him on political business; an occasion made memorable among his children by his remarking to Mabel Joyce that his name was 'Mr Kettle – what you boil the water in.' On hearing this, Eva remarked that he didn't know it was 'Mr Teapot' they boiled the water in – they had no kettle.

The date of repayment advancing on them, Joyce too felt constrained to appeal to Oliver Gogarty (a young man of some substance) for financial aid in March or early April. But help of another kind was at hand: a post of usher, or assistant master, arose in a private preparatory school in Dalkey. I suspect that this post at Clifton

House School was gained through the kind intervention of Mr Dempsey. To be near his work, but not out of town, Joyce moved to rooms in 60 Shallowing Road, a house occupied by a young couple with two small children called McKernan. They were Protestants and connections of some kind with the McKernans who had been the Joyces' neighbours in Drumcondra years before. They let him have the long room on the front of the house as his own.

The post in the school was basically for the Easter term which ended in July. The owner and headmaster was Francis Irwin, a Protestant and graduate of Trinity College, who catered for the sons of wealthy folk living along the Vico Road and the avenues of Dalkey. Here Joyce was to set the 'Nestor' episode of *Ulysses*, recalling some of the schoolboys he taught for so brief a period.

Easter fell that year on 3rd April, and John Joyce's creditor cannot have been pleased that his money was not repaid. In his diary Stanislaus presents a cruelly realized portrait of John Joyce at the age of 54. Drunk and belligerent, and dangerous to his infants, the remains of a fine, light tenor voice now given to abusing the young puppies that his sons had become: Jim aloof, Stanislaus grim and withdrawn, Charles pious, sentimental and given to whoring (he would spent 4 days in jail in May). John absented himself from home for more agreeable activities, such as attending funerals.

The end of April was enlivened by another Royal Visit, but – for some critical souls at least – the glitter and pomp of this were tainted by such social facts as the city's slums and the emigration figures for 1903 published on 11th May: these showed that 40,657 people had emigrated, some 870 of whom were not natives, presumably Jews.

Amid these passing events Joyce struggled on. He sang in the Feis Ceoil in 16th May, having pawned some of his books to enter. He sang well, and would have won first prize but he walked off unable to sight-read a piece of music. In disgust he threw the bronze medal he had won into a nearby area, but later retrieved it and gave it to his aunt. Nevertheless the judge thought very highly of Joyce's talent, according to Joyce's friend Palmiere who offered to train him for a share of his eventual earnings. But Joyce could not afford the modest term he suggested.

Despite his poverty, the young poet with the pleasant voice was now attracting the notice of others. On the evening of Wednesday 8th June, Joseph Holloway called on the Northern poet James Cousins and his wife, who lived at the Bungalow, Dromard Terrace,

Sandymount. 'You are always sure to find some interesting people there,' Holloway records in his diary.

> Miss Cousins played a couple of beautiful pieces beautifully, and Mr Joyce – a mysterious kind of youth with weird penetrating eyes (which he frequently shades with his hands) and a half-bashful, far-away, wistful expression on his face – sang some dainty ballads most artistically and pleasingly, some to his own accompaniment. As he sings, he sways his head from side to side to add to the soulfulness of his rendering. He is a strange boy; I cannot fathom him.

Two days later, on 10th June, the diarist encountered Mr Joyce again when he visited the hall in Camden Street where the Irish National Literary Society – of which Cousins and Padraic Colum were leading lights – was rehearsing under Willy Fay's direction Synge's plays *In the Shadow of the Glen* and *Riders to the Sea*. Synge himself was present and 'Mr Joyce put in an appearance.'

That afternoon Joyce was singing at a garden fête, but during the course of the day he had a memorable encounter when in Nassau Street he met a striking young lady with a memorable head of auburn hair. He was perhaps on his way to or from the offices of George Russell's paper the *Irish Homestead* at 22 Lincoln Place – facing the minaretted Turkish baths which Mr Bloom patronizes in *Ulysses*. She worked in Finn's Hotel, only a few doors away at the beginning of Leinster Street.

The dreamy young man whom Holloway described at once made an impression on the girl, whose name he discovered was Nora Barnacle. For Joyce the name Nora would have had old echoes from Ibsen, but she was a person more substantial than the captive of *The Doll's House*. The next day he wrote her a note, suggesting an assignation. This she failed to keep. But he wrote again on the 15th and this time they did meet on the following evening.

It was a Thursday, 16th June 1904. Joyce was to set *Ulysses* on this day, perhaps out of silent tribute to Nora: it is perhaps significant that Stephen vanishes from the action of the novel at just those hours when James and Nora would have been out walking. At the close of the 'Circe' episode, while Bloom stands guard over the fallen and deserted Stephen, he thinks he hears the young poet murmur a name. *Something about a girl. Some girl. Best thing could happen to him.* What Stephen had been trying to repeat were the lines from Yeats which had been troubling him all day, ever since Malachy Mulligan had recited them on the parapet of the Martello tower overlooking that green sea which had recalled to his memory the bowl of green bile torn from his mother's rotting liver.

> Then turn no more aside
> And brood upon love's bitter mystery.

Stephen's mother had once hoped he might learn what the heart was and what it feels. So too had Joyce's. That evening walking out with Nora, remembering the agony of his dying mother's love, Joyce's mind may well have turned aside to brood upon the bitter mystery of love – the perennial theme of all his work.

Meeting on the corner of Merrion Square, outside what Dubliners still call Sir William Wilde's house, they took a tram which let them off at the corner of Lansdowne Road. From there in the waning light of the long summer evening, they walked east past the Botanical Garden and the grand houses, coming out at last on the wide fields by the banks of the Dodder.

These were the very fields where the young housemaid had been murdered, the crime for which Henry Flower had been suspected, and moreover where James and Stanislaus had had their own strange encounter with the admirer of Walter Scott on another June day a decade before. Joyce was laying a new emotional experience over an old one. Here they paused, and here with the twilight gathering around them, Joyce was taken by suprise. Nora made the first approach and he was left in little doubt about her feelings for him. There was no intercourse – that would have been unthinkable – but Nora was knowledgeable enough to manipulate her partner to a climax.

Like so many of Joyce's experiences, this event also made its way into *Ulysses* transferred to the memory of Molly Bloom:

> . . . how did we finish it off yes O yes I pulled him off into my handkerchief pretending not to be excited but I opened my legs and I wouldn't let him touch me inside my petticoat I had a skirt opening up the side I tortured the life out of him first tickling him . . . he was shy all the same I liked him like that morning he I made him blush a little when I got over him that way when I unbuttoned him and took his out and drew back the skin . . .

Joyce never escaped from the consequences of this new encounter;

as he had imagined in that last long summer in Blackrock, brooding on the image of Mercedes, hoping for some future encounter that would transform his life, 'weakness and timidity and experience would fall from him in that magic moment'. This was that magic moment.

Here was a girl who, literally, took him in hand. Here was none of the trade in sex he was used to from the prostitutes Fresh Nellie and Annie Langton, nor any of the delusive virginal posturing which he thought epitomized the girls of his own class. Nora was the first woman with whom he found he could be open and free, each giving because each desired.

In summer the Dodder runs shallowly over a bed of rocks. By Lansdowne Bridge the trees bend over the water gurgling by. Until quite recently it reminded one a little of that poem by Yeats which Joyce loved to sing, and which he may even have recited to Nora as they walked through the summer grass on the bank above:

> In a field by the river my love and I did stand
> And on my leaning shoulder she laid her snow-white hand.
> And she bid me take life easy as the grass grows on the weirs,
> But I was young and foolish and now am full of tears.

Six weeks later he would copy out these verses and send them to her (by then his 'precious darling'), for he said they expressed 'very delicately and musically the vague and tired loneliness' which filled his heart at that time.

He saw her back to Finn's, and made another assignation. On her days off through that summer, they pursued their courtship. Nora was indeed the best thing that had happened to him, for she pulled him slowly out of the life into which he had fallen since his return from Paris. But for Nora, Joyce would have become just another drunken failed poet, of which Dublin at any time has an abundant supply. Soon they were meeting regularly, every second evening that she had off from work and on her week-ends.

Yet initially Joyce was not totally committed to her. On 22nd June he had a fight in Stephen's Green with the escort of a girl whom he had approached too easily, which left him with a cut eye. (The shaded walk around the Green was a well-known haunt of prostitutes.) He related this sad adventure when he wrote the next day to Con Curran, enclosing some of his novel. Curran was now among Joyce's creditors, for a few days later Joyce called on him at his office near the Four Courts to borrow money. He was writing his novel at the rate of about a chapter a week – the chapters written at this time would have dealt with his schooldays at Belvedere. What had been completed, perhaps some six or seven chapters, he gave to George Russell at the *Irish Homestead* to read. Russell now commissioned him to write a series of stories, 'epicleti' Joyce called them, for the paper, for which the editor would pay £1. Russell wanted 'anything simple, rural? livemaking? pathos?' which would not shock the readers. What he got were the first stories of *Dubliners*, which were all to be symbolic, urban, realistic, and ironic.

During much of this summer Joyce was a constant reader at the National Library. The episode of *Ulysses* which he sets there reproduces much of the kind of conversation in which he and his friends indulged. T.W. Lyster, the director, had on the mantelpiece of his office (where the discussion takes place) a copy of the portrait of Shakespeare from the First Folio: the discourse on *Hamlet* which Stephen gives to his friends would not (as Richard Best thought) have been at all unusual. Richard Best and William Magee (the writer John Eglinton) were on the staff and came to know Joyce at this time. The friendships were literary rather than personal, and not very close; neither man then regarded Joyce as being in any way more remarkable than any of the other young literary men who frequented the library to read and talk; but Joyce was to be one of the few who got around to actually writing.

Joyce saw much of Con Curran during the summer of 1904. It was Curran who took the most famous photograph of Joyce with hands in pockets, legs apart, standing in front of the glasshouse in the back garden of Curran's residence, his father's house at 6 Cumberland Place (now 211 North Circular Road), which was not far from Joyce's own less grand home. Asked what he was thinking about when the picture was taken, Joyce said he was wondering if Curran would lend him five shillings. Though widely reproduced, the picture gives a false impression of Joyce, for it shows him as Stephen Dedalus – proud, cocky, alert. But the real Joyce (the dreamy poet enountered by Holloway) should be seen as part of a social group (as he is in this book), a schoolboy, a Sodality member, a college student among other students. Curran's photo shows the Joyce of literary legend; these other pictures the Dublin Joyce of real life.

This was to be a summer of encounters for Joyce. On 13th July he and his father attended the funeral of Martin Kane, an old Kingstown friend of John Joyce who had been tragically drowned in Dublin Bay when he suffered a heart attack while swimming. The body was not recovered for several days, and to add to the sorrow he left a wife and young family, for whom a collection was organized. The funeral started in Kingstown, and made its way across the city to Glasnevin. As was so often the case at Dublin funerals, many figures familiar from Joyce's fiction attended, but among them was a new person, one Alfred H. Hunter.

Hunter, a tall, dark-complexioned man in his late thirties, caught Joyce's interest. From his father he learnt that this person was supposed to be Jewish and to have an unfaithful wife. Of the wife's actual infidelity I have been able to discover nothing as yet, but Hunter was certainly not Jewish. Alfred Henry Hunter (I discovered) was born at Mount Pottinger, Ballymacarret, then on the edge of Belfast, on 30th August 1866. His father was a Presbyterian leather merchant, who later had a shoe shop in Dublin; his mother was a Maria Lockhart. Hunter became a nominal Catholic when he married, on 1st February 1898 in Rathmines Catholic church. His wife was Margaret Cummins, whose mother ran a stationery shop in Castlewood Avenue; her father had been a bricklayer.

Significant now only for the rumours about him, Hunter would eventually provide Joyce with a model for Leopold Bloom. And given her rumoured infidelity to Hunter, his wife Margaret (?Molly to her friends) must be numbered among the models for Molly Bloom.

That evening Joyce wrote to George Roberts, a friend involved with the Camden Street group, to meet him the next day in The Ship, a pub in the city centre, with the loan of £1. The following day, while waiting for his friend, Joyce would have seen the *Freeman's Journal* which carried a report of the Kane funeral, with the names of his father and himself included among the list of mourners. On another page of that issue he would also have found an account of an accident at Sydney Parade station on the Dalkey line, in which a Mrs Sarah Bishop had been killed: this was the germ of 'A Painful Case'.

August was devoted to his pursuit of Nora, though it also saw the appearance of a poem in *Dana*, following on one a few days before in the London *Speaker* – both oblique verse tributes to his beloved.

On the 13th his story, 'The Sisters', appeared in the *Irish Homestead*. He sang at a concert in the Antient Concert Rooms on 26th August, a badly organized event which caused much bickering among the musical fraternity who were involved, and which inspired another story, 'A Mother'. This lady in life was Mrs Kearney, an old acquaintance of the family from earlier years, a figure well-known in musical circles in Dublin whose family had a music shop in Capel Street – that street which Joyce thought the most beautiful in the world. Nora went to this concert, escorted there by his friend Vincent Cosgrave with whom she was on ambiguously friendly terms. She never forgot this occasion, at which Joyce sang with John McCormack, and in later years would remark that it was a pity Jim did not persist in his career as a singer and become a rival to that great Irish tenor.

As his landlords the McKernans were going away in September for their summer holiday, Joyce had to leave his rooms in Shelbourne Road on 31st August. The following night he stayed with the Cousins at the bungalow off Sandymount Green. He did not care for their vegetarian diet, but the house itself was to furnish him with the setting of the first and third acts of *Exiles*. He stayed one night with his friend Maurice O'Callaghan, a medical student, off the North Circular Road. Rather than return to his father's house, he found refuge for a few days with his Murray relatives in their house at 103 North Strand.

Now came a move, on 9th September, to the Martello Tower in Sandycove, which was to provide him with the setting for the opening episode of *Ulysses*. He stayed there with Oliver Gogarty and another acquaintance of Gogarty's, Samuel Chenevix Trench (the model for Haines in the novel), a connection of a former Anglican Archbishop of Dublin. As a consequence of the use Joyce made of it, this week-long sojourn was to remain the subject of continuing controversy. Both Joyce and Gogarty claimed that Joyce paid the rent on the tower, but the surviving documents are all in Gogarty's name and it is difficult to imagine Joyce readily paying the rent on any premises.

Gogarty was one of the medical set with whom Joyce was accustomed to pass his time. Their ribald outlook and irregular hours contrasted to their benefit with his other friends with their regular hours and temperate habits. Gogarty was a relatively new friend of Joyce's – their accounts of how they met are also irreconcilable. Gogarty had ambitions as a poet which were only partly achieved, for both his medical career and his political involvements with Sinn Fein and later with the Free State government as a Senator, meant that he stayed an amateur writer to a late age. He was not able, either, to take Joyce's developing ambitions as seriously as Joyce himself did. His joking unseriousness (which made him so attractive then and later to many others) diminished him in Joyce's estimate. Joyce presents in his fiction a Gogarty who bears only a partial relationship to the real man. Gogarty was a skilled surgeon, a fine poet and a public man of courage and honour. This clash of personalities – triggered by the eccentric behaviour of Trench, who had a nightmare about being attacked by a panther in the night and which Gogarty disposed of by shooting down the pots hanging over Joyce's bed – came rapidly to a head. Joyce loathed violence, and thought that he was unwanted. He was ejected (as he liked to think) from the tower on 15th September.

Five days earlier the *Homestead* had published his second story 'Eveline', in which the choice of going abroad or staying at home faces a young girl (modelled a little on both Nora and his sister Margaret). He too was posed this choice over Nora: to stay, or to go abroad to a new life. One more episode proved crucial.

It is likely that on the evening when he was expelled from the tower he went out with Nora, and that having returned with her he visited his medical pals in Holles Street maternity hospital. One of the group described in the 'Oxen of the Sun' episode of *Ulysses*, 'Punch' Costello, Dr Francis Xavier Costello, certainly was there at this date.

From there an adjournment would have been made to the Kips in the Monto brothel quarter behind Talbot Street, to continue drinking. This too was used in *Ulysses*. There was nothing romantic about the Kips, as Joyce realized: it was a disease-ridden phantasmagoria. The girls in these houses were all quite young, in their twenties, the madames in their fifties. Many of the girls came from Liverpool and Glasgow, those other sea-ports on the coast of the Irish Sea. While sailors and soldiers were said to have been the main customers of these houses, they were in fact resorted to widely by men of all classes. The landlords of such slums were often Nationalist members of the City Council. The madames were said to own large houses in the suburbs and to send their own children to good schools. While in the Kips Joyce yet again got into a fight, during which his friend Vincent Cosgrave refused to help him and stood idly by watching the fracas.

Instead, out of the night came Mr Alfred Hunter, who picked Joyce up and took him home – either to his own house, at 28 Ballybough Road, or to his Uncle William's house nearby in North Strand, where he was staying and which was only a step away. This would have been one night between 16th and 19th September.

Joyce never forgave Vincent Cosgrave his betrayal, nor did he forget Hunter – his Judas and his Good Samaritan. Hunter was to be one of the Dublin models for Leopold Bloom; other elements were derived from Joseph Bloom, his father, and from his uncle William. Joyce only met Hunter on these two occasions, once at the Kane funeral and once when he rescued him. What little he learnt about the man from his father and from Hunter himself that evening (perhaps over a cup of Epp's cocoa) was all he needed.

At the time of his encounter with Joyce, Hunter was living on the Ballybough Road. Later he lived (as Joyce seems to have been aware) in May Street, off the Clonliffe Road, up to 1916. In 1921 Joyce asked his aunt Josephine specifically if she knew what had become of Hunter, but it is likely that by then he had passed out of her knowledge. An advertising agent by trade (as was Leopold Bloom), Alfred Henry Hunter died on 12th September 1926 in rooms at 23 Great Charles Street (off Mountjoy Square, by then a slum). He was only sixty.

Eventually Joyce's second, emotionally charged meeting with Alfred Hunter would become the climax of a story which he planned but never wrote, about Mr Hunter's day, called 'Ulysses'. Like most Dubliners of his kind, Joyce knew little and cared less for Ulster Presbyterians. Hunter, though a convert to Catholicism, would have been out of place in Dublin society. In evolving his character Joyce had recourse to another group of outsiders in Dublin, the Jewish community which he knew better. The Jewish identity which Joyce cast over the obscure Ulsterman came from that other Dublin character Joseph Bloom. Yet given the place of Leopold Bloom in the modern mythology of Dublin, it is a nice irony that the original model for the character should have been a Belfast Protestant – that was one cultural divide which Joyce could not cross.

Yet all of this was for the future. At the end of September Joyce moved back to St Peter's Terrace, but not for long. He and Nora had decided to go away. During the summer and autumn their relationship developed new depths. His seriousness surprised his brother. His aunt Josephine thought he was mistaken, but Joyce brought Nora to see her and she realized that she had been wrong: Nora was the right girl for Jim. Eventually they decided that as they would not marry in church they must go away. He would write and give language lessons. Perhaps through the Berlitz Schools. Preferably in Paris, the city which Joyce said 'was a lamp for lovers hung in the wood of the world'.

In *Ulysses* Bloom proposes to Molly on the bracken-covered slopes of Howth Head above the Baily: it is not too much to suppose that Nora's 'Yes I will, Yes' in acceptance of the future Joyce offered her was also uttered there. As a student Joyce had considered throwing himself into the sea from these same heights in the environs of Howth Castle; now they had restored him (by a commodious vico of recirculation) to the realities of life.

On 26th September he wrote to Grant Richards in London about the publication of his poems. In the course of the letter he mentions that he is planning to go to Holland in two weeks' time. Holland was a second choice after Paris, but even that would prove to be a vain destination. The couple would have to go first to Zürich where the Berlitz School (he was told by an English agent) had a post on offer.

Their plans made, frantic preparations followed. The fare (for two) to Zürich was £7.10.0. Nora had little or no money, Joyce had only £1 from the *Homestead* for his third story 'After the Race'. There were many last-minute appeals for aid and for money to his few remaining friends. George Roberts and Fred Ryan gave him £1 between them. George Russell also gave him money, and the poet James Starkey (Seumas O'Sullivan) gave him boots and a toothbrush from his father's pharmacy.

John Joyce and other members of the family came to see James off at the North Wall on 8th October 1904. Nora went on board by herself, as John Joyce was not to know about her. At last, on that bleak evening, Joyce climbed the gangway to the steamer, leaving behind him the city which would remain for ever the epicentre of his imagination, from which the shock waves of his fictional earthquake would rock and overthrow the genteel traditions of the nineteenth century. Daedelus took flight, forgetting that the revenge of Minos would find him out wherever he fled.

PART VII

'Perhaps she had not told him all the story?'

'The Dead'

16

'Nora'

The soul like the body may have a virginity. For the woman to yield it
or for the man to take it is the act of love. Love (understood as the desire
of good for another) is in fact so unnatural a phenomenon that it can
scarcely repeat itself, the soul being unable to become virgin again and
not having energy enough to cast itself out again into the ocean of
another's soul.

James Joyce, in the private notes on *Exiles*

Who was this girl with whom Joyce had thrown in his lot by going
away with her to Europe? As of now, as they came together on
the deck of the boat taking them away from Ireland, he knew little
about her except that she was a provincial girl, from Galway in the
west of Ireland, that epitome of backwardness to the knowing
Dubliner.

Joyce's friends and biographers have written of her simplicity, but
this leaves perhaps the wrong impression of her personality, for she
was neither simple nor naïve. Her background was as haunted as
James Joyce's; she had seen aspects of life unknown to him.

Her background was very different from Joyce's, however. The
Barnacle name is an old Irish one, said to be originally O Cadhain.
The medieval legend of the Barnacle goose has been mentioned
constantly by critics, as has the theme of the Wild Geese, and John
Joyce's comment when he heard Nora's name: 'Well, she'll always
stick to him.' But it was not her father's family – rural people –

who were influential in her life. Her upbringing was as urban as Joyce's.

Her mother Annie Healy was born in 1856. Annie's people from Galway city were fairly prosperous: her father Patrick was a merchant owning his own shop; her mother, born about 1826, was a Catherine Mortimer. Patrick Healy died while Annie was growing up. There were three other children in this family: Michael, Thomas, and Joseph.

Annie was educated by the nuns in the Convent of Mercy and her brothers were sent to the Patrician Brothers on Nun's Island – where Michael was recognized as an exceptionally brilliant pupil, eventually passing his Civil Service Commission exam in 1883 and rising to become Inspector of Customs in Galway. Thomas was a sort of jack-of-all-trades, but seems to have had no trouble earning a living as a general handyman. Joseph, who died in May 1896, was a cabinet-maker.

After Patrick Healy's death, the Healys lived at 6 Whitehall, a short side street (now reconstructed) leading into the police barracks off Lower Abbeygate Street in the town centre. It was a large house with a yard which they shared with a woman called Honour Walsh. Annie had a taste for dressmaking, which the nuns had encouraged; this was a good trade in the days before ready-made clothes, but it was hard and often unprofitable work. Indeed, until her children were grown up she supported herself by working as a seamstress.

Part of her father's business had been a bakery, a trade which her brother Thomas followed after their father's death. Annie became friendly with Thomas Barnacle, who had been her father's foreman. Thomas, born in 1846, was a baker, as his father Patrick had been. Patrick Barnacle is recorded as living in 16 New Road, on the north side of the city, in the 1860s. The family then had a shop in Williamsgate Street (now incorporated into Corbett's). Thomas Barnacle lived with his parents in 10 Lower Abbeygate Street, a house just opposite Whitehall on the corner of St Augustine Street. Thomas Barnacle was said to have been delicate as a child and to have received little schooling, but he grew up to learn his father's trade, which was as good an education as any.

On 28th February 1881 Thomas and Annie were married in the Catholic parish church of St Nicholas. The witnesses were their friends Thomas Carroll and Mary Daly. Annie, then 24, could read and write a tidy convent hand. Thomas was 35 and illiterate: the marriage register is signed with his mark. He gave his address as Abbeygate Street, she as Whitehall. It was not a necessary marriage as their first child was born eleven months later. But it was certainly thought a come-down by her family for her to marry an employee of her father's, and they never really approved of the marriage; that she went through with it suggests a certain reckless determination, and strength of character with a strong will.

At first the couple lived with the Barnacles in Abbeygate Street, where their first daughter Mary was born on 24th January 1882. Thomas, however, was over-fond of his drink and money was always short. For fifteen years while her husband drank himself from job to job and out of his marriage, Annie Barnacle was to rear her family in increasing poverty. Often they were quite destitute. The course of the marriage was marked by frequent moves, doubtless due to unpaid rent. From Abbeygate Street they went to Sullivan's Lane, where they were living when Annie became pregnant again. As they had no money, she did the only thing then possible to gain some proper attention for her second child in the circumstances.

Thus Nora Barnacle was born on 24th March 1884 in the Galway workhouse. Today the workhouse is gone, replaced in 1956 by a modern regional hospital with a well-equipped maternity wing. But a century ago the Union Workhouse was the last hated hope of the really poor. The regimen prescribed by the Poor Law demanded 'regularity, orderliness, strict enforcement of cleanliness, the preservation of decency and decorum, and the exclusion of all irregular habits and tempting excitements.'

Having a child in the workhouse was not like going into hospital now. Babies were born at home, the workhouse being the refuge of the destitute. (The local author Father O Laoi who wrote about Nora's early years, disagrees with this, saying that the workhouse was in fact a local general hospital and there was no stigma in having one's baby there. But in fact it was the custom to have children at home, if there was one.)

The pattern of Annie Barnacle's marriage was set, and it included few 'tempting excitements', aside from the dubious pleasure of sexual intercourse with her husband. For a while her mother Catherine Healy took the couple into the house in Whitehall, where their next child Bridget (later known as Delia) was born on 15th January 1886. Soon, however, they moved out, perhaps because of dissension between Thomas Barnacle and the Healys. Their next home was another lodging on Prospect Hill, where twins Annie and Margaret were born on 12th March 1889.

At this time, with four small children on her hands, Annie must have been hard-pressed indeed. She needed the eldest Mary to help with the infants, but Nora was sent to live with her grandmother in Whitehall. Intended only as a temporary arrangement, after a while it became permanent and Nora was to live with her grandmother for nearly eight years.

This was perhaps as well for her, since the family's fortunes did not change for the better. The Barnacles now lived in unrelieved poverty in one of the primitive cottages in the Claddagh, a Gaelic-speaking fishing village beyond the harbour on the edge of the city. A son Thomas Michael was born on 23rd August 1891. From there Thomas removed himself to lodging in Newtownsmith, into a ten-ement shared by several families. Annie had her next child, a boy named John, in the workhouse, and there he died 21 months later of convulsions on 12th October 1895. A year later Catherine (later Cathleen) was born in the workhouse ward on 12th October 1896; the parents' address is given as Newtownsmith.

This was to be Annie Barnacle's last child. Thomas had virtually abandoned his family and would go off for long periods, looking for work in bakeries, but mostly drinking what he managed to earn in one way or another. He returned to Annie now and again, leaving after a day or two with another child on the way. Some time late in 1896 they moved into a house in Bowling Green. Annie had had enough of poverty, drink and constant childbearing, and she now refused to oblige Thomas with his marital rights. When he beat her and threatened her with a knife, she took refuge with the neighbours and then went home to her family. Supported by the Healys, she went to the parish priest and got a separation with custody of the children. (These details are reflected in the sketch of Mrs Mooney in Joyce's story 'The Boarding House', in which the character of Polly Mooney, 'a little perverse madonna', is based on Nora Barnacle.) Annie moved with her family into three rooms of 1 Bowling Green, part of a house let out by a retired soldier named Hughes and his wife. Thomas meanwhile was working in various bakeries, eventually removing himself to Oughterard. Annie had escaped.

The wretchedness of the Barnacle family was not uncommon. Their plight arose out of the general poverty and hardship of the west of Ireland in which Galway shared. At this date Galway was a decaying provincial centre, the English-speaking capital of Gaelic Connaught. Once it had been a prosperous sea-port, but over a century trade had declined. When a scheme to enlarge the harbour and obtain the landing of the American mails failed in 1859 (due, it was locally believed, to the machinations of a cartel of Liverpool merchants), most of the transatlantic ships ceased calling at Galway. Only the emigrant ships still came. The local fishing industry, mostly in the hands of Claddagh men, also declined. Jobs were few and far between – indeed, Nora's uncle Michael Healy with a good position in the Customs and Excise was very well off, and a person of some local weight. The setting up of cloth mills, distilleries and a small factory or two did little to improve life in the town. In 1851 the population was 16,000; by 1901 it had fallen to 13,000. One writer complained in 1902 that the only new buildings in Galway were convents and churches, and they did little to create wealth in the city. Galway had become what Joyce was later to describe as 'a beautiful dying city in the west'.

Yet Galway still retained its connections with the maritime traditions of western Europe, and its people were still romantically attached to their past. They fancied their dark features were of Spanish origin, and claimed that Christopher Columbus had called there to pray in the Abbey before sailing the Atlantic (with a Galway man among his crew, it was uncritically believed). In Eyre Square the city fathers had erected the elaborate façade of a medieval merchant's house as a memorial to the town's ancient glory. Along the quays the Moorish-looking Spanish Arch facing the fish market recalled Gibraltar to some, and the tall narrow streets were a visible reminder of the city's old trade with the sultry Mediterranean.

Near Eyre Square, in Castle Street, they also pointed out to visitors the house of Judge Lynch, who hanged his own son and so added Lynch-law to the English language, though this too was a legend. Not that there were many visitors in those days. Galway was a poor city in an impoverished province. In the 'Hungry Forties' of the nineteenth century Connaught had suffered worst of all from starvation and disease. Emigration and exile were the common lot of young men and girls of any spirit. In the eighties, however, districts of Connaught were still congested with indigent tenant farmers. The Land War against increased rents and absentee landlords was fought hardest here. 'Boycott' was another term added to the language, derived from the name of a land agent in the Joyce Country beside Lough Mask with whom the people, urged on by Land League organizers, would have no truck.

Lynch-law and boycott: violence and intimidation were the very way of life in Galway. Agrarian outrages – as they were then called – were commonplace, and justice not always was seen to be done, as the terrible events surrounding the murder of the Joyce family at Maamtrasna had revealed, when the old man Myles Joyce was convicted back in the 1880s at Dublin and brought back to be hanged in Galway. As he spoke only Irish he was unable to defend himself in the English-speaking court, and no interpreter was provided. He was taken over the River Corrib and hanged in Galway gaol. That dreadful place was on Nun's Island, its grim walls towering over the convent and Perse's Distillery. (This was where Joyce set Gretta Conroy's childhood home in 'The Dead', another story which drew upon Nora Barnacle's early years.) Lady Gregory's play *The Gaol Gate* was set outside this infamous place, on the site of which Galway Cathedral now stands: her plot was drawn from the hanging of a Connemara boy. Religion, drink, and gaol: an awful trinity, it seemed to some, brooded over Irish life.

Country people from Connemara and the Aran Islands – these proud silent men and women dressed in grey homespun and red petticoats, so admired by the writers of the Irish Revival – were often to be seen in the city streets and markets, reassuring the city folk that there were some worse off than they. Outside the city, in the Claddagh village, the fishermen still lived under their own law.

*

Surrounded by such sordid poverty and squalor, and deeply affected by the breaking up of her family, Nora Barnacle still seemed a happy enough girl, outgoing and full of pranks and fun. At the house in Whitehall, where she was partly protected from the worst of things, she must have been spoilt by her grandmother and her uncle Michael, who had now taken over the support of the Barnacles. As her favourite, Nora was promised by her grandmother that when she died the little girl would not be forgotten: there was money coming to her.

For some eight years Nora was completely happy. At the age of five she was sent to school with the nuns in the Convent of Mercy at Newtownsmith, where she was prepared for her First Communion. In June 1891, at the age of eight, she was transferred into the National School, where she stayed until the spring of 1896. The family were then living on Prospect Hill.

Her memories of this childhood were vivid. Years later in Trieste, by means of free association, Joyce was able to recreate, from what she told him, some vignettes of those years before he had known her and about which he was insatiably curious. These sketches were among the notes for the play he was then writing, but they have something of the quality of his own epiphanies. The images and words he used are simple enough:

Snow:
> frost, moon, pictures, holly and ivy, currant-cake, lemonade, Emily Lyons, piano, window sill.

Tears:
> ship, sunshine, garden, sadness, pianoforte, buttoned boots, bread and butter, a big fire.

But the scenes he created were more than evocative:

> In the first the flow of ideas is tardy. It is Christmas, in Galway, a moonlit Christmas Eve with snow. She is carrying picture almanacs to her grandmother's house to be ornamented with holly and ivy. The evenings are spent in the house of a friend where they give her lemonade. Lemonade and currant-cake are also her grandmother's fare for her. She thumps the piano and sits with her dark-complexioned gipsy-looking friend Emily Lyons on the window sill.
>
> In the second the ideas are more rapid. It is the quay of Galway Harbour on a bright morning. The emigrant ship is going away and Emily, her dark friend, stands on the deck going out to America. They kiss and cry bitterly. But she believes that some day her dark friend will come back as she promises. She cries for the pain of separation and for the dangers of the sea that threaten the girl who is going away. The girl is older than she and has no lover. She too has no lover. Her sadness is brief. She is alone, friendless in her grandmother's garden and can see the garden, lonely now, in which the day before she played with her friend. Her grandmother consoles her, gives her a new clean pinafore to wear and buttoned boots, a present from her uncle, and nice bread and butter to eat and a big fire to sit down to.

The tone of sad nostalgia here is Joyce's, but the images of life are Nora's own. At that date, when Galway was a smaller place and more people lived in the centre of the town, there was more coming and going, more easy friendship with neighbours than now. Today 6 Whitehall has been rebuilt, but when I visited it, in the early 1970s, it had become a builder's yard and little could be discovered of what it was like when Nora lived there. The cottages on the other side of the street were due to be pulled down when the last old lady living there died. Once it must have been a street alive with children's voices on a summer morning, or sparkling with snow on a winter evening, as Joyce describes. But today what had been sad and desolate becomes again an area of modernized houses and smart offices.

After her grandmother died on 1st January 1897 Nora did not go back to her mother. At the Convent of Mercy and the free National School in Newtownsmith, she was taught to read and write a fairly clear hand; her attendance was excellent, though her results only middling, and her marks for grammar were good, though she was hopeless at Geography apparently. Her learning of the basics of the Catholic faith, the nuns would have considered just as essential. The instinctive attachment which Nora received in these early years of education was never to leave her. She carried in her heart the native feelings of her country towards the Catholic faith which her husband claimed to reject with such vehemence.

On leaving school at the age of 12 in April 1896, she was taken into the Presentation Convent on Nun's Island where she worked as a porteress and in the laundry. This was an enclosed order, and she must have come well recommended. She would stay there for four years, until 1900, when she was 16. Here she would have had presented to her the refinements of the Catholic faith as only nuns practise them. There was no more money after her grandmother's death to continue her education. A job in a convent was then thought safer for girls who had to earn some sort of living. Her slight resentment against her mother because of their long separation gave her an independent air at an early age. She was a pretty girl by now, with good features marred only by a slightly receding chin, with lovely auburn hair and a lilting voice.

It was at this time that she had her first experience of love. Her admirer (so her sister Cathleen told Patrick Henchy) was a young man of 16 named Michael Feeney. A school monitor, Feeney lived on William Street West and in February 1897 contracted typhoid complicated with pneumonia from which he died in the workhouse infirmary. He is buried in Rahoon Cemetery. His family name suggested that of Michael Furey, the lost love of Gretta Conroy in 'The Dead'.

So Nora worked in the convent for four years until 1900, when she left to rejoin her mother and family. Until 1900 the family were living in the lodgings in 1 Bowling Green; this was a large house with 12 rooms, but into these were crowded some 18 people. Mr Hughes and his wife had three rooms on the ground floor; the Barnacles had another three, and various lodgers occupied one each. The street was a narrow, crowded, working-class one. At the far end was a woollen factory in which some of the local men and girls were employed. Nearby was a slaughter-house, from which the smell of blood and offal pervaded the area. A little later the Barnacle family moved into 9 Bowling Green with Thomas Healy (where they were until 1905); then he left and Annie and her family moved in 1910 to 7 Bowling Green and then 12 Bowling Green (now a small museum styled the childhood home of Nora Barnacle, despite the fact that she never lived there), a small house, where they settled permanently. (Due to demolition, this was later called 4 Bowling Green, the address which appears in Joyce's letters, but in the local government and Census returns it remains number 12.)

Nora's life was one of small and simple pleasures. She and her friend Mary Halloren (who was also the daughter of a baker and lived at number 27) would spend their pennies, when they had them, on cream sweets, stealing as many more from the old women who owned the sweeteries, such as old Mrs Francis on Prospect Hill.

Sometimes the fun went too far. One evening they bought a card of black jelly babies, which they put into an important-looking envelope and sent across the road to a young man named Jim Connell. Jim had been waiting anxiously for a relative in America to send him his passage money so that he could emigrate as well. When he got the letter sent by the girls he was very excited, and came running into the Halloren house to ask someone to read it to him. When he found that it contained nothing but sweets he was furious with disappointment. He put the blame for the prank on an old sweetheart from the country and never spoke to her again.

Some of the girls' other pranks were stranger. When they were just a little older, they would dress up in the evenings in men's clothes borrowed from their brothers, tucking their hair under tweed caps and sauntering out for a stroll around Eyre Square. They were never caught at this, even though one evening they met Nora's uncle

Tommy and Mary said 'Good night' to him in a gruff voice as they passed.

There were other happy times, to rival those Christmas evenings at her grandmother's. At Hallowe'en, for instance, there was a party at the Hallorens'. The small children would play at cross-sticks, Nora often getting the soap in her mouth and having to wash it out. Afterwards they would fill their mouths with wheat and go round the houses in the street, listening at the open doors to catch some boy's name: it might be the name of the boy one of them would marry. If by chance they heard a name, they would burst out laughing and run away, afraid that the boy would catch them. But they never did.

At another friend's house they would try charms to tell their fortunes. They would stick nine pins in part of an apple, and throw away a tenth. Then they would wrap the apple up in a left stocking tied with a right garter. Nora would leave this under her pillow, hoping to dream in the night of the man she would marry.

Love had other oracles for the young, and at times they tried other kinds of fortune-telling. Once they stole a head of cabbage out of a stranger's garden, went into a field at night and, standing on a dung-heap, ate the raw cabbage leaves while staring into a mirror, hoping to see in the dark glass the face of a future husband. If Nora ever dreamed then of a man's face, it would not have been a stranger's or even that of her future husband, but a more familiar one, a face never dimmed even by other love affairs or marriage – the face of Sonny Bodkin, whom she thought of often in later life.

Nora was quite young when she knew Sonny, for she was still living with her grandmother in Whitehall and had not gone to work in the convent. Michael Maria Bodkin was about 17 at the time they met, and a student at Queens University in Galway. He was a dark handsome boy, with big expressive eyes: Nora particularly remembered his eyes. They would go out walking together, perhaps along the wooded lovers' walk between Tailors Hill and Dalysfort Road; Nora was 'great with him', as they say in Galway, the phrase being taken from the Gaelic. He was a very devoted admirer of the auburn-haired girl, but she was very young and afraid to be seen about with a boy by her uncles. Michael had a very good voice and, but for his bad health, would have studied music. At home he would accompany himself on a black upright piano which his family still own.

Sonny's father, Leo P. Bodkin, was a prosperous merchant with a shop at 1 and 2 Prospect Hill, on the corner with Eyre Square. He was well off, owning land and houses in other parts of the city, and in keeping with his status the family had a live-in maid. The Bodkins were one of the 13 Tribes of Galway, the old Norman settlers among whom were also the Joyces and the Lynches.

Bodkin was ambitious for his family; Sonny was sent to the University at a time when Catholics were discouraged from going there. Most of the 97 students in 1900–1901 were Protestants, and only 38 Catholic. Leo Bodkin, Sonny's elder brother, was well known in his time as a debater at Queen's College, and in 1904 he became the youngest councillor in the country when he was elected at the age of 21 to Galway Urban District Council. In 1906 he attempted to get the Nationalist candidacy for Galway City, which had been Captain O'Shea's, but the seat went to the writer Stephen Gwynn, who was duly elected. (Bodkin is mentioned but not named in Gwynn's memoirs.) Leo Bodkin's political career did not prosper; he became a solicitor and may have met Joyce while he was studying in Dublin in 1909, or so a tradition in the Bodkin family has it. The father's business declined and he died in Nun's Island in 1928. (Violet Cunningham, Sonny Bodkin's niece, was brought up in the house on Nun's Island after her parents left the city. She was struck herself by the coincidence with 'The Dead' and wondered if Joyce had heard about her in 1909 from her father Leo.)

To talk to Sonny, Nora and her friend Mary Halloren would go up to the shop on Prospect Hill and buy conversation lozenges, those old-fashioned sweets now found only in Ireland, with 'Meet Me Tonight' and 'I Love You' written on them. How long she knew Sonny is not clear, but it was long enough for his kindness and gentleness to make a lasting impression on her. He was a delicate boy, and she assumed he was 'weak in the chest' as they used to say in those days about consumptives. When her grandmother died in 1897, he seems to have heard something about her going into the convent, and one evening he came over after dark to the house in Whitehall. She was in her bedroom, packing her clothes, if we can believe the details related in 'The Dead', when she heard gravel being thrown against the window-panes. The window was so wet that she could not see through it, so she ran downstairs and slipped outside. There he was, shivering in the cold rain, his eyes bright in the shade of the wall at the end where there was a tree. She implored him to go home or he would get his death in the rain. All he could talk of was his love for her, but in the end he went away.

She never saw him again. He contracted rheumatic fever from the wetting that night and it left him with rheumatism and a weak heart. After leaving the college he became a clerk with the Galway Gas Company, in which his father had shares. Eventually in the autumn of 1899 he became bedridden, and during the winter his health declined. On Sunday, 11th February 1900, he died in his father's house on Prospect Hill.

When she heard he was dead Nora was deeply affected and took to her own bed with grief. She felt that he had really died for love of her. He had indeed died of a condition of the heart: not of love, as she believed, but of what his doctor called 'primary valvular heart disease of four months duration'.

His mother, Winifred Bodkin, was also deeply affected by her son's death. After Michael's passing she locked his room and it was never reopened until after her own death in 1915. Sonny Bodkin was buried in St Joseph's Cemetery in Rahoon outside the city, in a large tomb vault which the family had specially built which dominates the entrance path, shaded now by a row of dark cypress. The graveyard is on a low hill overlooking the city, on the edge of the countryside. Nora would often think of his lying there, and beyond his grave the rough fields of Connemara: this scene inspires Joyce's moving poem 'She Weeps over Rahoon'.

Young love was very sweet, as were her dreams of future happiness. The longings of her body were more immediate, and she learnt to soothe them by what Joyce later called 'the genteel art of self-satisfaction'. She was ripe with sensual appeal, albeit half conscious of it herself. If love had its mysteries, it also had its bitterness. Not all the charms in the world or hopes of happiness would keep a man's attentions from her.

The Presentation Convent where Nora worked was in Rahoon on the edge of the city, where it had been established in 1815. In 1882 the parish priest of Rahoon, Father Patrick Lally, built a new parish church dedicated to St Joseph on a site beside the convent. He was still the parish priest in 1895 when a newly-ordained priest, Father John Moran, joined him as a curate. Moran, typical of the ordinary Irish priest at the time, was the younger son of a strong farmer from Brownsisland near Tuam. Educated at St Joseph's Boys School in Galway, 'where his sterling character and honourable nature was known to all his companions', he completed his education under the Jesuits at St Ignatius College in Galway before going on to study for the priesthood in the Irish College in Paris. He was nothing exceptional, just an ordinary Irish priest.

In Rahoon Father Moran was a popular curate. He took a vigorous part in the election in South Galway in 1900 in the interest of the Irish National Party against the well-known local judge Lord Killanin. His great love, however, was music. He had a cultivated singing voice and a passion for religious music unusual at that time in Ireland. Wherever he went, he took a keen interest in the training of choirboys. Writing of him many years later, after his death, a local friend said that, 'In heart and ideals he was a child of all that was best in the culture and kindliness of the Gael. Sensitive as an Aeolian Harp, he trod the harsh paths of life with a light foot and shrinking nature, but when necessity arose a heart that never altered in doing good gave him the courage of a lion.'

While ministering to the spiritual needs of the Presentation Convent, Father Moran came to know Nora Barnacle. He was then a thin, ascetic-looking man of twenty-nine with brown hair. She was pleased by the kindness of this nice young man with the thick curly hair, who soon began asking her to tea at his lodgings in Sea Road. On these evenings they would have long chats; perhaps he told her of his time in Paris and what a lovely city it was. There was a growing familiarity. Flirting with good-looking young priests was something lots of girls did, and harmless enough it was most of the time. Eventually it went further as Joyce himself relates:

> One evening at tea he took her on his lap and said he liked her, she was a nice little girl. Then he put his hand up under her dress which was shortish. She however, I understand, broke away. Afterwards he told her to say in confession it was a man not a priest did 'that' to her. Useful difference.

So Joyce himself wrote in a letter to his brother nine years later, in which he does not name the priest. But he did not forget him: he gave his name and his curly hair to the young Gaelic League priest Emma Clery flirts with, much to Stephen's great disgust, in *Stephen Hero*.

The reaction of Nora herself, then nearly 16, seems to have been calmer and more sensible; at times she could be very self-possessed.

Perhaps she even felt sorry for the young priest, with a life of dedicated chastity before him. At least she did not have to live that way. However she felt, the week before Sonny died in February 1900, it was announced that Father Moran was being transferred as a curate to rural Ballyvaughan. (He returned to Galway as a priest of St Nicholas in 1919, so she might well have seen him on her visit to the city with her children in April 1922. He died suddenly at his mother's home in June 1923; some 300 people attended his funeral.)

Nora's life seemed strangely haunted by ill-luck. Bodkin had died. Another boy she knew named Kearns, the son of neighbours in Bowling Green, also died – perhaps serving with the British Army during the Boer War – of enteric fever at Bloemfontein. (He survives in *Ulysses* as Lieut. Stanley Gardner whom Molly Bloom fondly recalls kissing her by the canal before he left, as perhaps Kearns had kissed Nora by the Eglinton Canal bank before he left Galway.) When they heard that Kearns was dead the girls in the convent teased her. Because she was so fond of boys they nicknamed her 'the man killer'. But the name now had a more sinister ring to it. Would she always be so unlucky in love?

That was in 1900: doubtless there were other boys, but not as many as Joyce may have liked to imagine. One at least we can be certain about. A couple of years later, Nora became friendly with a youth named Willie Mulvagh. (He also appears in *Ulysses*, as Lieut. Mulvey with whom Molly had a more than friendly relationship while living in Gibraltar.) She met him quite casually, crossing one of the bridges over the Corrib. He worked in the soda-water factory owned by Joseph Young in Eglinton Street; they lived in Mary Street, across the road from Bowling Green. He was not a Galway man, it seems, but a Protestant from Tuam. He asked to meet her again and Nora asked Mary Halloren what she should do; Mary told her not to worry and to go out with him. But as they were only allowed out at night if they went together, what was Mary to do with herself while Nora went courting? She said she would sit in the Abbey Church and wait for Nora. Not only were the girls more tightly disciplined in those days, there really was not much to do in Galway then except walk around and talk. In any case, they had to be in by 10 o'clock. If Nora were late her uncle Tommy, who was now living with the Barnacles in 12 Bowling Green in place of their father, would give her a good thrashing.

So Nora went out walking with Willie Mulvagh in the evenings.

Willie's sister later recalled that she 'was a handsome, beautiful girl, with lovely auburn hair, and Willie was deeply in love with her. She was a charming girl. She was the daughter of very respectable and highly respected parents. Willie was very upset when Nora left Galway.' She was not in love with him, not as she had been with Sonny; she had been more than fond of Sonny and he would always linger somewhere in her affections. Mulvagh, however, was good fun and she went out with him to pass the time. Whereas the relationships she had known with others were simply the crushes of boys and girls, it is likely that hers with Mulvagh was more truly sexual: 'Mulvey was the first', as *Ulysses* says. The wisdom of the flesh would have prevented Nora from letting Willie Mulvagh go too far, but it is likely enough that she gained some experience from walking out with him.

However, her uncle Tommy was told about them and he did not approve. He did not care for Mulvagh, not because he worked in a soda-water factory – he was only a baker himself – but because he was a Protestant. There had been enough trouble over the Barnacles in one way or another without Nora losing her faith over a Protestant. This was not a trivial matter. Though Protestants were tolerated in a social sense, marriage implied obligations which the Catholics were careful about.

On the summer evenings of 1903 when she went out, her uncle Tommy would be out himself walking around the town and watching for her, trailing his blackthorn stick and whistling *My Mountain Maid Arise*. When she came in, he would be there before her. 'Well, my girl, out again with your Protestant,' he would remark. Eventually she was forbidden to see Mulvagh again ... but out she went.

There was something wilful, if brave, about this show of independence. Nora seems to have inherited something of her mother's reckless character that made the match with Thomas Barnacle. Walking out with a Protestant was not the most popular of pastimes in rural Ireland then or now. This time when she came home, uncle Tommy was waiting for her once again. Annie Barnacle was ordered from the room, then Tommy proceeded to thrash the girl with his blackthorn. Nora fell to the floor, almost fainting, clinging to his knees.

She was then 19. Uncle Tommy was in his early forties and a married man since 1898; he could not have set about the girl in this way without there being some slight edge of sexuality to his motives. In her situation, Nora was only too open to sexual and physical abuse.

By now Nora had had enough of this kind of treatment. It was not as if Tommy had the rights over her of a father. Since the separation, the children had seen little of Thomas Barnacle. He had become a shabby, stooped little drunkard with a white face and a white moustache and white eyebrows, above little eyes which were pink-veined and raw. Whenever he appeared on the street the Barnacle children would run in and close the door on him just as their mother had told them to do. There was no room for a father in that small four-roomed house, nor soon after for uncle Tommy either.

Nora could bear it no longer and the next week she left for Dublin, putting that long train journey eastward through the bogs of central Ireland between her and the scenes of her childhood. She may have secured her position in Dublin through a domestic agency, perhaps that run by Mrs Finn.

Nora rarely wrote. What was the point? To Mary Halloren she simply sent a postcard: 'My old pal, here I am in Dublin and my uncle Tommy won't follow me anymore.'

She came home to Bowling Green for only one visit after that, perhaps at Christmas 1903. She had got herself a job as a chambermaid in Finn's Hotel in Leinster Street – a respectable establishment owned by a Limerick family which catered to residents, country visitors to Dublin and the occasional commercial traveller. One of these, a man named Holohan, attempted to court her sexual favours and produced a French letter to encourage her, but she resisted. This Holohan may well have been the model for Hoppy Holohan, in Joyce's fiction.

The hotel was part of a newish red-brick building overlooking Trinity College Park, and just opposite were the Turkish baths with their curious Oriental onion domes and minarets. From her bedroom window at the back of the house she could see the students in their white flannels playing cricket in the summer or riding round the cinder track on their sports cycles. She was happy enough there. She had new friends in the hotel, where there was the occasional party. Dublin was very different from Galway and very exciting to a young girl. She had escaped.

*

One day in June 1904 Nora was walking back to the hotel along the wall of the college park in Nassau Street, when a young man stopped and spoke to her.

Within six months she was to commit her life to this same, strange young man, and happily leave Ireland with him for their great adventure in Europe.

PART VIII

Per questa andata, onde gli dai tu vanto,
   intese cose che furon cagione
   di sua vittoria. . . .

Dante: *Inferno* (Canto II, 25–27)

17

DUBLINERS ON THE ADRIATIC

The steamer from the North Wall took the couple to Holyhead, whence the long night journey by train brought them into Euston station early in the morning of 9th October. But they barely paused in London before catching the Paris train, via Newhaven and Dieppe, the cheap route already familiar to Joyce. Overnight this brought them in the morning of 10th October into Paris, Gare St Lazaire. There Joyce left Nora (whose new shoes were hurting her) to wait for him in a public park while he went to see if he could raise money from his few French friends, and to meet briefly with Constantine Curran and James Murnahan (later Mr Justice Murnahan of the Appeals Court): he was anxious that these respectable friends of his should not know about Nora.

In the afternoon the couple caught the Zürich train from the Gare de Lyon in the south of the city, and after yet another night journey arrived in Zürich early in the morning of 11th October. A porter at the Bahnhof suggested that they might be able to find accommodation – even at that odd hour – in the Gasthaus Hoffnung (Hotel of Hope), over the river in the Reitergasse. There they went and were accommodated.

The scene at the end of Joyce's story 'The Dead', in which Gabriel Conroy and his wife Gretta – the name being used by Nora on this journey was Gretta Greene – are shown to their rooms by candlelight by a night porter and have to undress by the feeble light from the street outside, was suggested by this grim arrival: it owed its underlying emotion for Joyce to this late arrival in Zürich.

Here at last, in the early morning hours of 11th October 1904, James and Nora consummated their marriage, in the words of the

Catholic doctrine of marriage, which *Ulysses* borrows for its explication of Leopold Bloom's marital state: 'with ejaculation of semen in the natural female organ'. Having breakfasted Joyce wrote to his brother Stanislaus, relating their hectic travels. Among his other items of news he announced of Nora (with perhaps a touch of vulgarity): 'Alors elle est touchée.' Nevertheless, this was to remain a special place and a special day.

Then he went round to the Berlitz School and discovered that there was not, as he had been led to believe, a position available for him. He had (he thought) been deceived by a British agent who claimed to act for the Berlitz Schools. But after several days of costly waiting, pleading and negotiation, he was told to proceed through Trieste to the port of Pola (now Pula) on the Adriatic coast of Austria, where there was an opening for a teacher of English.

The Joyces arrived in Trieste, tired and travel-worn, on 20th October and reached Pola by ferry the next day. Here they were to stay until March 1905. Joyce's first letters home were from Pola and full of complaints. The news from Dublin which he may have received would have included the announcement of Ellen Callanan's death on 4th December at the family home, 41 Aughrim Street, which the Joyces had so often visited from Cabra. Also he heard that his story 'After the Race' had appeared in the *Irish Homestead* on 17th December.

Unsettled and not completely happy in his circumstances, Joyce wrote an angry New Year's letter to his aunt Josephine. He was busy with all kinds of drudgery, though his lovely laziness of temper also played a part in his failure to write long letters to those at home, from whom nevertheless he would always expect long and detailed dispatches. By now he hoped she had read 'After the Race', for he had completed chapters XII, XIII and XIV of his novel, and would be sending them to her.

Nora was pregnant by now, and he hoped his aunt could see her way to writing to her with advice, as she was 'of course adorably stupid on these points'. Her husband, like most Irish males, was even more ignorant of the sexual facts of life.

He remained highly amused by what news he did hear from Ireland – Stanislaus had sent him a diverting account of some mourners near the cattle market – perhaps in the City Arms Hotel, which features so mysteriously in *Ulysses*.

I am trying to move on to Italy as soon as possible as I hate this Catholic country with its hundred races and a thousand languages, governed by a parliament which can transact no business and sits for a week at the most and by the most physically corrupt royal house in Europe.

Joyce was still alert to the effects of syphilis which had so fascinated him in Dublin: Prince Rudolf and Maria Vetsera, his lover, were said to have killed themselves because they were diseased. Josephine would soon be unable to take these references in her stride. However:

Pola is a back-of-God-speed place – a naval Siberia – 37 men of war in the harbour, swarming with faded uniforms. Istria is a long boring place wedged into the Adriatic peopled by ignorant Slavs who wear little red caps and colossal breeches.

Pola in fact was an ancient city, already in existence in the third century BC, with many Roman remains, and a thriving varied modern life. Even though he was quickly disillusioned with many things in Europe, with one thing he was still content: 'I have not been able to discover any falsehood in this nature which has the courage to trust me. It was this night three months ago that we left the North Wall. Strange to say I have not yet left her upon the street, as so many men said I would. In conclusion – I spit upon the image of the Tenth Pius.'* With disdain he reassured himself of his rupture from the Church by these kinds of remarks, which his poor aunt had to bear with the patience of a saint. Pius X would also be judged a saint in 1954.

*

In March 1905 Joyce was transferred from Pola back to Trieste. He himself spoke of a nest of spies being discovered, but according to his friends it was a simple matter of business. They took an apartment at 3^{III} Piazza Ponterosso where they stayed until the end of April 1905, when they moved to 30^{II} Via S. Nicolo. They were living there on 27th July when their son Giorgio was born. Joyce telegraphed his family: 'Son born Jim.' This was duly amended in verbal transmission by Vincent Cosgrave to 'Mother and Bastard doing well.' Joyce gave his son the name of his dead brother, the name too of the distant founder of their clan, but the infant was not baptized.

* Giuseppe Sarto had been elected Pope on 4th August 1903 on the death of Gioachino Pecci, Leo XIII, in July of that year.

Joyce claimed that he and Nora, using the name Gretta Greene again – a play perhaps on the Scottish village, Gretna Green, where runaway couples from England could be married by the blacksmith – went through a form of civil ceremony before Il Cavallerie Fabbri, a local official in Trieste; and also that another official, Il Conte Dandino ('the last gentleman in Europe' Joyce nicknamed him), had issued the Joyces with a certificate of legitimacy for Giorgio, a commonplace when the father marries the mother after the birth of the child.*

From Dublin there would have come news to which Joyce nowhere refers in any surviving letters: the death on 25th August of his great-aunt, Julia Lyons (the 'Julia Morkan' of 'The Dead'), in St Monica's home for old women in Belvidere Place, near the Joyces' former home off Mountjoy Square. Though letters from Dublin all too often brought news of deaths of people in the older generation, which depressed Joyce, he would in due course put the elegiac mood they induced to good purpose in his short stories.

In September 1905 Grant Richards, the London publisher to whom he had submitted them before leaving Dublin, wrote to Joyce rejecting the poems he had collected as *Chamber Music* – only with a subsidy from the author would he be able to publish this. Joyce had to confess, when he wrote to thank Richards for his interest, that he had no money for such a scheme.

This rejection was the beginning of a long struggle to get not only this slim volume of poems, but also his stories and the novel on which he was still at work, into print. Joyce was grateful to the enterprising if slightly piratical Richards, nevertheless, for his interest in the poems. For all his failings, Richards was a judge of literature.

In October 1905 Stanislaus Joyce was finally persuaded to come out to Trieste, initially to keep James and Nora company, eventually just to keep them. He had abandoned his studies in the Apothecaries' Hall (which provided many with a short cut to a medical career, among them Joyce's friend John Ellwood), and sought to make a living if not a fortune in Austria. By now, the former Prefect of the

---

* Nevertheless, his British lawyers – to ensure succession under British law, and horrified at this quaint Continental solution of using a false name, made the Joyces undergo the indignity of a civil ceremony in London on 4th July 1931.

Sodality of Our Lady in Belvedere had joined his brother in apostasy, but his would be more complete and more bitter.

The following month, November 1905, Joyce dispatched to Grant Richards the first manuscript of *Dubliners*. The inevitable delay followed, and in February 1906 Joyce had to write to Richards, but was then delighted to have the book accepted. He explained that he had also written 1,000 (actually 914) pages of a novel. *Stephen Hero*, begun with such ardour, would never be completed. He would write no more of it, and the draft would lie neglected in his desk for two years. He had also written a thirteenth story, and would send it. Though he made a joke about the number thirteen, it was an omen of the ill-luck which now began to haunt his little book.

That month the family moved, on 24th February 1906, to a flat on the second floor of 1 Via Giovanni Boccaccio. Richards now announced that he was having difficulty with his printers, who were objecting to the content of Joyce's stories. On 26th April Joyce wrote to Richards in reply to this troubling news, and again on 20th May. In yet another letter on 23rd June – Richards now had the revised manuscript – Joyce defended his point of view and his method:

> It is not my fault that the odour of ashpits and old weeds and offal hangs round my stories. I seriously believe that you will retard the course of civilisation in Ireland by preventing the Irish people from having one good look at themselves in my nicely polished looking glass.

And there the matter of *Dubliners* rested when the Joyces moved at the end of July 1906 from Trieste to Rome, Joyce at last fulfilling the wish he had imparted to his aunt Josephine when he and his companion first arrived in Austria two years before. Rome, however, was to prove a strangely mixed experience for them both, at once a great disappointment and a great creative opportunity, which would affect not only the stories on which he still worked but the novel he had hoped to complete.

18

Rome: An Infernal Machine

On 30th July 1906 the Joyces left Trieste by train for the Hungarian port of Fiume; there they caught the night boat across the Adriatic to the Italian port of Ancona. Fiume was, so Joyce thought, 'a clean asphalted town with a modern go-ahead air', far finer for its size than Trieste. They spent the whole night on the deck of the boat, the cheapest way to travel. This left Joyce out of sorts, for the next day, by contrast, he saw Ancona biliously, as a filthy hole – 'like a rotten cabbage' – where he was swindled three times: by the money changer, the cabman and the railway official at the station. They had to drive three miles from the pier to the railway station, through a fine panorama of houses, yet there was something almost Irish in Ancona's bleak, gaunt, beggarly ugliness. Italy did not auger well.

On 1st August they arrived safely by train at Rome. James and Nora were very tired, but it was only in the last few miles that the infant Giorgio got restless, having taken the journey so far in his stride. Descending upon the traditional Strangers' Quarter between the Corso and the Piazza di Spanga, they found an apartment (only a single room for the three of them) at Via Frattina 52, where Signora Dufour (surely not an Italian) would have charged a stiff rent. From centuries of catering for tourists, this area was by far the most expensive district of Rome.

Joyce then set out to locate the premises of his new employers, Nast-Kolb & Schumacher, one of the leading financial institutions in Rome. The width of the Tiber frightened him, the bank building – an immense palazzo on the Corso – terrorized him, and he thought Rome would please Stanislaus more than him. While searching for the bank, he passed a palazzo on the corner of the Corso on the front wall of which there was a plaque:

'In this house Percy Bysshe Shelly
wrote the *Cenci* and *Prometheus Unbound*.'

At least one writer had achieved something for literature in Rome.

That evening in the Piazza Colonna they heard a military band play a selection from Wagner's *Siegfried*. Here they had a chance to observe the citizens at their leisure. Joyce, like many Dubliners, valued informality as a test of sincerity: the Romans he thought were 'excruciatingly well-mannered'.

The next day, 1st August, he went into the bank for his interview with Schumacher, the manager, whom he found grimly Germanic in his outlook; he was Consul for the Austro-Hungarian Empire. Joyce had sent him a copy of the letter Timothy Harrington had given him in 1902. As a city mayor on the Continent was a powerful figure, Joyce was now quizzed about this document: was the Lord Mayor a friend of the family, Schumacher asked; was Joyce's father alive; and so on, for some time. Finally, the interview over, Joyce was placed in the Italian Correspondence department of the bank.

The bank offices were in the ground floor of the Palazzo Marignoli on the Corso, fronted by the Caff'è Aragno. The actual entrance, however, was at 87 Via San Claudio. There were about fifty employees in the firm, and the atmosphere was more apathetic even than the Berlitz School in Trieste. His hours of work were to be the usual Roman ones: 8·30 to 12, and 2 to 7·30, nine hours a day in all. Though he was given little work to do, and that little very easy and mechanical, he was paid 65 lire for the journey and an advance of 100 lire (about £6 12s).

So far Joyce was safe financially. However, he found Rome confusing and twice lost his way en route to the bank: a remarkable achievement in so confined a locality. Though many items seemed cheaper, after a few days Rome was proving to be more costly than Trieste, and he expected to lose money for the first week or two. This would be 'Too damn long,' Joyce thought; he was too optimistic.

Whenever he was free over the next five days they went to see St Peter's, the Pincio (the fine garden overlooking one of the city gates with a magnificent view of the Vatican), the Forum, and the Colosseum. The museums of the Vatican were, alas, closed on

Sundays, the only whole day he had off; but as Joyce did not care for art, this was little loss to him. St Peter's did not impress him: it was not much bigger than St Paul's in London, and from the inside the dome did not give the same impression of height as it did from outside. This was not true, of course, but Joyce was already determined to denigrate everything he found in the Eternal City, the seat of the Pope. The first Pope, the Apostle Peter, the founder of the Church at Rome, was buried in the crypt of the basilica: a fact which surprised him, despite all those lessons in church history at Belvedere. He had expected to hear fine music in St Peter's, though there was not much of that; but then he was at one of the twenty side altars for mass, not at a major ceremony on the main altar. That Joyce went to mass in Rome, albeit for the music, does not detract from the fact that he actually went to mass still, five years after he had broken with the Church.

Rome was not the city state it had been in the heyday of Papal power. Since it had become the capital of Italy and the Pope had withdrawn within the Vatican, it had become shabby and run down in the opinion of well-informed travellers such as Augustus Hare. Joyce felt this too. The neighbourhood of the Colosseum was like an old cemetery with broken columns of temples and slabs. The British tourists quoting Byron from their guide-books and the parties of American schoolgirls annoyed him. English and Americans abroad talked at the top of their voices, he found, and he did not care for their accents. Indeed, they were a taste he was not to acquire until it was useful to do so in the 1920s. Ancient Rome bored him. He had had enough, he told his brother, of stupid monuments. Giorgio, however, tried the echoes of both the Colosseum and St Peter's, calling out 'Iga, Iga' when the priest began to chant.

Joyce hoped to find an agreeable café, such as those which existed in Trieste, but he did not care for the Caff'è Aragno, which served cold lunches only. (He explained to his brother that there was only one café in Rome; the guide-books of the day list at least seven. But again he had no desire to be satisfied.) He was forced – so he claimed – to go to the Caff'è Greco on the Via Condotti, which had been frequented by Henri Amiel, Thackeray, Byron, Ibsen and the like; even today it is where one is most likely to meet non-Romans. Here the menu was in English, 1½d for coffee, a 6-cup pot of tea for 6d. There were papers too: the *Continental Daily Mail*, the *Herald Tribune*, and the *Journal*. In these he could keep up with the state of the world, but he depended on Stanislaus to keep in touch with the real news, that is to say news from Ireland. He would have to wait upon the return of Wyndham, an Anglo-Irishman resident in Rome to whom he had an introduction, to find something better in the way of accommodation.

Debts pursued him from Trieste, but he was more anxious to hear from Grant Richards in England than he was from the baker, the landlord, the tailors and the doctors to whom he owed money in Austria.

Her husband does not seem to have given much thought to Nora's feelings about her new situation. Giorgio, however, liked Rome and was well pleased with the attention which the Romans paid him. Their landlady liked him too. As the late Maria O'Donohoe in Dublin would have said, Signora Dufour was a 'very nice person'.

The news from Dublin which Joyce eventually received included the election of his college friend Thomas Kettle for the Ulster constituency of East Tyrone on 25th August 1906. But Joyce did not believe that Ireland's problems would be solved by parliamentary means: his Fenian views (now disguised as socialism) were still too strong for him to be a ready advocate of mere democracy. What other news about people he knew was he missing, he wondered. Another surprise was Oliver Gogarty's marriage in September. Joyce's comments to his brother on this event suggest that he hardly saw Gogarty as the marrying kind: 'I fancy as he emerged from the church door his agile eye went right and left a little anxiously in search of a certain lean myopic face in the crowd, but he will rapidly grow out of that remaining sensitivity.' The conformities required by marriage and society annoyed him. He saw in Gogarty's church wedding a new tide of religious conformity, and felt that the establishment of the Catholic Church in full power in Europe would mean 'the renewal of the Inquisition'.

Joyce was now writing 'A Painful Case', for which he needed the manuscript and the book of notes he had made in Paris and the Latin quotations he had copied from the prophecies of the Abbot Joachim of Fiore in Marsh's Library. These Stanislaus sent him. Money remained a problem: would Stanislaus send him some? He had spent 42 lire on clothes for Nora, Giorgio and himself, paid the rent in full and was left with 52 lire. Four days later he had only 25 lire. 'The real reason the money goes so quickly,' he explained in a letter to Trieste, 'is that we eat enormously.' Nora was getting healthier-looking, as well she might considering that for dinner she would eat two slices of roast beef, two polpetti, a tomato stuffed with rice, a salad and some wine. The meat they bought already cooked and took along to eat in a little wine-shop. One evening, for instance, they ate an entire roast chicken and a plateful of ham, yet went to bed hungry.

From Stanislaus Joyce expected money, yet he claimed he would both repay this loan and add money for his savings account. He was reading Oscar Wilde's *The Picture of Dorian Gray*, and felt that if Wilde had had the courage to develop the allusions to the underlying homosexuality the book would have been better. Joyce valued frankness for itself, as his own stories would show.

On the evening of 15th August they went to see the New Protestant Cemetery, beside the Porta San Paulo, in the south of the city. Here the ashes of Shelley had been laid up near the eastern wall, with a recent monument over them, shaded by sombre cypresses, which greatly affected Joyce's imagination. He was troubled every night, now, by horrible and terrifying dreams: 'Death, corpses, assassinations in which I take an unpleasantly prominent part.' Death and burial was a theme beginning to run in his imagination. He looked for a notice in the paper of Gogarty's arrival in Rome on his honeymoon tour, but saw none. He arranged to take lessons in his language from a Dane named Pedersen. Meanwhile, they muttered to each other in German mixed with Danish.

By the middle of August he was still fretting about Grant Richards, adding paragraphs to 'A Painful Case', and thinking he would rewrite 'After the Race'. Yet if Richards sent proofs now he would pass them without radical revision, he thought. A picture of Archbishop Walsh exposed on the street also reminded him of Ireland. He was reading the anti-clerical paper *L'Asino* and shocking the other bank clerks with his liberalism. Joyce as a socialist believed in revolution, they believed in beating their children. His own son was a delight to him, blowing soap bubbles with his mother while he read Wilde; he would never be able to beat him. Nora too was skilled at this game: some of her bubbles reached the size of a football.

He borrowed 100 lire on 20th August, received 50 lire from Stanislaus on 31st August, but had to pay his landlady 40 lire. His trousers, worn through and patched, disgraced him at the bank. It was not pleasant to live in this way. News from Ireland told of Kettle, Skeffington, Father Delany and J.M. O'Sullivan all in the public eye.

And here am I (whom their writings and lives nauseate to the point of vomiting) writing away letters for ten hours a day like the blue devil on the offchance of pleasing three bad-tempered bankers and inducing them to retain my position while (as a luxury) I am allowed to haggle for two years with the same publisher, trying to induce him to publish a book for which he has intense admiration. Orco Dio.

From Wilde he had passed on to reading George Moore's novel *The Lake*, about a priest's loss of faith in his vocation; he failed to note that the preface was by Edouard Dujardin, whom he later claimed gave him the notion of interior monologue.

One evening they dined with the proprietor of the little wine shop where they ate, on a pudding supplied by a Sicilian priest. The cafe owner had a revolver to protect himself from assault, for Rome was a dangerous and violent place. A few days later Giorgio was struck on the face by a careless carter's whip, an incident which deeply angered Joyce. But that was the least of his worries: money, as always, was the most pressing problem. He had no desire to sponge on his brother, only to be helped over the coming month. He needed the money to retain his position. On 3rd September he had only 10 lire. He answered an advertisement for a language teacher. Wyndham, his Irish connection, was away in Naples and there was no chance of lessons. A student ready to pay turned up, so there was a chance that he might yet get through to the end of the month.

His male friends, he observed to his brother, failed to understand him in the same way that Nora or Josephine Murray did, despite being simple and uncomplicated women. He longed to be accepted and to live in comfort; he dreamed of being in a seaside place in England or Ireland, eating rashers and eggs in the morning, of English sunshine, beefsteak and onions, and a pier at night. This dream, which owed much to a childhood in Bray, was one he would indulge to the full in later years.

In September he was moved to the reception desk where the work was lighter, and he had such agreeable tasks as cashing a *Freeman's Journal* cheque for their Rome Correspondent P.J. Connellann. Again he wrote to Grant Richards. Money worries, keeping up appearances and fretting about Richards: all these consumed mental energy.

Amid all his troubles, by the end of September he reported that he had 'a new story for *Dubliners* in my head. It deals with Mr Hunter.' This story of Mr Hunter's days' wanderings through

Dublin was to be called 'Ulysses'. Although it was never written as a story, in time it provided the essential structure of his novel. Hunter, as his father had perhaps suggested to him when they met the man at Martin Kane's funeral in 1904, was a non-Catholic who had married an unfaithful Catholic wife. As this Hunter was a Belfast Presbyterian, it is unlikely that Joyce's fictional Hunter was as yet Jewish in his mind. But since Presbyterians were of little interest to Joyce's Catholic imagination, the attraction of a Jewish hero would soon develop on him.

However, future literary schemes depended on present success with Grant Richards. He talked to the rather appalling Wyndham, who was married to an English woman and was a most foul snob. He took legal advice from a local attorney about Richards and replied to Gogarty rejecting his advances. In a letter to Stanislaus he admitted, significantly – given the importance it was to assume for him in his ideas about Dublin – that he knew little about venereal disease.

A major event in Rome during Joyce's stay was the ninth congress of the Italian Socialist Party; this took place between 7th and 10th October, and he followed its proceedings in the papers with some interest. The party was divided: a Syndicalist faction led by Arturo Labriola was dedicated to a Marxist revolution in the industrial towns of the north; Labriola, however, was from Naples. The other main wing was a reforming group led by Signor Turati which believed in parliamentary reform (and to an Irish mind would have seemed like John Redmond's party). Between these were the Integralists led by Enrico Ferri, editor of *Avanti*, and widely considered a mere opportunist. Though Joyce admired Labrioli, the congress ended with his defeat (by 5,000 to 27,000), the party as a whole preferring a *rapprochement* between the other wings. No clear political policy in fact emerged; it was exciting, colourful and ineffectual. Observers noted that the Socialist vote was already in decline, and Labriola's main device of general strikes was not welcomed by the urban workers.

Joyce shared some Italians' dislike of parliamentarians, and of course many of these socialists were eventually to burgeon into the Fascisti of the Mussolini era. But politics for Joyce was mere play-acting. As his brother pointed out, he was a feeble socialist at best, his individualism being too well developed for him to be carried away by dreams of collective action.

On the evening of 14th November, at about twenty minutes past six, an individual approached the Caff'è Aragno and placed on the steps a small briefcase which he covered with a coat. He then left. The customers were looking curiously at the case when it exploded. The café was showered with debris and filled with thick smoke, and windows nearby were shattered. Next door to the café, in the same building, Joyce was sitting at his desk, heard the explosion and felt the palazzo shake. Soon the street was filled with people running about and shouting 'Bomba, Bomba,' the pavement of the Corso littered with broken cups.

Five days later, on Sunday 18th November, another bomb went off, this time in St Peter's. Joyce had planned to go there for morning mass and would have been in the church when the bomb went off, but changed his mind and arrived in the afternoon. The next day, a third bomb was thrown in Piazza di Spanga, at the head of Via Frattina, only steps away from the Joyces' flat.

At first he could pass this off as a matter of things getting pretty lively, but he was scared that the forthcoming visit by the King of Greece might mean a serious explosion in the neighbourhood. It did not matter to him if it were anarchists or *agents provocateurs* who were responsible for the bombs; his fears were real.

Revolutionary talk at the Socialist Congress was all very well; bombs in his office building were another matter. Joyce's socialism, which had been on the wane, by the end of his stay in Rome was extinct. He would not wish then to class himself as either a socialist, anarchist or reactionary. The political Joyce was dead, killed off by these Roman outrages, and would never be revived.

November passed into December, and to Joyce's surprise their landlady threw them out. This, though he denied it, was because of his drinking. At 11.30 one night the family had to take a cab and search for a place in a hotel. Joyce had little experience of hotels, this being only the second time he had stayed in one with Nora. The first time had been in Zürich, when they had consummated their relationship and he had learned a little about her past. Now, with snow falling on Rome, his mind may have reverted to that scene, and then to his present feelings of anguish and impotence. Arriving late, they were presumably shown to their room by a servant with a candle: this detail from 'The Dead' fits this experience better than it does the well-appointed Gresham in 'The Dead'. From the room in Rome the chain of association led back to the Gresham and then to the better times in the Dublin of the old days, and to ruminations on the long Dublin history of the Flynns. The materials of 'The Dead' were presenting themselves to his imagination, but they would not yet be written. The revelations of Zürich now combined with the despair of Rome into a fruitful union.

With immense difficulty he secured a room and they moved there a week later. This was at 51^{IV}, Via Monte Brianzo, running along the Tiberside with a view towards the Vatican. They had only one room and one bed, in which the Joyces, like the Blooms, had to sleep head to toe. He did not forget his brother's birthday, nor did his father forget him, writing to seek a £1 note for Christmas. Yet Christmas Eve found them reduced to 11 lire and the prospect of dining off pasta for the holiday. With his long hours at the bank, his further hours of teaching, and his drinking, this was 'the low-water mark in Xmases this 'ere time'.

Nevertheless, by January he had the idea for three or four immortal stories in his head, though he was too cold to write them.

Scene: draughty little stone-flagged room, chest of drawers to left on which are the remains of lunch in the centre, a small table on which are *writing materials* (*He* never forgot them) and a saltcellar: in the background, a small-sized bed. A young man with a snivelling nose sits at the little table: on the bed sits a madonna and a plaintive infant. It is a January day. Title of the above: *The Anarchist*.

The madonna on the bed was, Joyce now knew, expecting a second child.

Rome meant little to Joyce because he could not and did not want to participate in its life; only the dramas of religion caught his real attention. In the second week of January the Vatican was celebrating the Union of Rites, and he longed to attend and witness the Coptic, Greek, Chaldean and other Oriental rites. 'But I might as well be in Cabra.'

A small relief in these days was the arrival of a contract from Elkin Matthews for *Chamber Music*. John Long, however, now added his name to those who had rejected his stories. The appearance of the first issue of *The Belvederian* was welcome: he sent George Dempsey, the editor, a poem for the Summer 1907 issue.

However, the great excitement was the news of the riots in Dublin over J.M. Synge's brutal play *The Playboy of the Western World*. Here was yet another artist, another acquaintance, making his mark while Joyce rotted abroad. The initial demonstrations were followed a few days later by a debate in which his medical friend Daniel Sheehan shone forth with the frankness of his speech. Sheehan had stayed the course, and now had the economic freedom to speak out. It was what Joyce had wanted but not achieved.

This disturbed and distressed Joyce, giving him stomach pains. He went one evening to *The Dusk of the Gods,* but did not enjoy it. Wagner had marked their arrival at Rome; now he would mark their departure. The same day he gave in his notice at the bank. Since being in Rome he had not put pen to paper. He would achieve nothing living the way he was; there was no future for him in commerce. He hoped he might return to Trieste and give lessons – and had Artifoni not promised him his position back? He felt that life was slipping away while his friends, even that minor fellow Coppinger, were making their way. Even the annual commemoration of Giordano Bruno left him cold, again the accents of the American scholars in attendance disgusting him. Nora, on her own initiative, had taken another flat on which they had to pay rent, which added to their troubles in Rome.

Joyce had fallen out of sympathy with a country which had held his imagination since his schooldays. The Italians, he decided, had no delicacy – this from the future author of *Ulysses!* At the Giordano procession he was idly watching a young woman when he was startled to see that attached to a ring round her neck she had a small gold phallus which she carried unthinkingly to her mouth now and again. In his puritanical Irish way he was shocked, for he thought it required either a great deal of talent or a great deal of courage to render such facts of life as the sexual organs in any way interesting. The clerks at the banks talked casually of '*cazzo, culo* or *coglioni*' and drove him to distraction. The little phallus was intended not to shock but to ward off the evil eye, and was part of the hearty, earthy, pagan culture of the Mediterranean which the cold, Catholic, Hyperborean Joyce would never be able to enjoy. His soul was frozen in the sins of his youth.

Casting around for another post, Joyce thought of Marseilles – shades here of *The Count of Monte Cristo* which he had read as an impressionable child. There was an agreeable job in the port which would suit him. Stanislaus urged him to be sensible and withdraw his notice, but Joyce refused. 'My mouth is full of decayed teeth and my soul of decayed ambitions.'

At the end of the month he cast his die: 'I have come to the conclusion that it is time I made up my mind whether I am to become a writer or a patient Cousins. But the verses are not worth talking about: and I begin to think neither are the stories.'

The sojourn in the Eternal City had lasted a mere nine months, but as it gave birth to his greatest story, 'The Dead', the interlude was not without its bounty. He had lost his faith in politics, which meant that only in literature was there any hope of saving his soul. In Rome, too, his emotions had undergone a painful change, for Rome was largely his inspiration for *Exiles* when he came to write that drama nearly a decade later, as the references to Nora's past and to their visit to Shelley's grave in the notes for the play show, connecting it directly with 'The Dead'. The extreme isolation of Gabriel Conroy's soul, described at the conclusion of 'The Dead', represented the nadir of Joyce's life on the Continent. But the determination to become his own kind of writer which took him back to Trieste was the beginning not of better days but of a new stage in his struggle with fortune.

A Portrait of
the Artist

March 1907—24th July 1909

Having made his arrangements to leave Rome, Joyce slipped away from Nora to celebrate by drinking in the Pincian Gardens. He was reckless enough to expose his wallet to his companions and they duly relieved him of it, adding insult to injury by pretending to be patrol officers and taking him off to the police station to report the crime. Enough was enough. The Holy Family fled from the Eternal City, this time by train overland by way of Florence, that city whose history had so fascinated him as a schoolboy, but they did not stop to look at the city of Dante and Bruno. Joyce had had enough of the Italians.

When they arrived back in Trieste on 7th March, they returned to a new apartment (courtesy of the efforts of the ever-patient Stanislaus) at Via S. Nicola 32^{III}. Joyce now resumed his old routines of private language lessons, now adding to them more journalism and public lecturing.

In March he wrote an article on Home Rule for the *Piccolo*. The paper had been founded by Theodore Mayer in 1881, and at this time was edited by Roberto Prezioso, to whom Joyce had given lessons in the early days of his time in Trieste. Short of money after his stay in Rome, Joyce agreed with Prezioso to write a series on Ireland under British rule. The paper supported the cause of the Italian Irredentist movement in Trieste, and the parallels between two different empires would prove congenial reading for the newspaper's patrons.

The political situation in Trieste was as complicated as that in Dublin. The original Latin population which spoke Italian wished to be united with the Kingdom of Italy, and were Liberals. Then there were others – of German origin, connected with the new industries and shipping companies – who supported the Austrian cause and voted Catholic. The Slavs who had moved into the city from the hinterland of the Balkans in search of work resisted unity with Italy. So too did the local Socialists, who resisted the claims of Nationalism from a dedication to the international workers' cause; they too supported union with Austria. Joyce, as a quasi-Socialist supporting the Irredentist cause, was in the ironical situation of supporting politicians who hated Socialism.

Joyce's first article appeared on 22nd March, and dealt with the Fenians, the newsworthy occasion being the death in Dublin on St Patrick's Day of John O'Leary. To Yeats O'Leary had been an heroic figure, the man who had done much to inspire the literary movement. At least he had inspired Yeats. To Joyce, however, he was 'a figure from a world that had disappeared'.

> He would often be seen walking along the river, an old man dressed in light-coloured clothes, with a shock of very white hair hanging down to his shoulders, almost bent in two from old age and suffering. He would stop in front of the gloomy shops of the old-book dealers, and having made some purchase, would return along the river. Aside from this, he had little reason to be happy. His plots had gone up in smoke, his friends had died, and in his own native land, very few knew who he was and what he had done.

Apart from this personal glimpse of the patriot, Joyce's article ran along the well-known lines of nationalist complaint. He remarks on the twofold struggle, between Ireland and England and between revolutionaries and democrats, Joyce naturally supporting the revolutionaries. However, he wrote also of the rise of Sinn Fein, and its attempt to force separation by economic rather than military means. (Sinn Fein had been founded by Arthur Griffith specifically as a non-violent constitutional, indeed monarchist, party which wished to achieve a dual monarchy similar to that enjoyed by the Hungarians under the Emperor Franz Joseph. But by 1914 it had been subverted by members of the I.R.B. who were intent on fomenting another revolution.) Joyce does not advert to the simple fact that the Fenians, for all the romance which surrounded them in the eyes of some, simply did not command the support of anything but a small number of Irish people at any time. A further article dealing with the Home Rule Bill, then engaging the attention of Parliament, dealt again in extreme nationalist terms with the history of Gladstone, Parnell and the (to Joyce) contemptible Irish Parliamentary Party. Even in distant Austria he remained true to the politics of his father and John Kelly, the politics that still impose upon unhappy Ulster the burden of revolutionary violence and community hatred.

From these excursions into current affairs Joyce returned to literature, his next task being to correct and return the proofs of *Chamber Music* to Elkin Matthews in London. He was not encouraged to receive a letter from his father in Dublin, who talked of his eldest son's blighted promise. But that appearance of failure might now be a thing of the past. Joyce had an invitation from a former pupil, Dr Attilio Tamaro, to give a series of lectures on Ireland to Universita del Popolo, a sort of Socialist free university for night students.

These began in April with lectures on Ancient Ireland, continued with a talk on the poet James Clarence Mangan (deftly plundered from his college essay), and concluded with an account of the Irish Literary Revival (the text of which is now lost). In these lectures Joyce was refocusing his own relationship with the matter of Ireland, especially as laid out in the manifestations of the Yeatsian Revival. Though he never cared to advert to it, he belonged to the realistic side of the movement influenced by George Moore, which would in time produce a number of novelists concerned with the social realities of Ireland to counter the romantic dramatists of the Abbey Theatre.

In May *Chamber Music* appeared, and copies were sent off to Curran, Price, Josephine Murray and John Joyce. This was Joyce's first published book. These delicate, lyrical verses were the work of the young poet of the college years and later. Yet Joyce was now engaged with stories and fictions which were not so much an advance on but a reversal of the earlier mood and view of the world. His poetry was a thing of the past; in future he would resort to poetry only at moments of great emotional distress. The dozen or so reviews, though few in number, were appreciative. Among the reviewers were old college friends, Thomas Kettle in the *Freeman's Journal* and Arthur Clery (writing as 'Chanel') in the *Leader*. Arthur Symons, another old ally, finished his review in the *Nation* on a graver note: 'But if anything in art is small, and merely good, without anything but that fact to recommend it, it has usually to wait a long time for recognition. People are afraid of following even an impulse, feeling that they may be mistaken. How unlikely it seems, does it not, that any new thing should come suddenly into the world, and be beautiful?' The special beauty to be found in Joyce's stories would indeed be a long time seeking recognition, and he would not be able to publish another book until 1914.

That summer Joyce fell ill and in July and August was laid up in the Municipal Hospital with rheumatic fever. While he was there, Nora gave birth to their second child, conceived during the months of their Roman autumn in the Via Frattina. It was a girl, who was not to be baptized but to be named Lucia Anna. St Lucia was the patron saint of light, and had a special significance for Joyce whose own sight was now affected by his recent illness. Nora sourly commented that the child was almost born on the street. When she went home with her baby, the nuns gave her twenty crowns as charity. Mother and infant arrived home to chaos – father ill, brother surly, mother nursing and babies bawling. The Berlitz School was now sold off and Joyce was forced into taking private lessons. Money was always short, and debts old and new harassed them.

For Joyce, however, his illness was a time of work and rest. By September 1907 he had almost finished the story that had also been conceived in Rome, 'The Dead', where some of his life with Nora, his Dublin past and his Roman days found new expression. The death in Dublin of Ellen Callanan and Julia Lyons (in the first years of Joyce's exile) had brought to mind more details of those musical evenings in Usher's Island in the old days. The pattern of the story brought together many disparate pieces of his own family experience, but holding them all together were Nora's childhood emotions. Nearly all the details of the story, even down to Bodkin's job in Galway gasworks, were drawn from life. The figure of Gretta Conroy remains elusive; Joyce's interest is concentrated on her husband Gabriel, so we see her only through his eyes:

> She was walking on before him so lightly and so erect that he longed to run after her noiselessly, catch her by the shoulders and say something foolish and affectionate into her ear. She seemed to him so frail that he longed to defend her against something and then to be alone with her. Moments of their secret life together burst like stars upon his memory. A heliotrope envelope was lying beside his breakfast-cup and he was caressing it with his hand. Birds were twittering in the ivy and the sunny web of the curtain was shimmering along the floor: he could not eat for happiness. They were standing on the crowded platform and he was placing a ticket inside the warm palm of her glove.

His first present to Nora had been a pair of gloves: the man toiling over the glass would have been in the Dublin bottle works; the heliotrope letter was that very first one which she had written him in the summer of 1904; the ticket was her passage to Europe, as they parted to board the boat at the North Wall separately on the night they left Ireland in 1904: all moments of their secret life together.

The conviction of this is made more certain when Joyce refers to his own letters to Nora, quoting his own words. Like distant music, these words that he had written years before were borne towards him from the past.

*

Chamber Music proved to be a *succès d'estime* and led to offers from a variety of composers to set the verses to music. It was time for a renewed effort on the stories, which were now complete. Elkin Matthews refused the book, but now came an inquiry by way of a letter from Joseph Maunsel Hone, the monied partner of the Dublin firm of Maunsel and Company, John Synge's publishers, where his friend the Ulsterman George Roberts was managing director. Joyce did as requested early in 1908.

Now, too, Joyce began the task of recasting *Stephen Hero*, that behemoth, into the elegantly impressionistic *Portrait of the Artist*. The manuscript of *Stephen Hero* was said to have been thrust on the fire in a fit of despair by Joyce after its rejection for the twentieth time; but it must be more likely that this was a script of his short stories rather than his novel, for the surviving pages of the draft novel show no sign of damage. Ettore Schmitz was among the few to read the first three chapters of the book. Gorman, writing under Joyce's eye, dates this incident to 1908, though other evidence points to a later date. But the matter is confused, not least because of Joyce's lack of interest in clarifying it.

It was no mean thing to abandon over 500 pages of hard work, and begin again. The artistic decision must have grown out of the completion of *Dubliners*. *Stephen Hero* had been a traditional *bildungsroman*, paralleled in fact by contemporary novels such as *The Way of All Flesh* or *Buddenbrooks*. The massive social data and the extended treatment no longer appealed to Joyce after the concise achievement of 'The Dead'. So he began again, commencing and rearranging the material to achieve a far greater effect. His panorama of Dublin life was finally reduced to the dimensions of a portrait, *A*

Portrait of the Artist as a Young Man. He wrote three chapters and then paused, unable for the moment to continue. Until *Dubliners* had appeared, what was the purpose? Yet the conception of the book as it stands grew naturally out of the conclusion of *Dubliners*, and the wider panorama would eventually fall into place when he began *Ulysses* in 1914.

He now suffered yet another attack of iritis, but otherwise he was well occupied with lighter things – going to the opera, following the career of several local musicians, and reading with attention the musical criticism of Giovanni Pozza in the *Corriere*. He also took singing lessons from Romano Bartoli. September saw the appearance of another article in the *Piccolo*, on Ireland at the bar of international public opinion pleading her case for independence. Again Joyce adopts an extreme viewpoint, beginning with the tangled tale of the Maamtrasna murders, and the injustice of the execution of old Myles Joyce. Nevertheless Myles – whatever Joyce might have thought – was guilty of killing his relatives.

November brought another move, to Via S. Caterina 1^I. This was perhaps the dreariest time of Joyce's life, 1907 passing into 1908 with little to mark them. Aside from his language lessons, Joyce translated into Italian Synge's *Riders to the Sea*, and with his friend Dr Nicolo Vidacovich he began a version of Yeats's play *The Countess Cathleen* as well.

On 4th August 1908, Nora miscarried a 12-week child. She was unmoved, but Joyce mourned his lost son and transferred his emotions over the little foetus (which he examined with care) to Leopold Bloom. Miscarriages, let alone abortions, dismayed and distressed Joyce.

In December 1908, now more or less recovered from his rheumatism and eye troubles, he wrote to his sister Poppie in Dublin proposing that he would send Giorgio to Ireland with Stanislaus for six weeks from the end of the following July. The family moved in April 1909 to a new flat Via Vincenzo Scussa 8^I. Yet still the siren call of Dublin lured, as did the more practical matter of dealing with the dilatory firm of Maunsel and Co. from whom he had heard nothing about the possibility of publishing his stories.

In the event, it was Joyce who accompanied the small boy to Ireland in the summer of 1909, on a visit not only to his own Dublin but also to Nora's as yet unknown Galway.

The Haunted Inkbottle

25th March 1909—6th January 1910

His decision made to go to Ireland, Joyce's mind was now running on the fate of Irish men of letters: in March he contributed an article to the *Piccolo della Sera* on the misfortunate Oscar Wilde, occasioned by the first performance in Trieste of Richard Strauss's opera *Salomé*, based on Wilde's play written in French for Sarah Bernhardt. Oscar Wilde, though shrouded by scandal in Ireland and England, was then at the height of his fame on the Continent. Wilde, with Yeats, was one of the writers he aimed to challenge with his own work.

A month later, before moving to a new flat at Via Vincenzo Scussa 81, he sent off the manuscript of *Dubliners* to Maunsel and Company in Dublin. The firm was then enjoying great commercial success as the publishers of John Synge and other writers of the Irish Revival. They were also the publishers of lighter, more popular work such as Lynn Doyle's Ballygullion stories, which were to remain in print for over fifty years. As George Roberts was an old acquaintance from 1904, Joyce thought he could hope for a friendly reception. He had been asked to submit the material by Joseph Maunsel Hone, a young man of 26 who had lent his name and capital to the firm. Oddly, in view of this personal approach, Joyce was to have no direct dealings with Hone, and this may have been the real cause of his problems with the company.

Hone had been given the cheap school copy-books in which the stories had been written out in Joyce's finest copperplate handwriting 'that would have won a schoolboy a prize in calligraphy', Hone later remarked. Roberts was concerned (as Hone recalled) by one story, 'Ivy Day in the Committee Room', and in discussion with him Hone obtained the mistaken impression that Roberts feared publishing its anti-royal sentiments would lose the firm a contract from Lady Aberdeen to publish pamphlets for her anti-tuberculosis campaign. This seems very unlikely. Hone sought the opinion of his friend Victor Le Fanu, nephew of the author of *The House by the Church-yard*. Le Fanu was a man of taste and well-read, and though the stories dealt with a life out of his way he recognized their 'remarkable quality and took more interest in them than in the usual Maunsel publications'. Much later, in 1923, Hone astutely commented on the real qualities of Joyce. He refers to Synge's 'original and provocative interpretations of the peasant life of Aran and Connemara'. But Joyce was different:

> Mr Joyce's books exhibit a type of young Irish-man of the towns – mostly originating from the semi-anglicised farming and shopkeeping class of the east and centre – a type which has been created largely by the modern legislation which provides Catholic democracy in Ireland with opportunities for an inexpensive university education. This young Irish-man is now [1923] a dominating figure in the public life of Ireland; he was less important in Mr Joyce's day, but had already exhibited a certain amount of liveliness. Daniel O'Connell described him, before he had come to the towns and got an education, as smug, saucy and venturous, and the portrait is still recognisable, though he was then only in the embryo stage of self-consciousness.

Hone realized that Joyce's books were more important than Synge's, one writing of a dying culture, the other of one on the rise. 'When I first read *A Portrait of the Artist as a Young Man*, it seemed to me that the book announced the passing of that literary Ireland in which everyone was well bred except a few politicians.' (Hone lived to be President of the Irish Academy of Letters in 1957.) 'For us in Ireland Mr Joyce's significance lies in this, that he is the first man of literary genius, expressing himself in perfect freedom, that Catholic Ireland has produced in modern times.' However, this was not how it appeared to Mr Hone's own firm in the autumn of 1909.

There were other matters that Joyce intended to deal with on this visit. Though he was taken up with the musical settings which Molyneux Palmer was doing for his poems, he was also concerned to obtain the rights to translate John Synge's *Riders to the Sea* – the one play of Synge's that he now admired without reservation – into Italian.

The Church political: the anti-Parnellite Cardinal Logue (derided in *A Portrait of the Artist*). *Author's collection*

The Capuchin church, Church Street, where Stephen Dedalus confesses his sins. *Author's collection*

Certificate of Sodality membership signed by James Joyce for Patrick O'Dwyer (mentioned in *A Portrait of the Artist*). *University College Dublin (Curran Papers, Special Collections)*

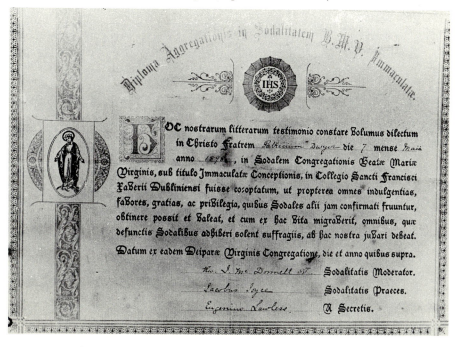

Her image had passed into his soul for ever and no word had broken the holy silence of his ecstasy. Her eyes had called him and his soul had leaped at the call. To live, to err, to fall, to triumph, to recreate life out of life! A wild angel had appeared to him, the angel of mortal youth and beauty, an envoy from the fair courts of life, to throw open before him in an instant of ecstasy the gates of all the ways of error and glory. On and on and on and on!

He halted suddenly and heard his heart in the silence. How far had he walked? What hour was it?

There was no human figure near him, nor any sound borne to him over the air. But the tide was near the turn and already the day was on the wane. He turned landward and ran towards the shore a

The hand of James Joyce: the liberating encounter with Lucy, the Bird-Girl on the strand of the North Bull, from the author's fair copy manuscript. *National Library of Ireland*

Newman House and the other buildings of University College on St Stephen's Green in Joyce's time. *Author's collection*

Some members of the Class of 1902, photographed in the garden of Newman House. Front row, left to right: Felix Hackett, Seamus O'Kelly, Michael J. Lennon, Constantine P. Curran; second row, left to right, George Clancy, Father Edmund Hogan S.J., Prof. Edouard Cadic, Father Joseph Darlington S.J.; back row, left to right, Father George O'Neill S.J., James Joyce, John Marcus O'Sullivan, R.J. Kinahan, James Clandillon, Patrick Semple. *Author's collection*

Mary Elizabeth Cleary ('Emma Clery'), Mrs James Nahor Meenan, from a photograph taken in 1912. *Courtesy of the late Prof. James Meenan*

Above right: The Dublin headquarters of the Gaelic League in Sackville Street (describ in *Stephen Hero*), where James Joyce attended language lessons with Miss Cleary a others. *National Museum of Ireland*

'O, Mr. Conroy, will you come for an excursion to the Aran Islands this summer?' ('The Dead'). Mary Cleary and Mary Wyse Power outside an Aran cottage in the summer of 1901. *The Loreto Magazine, courtesy Sister Mary Burke*

Nora Barnacle, photographed shortly before she left Galway for Dublin. *Southern Illinois University Library*

Father John Moran, a Catholic curate in Galway, whose relationship with Nora confirmed Joyce's anti-clericalism. *Author's collection*

'Rain on Rahoon falls softly, softly falling,/Where my dark lover lies.' (*She Weeps Over Rahoon*). The tomb of Michael Bodkin, Nora Barnacle's early love, in Rahoon Cemetery outside Galway, evoked in the closing passage of 'The Dead'. *Photograph Peter Costello*

The necklace which Joyce had made for Nora as a special present in 1909 after the Cosgrave affair. *La Hune Catalogue*

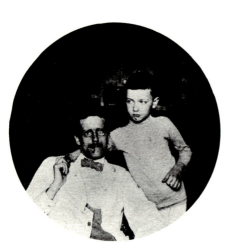

'Richard and Archie Rowan' (*Exiles*): James Joyce in Trieste with his son Giorgio, about 1914. *Southern Illinois University Library*

The Volta Cinema, the first in Dublin, opened by Joyce in 1909. *Courtesy Liam O'Leary*

The North Wall station from which the boat for England, taken by Joyce and Nora in 1904 and 1912, departed; and which is the setting for the end of 'Eveline'.
Irish Architectural Archive

Nora Joyce (in the aspect of Bertha Rowan), painted in Trieste by Tulio Silvestri, 1914. *La Hune Catalogue*

Roberto Prezioso, the Triestian model for 'Robert Hand' in *Exiles*, who was a passionate admirer of Nora. *Giornalfoto, Trieste*

James Joyce in Zürich, contemplating the mysteries of the past for *Ulysses.*
The Poetry Room, Lockwood Memorial Library, State University of New York
at Buffalo

At the end of July James and Giorgio left for Ireland, arriving in Dublin on 29th July. On the boat quay at Kingstown he saw Oliver St John Gogarty in the distance, but did not speak to him, escaping on to the train into the city. Arriving at Westland Row station, he was met by his family. A postcard to Nora in Trieste announced their safe arrival.

For the month of August he intended to stay with his family in the small cottage that they now occupied at 44 Fontenoy Street, lying behind Dorset Street, in a poor but not totally impoverished quarter of the city. His sisters were delighted with Giorgio and John Joyce doted over his grandson, who reminded him distinctly of James at that age, a comparison he demonstrated with a photograph he gave Joyce. In the days that followed their reconciliation was completed. They took a walk out into the country and, stepping into a public house, settled down to play the pianos there, countering each other's operatic arias – one of which dealt with a son's love for his father. They understood each other without putting it into words of their own. Joyce now bustled about his business, calling on relatives like his aunt Josephine. She thought that he had lost his old boyishness – as well she might.

Though some of his old acquaintances cut him in the street, others were glad to see him. The Sheehy-Skeffingtons invited him round to their house in Sandymount, but he did not go. He went to see Curran, but found he was disposed to be unfriendly. George Russell and William Magee were encountered on Merrion Square and were very friendly. Magee thought he looked very ecclesiastical; Russell, however, saw a man of business. William O'Leary Curtis considered he was more mature, while Keohler said he looked nearly ten years older than he was. Richard Best and James Cousins were away. Kettle, too, was away, but Joyce nevertheless wrote to him asking for help about a position as an examiner in Italian for the Intermediate Board of Ireland.

Calling in to Maunsel's Abbey Street office early the next week, on 2nd August, Joyce found that Hone was away in Belfast. On leaving he met George Roberts in the street, and over a drink he smoothed him down. ('I took lithia' he carefully told his distant brother.) He agreed to go round to the office on the following Monday (9th August) to hear the the firm's verdict about his manuscript of *Dubliners*.

Then at last he encountered Gogarty on Merrion Square and tried to pass him by without a greeting. But Gogarty ran after him, caught him by the arm and made a long confused speech. He took Joyce over to his house in Ely Place, the street on which George Moore also lived. To everything Gogarty said, Joyce replied, 'You have your life. Leave me to mine.' Lunch in Enniskerry with Mrs Gogarty was offered; so too were spirits, wine, coffee, tea. All these Joyce declined, staying quiet and sober.

'Well, do you really want me to go to hell and be damned?' said Gogarty at last.

'I bear you no ill-will. I believe you have some points of good nature. You and I of six years ago are both dead. But I must write as I have felt.'

'I don't care a damn what you say of me as long as it is literature.'

'Do you mean that?'

'I do. Honest to Jaysus. Now will you shake hands with me at least?'

'I will, on that understanding.'

Naturally, reporting back as he was to the critical Stanislaus in Trieste, Joyce cast himself in the best possible light, for Gogarty's recollection of the encounter was very different. According to this he wrote asking Joyce to lunch with him in the Dolphin on Monday (2nd August), but before that had asked him to come round to Ely Place for a chat, as they had a lot to discuss and he had some diversion in mind for the returned poet. He offered to send his driver to collect him in his car, but Joyce came on his own. After sitting looking out at the fine display of roses blooming in the garden below the bay window, he asked him, 'Is this your revenge?' Revenge on what, Gogarty wondered. 'On the public,' was the enigmatic reply.

The sight of those roses must have hurt Joyce very badly. If he had only persisted in his own medical studies and made his fortune in three years, he too might be as well established as Gogarty, Coppinger and Sheehan, and free to write as he liked. As it was, by going into exile he merely made hostages to fortune of himself, his wife and his infants.

In view of Joyce's indifference to convivial entertainment, Gogarty later sent him a short note cancelling their lunch, pleading a surgical consultation and saying he would let him know a new date. But he failed to do this and the two men never met again.

The list of those Joyce met included Daniel T. Sheehan, the outspoken medical critic of *The Playboy*, and Vincent Cosgrave, who thought he looked in splendid health. On Friday, 6th August, he fell in with him again while making his rounds of the city. Cosgrave, having given up his medical studies, had little to do and was always free for a drink. Joyce, who was being affable in formal manner as befitted a travelled man of the world with a family and position, little realized the sharp resentments that constantly pecked at his friend's heart. Cosgrave hated Joyce. He had failed with Nora in the summer of 1904, she had refused to believe him when he said Joyce was mad, and now he was a falling failure while even Joyce was rising. He may also have resented his appearance under the name of Lynch in Joyce's novel. Joyce seemed so confident of life that Cosgrave determined to shake him, and on the evening of 6th August he succeeded better than he could have hoped.

They must have been talking of Joyce's new life and Joyce would have mentioned Nora's loyalty. Loyalty, said Cosgrave, perhaps with a laugh. Joyce remembered how she said she could only see him every other night? Because she was busy in the hotel? Not at all, said Cosgrave. On those other evenings she would meet Cosgrave outside the National Museum in Kildare Street and they would walk down to those fields by the Dodder.

He had said enough. Joyce's whole world seemed to be collapsing around him. The one steady person in his drifting life had now betrayed him. She was no better than the others in this country, this nation of informers, traitors, deceiving hypocrites. In the first flush of his unhappy anger he wrote a letter which he posted that night.

I have been frank in what I have told you of myself. You have not been so with me.

At the same time when I used to meet you at the corner of Merrion Square and walk out with you and feel your hand touch me in the dark and hear your voice, (O, Nora! I will never hear that music again because I can never believe you again) at the time I used to meet you, *every second night* you kept an appointment with a friend of mine outside the Museum, you went with him along the same streets, down by the canal, past the house with 'the upstairs in it', down to the bank of the Dodder. You stood with him: he put his arm round you and you lifted your face and kissed him. What else did you do together? And the next night you met *me*!

I have heard this only an hour ago from his lips. My eyes are full of tears, tears of sorrow and mortification. My heart is full of bitterness and despair. I can see nothing but your face as it was then raised to meet another's. O, Nora, pity me for what I suffer now. I shall cry for days. My faith in that face I loved is broken. O, Nora, Nora, have pity for my poor wretched love. I cannot call you any dear name because tonight I have learnt that the only being I believed in was not loyal to me.

O, Nora, is all to be over between us?

Write to me, Nora, for the sake of my dead love. I am tortured with memories.

Write to me, Nora, I love you only: and you have broken my faith in you.

O, Nora, I am unhappy. I am crying for my poor unhappy love.

Write to me, Nora.

He passed a sleepless night, racked by confused doubts. Was Giorgio his son? That first night in the Zürich hotel he had thought she was a virgin, yet now he came to think of it, there had been too little blood. Had she made love with anyone else, with that Holohan man in the hotel perhaps? Had she told him the whole story?

The rumour in Dublin was (so he improbably claimed) that he had taken the leavings of others. Perhaps they laughed to see him parading his 'son' around the streets.

Tell me. When you were in that field near the Dodder, on the nights when I was *not* there) with that other (a 'friend' of mine) were you lying down when you kissed? Did you place your hand on him as you did on me in the dark and did you say to him as you did to me 'What is it, dear?' One day I went up and down the streets of Dublin hearing nothing but those words, saying them over and over again to myself and standing still better to hear the voice of my love.

His imagination ran to morbidity. Gogarty had said that he was consumptive. Would there be any hope of happiness?

In his unhappiness Joyce did not pause to consider how probable the story was. Given what he knew of Nora's character, could she have deceived him? No reply came from Trieste, though he sent a postcard to Stanislaus to forward his fare back at once. In his grief he searched the city for consolation, a familiar friend to help him in his hour of need.

When Joyce arrived in Dublin his other old friend John Francis Byrne had been away in Wicklow with his family at Dundrum. Hearing of Joyce's return, he hurried back to Dublin. He and Joyce passed the afternoon of Wednesday, 4th August, talking in the back sitting-room of his house in 7 Eccles Street, where he and his aunt now lived, while Giorgio played around the apple tree in the back garden with Byrne's dog, Boy.

On Saturday afternoon, 7th August, Byrne was surprised by Joyce's return to Eccles Street. He was now in a state of utter perturbation and poured out the whole unhappy tale to his friend. Byrne had always known that Joyce was highly emotional, but never before had he seen anything like the frightening condition that now convulsed him. Joyce cried, groaned, gesticulated in what seemed futile impotence to Byrne as he related the details of what had happened. Never had Byrne seen any human being more shattered by his emotions. The sorrow he now felt for Joyce was more than enough to obliterate the unpleasant memory of the postcards from Paris in 1902 that had left a certain distance between them.

Byrne's opinion on the affair was definite. Cosgrave's claim was 'a blasted lie'. Did Joyce not realize that Cosgrave was a trouble-maker and a friend of Gogarty? The pair of them must have concocted the story as part of a plot against Joyce. Cosgrave was a half-crown Judas. Joyce was convinced. Of Gogarty he was prepared to believe any treachery, and Cosgrave was a devious little person at any time. He stayed to dinner with Byrne, and to supper, and spent the night at 7 Eccles Street as well. The next morning, quite free of self-pity and gloom, he departed after breakfast humming to himself.

Some days later Joyce returned with something to show Byrne. With almost childish pleasure he produced a jewel-box in which lay a gold necklace with ivory pieces. It was a present for Nora.

'It's beautiful,' Byrne said, adding, 'You got one ivory for every year you have been with her.'

'I never thought of that,' Joyce observed. 'But it's a splendid idea, and I'll add one to it every year.'

Joyce did not forget Cosgrave. Already he was rankled by the way in which Cosgrave had stood aside while he had been attacked that night in the summer of 1904. In due course this incident, coloured by the even greater hatred engendered by the summer of 1909, was used in *Ulysses*. There, in the 'Circe' episode, Lynch also fails Stephen in the fight with the British soldiers, though he does urge Bloom to save him before departing with the whore Kitty Ricketts.

STEPHEN

(Points.) Exit Judas. Et laqueo se suspendit.

Cosgrave never saw Joyce again. Though he persisted with them for many years he never completed his medical studies, and eventually gave up trying. He lived at home with his mother until she died in 1926; then the house was sold and he found himself in difficulties. Crossing to England, he visited Manchester and then London. He stayed in a hotel in Russell Square where his drinking dismayed the staff. At the end of August he disappeared, on 1st September his body was taken from the Thames at Rotherhithe. He had killed himself at the age of only 48.

His brother gave evidence at the inquest on 4th September that 'literary work' had taken Vincent to England. He had only one story to tell, however, and the inference must be that he had tried to interest the *Manchester Guardian* and other papers in his connection with James Joyce, though no evidence of this was offered. If it had not been for that meeting with Nora in the same summer of 1904, Joyce too might well have descended this path of perdition with his friend. As it was, his Judas died alone.

*

Joyce had been prepared to go back to Trieste, and had written to Stanislaus for the money. Now he returned to his business in Dublin. On Monday 9th August he called on Maunsel's. Hone and Roberts felt that the book would not be a commercial success. Joyce offered to bear part of the cost if a royalty was paid to him from the first, which they said they would consider. He also wrote to Arthur Clery, whose review of *Chamber Music* he had just seen, to thank him for his kindness.

The next day, 10th August, he made inquiries about a possible professorship of Italian at the new National University of Ireland, of which University College Dublin was now a constituent part. He made efforts to gather impressive-looking testimonials from Trieste and Rome to support him. When he called on the secretary of the university he was told that the post was worth £100 a year, but it was for commercial Italian, with no literature or philology.

The following week a further meeting with Maunsel's produced a draft contract for terms 5 per cent better than Grant Richards had offered him originally. The book was to appear before March 1910. Joyce still hoped for the Intermediate examinership, under which the scripts would be sent to him to correct in Trieste. He planned now to bring his sister Eva back with him, so as to relieve Nora of the burden of housekeeping and child-minding.

Meanwhile in Trieste Nora was puzzled about what she should do. Joyce's letter had upset her, leaving her feeling wretched and helpless in a foreign city. Then she brought herself to write to him. She was only a poor uneducated girl from Galway with whom he had been foolish to get involved. He had been too kind to her. Perhaps it was for the better that they should separate before they caused each other any more unhappiness.

In her own unhappiness she had turned to Stanislaus and sought his advice. Always a steady and sensible man, he was now an unexpected source of reassurance. Like Byrne, he had long suspected Cosgrave's good-will. During that summer of 1904 he had met Cosgrave one evening looking very downcast, and had asked him what the matter was. Cosgrave explained in strict secrecy that he had been trying to get inside Joyce with Nora, but that she had rebuffed him. At the time Joyce had known something of this and had faced Cosgrave with it. But Cosgrave, who had after all been escorting Nora for Joyce, explained it away as merely concern for the girl. Stanislaus had often hinted to his brother that Cosgrave was no true friend of his, though he never revealed why he thought so. He now wrote to Joyce in Dublin telling him the facts in his usual blunt way.

This universal denigration of Cosgrave is odd, for he emerges in Gogarty's memories as a more attractive fellow. And indeed what more had he said to Joyce than the truth? He had gone about with Nora, accompanying her to Joyce's concert. He would not have been the first man to make a pass at a friend's new floozy. But even after Joyce and Nora had gone to Austria, she was in contact with Cosgrave, as he notes in a letter to Joyce. He was not to know the role in which life and literature were to cast him and Joyce and Nora. As we have only Joyce's version of this history, we can allow Vincent Cosgrave a generous thought or two.

By now Joyce had fully recovered his composure. His negotiations with Hone and Roberts came to a successful conclusion and he signed the contract with them on 19th August. The book was to be bound in grey, with dark red lettering, he reported in triumph to Trieste.

Now he turned his mind to Nora. To restore her health he dispatched a half-stone of shell cocoa; this was intended to fatten her up, Joyce belonging to a generation that preferred their ladies plump.

He wrote that he was absurdly jealous of her past, which had always been true. Now, despite his jealousy, he began again to build a relationship with Nora.

The letters from this period contrast with those later in the year. He wrote pleading his case.

> My darling, forgive me. I love you and that is why I was so maddened only to think of you and that common dishonourable wretch.
>
> Nora darling, I apologise to you humbly. Take me again to your arms. Make me worthy of you.
>
> I will conquer yet and then you will be at my side.
>
> Good night 'my dearest' 'my precious'. A whole life is opening for us now. It has been a bitter experience and our love will now be sweeter.
>
> Give me your lips, my love.

He closed with some lines from *Chamber Music*:

> My kiss will give peace now
> And quiet to your heart
> Sleep on in peace now,
> O you unquiet heart.

A couple of days later he was writing to her trying to explain the changes in himself which he felt as a result of this terrible trial. From the pale passionless beauty of a pearl he had become an opal full of strange uncertain hues. He had written to her mother, but he felt that he could not go down to Galway, as that city would be too full of stories of her childhood.

To recall the sound of his voice, Nora was reading over the poems in *Chamber Music*. She wrote wondering what he had been like then, before she knew him or he knew her. He was touched. Five years earlier he had thought she felt nothing for his art, only to have her quote (or rather misquote, for even love has its failings) a line from one of the poems, while they were talking together one evening. Now he was trying to explain what he had been like when he wrote them.

> My dear little Nora I *think* you are in love with me, are you not? I like to think of you reading my verses (though it took you five years to find them out). When I wrote them I was a strange lonely boy, walking about by myself at night and thinking that some day a girl would love me. But I never could speak to the girls I used to meet at houses. Their false manners checked me at once. Then you came to me. You were not in a

sense the girl for whom I had dreamed and written the verses you find now so enchanting. She was perhaps (as I saw her in my imagination) a girl fashioned into a curious grave beauty by the culture of generations before her, the woman for whom I wrote poems like 'Gentle lady' or 'Thou leanest to the shell of night'. But then I saw that the beauty of your soul outshone that of my verses. There was something in you higher than anything I had put into them. And so for this reason the book of verses is for you. It holds the desire of my youth and you, darling, were the fulfilment of that desire.

Joyce's reappearance in Dublin was attracting attention among the few who recalled the student. Joseph Holloway records in his diary a discussion about Joyce with D.J. O'Donoghue (a leading candidate for the post of university librarian at the new University College), and the following evening he met him in the foyer of the Abbey Theatre, at a performance of *The Playboy of the Western World*.

Joyce explained rather grandly that he had come over from Trieste to cover the controversial first night of Bernard Shaw's play, *The Shewing-U of Blanco Posnet*, for the Italian press. This took place the following evening, on 25th August. The play had been refused a licence in London by the Lord Chamberlain, and the Abbey Theatre (that is, Yeats and Lady Gregory) had agreed to put it on in Dublin where there was no theatre censorship. Given the playwright and the controversy, this was an international occasion and Joyce played his part well as the cultivated cosmopolitan. That evening he also met young Piaras Béaslai, a journalist on the *Evening Telegraph,* and promised to call on him.

This he did the next morning, before getting a train to Galway, where he planned to stay the weekend with Nora's family. Though he was a mere two days in the city, he was able to indulge his sentimental emotions to the fullest over the scenes of Nora's childhood and early womanhood.

On 5th September his article on the Shaw play appeared in the *Piccolo*. The evening of 7th September he spent with Thomas Kettle, who was to be married the next day to Mary Sheehy. Holloway records this as well.

Joyce did not, however, go to the Kettle-Sheehy wedding. But that evening he put in an appearance at the Abbey Theatre to give the manager the cuttings of his article that had come from Austria. He had concluded that the play suggested a crisis in the playwright's mind: an echo of his own position. This resulted in a paragraph about Joyce himself in Béaslai's paper on 8th September. That evening he passed agreeably with Jeff Byrne, concluding with a long walk through the streets of the deserted city. This walk was to form the basis of the Eumaeus episode of *Ulysses*, in which Bloom and Stephen undertake a similar peregrination, even to the details of Mr Bloom's weight on the chemist's scales and the height of the drop into the area at number 7 Eccles Street.

On 9th September Joyce left the North Wall with Giorgio and his sister Eva, and the promise from his publishers that his book would appear. As an earnest of their good faith they had advanced him £3 to pay for his tickets back to Trieste.

*

The party did not reach Trieste until 14th September. Nora was delighted to see him, even though his sister Eva was an added burden to their domestic problem.

The autumn passed. Still his mind ran on a job in Dublin. On 4th October he wrote to David J. O'Donoghue, who had asked him about *The Holy Office*. Joyce now sent him a copy he had come across one morning while rummaging through his papers, remembering that O'Donoghue had wanted this for his store of literary curiosities. 'I send it to you for yourself, not that I regret in the least having written it but it served its purpose at the time I wrote it and would serve no purpose now.' He asked to be remembered to O'Leary Curtis and inquired also what had happened about the post of university librarian. O'Donoghue – then the leading authority on James Clarence Mangan and the mysteries of his life – had got the post, which Joyce himself seems to have considered. That Joyce should disown the satire of his younger self was perhaps a signal of his maturing vision.

Now there came a sudden interlude in his literary plans. About this time Eva commented on how odd it was that in Trieste there were several popular cinemas, while in Dublin there was not a single one. Joyce as proto-businessman at once leaped on this idea. On 18th October he started again for Dublin. He had made arrangements with Giovanni Rebez, Giuseppe Caris and Francesco Novak, who owned – as the International Cinematograph Société Volta – the *Edison* and the *Americano* in Trieste and the *Cinema Volta* in Bucharest. They also owned 23 film-producing factories from which it would be possible to supply the Dublin theatre with the newest films at all times. Joyce was to return to Dublin to see what might be done about opening there a Continental-style cinema with low prices, new films and a constant change of subject.

Travelling by way of Paris and London, Joyce arrived in Dublin on 21st October; he had left Nora fretful at this new departure. He had to kick himself out of Paris, he claimed, or he would have remained there a week. In Paris, however, on one of the new recording machines, he heard Caruso and a lady sing the love duo from *Madam Butterfly*, and urged Nora to hear it in Trieste. Some day *her* love would also return. He was very sick on the sea crossing from Dieppe, but was cheered by his skill in wangling a free pass from the manager of the London and North-Western Railway. He arrived on the morning of 21st October, and moved in once again at 44 Fontenoy Street with his family. He now set about finding a suitable city centre site for the theatre he planned, and interviewed the inspector at Dublin Corporation about a theatre licence on the 23rd.

His days were devoted to business, his many lonely evenings to writing increasingly explicit letters to Nora, whom he had left unhappy and doubtful of his affections.* He felt a stranger in Ireland, and loathed both the country and its people ... or so he told Nora.

Planning only a setting-up role for himself in this matter, he soon found a possible site at 45 Mary Street (premises which had formerly been Graham's ironmongers). But he also investigated with the Dublin Woollen Company to act for them in Trieste. A scheme to import sky rockets came to nothing too.

Bereft of Nora, he suffered from sciatica in his leg, and what he described to her as 'a damned dirty affair' and a fear that he might have infected her. Though Joyce had made all haste, his partners were delayed in their arrival for nearly three weeks. The money Machnich sent proved useful in keeping the whole Joyce household going. He talked again with Maunsel's about the publication of the settings of his songs; they were not eager. The appearance of James Stephens as a writer was the latest sensation.

---

* These letters, which have received much excited attention, distort what we know about Joyce. Written by an unhappy, ill-nourished man, living under great emotional and financial stress, they are *exceptional* documents. The obsessions they reveal are carried over into *Ulysses* (masturbation, coprophilia, sado-masochism, unusual forms of sexual congress, pornography); but those are topics of wider interest.

Joyce paid £40 earnest money on the premises with Coates the landlord, and had his solicitor Charles Murray (a distant relative) draw up the contract which was signed and had to be stamped. His own younger brother Charles wailed from America about his hardships, and his father had to go into hospital. His sister Margaret (Poppie) was off to join a convent in New Zealand. And in December there was notice to quit on 44 Fontenoy Street; as usual the Joyces had neglected the matter of the rent. On 19th November his partners Machnich and Rebez arrived and he put them up in Finn's Hotel. When they left, he took the opportunity to inspect Nora's little room, which induced in him yet more sentiments about her girlish past.

On 27th November the partners made an excursion to Belfast to explore the possibilities of a cinema there. On 2nd December other Italians arrived. Despite a bout of iritis, Joyce trailed down to Cork for a day on 12th December to investigate business opportunities there. Nothing came of this: in fact, Ireland's second cinema opened in Cork the day after the Dublin venture. There was a hope of opening the Dublin cinema on 11th December; the day before, the Italians had moved from Finn's Hotel to rooms over the show. There was trouble with the electricians, and through O'Leary Curtis Joyce had to find others. One of them was Lennie Collinge. His employer got the job of wiring the house – which had to be largely rebuilt for its new use – but went bust and Collinge completed the job; he was retained when the others walked out on the opening night, and was taken on as a projectionist.

On Monday, 20th December, the *Cinematograph Volta* finally opened. Posters (designed by Joyce himself) were pasted up around the city, and sandwich-board men (their services hired at a cost of £50 from David Allen's Advertising Co. of D'Olier Street, which is featured in *Ulysses* as Blazes Boylan's firm), paraded the streets like the H-E-L-Y-S men in *Ulysses*, announcing the opening of 'the most elegant hall in Dublin'.

The cinema was fitted with hard wooden benches and with kitchen chairs at the front for an elite who could afford the top price; though the best view was to be had from the cheapest seats at the back. The colour scheme was crimson and light blue, but to at least one visitor the hall seemed plain and comfortless. The admission charges were 2d, 4d, and 6d; children were half-price and babies in arms free. Though the company was Italian, Joyce had the tickets printed at the nationalist Dundalgen Press in Dundalk, and they carried the logo of the 'Made in Ireland' movement of the day. The cinema hall itself had electric lights along the side walls, though the projector was hand-cranked.

The *Volta* showed a programme of Continental one-reel films, about three or four to the hour. As these had Italian continuity titles the Dublin audience would have been puzzled by them, so they had to be given printed hand-bills providing a translation of the titles and a plot summary. Language was a difficulty in every respect. Collinge had only a little French (learnt from the Christian Brothers); Joyce and the owners spoke German and Italian among themselves; the workmen spoke only English.

From 5 o'clock on there was a continuous performance until 10 p.m., with a Saturday matinee starting at 3 p.m. The general management was in the hands of Signor Novak and the projectionist was Guido Lenardon; the projection booth was in an overhead room. The current, however, was alternating, which made it very difficult to control the quality of the pictures: these, as Lennie Collinge recalled, were 'real flickers'. A small orchestra under Mr R. Morgan (and later under the now better-remembered Dr J.F. Larchet) provided music for the intervals, and to accompany the films. Morgan would play his piano for the afternoon shows, sustaining himself with Guinness stout from a tea-cup on a saucer, which he replenished in the intervals. His music for galloping horses was much appreciated by the young, as he really made the hall rattle.

It seems to have been the intention of Joyce and his partners to introduce Dublin audiences to the popular Italian genre of 'Opera' films, in which the story of the opera on film was accompanied on disc by extracts from the score. This certainly sounds like an interest of Joyce's. But in the event a more popular programme, similar to those in the company's other cinemas in Europe, was shown.

The first programme consisted of *The Bewitched Castle*, *The First Paris Orphanage*, *Beatrice Cenci*, and *Devilled Crab*. In the second programme (27th–29th December) the Volta showed *The Waterfalls of Tanfornan*, *The Fascination of Snowy Mountain Peaks*, *Little Jules Verne*, and *The Interrupted Appointment*. The third programme (from 30th December) consisted of *The Athlete*, *An Interesting Journey to Marseilles*, *Nero: a sensational dramatic story of Ancient Rome*, and *His Dainty Lordship*.

In these choices made under Joyce's direct management, we can perhaps detect some of his own personal interests. Mario Caserini's

Beatrice Cenci was a landmark of the current Italian cinema, along with Guiseppi Liguoro's version of Dante's *Inferno* and Homer's *Odyssey*, subjects also of interest to Joyce. The mixture of the serious with the comic in the programmes is also very Joycean. This time of involvement with the cinema was to leave its mark eventually on the writing of *Ulysses*. Where the early epiphanies had been like snapshots, and the stories in *Dubliners* realistic genre photographs, *Ulysses* as a novel developed a rapid cutting style – 'The Wandering Rocks' is especially cinematic. (And by extension *Finnegans Wake*, in which the new medium is mentioned in fiction for the first time, is completely televisual.)

That first showing was before a specially invited audience.* The *Freeman's Journal* provided a review the next day in which Joyce's efforts were duly praised. This drew crowds to the show, so much so that the Dublin Metropolitan Police had trouble controlling them. A constable was posted at the *Volta* on special duty for Christmas; invited upstairs by Joyce, he turned out to be from Galway and to have known Nora, 'a handsome girl with curls and a proud walk', as he recalled. This encounter induced in Joyce a further fit of moody longing for Nora and a helpless fear of her past. Was this polite young man yet another of her admirers?

This initial success pleased the Italians and they returned to the Continent for the New Year on 25th December, leaving Novak in charge. Before Joyce could leave, however, he had still to appear before the Recorder of Dublin to secure the music licence on 29th December.

There was a discussion among the technicians working in the cinema about the sandwich-board men. They felt it was degrading work; Collinge thought they were just making a living. When they put the case to Mr Joyce, 'he said there was nothing degrading about men who worked honestly. But there was something degrading about people who did not work at all ...'

Lennie Collinge's impressions of Joyce were vivid: though he was a very quiet-spoken man, he was the boss. He looked clerical in appearance, and seemed unapproachable; he wouldn't laugh, or talk about anything that kept him away from his business. Hearing he

* Flann O'Brien in one of his Myles na Gopalleen pieces claims to have seen in a dealer's shop a photograph of the proprietors and staff of the *Volta*, taken on the opening night, on sale for three shillings. This interesting document remains to be traced.

was a writer, Collinge confused him with P.W. Joyce, the historian.*

A contrasting view of Joyce is provided by the writer Charles Duff, then a boy of 15 at boarding-school in Dublin. In the Phoenix Park he made friends with an Italian chocolate-seller from Trieste, who asked him one day if he liked the moving pictures, as a relative of his was involved in opening a cinema down in the city. Duff was invited to the *Volta*, and so met Joyce: 'a tall, thin Irishman with glasses and wearing a long overcoat which, in my memory, seems to have been most of the time turned up round the collar [and who] usually kept his hands in the overcoat pockets, and took them out only when the conversation in German or Italian demanded a gesture.' Duff was given a free pass and visited the cinema several times, and after the show would go with Joyce to a nearby tea-room to talk Italian and German over a bun and a cup of tea, occasionally in company with the chocolate-seller. Joyce announced to Duff that 'who ever cannot speak and understand a language when spoken does not know it', and Duff took a lifelong interest in languages from this initial encouragement. Joyce's kindness and humanity to a mere schoolboy surprised and pleased Duff, who later returned the favours of 1909 by writing *James Joyce and the Plain Reader* (1932).

The *Volta* was not the only business that presented problems for Joyce. In December George Roberts, having the author to hand, asked for changes in the text of *Dubliners*. But these difficulties were soon overcome (as Joyce thought), and the plans for publication went ahead. On Christmas Eve, Joyce was observed with a man and woman in Fleet Street by the ubiquitous Joseph Holloway; other aspects of his life at this time are lost, a reminder that his surviving letters clearly do not give a complete picture of his activities in Dublin.

On 2nd January 1910 Joyce departed from Dublin, arriving in Trieste four days later.

*

---

* The cinema did not last much longer under Italian management. Joyce urged his father to negotiate with the British Provincial Cinemas, who were opening their own theatres in Dublin, to sell the *Volta* for £1,000, a 40 per cent loss on the investment. But John Joyce was dilatory. Eventually the Italians had to sell to the British, but his father failed to gain the commission he might have had. It was a condition of the contract of sale that young Lennie Collinge's services were retained. The hall itself survived as a cinema down to 1948.

Back in Trieste, though there were difficulties (as usual) with their flat and with Stanislaus, by March 1910 George Roberts was writing from Dublin to promise proofs of *Dubliners* very soon.

The summer dragged out; John Joyce was in Fermoy, piously visiting the home of his ancestors. But what Joyce called – in a letter in July – his bitter and sordid stories were further delayed. In December he wrote an article for the *Piccolo* on Home Rule which he saw as being like Haley's Comet of that year, a spectacular but passing thing. At about the same time they moved to another flat.

The new year came and in July 1911 Joyce's sister Eva returned home to Dublin and his sister Mabel died of typhoid in hospital, much to his father's distress. This disaster was followed in July by Maunsel finally deciding to postpone his book. More objections had now been raised as to the content of the stories; the Royal references which had bothered Roberts were only one matter. Joyce attempted to sort this out by writing to the King's secretary, but that ploy was no real help against the Ulster stubbornness he faced.

He resorted to the device of an open letter to the press, published only in *The Northern Whig* and *Sinn Fein*, both of which wished to reveal the squalor of Dublin life from different points of view. But the firm of Maunsel was unmoved, and another new year came with publication still unadvanced.

In March 1912 Joyce gave a popular series of lectures on Daniel Defoe and William Blake, a combination of writers he had always admired for their realistic detail and structured symbolism. Then in April 1912 he went to Padua, to sit a state examination enabling him to teach in Italy. But his papers in which he had discussed Dickens failed to gain him the certificate he needed. That May he published yet another article in Trieste, this time on Parnell and his meaning for Ireland. The theme of treachery, too close to Joyce's nerves, emerged again. For him it was now time to return to Ireland, that Garden of Gethsemane, that place of suffering and betrayal.

21

EXILES

In the summer of 1912 Nora, now eight years away from home, decided to take the children back to Galway for a holiday so that they could see their Barnacle grandmother. It was planned that she should go on ahead with Lucia, and send some money from the ever-generous Michael Healy so that Joyce could join them, bringing Giorgio with him. There was, of course, the small matter of Nora's wedding-ring; Joyce forbade her to wear one, but she ignored him. Rather than distress her mother she provided herself with a wedding band, whatever James might think about it.

Nora arrived in Dublin on Monday 8th July, where her main task was to inquire from Maunsel's about *Dubliners*. She put up in Finn's Hotel, and went to see Roberts at his office on the Tuesday, but made the mistake of taking John Joyce and Charles with her. Though she started in fine fashion to take Roberts to task for his treatment of her husband, John Joyce then interrupted. Roberts naturally ignored her and addressed himself to the elder Joyce. When Nora and Charles called the next day, Roberts avoided them. Though he knew nothing about the matter, she left the business of the book in Charles's less than capable hands and departed for Galway.

In Trieste, Joyce heard nothing from Nora except for a hasty postcard noting her safe arrival. He wanted to imagine her visiting the scenes of their early love that meant so much to him, but less to her. Yet she said nothing, she was unmoved by such nostalgia. When she said nothing, all his old hysterical longings returned. He had a pain in his side, could not sleep, and was afraid to stay alone in Trieste, 'afraid of myself'. He followed her at once from Trieste, without waiting for the money to come. 'What are Dublin and

Galway compared with our memories?' he asked. Engaging with the *Piccolo della Sera* for a set of Irish articles, he left Trieste for Dublin on 12th July, intending then to be back by 24th August.

His letter crossed one from her, written from Bowling Green on 11th July 1912, in her best wandering style.

> My darling Jim since I left Trieste I am continually thinking about you how are you getting on without me or do you miss me at all. I am dreadfully lonely for you I am quite tired of Ireland already well I arrived in Dublin on Monday night your father Charley Eva and Florrie were at the Station all looking very well we all went to Finn's Hotel I stayed two nights in the hotel but I got very sick of Dublin its a horrible place its quite true what you said I would soon get tired of it, now I am in Galway I find everyone very well my Mother is very fat and looking very well also all my sisters and brother I feel very strange here but the time won't be long slipping round till I am going back to you again.

Nora's uncle had recently had an expensive nasal operation and she thought he would be unable to pay Joyce's fare to Ireland. But Joyce was already on his way across Europe.

Passing though London on 14th July he saw Yeats, and was surprised to find him polite – though Yeats was never less than that with Joyce. The discussion on the Italian translation of Yeats's play might prove useful in later days. Arriving in Dublin, he put up with his sister and went to see Roberts himself. The evasive Ulsterman remarked that the Giant's Causeway, that familiar landmark of his Northern homeland, was as putty compared with Joyce. The new proposals for the book were simple. Deletions were to be made in 'Ivy Day' and 'An Encounter', replacing the removed text with asterisks, with a prefatory note of explanation from Joyce. Or Joyce could take over the sheets and issue the book himself through Simpkin Marshall of London on commission. Uncertain as to which he would choose, Joyce hurried on down to Galway.

Nora was delighted with his arrival. As she noted in a letter to Eileen Joyce: 'What have you to say to Jim after all our little squabbles he could not live without me a month.' His telegram announcing his arrival had been a joy to her. It seemed that Joyce could work wonders, as he had sent it at midnight while the boat was on the deep sea.

This western holiday was very enjoyable. There was a lot of rain, as there always is in the west of Ireland, but when it was fine they spent the days on the beach at Salthill. The air and the food were splendid and the children throve on the new sights and the affectionate interest of their Irish relatives. Joyce and Nora with Giorgio stayed with Michael Healy in his larger house in Dominic Street, while Lucia stayed with her grandmother in Bowling Green: every night after her parents left, she would say good-night and go up to bed singing. 'She is a wonderful [Nora wrote to Eileen] she is as rosey the two children love the place they are out all day they don't give themselves time to eat.'

Joyce also improved in the fresh western air; he rowed on the Corrib River some days. The pains he had complained of in Trieste were not heard of here. They went to Galway Races, the biggest event in the county calendar, with parties and a great ball in Eyre Square. But for Joyce, as for Yeats in his poem 'At Galway Races', written in 1908, the sight of the crowds brought on a melancholy sense of social exclusion and he spoke to Nora of his fears. He told her of his grief, a grief he still felt weeks later.

Cycling 100 miles, through the Joyce Country to the western seaboard, Joyce interviewed the Italians involved with the Marconi transatlantic Radio Station at Clifden – Marconi's mother was an Irishwoman, and it might provide a nice article with Italian echoes in Ireland. He also wrote two articles, one on Galway city, and one on the Aran Islands – which he visited at the end of July – for the *Piccolo*, where they appeared in August and September.

Galway city's history and its ancient and medieval associations were briefly run over by Joyce for his Italian readers, but he could not but observe the decayed buildings sprouting weeds. He saw here too an epiphany of potential change: a pipe band swinging through the evening streets watched by nuns discreetly from their convent windows, the new order challenging the old.

The visit to Aran echoed the advice which Miss Ivors had given Gabriel Conroy in 'The Dead'. Joyce and Michael Healy sailed out in the ferry from Galway Harbour, which gave the old customs man the opportunity of showing Joyce the intended site of the transatlantic harbour. This interested Joyce the nationalist – the tentacles of Ireland reaching round the world, and ironically supplying England in time of war. Landing at Kilronan, the harbour on the main island, they set out to explore. Meeting a man named O'Flaherty, Joyce recalled Oscar Wilde's numerous names among which was O'Flahertie; this man could as easily have been a relative of the Aran novelist of the future, Liam O'Flaherty. They were invited into a cottage where they were given tea, for which payment was refused. Joyce, unlike Synge, lingered only long enough to savour the culture of the islands which had inspired so much of the Romantic side of the Irish Revival. Yet Synge he did admire, writing later in Zürich of *Riders to the Sea* that 'the heart and the ear mislead one gravely if this brief scene from "poor Aran" be not the work of a tragic poet.'

For Joyce there was a different kind of tragedy in the west of Ireland, a tragedy which suited his more realistic temper. On Sunday, 4th August, he took himself out on his bicycle to visit the graveyard in Oughterard where he had imagined Michael Bodkin was buried. It was just as he had imagined it to be for the conclusion of 'The Dead', and he was morbidly satisfied to find a grave of a J. Joyce. He must have told Nora about this trip, and she must have told him where exactly her lover was buried. In the notes written later in the next year for *Exiles*, he related Bodkin's grave to that of Shelley in the Protestant Cemetery in Rome.

Moon: Shelley's grave in Rome. He is rising from it: blond she weeps for him. He has fought in vain for an ideal and died killed by the world. Yet he rises. Graveyard in Rahoon by moonlight where Bodkin's grave is. He lies in the grave. She sees his tomb (family vault) and weeps. The name is homely. Shelley's is strange and wild. He is dark, unrisen, killed by love and life, young. The earth hold him.

In Rome that grim winter they had, apparently, visited the grave of the Romantic poet. Nora must have been touched by the strange tale of his death, as told by Trelawny and recounted by Joyce. Now revisiting Bodkin's grave in Rahoon with Joyce she wept again, this time for the lost days of her own youth. 'There are tears of commiseration. She is Magdalen who weeps remembering the loves she could not return.'

On his return to Trieste, at the beginning of what was to be one of his most creative periods, Joyce was writing poetry again. One of the poems was inspired by their visit to the tomb of the Bodkins; a draft was begun in Dublin. He called it simply *She Weeps Over Rahoon*.

> Rain on Rahoon falls softly, softly falling,
> Where my dark lover lies.
> Sad is his voice that calls me, sadly calling,
> At grey moon rise.
>
> Love, hear thou
> How soft, how sad his voice is ever calling
> Ever unanswered, and the dark rain falling,
> Then as now.
>
> Dark too our hearts, O Love, shall lie and cold
> As his sad heart has lain
> Under the moongrey nettles, the black mould
> and the muttering rain.

He had set out on his journey westward. Always at the heart of his own love would lie the memory of Nora's early loves, which in their simplicity had transcended both the carnality and the spirituality that he offered Nora. She would always remember that Michael Bodkin died for her. Joyce still resented this. After seeing a review of *Chamber Music* which spoke of his 'exquisite and passionate poems', he asked her if 'your friend in the soda-water factory or the priesteen' could write his verses.

He was sent letters every day by his friend Price, an enthusiastic Ulsterman who had a cure from Styria for foot-and-mouth disease, then ravaging parts of Ireland. Joyce sent these on to William Field, the Blackrock butcher whom his father had known, and who was then president of the Irish Cattle Traders Association. Field included Price's letter with one of his own in a communication to the *Evening Telegraph* on 17th August. Here yet another small mosaic for *Ulysses* had fallen into place, for Price was to become a model for Mr Deasy in the 'Telemachus' episode. Joyce himself would contribute a second leader to the *Freeman's Journal* on the question of politics and cattle disease on 10th September, thus completing the pieces for a fragment of the matter of *Ulysses*.

Joyce returned to Dublin to wrestle with the problem of his book; he stayed with his brother Charles – then standing in danger of arrest for debt – at 17 Richmond Place, on the North Circular Road, in the very area where the earliest of his stories are set. Roberts and Hone had given further consideration to the matter, and had written to Joyce in Galway suggesting that Grant Richards, whose printers would not print the book for him, should take over the already printed sheets which Maunsel's would not publish. Joyce engaged his father's employer George Lidwell to act for him as his solicitor. After extensive discussion nothing was settled on 20th August, though Roberts now began to suspect other areas of discreet obscenity. He asked Joyce what 'simony' was, whether the priest in 'The Sisters' was suspended only for breaking his chalice, and was there more to 'The Dead' than appeared.

The book was given to Lidwell to read and give his opinion on. He did this, but his letter was by no means satisfactory and C.P. Curran thought that Joyce's case was weakened by Lidwell's presentation of it. Joyce went to speak to Lidwell in the Ormond Hotel, where he found him with John Joyce and other cronies exchanging ribald stories of the Irish clergy. Here is another source for material in *Ulysses*; this time 'Sirens' fell into place. Doubtless Joyce visited Barney Kiernan's at this time as well.

Despite his taste for ruderies about parish priests, Lidwell felt that Joyce's book was a disgusting one, and gave him little real support. From Trieste, all Joyce heard were tales of threatened eviction. Nora was still in Galway. Feeling depressed and lonely, he sent her a draft of the verses about Rahoon which he thought she would like, though they too shared his bitter mood. He could only talk of Nora, 'even very intimate things' with his aunt Josephine: how she sat at the opera in Trieste and was admired by other men. 'I told you of my grief at Galway Races. I feel it still. I hope that the day may come when I shall be able to give you the fame of being beside me when I have entered into my Kingdom.'

Nora arrived in Dublin on 22nd August, and took a room for them both with two beds in 21 Richmond Place, hoping for some time together. But business dominated his days and worried his nights.

Lidwell had thought that the advisers to the Crown would not take action on the passages he had been shown, but the indelicacy remained. Joyce agreed to remove 'An Encounter', to add a note that the book was incomplete, that no more changes be made and that it appear not later than 6th October 1912 (this being Ivy Day, of course). They even discussed the binding that day.

Joyce returned at noon on 23rd August to find that the firm had finally steeled itself to reject the book. He then talked with Lidwell and with his father, who told him to buck up and find another publisher. Joyce's thought was to buy a revolver and shoot Roberts.

However, he returned to Maunsel's and for two hours until 5 argued with Roberts who remained resolute, having received advice from his own solicitor, the poet Charles Weekes. Indeed, Weekes actually suggested that Maunsel's sue Joyce for breach of contract in that he offered them a book he knew to be libellous. And, as there was little chance of them recovering their costs by selling the sheets to another publisher, Joyce must compensate the firm for its loss.

Further pointless meetings followed. Joyce talked to Richard Best, at the National Library, who suggested he speak to Longworth, the editor at the *Express*. Colum came with him to support his case, but on looking at the proofs, wondered whether the book was all about pubs, and thought 'Counterparts' terrible. Later still, Roberts wanted more name changes. Joyce now talked to Keohler, and to Arthur Griffith who was most supportive and said that Roberts had been playing this game for years. He gave Joyce the name of another solicitor named Dixon on Westmoreland Street, but he too was hostile.

Joyce suspected that there was a plot against him, or that the firm wished to keep in with the 'Castle Establishment', for it was involved with Lady Aberdeen's various disease-eradication schemes. This sounds like a suggestion from Griffiths, but Joyce does not seem to have realized the real shock his stories could give. In the case of Synge, Maunsel's had Yeats to fight their battles for the play before they published it; then they could take the controversy, for the jibes were aimed at the Abbey Theatre rather than at them. But in Joyce's case the air of innuendo that surrounded the stories made them uneasy; this was not a life they knew, the hidden aspects of the stories made them fearful. And the first Irish reviews, full of distaste for the book, were to prove them right about local reactions.

On the matter of censorship, all publishers were aware of the recent case when Scotland Yard detectives had called upon John Lane, founder of the Bodley Head and future publisher of *Ulysses*, and he had to withdraw Hermann Sudermann's novel, *The Song of Songs*, for both its content and the raw language used. Lane canvassed the opinions of a host of eminent writers about Sudermann's high status. But the matter had been a serious one, and a police prosecution was a possibility.

Joyce then gave thought to buying the sheets and issuing the book himself in Dublin under his own imprint as The Liffey Press from two rooms at 2 Jervis Street. But the printer, John Falconer, had by now read the proofs himself and refused to have his firm associated in any way with the book. Joyce went to see them; but they preferred to burn the sheets and break up the type. And that, within an ace of publication, was the end of the Dublin edition of *Dubliners*. On the morning of 11th September 1912, Joyce salvaged from the disaster a set of the proofs with the title page; and it was from these that the first edition would eventually be set. But at that moment there seemed to be no future.

He went back to the Murrays, where he and Nora were eating. His aunt had prepared a special supper but he ignored it, going upstairs to play a plaintive song on the piano. Nora, put out by this display of petulant bad manners, stayed downstairs until Josephine cried out, 'Ah, do go up to him. Can't you see all this is for you.'

They left Ireland by boat on the evening of 11th September 1912. This was to be Joyce's last sight of his country and his native city – henceforth he would travel home only in his imagination. He had done, so he thought, with Dublin and its treacheries. These last encounters in 1904, 1909 and 1912 had, however, provided him with nearly all the material for *Ulysses* and *Exiles*.

Dublin as an immediate experience was now behind him. Rejected in all his efforts to re-establish himself there, he was now exiled for ever from the kingdom. From now on his memory would have to suffice the artist. As the city and the mountains slipped below the sea from the night boat to England, Dublin became immutable, fixed for ever in his mind in its late Victorian and Edwardian heyday.

PART IX

22

The Living and the Dead

September 1912—July 1915

The long, dreary, dirty journey, the all-too-familiar and painful journey back to Trieste began yet again.

While passing through London on 12th September Joyce went to see Padraic Colum's publisher, Mr Boon of Mills and Boon. Colum had written commending Joyce and his books, but Joyce himself felt that however strongly Colum had put him forward, the fact that the Ulster critic Robert Lynd was no longer the firm's reader would prevent Boon from taking an option on *Dubliners*. He was right. A few days later Boon wrote rejecting the book, which he thought might 'give a certain amount of offence to readers'. But Joyce was grateful to Colum for his aid nevertheless. In later years Colum and his wife Mary would be among the closest and staunchest of the Joyces' friends through even more troubled times.

While waiting for their train connection in Flushing on 14th September, Joyce passed the long interval in the waiting room by writing out on the back of his contract with Maunsel's a hundred-line pasquinade against that obnoxious company and its partners. This was *Gas from a Burner*. Later, having polished his invective through three drafts on the train between Flushing and Salzburg, he would have it printed in Trieste. With harsh sarcasm, the lines spoke to his own immediate relationship with Ireland:

> This lovely land that always sent
> Her writers and artists to banishment
> And in a spirit of Irish fun
> Betrayed her own leaders, one by one.
> 'Twas Irish humour, wet and dry,

Flung quicklime into Parnell's eye . . .
O Ireland my first and only love
Where Christ and Caesar are hand and glove!

*

The Joyces arrived in Trieste on 15th September, to a new flat on the second floor of 4 Via Donato Bramante, which Stanislaus had leased from the beginning of the month. A few days later (on 19th September) Joyce wrote to W.B. Yeats regarding the translation into Italian of Yeats's play *The Countess Cathleen* which he had made with his friend Nicolo Vidacovich. Joyce was always ready to promote Irish literature which he admired:

> I suppose you will have heard of the fate of my book *Dubliners* [he concluded]. Roberts refused to publish it and finally agreed to sell me the first edition for £30 so that I might publish it myself. Then the printer refused to hand over the 1000 copies which he had printed either to me or to anyone else and actually broke up the type and burned the whole first edition.

The rejection Joyce had suffered contrasted with the enthusiasm he felt for Yeats's work. He asked Yeats if he could suggest another London publisher, and Yeats proposed Martin Secker, a younger man, to whom Joyce sent the book in December. He asked Yeats to put in a word for it as a service to Irish literature; it was difficult for Joyce to do anything for himself at a distance. Secker, too, refused the book.

In October there were difficulties over the flat. The gloom of this month of domestic difficulties was brightened for Joyce by the arrival through the post of 24 copies of *Chamber Music* for him to dispose of about Trieste.

Problems remained: in his teaching position he still hoped to get a licence to teach at university level. Meanwhile, he was engaged in classes at the Commercial Academy. December, however, was darkened by the news from Dublin of the death of his uncle William Murray. As he wrote to his aunt Josephine, 'We had many wild nights together, many arguments. He was the only member of my mother's family who seemed to take any pride out of my existence: and I can still remember the tone of his voice when he spoke of "my nephew". After all he was a man, like us all or like many of us, worthy of a better life than he had assigned him.'

Though given to tantrums, William Murray is the genial Richie Goulding of *Ulysses*. There had, it seems, been too many wild nights, for he died fortified by the Last Rites of the Catholic Church, after what his death notice calls a long and painful illness. However, his death certificate reveals this illness to have been General Paralysis of the Insane, the tertiary stage of syphilis – the very disease that had haunted the imagination of the youthful Joyce. His uncle's syphilis may indeed have taken on a symbolic value for him when he began to write *Dubliners* in the summer of 1904.

William Murray must have contracted the disease soon after the turn of the century; his last child was born healthy, unaffected by any syphilitic side effects, in 1899. Murray had been the model for the solicitor's clerk in 'Counterparts', who has a ready eye for a fast lady. Perhaps the tantrums in life and fiction were symptomatic of the disease. In *Ulysses* Richie Goulding is already confined to bed, where he continues to make up his cost accounts for Collis and Ward. This too may be indicative of an undermined constitution. Though Europe as a whole was witnessing a syphilitic epidemic, for Joyce the disease had a close familiar connection. His uncle's decay became symbolic of the decay of Dublin.

Joyce now explained to his aunt that he disliked the sight of a Dublin postmark as the letters seemed always to bring 'sad news of death, poverty or failure of some kind'. Yet he now retained only pleasant memories of her husband, 'a good-hearted and lively companion of my youth'.

The rejection he had suffered in Dublin had steeled Joyce in his resolve. At the end of March he wrote to Elkin Matthews (the publisher of *Chamber Music*), who had written to tell him of his inclusion in a new anthology of Irish poetry edited by Katharine Tynan, asking him if he would take on the publication of 'my famous book *Dubliners*', either at Joyce's expense or as a normal publishing venture. He would take 110 copies for sale in Trieste.

Joyce explained that he wished for a quick answer as he intended to push the matter. The edition would be prefaced by his account of the book's 'curious history'. His novel would be finished that year – 'a book about which you may have heard something from your Irish acquaintances'. (At this date only two chapters of *A Portrait of the Artist* remained to be written.)

One way or another Joyce was anxious to settle the matter. 'The later history of the book seems to be open to one interpretation only and that is, that there was a deliberate conspiracy of certain forces in Ireland to silence me. I can scarcely be accused of egoism in coming to this conclusion in view of the facts.' He was as determined as ever to detect the hidden hand working against his interests. Mathews refused the book, but suggested that John Long might take it. John Long did not.

Before leaving Dublin Joyce had received as a gift from his father the set of family portraits which had come into John Joyce's possession in the summer of 1881. Joyce arranged for them to be cleaned and restored by Daniel Egan of Ormond Quay, and early in 1913 they were shipped out to Trieste. They constituted Joyce's *lares et penates*, his household gods which he held in pious reverence and which would accompany him from flat to flat for the rest of his life.

It was to this spring and summer that the emotions recorded in such etiolated form in *Giacomo Joyce* reached their peak. Joyce's infatuation with one of his young lady students echoed in his fiction the image of Emma Clery and a little later of Beatrice Justice in *Exiles*. Indeed, *Giacomo Joyce* may be seen as a further series of notes towards the play. Whatever their nationality these girls remained the same type of person, the contrast with Nora or Bertha being even more strongly emphasized. The figure in the book has been identified (by Professor Ellmann) with an Amalia Popper, but even the evidence he adduces in support of his case undermines it; the dates simply do not fit.* Joyce had several girls among his group of students, and it may be that impressions of several of them coloured a portrait largely drawn from an Irish original.

The notes and outline of *Exiles* belong to November or at least to the autumn of 1913. Though it owed the local detail of its setting to Dublin, the emotional situation involving Joyce and Roberto Prezioso, Nora and his student belonged to Trieste. Yet the very name of Beatrice Justice – carrying as it did a hidden reference to those distant Cork relations of his father and Mrs Conway – suggests that the texture of the play has other aspects which have yet to be explored. The reference to Youghal recalls Joyce's visit made there with his father, on which he may well have met or heard of his Justice relatives.

This season saw the completion of Molyneux Palmer's settings of

---

* His evasive reply to the devastating critique by Helena Barolini provides a curious account of his research methods.

a number of Joyce's verses from his early years. There also appeared one of Joyce's rare later poems, 'Watching the Needle-Boats at San Sabba', which was published in the London *Saturday Review* on 20th September. This was suggested by the sight of his brother rowing in a racing skiff pulling towards the shore while the crew sang an aria, 'A pettera ch'io torni', from the Puccini opera, *The Girl of the Golden West* (*La Fanciulla del West*):

> Let her await my return.
> The days will pass away,
> and I shall not return ...

There was an echo here of that other aria in *Madam Butterfly*, which he had wanted Nora to recall during his stay in Dublin, in which the bereft Japanese girl longs for her American's return. Joyce now seems to have thought that there would be no return of love. He was at that age, 31, which the Romans had seen as concluding *adulescentia*, that period of youth which he had entered upon in the summer of 1898. The sexual life he had then embarked upon was now closed. We may suppose that complete sexual intercourse between James and Nora had ended at the age of 27 in 1910 (as it had for Bloom at that age), those letters from Dublin being the last dying flourish of a relationship which had not survived that stillborn child in August 1908. For the artist, too, an era was ending.

He sent the poem to his brother, with the comment that *Quid si prisca redit Venus*: What if an old passion should return. There would be no return of passion. Joyce's energies were now moving in the direction of sublimation, of artistic recreation. *Ulysses* had begun.

That winter he began to prepare a series of lectures on *Hamlet*, which he gave on 4th–10th February 1913, outlining the theory of which he was to make critical use in *Ulysses*. But it was the tidying-up of *Dubliners* and the preparation of a lengthy statement on its long and sorry history that brought November to a close.

Dublin at this date was an object of wide attention in the European press. Since the late summer the city had been disturbed by a labour dispute which had resulted in riots at the end of August 1913 when workers had been killed after clashing with the police. The squalor of the city had been emphasized on 2nd September by the collapse of a house in Church Street – near the Franciscan church where

Stephen had sought confession – which killed 7 people and injured 6. The man of the hour was James Larkin, and many of Joyce's friends such as George Russell and Frank Sheehy-Skeffington – still wearing his knickerbockers – were deeply involved in a crisis during which the Catholic Church took up an equivocal position on the social issues, while objecting strongly to Dublin slum children being sent to England. The whole social fabric of the city was laid bare. The eyes of Europe were on Dublin. So Europe should be interested in reading *Dubliners*. Joyce sent his 'Curious History' to Richards to stimulate his appetite for the book.

Joyce may have seen himself as isolated in Trieste, unable to come to terms with distant and indifferent publishers, yet the thoughts of others were turning to him. W.B. Yeats was now sharing Stone Cottage in rural Sussex with Ezra Pound, the American poet being at this time involved with the editorial side of an advanced journal of the day called the *New Freewoman*, later *The Egoist*. He was also looking for poems for an anthology he was putting together called *Des Imagistes*. Yeats suggested to him that Joyce might have work to hand that would suit his purposes.

On 15th December Pound wrote from London to Joyce asking him if this were the case, and would he care to submit some material. He did not know if they would be of help to each other, but from what Yeats had been saying he thought they might have a hate or two in common. Yeats emerged from the confusion of his own papers with Joyce's poem 'I hear an army' (from *Chamber Music*), and Pound wrote again to Joyce requesting to use it in the *Imagistes* anthology.

Joyce closed his novel, signing the end in the homely style 'Cabra, Dublin 1904. Trieste, Austria 1914.' It was a token of the way he had travelled, that the book linked Dublin and Europe and owed nothing to British taste. The new year came, and with it Ezra Pound's rising enthusiasm for Joyce's work, both for the short stories and for the novel which by now he had received. On 8th January Joyce wrote again to Grant Richards pressing him about the publication of the stories, and *The Egoist* (as it had now become) published on 15th January his statement 'A Curious History'. Pound meanwhile was absorbing Joyce's *A Portrait of the Artist*, and wrote of it to Joyce with the highest praise; through his influence it was accepted for serialization in *The Egoist*, which was then edited by Dora Marsden, and later by Harriet Shaw Weaver. Writers associated with the magazine included T.S. Eliot, Rebecca West, Wyndham Lewis, H.D. and her husband Richard Aldington.

Though Pound failed to place any of Joyce's short stories in America with H.L. Mencken's magazine the *Smart Set* at this time – two stories appeared later in May – this did not matter, for in February *The Egoist* published the first episode of 'A Portrait of the Artist as a Young Man'. This in itself was a statement of Joyce's status as a leading modern writer.

Grant Richards (alerted by the interest now being shown in Joyce, both in London and America) now sent a contract for the publication of *Dubliners*, which Joyce signed at the beginning of March. By the end of April he had hastily corrected and returned the proofs. He wished to have the Continental dash used for dialogue, but was unable to impose his wish on Richards; he successfully reassured him that no libel actions would follow the appearance of the book. While preparations for publication were in train, Joyce received one of his rare letters from his father, who was in hospital in Dublin and concerned about the forthcoming marriage of Eileen in Trieste to a young Czech named Frantisek Schaurek.

> I am and always was very fond of Eileen. She is the only one of my daughters now alive who never gave me insolence, or showed contempt for me so that I look to you to take my part and see after her interests. I had a letter from her telling me she is very fond of this young gentleman and of course that counts for a good deal, but it is not everything. As you know I had a good deal of experience in that respect.

John Joyce was thinking of his own broken engagements. His concern was justified, as Schaurek turned out to be an embezzler, and in 1926, a suicide whose death caused his wife intense agony and prolonged distress.

James wished to have a portrait of his father painted, and there was talk of his visiting Trieste, but this came to nothing. The portrait was eventually painted in 1924 by Patrick Tuohy, the artist son of old Doctor Tuohy who had looked after the infant Frederick William at the time of his death in 1895.

Joyce had no photographs of himself and had to have one taken for Grant Richards' use. Richards was not anxious to use Joyce's letter on the history of the book, and hoped he could arrange with Filson Young, the *Manchester Guardian* writer, for an introduction.

But this scheme too came to nothing. *Dubliners* was finally published in London on 15th June 1914, a fat little volume in red cloth binding with gold stamping. It was welcomed with a supportive review from Ezra Pound. Joyce took 120 copies to sell in Trieste; another 120 were sold in Ireland to his friends, relations, acquaintances and enemies. By April 1915 499 copies had been sold. This was not a great number – certainly nothing like the 8,000 copies he had once hoped would bring him £500.

At long last, however, Joyce had achieved the breakthrough he had longed for. After ten years he had, as he had promised, produced a work that pleased him, though the Irish reviews of the book were not welcoming. None appeared in the *Freeman's Journal*, the *Evening Telegraph*, or Arthur Griffith's paper *Sinn Fein* where Joyce might have hoped for a favourable notice. Though *The Irish Booklover* did not care for it at all, the reception in British periodicals was warm enough for Richards to ask about Joyce's new work.

The Jesuit bibliographer Stephen Brown, then living at Clongowes, a little later summed up the Irish reaction to Joyce's 'entire absence of reticence and of the regard for the ordinary amenities of publicity', rightly connecting him with George Moore in the Irish literary tradition. He wrote of *Dubliners*:

> Seventeen [actually fifteen] genre studies in the form of stories picturing life among the Dublin lower-middle class and lower classes, but from one aspect only, viz., the dark and squalid aspect. This is depicted with brutal realism, and though there is an occasional gleam of humour, on the whole we move, as we read, in the midst of painful scenes of vice and poverty. His characters seem to interest the author in so far as they are wrecks or failures in one way or another. He writes as one who knows his subject well.

The last remark was the comment of a priest privy to the secret history of the Joyce family. This 1915 notice in *Ireland in Fiction* did not escape Joyce's attention, for in July that year he sent the Jesuit (through his literary agent J.B Pinker) details of his family history for inclusion in a second edition.

The appearance of Joyce's book had one curious effect. It prompted Edward Martyn – now a complete outsider in the Irish literary revival which he had done so much to inspire originally with his Ibsenesque dramas – to write his last play *The Dream Physician* (produced at the Irish Theatre in Upper O'Connell Street on 2nd

November 1914). In this play he ruthlessly and unkindly parodies George Moore as George Augustus Moon, W.B. Yeats as Beau Brummell, and James Joyce as the affected young poet Otho, an 'artist', who says to Brummell (as in life Joyce had said to Yeats): 'Ah – I see you are too old for me to influence you.' That the young and almost unknown Joyce should be thought worthy of parody, and in such company, is significant. Few among the gossips and poseurs of Dublin literary life would have had any doubts about who it was that Martyn was guying. Having rejected Joyce, Dublin was now prepared to give him satirical recognition, but he may never have been made aware of this backhanded tribute.

If Dublin cared merely for the comedy of Joyce, Joyce himself was concerned only with the *commedia* of Dublin. Though he already had in hand some epiphanic material such as sketches of Gogarty and life in the tower, in the spring of 1914 Joyce had at last commenced upon *Ulysses* with a sketch of the final part, the semi-somnolent wanderings of Molly Bloom. For Joyce, Molly was the authoress of *Ulysses*, in much the same way that Nausikaa was for Samuel Butler the authoress of the *Odyssey*. Thus he commenced his most determined attempt upon the universality of Dublin's particularity.

Yet his main interest now was with his play *Exiles*, which he completed in three months. His friend Ettore Schmitz (one of the models for Leopold Bloom) had asked when thanking him for a gift of a copy of *Dubliners*: 'When will you write an Italian work about our town? Why not?' *Giacomo Joyce*, which seems to have been written out in its school copybook in July and August 1914, was in a secret way as much a response to Trieste as was the play.

Having concluded his work on *A Portrait* by the autumn, or more probably in the spring of 1915 (despite the dates at its conclusion – Joyce was anxious to fulfil the rash promise referred to in *Ulysses* to produce a work in ten years time), he then returned to the scheme of *Ulysses* and now wrote the first chapter. But this freshet of creativity was dammed by the outbreak of war.

In the Balkans there had been a long prologue to the Great War for the previous two years, with a war to which Joyce seems to have paid no attention. (Joyce Cary served in it under the illusion that it was the last war a civilized century would see.) Austria had annexed Bosnia and Herzegovina in 1908; then from October 1912 to September 1913, the Balkan War had raged between various states and

Turkey. In Bosnia on 28th June 1914, the heir to the Imperial throne and his wife were murdered by a Bosnian nationalist – encouraged by the Serbians to the south in a plot which can be traced back to disaffected elements in Trieste. From these local disputes a continental war developed in a matter of weeks. Germany, Russia and France put into effect long-planned operations. Great Britain declared war on Austria on 12th August 1914 – a week later than on Germany. As a British subject Stanislaus, who was on holiday in the Carso Hills behind Trieste, was arrested on 15th June 1915 and, with his typical luck, was interned at Katzenau; but James, equally typically, remained at liberty.

With the coming of war Joyce's private pupils vanished, though he retained his college position. Nevertheless he was at a loss. His enemy had been England; now he, as a British subject, was the enemy. Most confusing. As a free prisoner, his position was difficult. Friends such as Silvio Benco observed his troubles with sympathy: 'One would meet him in the street, his lips together in a firm, horizontal line. He would bow and regard one fixedly, and avoid stopping or exchanging a few words.' Benco thought that like many intellectuals he had lost his mental bearings in the Great War.

On 11th November 1914 Joyce wrote (by way of a difficult war-time route through Venice and Switzerland) to Harriet Shaw Weaver, sending on to her printer the last two chapters of 'A Portrait'. The serialization ran through to September 1915. The difficulties of this period were assuaged by Nora's uncle Michael Healy sending the family money from Ireland, again by the roundabout route through Italy, which he had arranged through an Ulsterman resident in Switzerland and a Triestine family with extensive English relations. This unlooked-for assistance was typical of the generosity which Joyce evoked throughout his life.

The literary business which Joyce was trying to organize through Pound and his agent J.B Pinker was also affected by the war. Pound was detailed by Joyce to deal with Pinker on his behalf. In America, H.L. Mencken placed two of the stories with his magazine *The Smart Set*: 'The Boarding House' and 'A Little Cloud' appeared in the May 1915 issue. The American edition of the stories had been delayed, but Mencken assured Joyce that he was in good hands with Ben Huebsch, 'one of the few intelligent publishers in New York'.

At that moment Huebsch felt that he could not bring out the volume successfully, yet in due course he would publish not only the first edition of *A Portrait* in December 1916, but his firm – later the Viking Press – would retain a long connection with Joyce and his work.

On 1st April 1915 Joyce finally completed the last draft of *Exiles*, an Ibsenesque drama which he described to Richards as 'a comedy'. The next day H. G. Wells wrote expressing his 'unstinted admiration' for Joyce's work: this was to lead to a review of Joyce's novel in *The Nation* in February 1917 which was critical in his final acceptance as a major writer of general rather than minority interest. It was Wells who had suggested in March to Pinker, his own agent, that he might be of assistance to Joyce.

Richards claimed to be not too distressed by the small sale of *Dubliners*, yet in May 1915 he concluded (with the support of his reader) that he could not bring out Joyce's *A Portrait of the Artist*. This was then taken over by the Egoist Press, who would issue a British edition in 1917.

Joyce's situation became even more complicated when war broke out between Italy and Austria on 23rd May 1915, resulting in fighting along the Alpine and Istrian fronts. Trieste was overwhelmingly Italian in population and Irredentist in political sympathy, hence an immediate object of the Italian military campaign. Yet the city's whole economy as a sea-port depended on its relationship with the Austrian provinces behind it. The Triestine nationalists were ready to sacrifice mere prosperity to achieve their dream of unity with Italy: Joyce would have been familiar with the type from Irish politics. For him the war between Franz Joseph's Austria and Victor Emmanuel's Italy was a nonsense. 'It was a difference of opinion between an old gentleman who is inaudible at twenty paces and a young gentleman who is invisible at the same distance' – the emperor had no voice and the king was very short. The citizens of Trieste would sit along the quay in front of the Café Miramar listening to the faint sound of the artillery on the distant front, shouting 'Avanti, Cagoia' ('Onward, Caterpillars') in mockery of the old Italian slogan of the Risorgimento, 'Avanti Savoia'. Nevertheless, the war was coming nearer. That month his sister Eileen finally married her Czech bank clerk. James stayed to witness the ceremony, but then it was time to go.

With the help of two of his students – both Greek aristocrats, Baron Ambrogio Ralli and Count Francesco Sordina – Joyce was able to obtain from the Austrian authorities exit permits for himself and his family to leave Austria and go to neutral Switzerland. He had some help too from his friend the Austrian Governor of the Littoral Province, Prince Conrad Hohenlohe, whose sons – by then cadets in the Royal and Imperial Army – had also been students of Joyce's. He had to give his parole that he would not take an active part in the conflict; an easy promise for an Irish intellectual to make. They could take nothing but hand baggage with them; his furniture, books, papers and the family portraits in their gilded frames would have to be left behind. Among these papers lay neglected not only *Giacomo Joyce*, but also his 1909 secret letters to Nora, which in their fearsome intimacy were in retrospect to provide such a distorted view of their lives.

By June, Joyce had written the first three sections of *Ulysses*, bringing him part way into the 'Proteus' episode. Writing of his literary *alter ego* Stephen Dedalus on the beach at Sandymount, he had reached the emblematical paragraph beginning:

> Houses of decay, mine, his and all. You told the Clongowes gentry you had an uncle a judge and an uncle a general in the army. Come out of them Stephen. Beauty is not there. Nor in the stagnant bay of Marsh's library where you read the fading prophecies of Joachim Abbas. For whom? The hundredheaded rabble of the cathedral close ... A choir gives back menace and echo, assisting about the altar's horns, the snorted Latin of jackpriests moving burly in their albs, tonsured and oiled and gelded, fat with the fat of kidneys of wheat.

The next 700 pages of the novel, in which he would achieve the almost total artistic recreation of his years of experience in Dublin, would have to wait for now. Yet he had begun: what moved him was not the fabric of the city, for that it hardly described, merely suggested. With his partial sight he had seen little of Dublin, but had smelled it and heard it, especially the voices of his family, his friends, his acquaintances and his enemies. There were to be few strangers in *Ulysses*; one way or the other, he knew them all, and would now use them to create the great masterpiece on which he was engaged.

On 21st June, the feast of the Jesuit St Aloyius Gonzaga, Joyce and his family left Trieste by train for Switzerland. Their ten-day journey through the intricate railways of Austria was not without its adventures, including a long, disturbing delay at Innsbruck, but at last they crossed the Swiss frontier. Their intended destination was

Lausanne, but they got only as far as the first large city they came to on the neutral side of the border. On the last day of June 1915, James Joyce and his family arrived in Zürich: for Joyce, this was the end of the beginning.

JOYCE'S HOROSCOPE

Prepared with the assistance of Mr Austin D.F. Byrne, Irish Astrological Society

Lord Raglan defined religion as 'ritual linked with theology', and magic as 'ritual which has lost its theology'. Once James Joyce had lost his Catholic faith, as the Irish expression has it, he was certainly left with rituals which had no belief to support them. His superstitions, which often amazed his more sophisticated friends and dismayed his Catholic ones, were in actuality pure magic. Like some Trobriand Islander, his life was a maze of special feasts, sacred days, little acts of propitiation, taboos and irrational fears. He often felt he had a special kind of second sight. Fate ruled his fortune.

This being so, it seems appropriate to set out details of his astral chart and the suggestions relating to his life's course which arise from it. At one stage in the early thirties he planned to have his horoscope cast, and tried to obtain from his father in Dublin the exact hour of his birth.

John Joyce's deathbed message to his son in December 1931 was: 'Tell Jim he was born at six in the morning.' This was on 2nd February 1882 in the Tenerure district south of the city of Dublin, approximately latitude 53° 20'38" North; longitude 6° 17' 30" West.

What follows is a brief summary of Mr Byrne's biographical-historical reading of Joyce's astrological chart, delivered after the composition of this book. It is an approximation of what Joyce's own astrologer in Paris would have told him, and reveals the tension between Joyce's free will, his upbringing, and the astrological conditioning of his birth-date.

First the chart itself. The Sun sign is Aquarius. The Moon sign is Leo. The Ascendant (an important definer of personality), lies very close to the division between Sagittarius and Capricorn, but is set in Capricorn (as the exact time of birth is known). This marks the Winter Solstitial position. The Southern (Mid-Heaven) sign is Scorpio. These represent the major influences at Joyce's birth.

The chart can be read for indications of (1) personality, (2) character,

(3) attitude of mind, (4) life and career, and (5) relations with others. Mr Byrne did not provide a reading through the Twelve Houses of the Zodiac, however; and it must be clearly understood that he was given only the date and time of birth, and no details as to the name and gender of the subject. In a few pages I can give only the gist of a long, seventeen-page report.

The subject would have been a strong disciplinarian in the sense of having great *self-discipline*, and an attitude of authority combined with an easy-going air. They would have been able to achieve what others thought impossible. They would have shown originality of dress within their own self-imposed conventions.

On the cusp of what might have been a conservative and conventional life, they would have been very innovative and self-expressive, and would not have ducked controversy if it came their way. Politically minded, yet not a complete anarchist, they would not have been over-influenced or coloured by the prevailing mores of the day.

They kept the upper hand, with a front-running role. Romantic, *avant garde*, eccentric in their mode of self-expression and description. Flamboyant, yet studied in expression, with a distinct flare for theatre and the performing arts; this would have been a special feature of their life.

A leaning towards science, in the sense of an interest in the new and unusual, verged towards the distinctly metaphysical. They would have had a following of their own, with an appetite for the social life, gregarious and good-humoured, with a liking for the public eye and the attention of the many. A capacity to manage people and social feelings created their own remarkable following.

An association with the Church is revealed – in the sense of a link with those active in religion. Had quite a fascination with Theology, for that which reflected a higher order of life.

In terms of character they would have been very generous, universal, one-for-all, all-for-one. Radical in their artistic interests. Had a fascination with the past, but with a tendency to rewrite history to their own perception.

Interested in the exploration of knowledge through books. In fact in astrological terms, it can be seen that they would have travelled a great deal in the mind. The writer/media person of the period would have been in evidence.

Involvement in the psychic, with mysticism, the dream-world, the unconscious; in fact, with a fascination for the whole area of psychology.

A quick ability with finance, making and spending money quickly. Would have done well in commerce if they had gone into it. They would also have been very successful with writing and communication – perhaps through early radio.

An esoteric approach to the politics of the time. Caught up in spirit of revolution. To the fore in change, the process of the breakthrough in thinking and attitude. Involvement in military matters suggests that they were put out of the struggle through some sort of incapacitation, which was rather more an inconvenience than anything else.

If they had been a female they would undoubtedly have been a suffragette and fought to find expression of the definitive energies in their chart. They would have attempted to establish their uniqueness and originality regardless of gender.

Their mental attitude was one of openness. Quick to respond to confrontation and criticism. A perfectionist with an artistic sensibility. A generator of public opinion, with a strong intellectual attitude. A tendency to break conventions.

A life of high risks is indicated. In tracing the indications of the life course, there is a distinct possible danger with regard to water and even drowning. This highlights a period of difficulty about age of 7–8, where an association of danger is shown with regard to mud or swampy ground. A spirit of adventure leading into danger and a serious accident, perhaps.

Another critical period can be seen at 18–20 with an indication of quite a lot of money, perhaps inherited, being seemingly squandered. Would have travelled and had an involvement with the sea. This indication is strong enough to suggest they might even have joined the Navy. They would never have lost this interest in and fascination with the sea. Around 29–30 is marked as a period of critical choice. This was quite a turning point. These were challenging, potentially dangerous years, involving almost a serious restriction of their continuance. This involved coming home and a public involvement there. They would take the challenge in hand and work very fully with it: this would have been a feature of their self-discipline.

The chart moves forward to about the 60th year. This saw a change of personal and financial circumstances with a reduction in living standards and material well-being – a dramatic turn of events about 1940. The year 1940–41 was a year of considerable and deep reflection. No date later than 1940–41 is mentioned by Mr Byrne.

Earlier dates are also significant: coming up to 6 years a change of security so great as to suggest moving to a different country. But this would have proved to be more of an advantage rather than a disadvantage. Around 7–8 years of age is also a special year. Harshness is a significant feature here with a traumatic effect on the child. Schooling divisive in terms of what was secure and what was comfortable. The chart suggests a pre-occupied student, one indeed who missed much schooling between 8 and 14, but caught up later. After 14 their originality is given an outlet and the course of life resumed. They are quite the inventor.

The years move in a great cycle of 12 years, with shorter cycles of 4 and 2 years, with significant years at 22, 24, 26, 30, and $33\frac{1}{2}$ years of age. There is a persistent feature of an initial creative movement, leading to greater depth of research and investigation, followed by a rapid pulling in of results, the making of discoveries. A graph of their life would be one of peaks and troughs with regard to finances. A restlessness would come into their life in cycles, but their creativity would then come to the fore again.

My Byrne concludes with regard to career, 'Artist probably, one can say that', but a strong feature of the chart is the wide, almost universal breadth of life interests.

The final area of inquiry was that of relations with others. Difficult relations with mother and father. Very reactive to the mores of the time, resulting in disputes with parents, leading them to go their own way in dramatic circumstances.

Well-to-do initially, a collapse of this to some degree, with a very considerable change of circumstance around about the years 3–7. The family situation would have changed rather dramatically, from plenty to not-so-plenty. A period of restraint, something akin to a period in jail, suggests a scandalous episode. A clash with the established Church in their lives, some sort of involvement-disinvolvement, a major swing of the pendulum, is indicated about the age of 29.

Not easy with female members of the family. Astrologically speaking, not at all getting along with females, period. Vocal and argumentative, their expression of opinion and ideas would have lead to a sharp response. They would have along very well with a particular brother, with whom they would have travelled and had money-related activities.

The area of health suggests a chest ailment. The strong possibility is death through a heart attack, though this could have happened as the result of something else, for what is indicated is some element of accident or shock, which brought about their demise. Their death, in any case, was likely to have been sudden, rather than protracted.

The chart shows someone with innovative drive, very creative on all levels, in tune with the changing times, spontaneous, making and spending money quickly, moving in peaks and troughs through life, the more dynamic aspects of their creativity and achievement falling into a three stage mode. Very well self-educated. If female, very tough. If male, someone who would have had an adventurous life, and would sought to have contributed to the ideas and the media that were coming up in the new modes of communication. To the forefront of the changing times.

I make no large claim for this astrological reading; the sceptical can have it repeated for themselves. Readers must decide just how significant or insignificant it really is, but to my way of thinking, as a biographical experiment, it has produced some strange results, which would have surprised even Joyce himself: that Daedalus and Ulysses, the inventor and the sailor, were written in his stars.

23rd March 1992

FAMILY TREES

These family trees are as complete as current information and space allow; I have had no room to include the descendants of Hugh Murray of Tulcon, though the data is in hand. As with all matters genealogical, further research will doubtless soon provide additional information about earlier generations, and more exact details about later individuals.

I am particularly grateful to Mr Michael Whelan for all the help he has given me on tracing the Murrays back to their origins. Mr Arthur Walls and Mr Ken Monaghan have aided me with details of the more recent generations of the Murrays and Joyces. Likewise Mr Charles McCarthy of Cork has been of invaluable aid with regard to the Joyces and the O'Connells. Professor Maurice O'Connell, and his kinsman Mr Maurice O'Connell, have also aided me with their suggestions and information relating to the researches of the late Basil O'Connell, the well-known genealogist of the O'Connell clan, who did not care for James Joyce and was far from anxious to detail in print the writer's links with the family of the Liberator.

Further information on the Flynn and Lyons families would be welcome.

TABLE I: THE PEDIGREE OF STEPHEN JAMES JOYCE b.1932

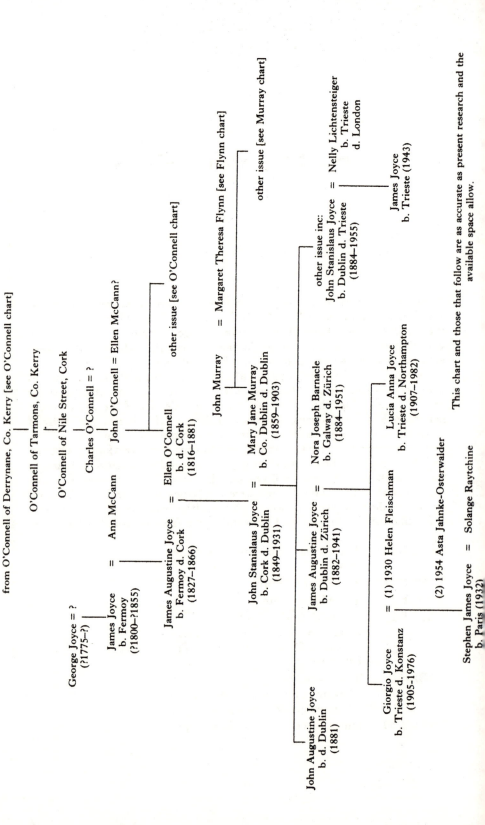

from O'Connell of Derrynane, Co. Kerry [see O'Connell chart]

This chart and those that follow are as accurate as present research and the available space allow.

TABLE II: THE FLYNN FAMILY

Persons in **bold type** figure in Joyce's work

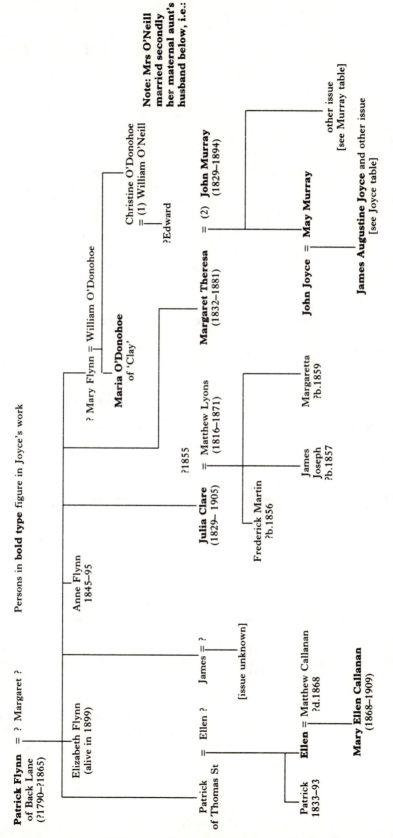

This table is less detailed than the others due to the obscurity surrounding several individuals and lines.

TABLE III: THE MURRAY FAMILY

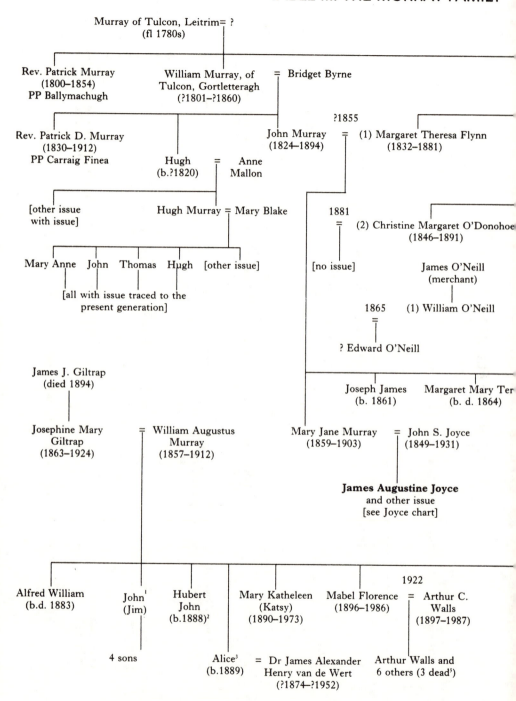

Murray of Tulcon, Leitrim= ?
(fl 1780s)

Rev. Patrick Murray
(1800–1854)
PP Ballymachugh

William Murray, of
Tulcon, Gortletteragh
(?1801–?1860)
= Bridget Byrne

Rev. Patrick D. Murray
(1830–1912)
PP Carraig Finea

Hugh
(b.?1820)
= Anne
Mallon

John Murray
(1824–1894)
?1855
= (1) Margaret Theresa Flynn
(1832–1881)

[other issue
with issue]

Hugh Murray = Mary Blake

1881
= (2) Christine Margaret O'Donohoe
(1846–1891)

Mary Anne   John   Thomas   Hugh   [other issue]

[no issue]

James O'Neill
(merchant)

[all with issue traced to the
present generation]

1865
=
(1) William O'Neill

? Edward O'Neill

James J. Giltrap
(died 1894)

Joseph James
(b. 1861)

Margaret Mary Ter
(b. d. 1864)

Josephine Mary
Giltrap
(1863–1924)
= William Augustus
Murray
(1857–1912)

Mary Jane Murray
(1859–1903)
= John S. Joyce
(1849–1931)

James Augustine Joyce
and other issue
[see Joyce chart]

Alfred William
(b.d. 1883)

John[1]
(Jim)

Hubert
John
(b.1888)[2]

Mary Katheleen
(Katsy)
(1890–1973)

Mabel Florence
(1896–1986)

1922
= Arthur C.
Walls
(1897–1987)

4 sons

Alice[3]
(b.1889)
= Dr James Alexander
Henry van de Wert
(?1874–?1952)

Arthur Walls and
6 others (3 dead[5])

This table has been prepared with the generous
assistance of Michael Whelan, Arthur Walls,
Fergus McNestry, and Kenneth Monaghan.

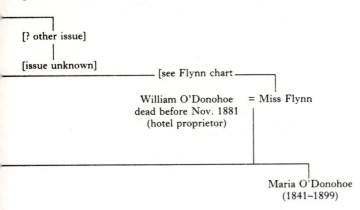

[? other issue]

[issue unknown] ————————————————— [see Flynn chart ——————————

William O'Donohoe   = Miss Flynn
dead before Nov. 1881
(hotel proprietor)

Maria O'Donohoe
(1841–1899)

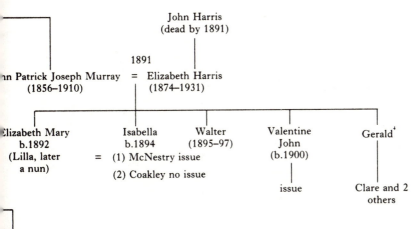

John Harris
(dead by 1891)

1891

ın Patrick Joseph Murray   =   Elizabeth Harris
(1856–1910)   (1874–1931)

| Elizabeth Mary b.1892 (Lilla, later a nun) | Isabella b.1894 | Walter (1895–97) | Valentine John (b.1900) | Gerald[4] |

Isabella = (1) McNestry issue
(2) Coakley no issue

Valentine John — issue

Gerald — Clare and 2 others

ıry (May)   =   Peter Cullen
899–1961)

(6 children)

NOTES
1 John, called Jim, married his wife Betty during the Great
  War in Liverpool, where he died; he had 4 sons.
2 Hubert, who joined the British Army, died in Wrexham in
  the 1950s, unmarried.
3 Alice, who nursed in London, married there; her husband
  was a doctor from Ceylon (now Sri Lanka), who had
  served in the British Army.
4 Later an officer in the Irish Army.
5 Peter H. Walls, died 27/7/1926, aged 1 year 7 months;
  Pauline Patricia Walls, died 15/3/1950, aged 1 year 2
  months; and Mary J. Walls, died 4/5/1936, aged 2 months
  3 weeks.

TABLE IV: THE O'CONNELL FAMILY

The names in bold indicate the connection between Daniel O'Connell ('The Liberator') and James Joyce through John O'Connell, the founder of Derrynane.

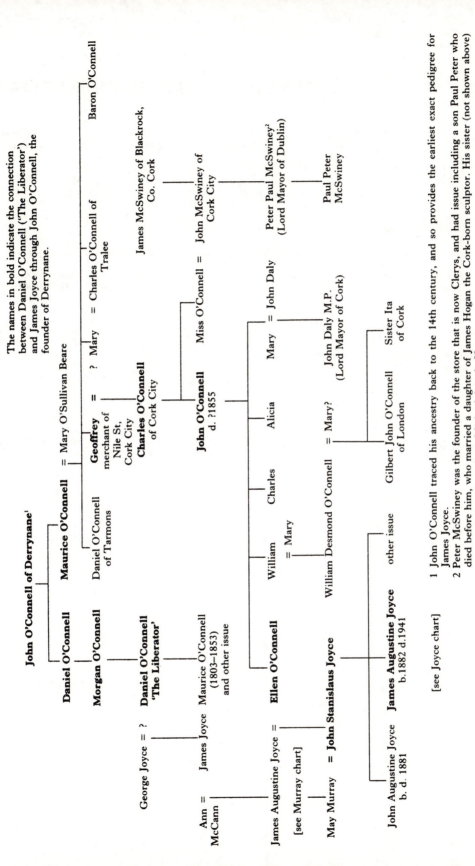

[see Joyce chart]

1 John O'Connell traced his ancestry back to the 14th century, and so provides the earliest exact pedigree for James Joyce.

2 Peter McSwiney was the founder of the store that is now Clerys, and had issue including a son Paul Peter who died before him, who married a daughter of James Hogan the Cork-born sculptor. His sister (not shown above) was married to the painter Michael Angelo Hayes.

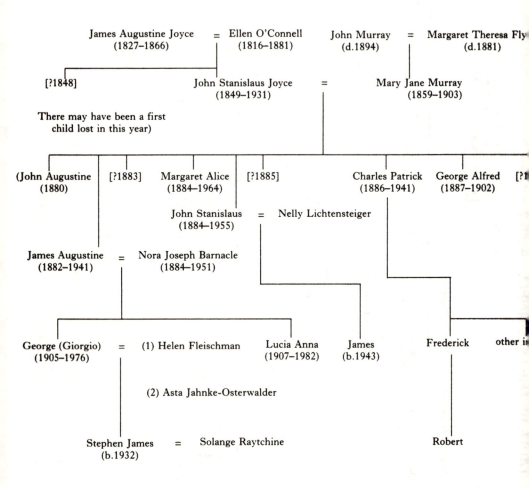

James Augustine Joyce (1827–1866) = Ellen O'Connell (1816–1881)

John Murray (d.1894) = Margaret Theresa Fly (d.1881)

[?1848]

John Stanislaus Joyce (1849–1931) = Mary Jane Murray (1859–1903)

There may have been a first child lost in this year)

(John Augustine (1880)

[?1883]

Margaret Alice (1884–1964)

[?1885]

Charles Patrick (1886–1941)

George Alfred (1887–1902)

[?1

John Stanislaus (1884–1955) = Nelly Lichtensteiger

James Augustine (1882–1941) = Nora Joseph Barnacle (1884–1951)

George (Giorgio) (1905–1976) = (1) Helen Fleischman

Lucia Anna (1907–1982)

James (b.1943)

Frederick

other i

(2) Asta Jahnke-Osterwalder

Stephen James (b.1932) = Solange Raytchine

Robert

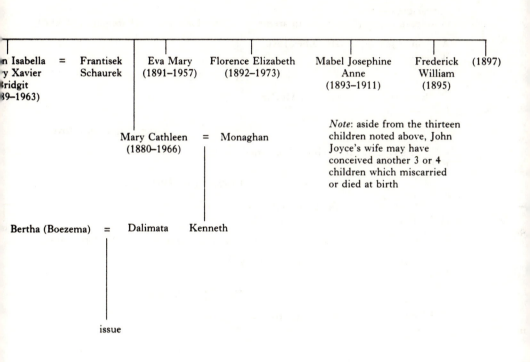

n Isabella = Frantisek Eva Mary Florence Elizabeth Mabel Josephine Frederick (1897)
y Xavier   Schaurek   (1891–1957) (1892–1973) Anne William
Bridgit   (1893–1911) (1895)
89–1963)

Mary Cathleen = Monaghan
(1880–1966)

Note: aside from the thirteen children noted above, John Joyce's wife may have conceived another 3 or 4 children which miscarried or died at birth

Bertha (Boezema) = Dalimata Kenneth

issue

TABLE VI: JAMES JOYCE'S GENETIC MAKE-UP

The letters represent schematically the transmission of genetic characteristics. 'Biologically an individual has no parents, but four grandparents and sixteen great-great-grandparents. This means that a child inherits through its parents the qualities of its grandparents, and through its great-grandparents the qualities of its great-great-grandparents.' (Dr Halliday Sutherland.)

(Great-great-grandparents)	(Great-grandparents)	(Grandparents)	(Parents)	(Child)
A George Joyce	ab James Joyce			
B ? ——				
		ABCD James A. Joyce		
C ? McCann	cd Ann McCann			
D ? ——				
			abcdefgh John Joyce	
E Charles O'Connell	ef John O'Connell			
F ? ——				
		EFGH Ellen O'Connell		
G ? McGann	gh Ellen McCann			
H ? ——				
				ABCDEFGHIJKLMNOP James Joyce
I ? Murray	ij William Murray			
J ? ——				
		IJKL John Murray		
K ? Byrne	kl Bridgit Byrne			
L ? ——				
			ijklmnop May Murray	
M Patrick Flynn	mn Patrick Flynn			
N ? ——				
		MNOP Margaret Flynn		
O ? ——				
P ? ——				

James Joyce thus inherited his genetic characteristics from James A Joyce (fecklessness); Ellen O'Connell (nervous disposition); John Murray (drink/sexuality); Margaret Flynn (musical taste). From an earlier generation came his will and determination, characteristic of George Joyce, Charles O'Connell, and Patrick Flynn. But with eight great-great-grandparents unknown, the full picture is not clear. The double input of genes from the McCann family (clearly connected with each other and with his godfather Philip McCann) also require further investigation.

BIBLIOGRAPHY

I The Writings of James Joyce

(by date of publication of edition used):

Chamber Music [1907]. Edited by William York Tindall. New York: Columbia University Press, 1954.

Dubliners: the Corrected Text [1914]. Edited by Robert Scholes in consultation with Richard Ellmann. London: Cape, 1968.

A Portrait of the Artist [1916]: *Corrected Text*. Edited by Chester G. Anderson and reviewed by Richard Ellmann. London, 1964.

Exiles [1918]. Harmondworth: Penguin Books, 1973.

Ulysses [1922]. Reset edition. London: The Bodley Head, 1960.

Pomes Penyeach [1927] *and other Verses*. London: Faber and Faber, 1966.

Finnegans Wake [1939]. Reset edition incorporating the author's corrections. London: Faber and Faber, 1958.

Stephen Hero [1944]. Revised and re-set edition. London: Cape 1956.

Giacomo Joyce. With an Introduction and Notes by Richard Ellmann. London: Faber and Faber, 1968.

Letters of James Joyce. Vol.I, edited by Stuart Gilbert. London: Faber and Faber, 1957.

Letters of James Joyce. Vols. II and III, edited by Richard Ellmann. London: Faber and Faber, 1966.

Selected Letters [containing the 1909 Dublin letters]. Edited by Richard Ellmann. London: Faber and Faber, 1975.

'Daniel Defoe'. Edited from the Italian manuscript and translated by Joseph Prescott. *Buffalo Studies* (Buffalo), vol.1, no.1, December 1964.

Joyce and Hauptmann Before Sunrise: James Joyce's Translation [of Gerhart Hauptmann] with an introduction and notes by Jill Perkins. Los Angeles: Henry E. Huntington Library, 1978.

Scritti Italiani. A cura di Gianfranco Corsini e Giorgio Melchiori, con la collaborazione di Louis Berrone, Nino Frank e Jacqueline Risset. Milano: Arnaldo Mondadori Editore, 1979.

James Joyce: The Critical Writings. Edited by Ellsworth Mason and Richard Ellmann, with an introduction by Guy Davenport. Ithaca, NY: Cornell University Press, 1989.

Poems and Shorter Writings. Edited by Richard Ellmann, A. Walton Litz and John Whittier-Ferguson. London: Faber and Faber, 1991.

Joyce's Notes and Early Drafts for 'Ulysses'. edited by Phillip F. Herring. Charlottesville: University Press of Virginia, 1972.

The James Joyce Archive. Edited by Michael Groden and others, in 63 vols. New York: Garland Publishing, 1977–79.

James Joyce's Manuscripts. An Index. Edited by Michael Groden. New York: Garland, 1980.

Recklinghausen, Daniel von. *James Joyce – Chronik von Leben und Werk*. Frankfurt-am-Main: Suhrkamp Verlag, 1968.

II Manuscript sources consulted

State Papers Office, Dublin
>   Chief Secretary's Office Registered Papers Index 1881–1905
>   Fenian Papers
>   Crime Branch Special Papers

National Archives, Dublin
>   Index of Wills and Administrations 1864–1922
>   Wills and Probates 1923 onwards
>   Chapelizod Distillery Plans
>   Intermediate Education Board Records
>   Census Returns 1901 and 1911
>   Valuation Office
>   Registry of Deeds
>   Registrar-General for Ireland, Births, Deaths and Marriages
>   Clongowes Wood College
>   Belvedere College
>   Jesuit Fathers Leeson Street
>   Catholic University College Archives 1882–1908

Sion Hill
O'Connell Schools, Richmond N. Street
University College Cork

University College Dublin
>   C.P. Curran Papers
>   D.J. O'Donoghue Papers
>   Kettle Papers

National University of Ireland
Glasnevin Cemetery Office Records
BBC Written Archives

National Library

Francis Sheehy-Skeffington Papers
Joseph Holloway Papers: diaries and theatre journals
Joyce Papers
Liam O'Leary National Film Archives
Padraic and Mary Colum Papers
William Fallon Papers

Dublin Public Libraries
    Records and Catalogues of Capel Street and Charleville Mall libraries
        1884–1916

Trinity College, University of Dublin
    Patricia Hutchins Papers
    Thomas McGreevy Papers

British Library (London)
    Harriet Shaw Weaver Papers and Correspondence

III Secondary sources
These books are those which contain essential biographical, background or
topographical information, or which are referred to in the Notes. Mere critical
studies are not included otherwise.
Anon., *The Story of the Parnell Crisis: told from Authentic Sources, Public
    and Private, a handbook for Politicians and Electors*. London: Pall Mall
    Gazette Office, January 1891.
Adams, Robert Martin, *Surface and Symbol*. New York: Oxford University
    Press, 1962.
Anderson, Chester G., *James Joyce and His World*. London: Thames and
    Hudson, 1967.
Anderson, Margaret, *My Thirty Years' War*. New York: Covici, Friede,
    1930; London: Alfred A. Knopf, 1930.
Atherton, J.S., *The Books at the Wake*. London: Faber and Faber, 1959.
Araby: the Official Catalogue, Dublin, 1894.
Arnold, Bruce, *The Scandal of Ulysses*. London: Sinclair-Stevenson, 1991.
Ball, F.E., *A History of the County Dublin*. Dublin, 1902–1920.
Barolini, Helen, 'The Curious Case of Amalia Popper', *New York Review
    of Books*, 20 November 1969, vol.13, no.9, pp.44–51. With a reply by
    Richard Ellmann.
Barrett, Edward Boyd, *The Jesuit Enigma*. London: Cape, 1928.
———, *Ex-Jesuit*. London: Geoffrey Bles, 1931.
Baedeker, Karl, *Central Italy and Rome*. Leipsig: Karl Baedeker, 1900.
———, *Southern Germany and Austria*. Leipsig: Karl Baedeker, 1891.
———, *Switzerland*. Leipsig: Karl Baedeker, 1913.
Beach, Sylvia, *Catalogue of a Collection Containing Manuscripts and Rare
    Editions of James Joyce, etc*. Paris: Shakespeare & Co., 1935.
———, *Shakespeare and Company*. New York: Harcourt, Brace, 1959;
    London: Faber and Faber, 1960.
Beckett, Samuel and others, *Our Exagmination Round His Factification for*

Incamination of 'Work in Progress'. Paris: Shakespeare & Co., 1929; London: Faber and Faber, 1936, 1957.

Beebe, Maurice, 'James Joyce: Barnacle Goose and Lapwing.' *Publications of the Modern Language Association* (Menasha, Wisc.), LXXXI (June 1956), pp.302–320.

———, 'Joyce and Stephen Dedalus: The Problem of Autobiography' in *A James Joyce Miscellany* (Second series), edited by Marvin Magalaner. Carbondale, Ill.: Southern Illinois University Press, 1959.

Benson, E.F., *As We Were*. London: Penguin Books, 1942.

Benstock, Bernard, *Joyce-Again's Wake. An Analysis of Finnegans Wake*. Seattle: University of Washington Press, 1965.

Benstock, Bernard and Shari, *Who's He When He's At Home. A James Joyce Directory*. Urbana, Ill.: University of Illinois Press, 1980.

Bérard, Victor, *Les Phéneciens dans l'Odyssée*. Paris, 1902.

Berrone, Louis, *James Joyce in Padua*. New York: Random House, 1977.

Bidwell, Bruce (with Linda Heffer), *The Joycean Way*. Dublin: Wolfhound Press, 1981.

Blake, Mr [Recollections of Joyce] in 'A Portrait of Joyce as a Young Man' in *Irish Literary Portraits*, edited by W.R. Rogers. London: British Broadcasting Corporation, 1972.

Blamires, Harry, *The Bloomsday Book*. London: Methuen, 1966.

Bowen, Zack, *Musical Allusions in the Works of James Joyce*. Dublin: Gill and Macmillan, 1975.

Bowman, John and O'Donoghue, Ronan (eds.), *Portraits: Belvedere College Dublin 1832–1982*. Dublin: Gill and Macmillan, 1982.

Boyd, Ernest A., *Ireland's Literary Renaissance*. Dublin: Maunsel and Co., 1916; New York: Alfred A. Knopf, 1922.

Bradley, Bruce, *James Joyce's Schooldays*. Dublin: Gill and Macmillan, 1981.

Brandabur, Edward, *A Scrupulous Meanness*. Chicago: University of Illinois Press, 1971.

Broeker, Galen, *Rural Disorder and Police Reform in Ireland, 1812–36*. London: Routledge & Kegan Paul, 1970.

Brown, Stephen, *Ireland in Fiction*. Dublin: Maunsel and Company, 1919.

Browne, Henry, *Handbook of Homeric Studies*. Dublin: Browne and Nolan, 1905.

Bryher, *The Heart to Artemis*. London: William Collins, 1963.

Budgen, Frank, *James Joyce and the Making of 'Ulysses' and other writings*. London: Oxford University Press, 1972.

———, *Myselves When Young*. London: Oxford University Press, 1970.

Bulfin, William, *Rambles in Eirinn*. Dublin: M.H. Gill, 1907.

Burgess, Anthony, *Here Comes Everybody*. London: Faber and Faber, 1965.

Burke, Sir Bernard, *The Landed Gentry of Ireland*. Tenth edition, edited by Ashworth P. Burke. London: Harrison and Sons, 1904.

Butler, Samuel, *The Odyssey Done into English Prose*. London: Longman, 1900.

———, *The Authoress of the Odyssey*. London: Fifield, 1913. (First edition 1895.)

Butler, William F.T., *Gleanings from Irish History*. London: Longman, Green and Co., 1925.

Byrne, J.F., *Silent Years: An Autobiography with Memoirs of James Joyce and Our Ireland*. New York: Farrar, Straus and Young, 1953.

Campbell, Joseph, and Robinson, Henry Morton, *A Skeleton Key to 'Finnegans Wake'*. New York: Harcourt, Brace and Company, 1944; London: Faber and Faber, 1947.

Campbell, Sandy, 'Mrs Joyce in Zürich.' *Harper's Bazaar* (New York), October 1952.

Cannadine, David, *The Decline and Fall of the British Aristocracy*. New Haven and London: Yale University Press, 1990.

Carpenter, Humphrey, *Geniuses Together. American Writers in Paris in the 1920s*. London: Unwin Hyman, 1987.

Catechism of Catholic Doctrine. Approved by the Archbishops and Bishops of Ireland. Dublin: M.H. Gill and Son, 1951.

Chart, D.A., *The Story of Dublin*. London: J.M. Dent, 1907.

Childers, E.S., *The Life and Correspondence of Hugh C.E. Childers*. London, 1901.

Cixous, Hélène, *L'Exil de James Joyce*. Paris: Bernard Grasset, 1968. Translated as *The Exile of James Joyce*. New York: David Lewis, 1972.

Clarke, Austin, *Twice Round the Black Church*. London: Routledge & Kegan Paul, 1962.

——, *A Penny in the Clouds*. London: Routledge & Kegan Paul, 1968.

Cole, Grenville and Praeger, R.L., *Handbook to the Dublin District*. Dublin: at the University Press, 1907.

Colum, Mary, *Life and the Dream*. New York: Doubleday, 1947.

——, 'A Little Knowledge of Joyce.' *Saturday Review of Literature* (New York), vol.33, 29 April 1950, pp.11–12.

Colum, Mary and Padraic, *Our Friend James Joyce*. New York: Doubleday, 1958; London: Gollancz, 1959.

Colum, Padraic, 'Dublin in Literature', *The Bookman* (New York), vol.63, July 1926, pp.555–61.

——, *The Road Round Ireland*. New York, 1926.

——, 'Introduction' in James Joyce, *Dubliners*. New York: Modern Library, 1929.

——, 'Portrait of James Joyce.' *Dublin Magazine*, vol.7, April–June 1932, pp.40–48.

——, 'Introduction' in *Exiles* by James Joyce. London: Jonathan Cape, 1952.

Connolly, Thomas E. (ed.), *The Personal Library of James Joyce: Descriptive Bibliography* (University of Buffalo Studies, vol.XXII, 1). Buffalo: The University Bookshop, 1957.

—— (ed.), *James Joyce's 'Scribbledehobble': The Ur-Workbook for Finnegans Wake*. Evanston, Ill.: Northwestern University Press, 1961.

Cope, Jackson. I., *Joyce's Cities: Archaeologies of the Soul*. Baltimore and London: The Johns Hopkins University Press, 1981.

Corcoran, Timothy, *The Story of Clongowes Wood*. Dublin: Catholic Truth Society, 1900.

Corcoran, Timothy, *The Clongowes Record: 1814–1932*. Dublin: Browne and Nolan, 1932.

Cork, City and County Directory. Edited by Francis Guy. Cork, 1894.

Cosgrave, Dillon, *North Dublin City and Environs*. Dublin: The Catholic Truth Society, 1909; Dublin: Four Courts Press, 1977.

Cosgrave, Ephraim MacDowel and Strangeways, Leonard R., *The Dictionary of Dublin*. Dublin: Sealy, Bryers and Walker, 1907.

Costello, Peter, *The Heart Grown Brutal. The Irish Revolution in Literature, 1891–1939*. Dublin: Gill and Macmillan, 1977.

———, *James Joyce*. Dublin: Gill and Macmillan, 1980 [*Gill's Irish Lives*].

———, *Leopold Bloom: A Biography*. Dublin: Gill and Macmillan, 1981.

———, *Clongowes Wood College: A History*. Dublin: Gill and Macmillan, 1988.

———, *Dublin Churches*. Dublin: Gill and Macmillan, 1990.

———, and van de Kamp, Peter, *Flann O'Brien*. London: Bloomsbury, 1987.

Craig, Maurice, *Dublin 1661–1860: A Social and Architectural History*. London: The Cresset Press, 1952.

Cowley, Malcolm, *Exiles Return*. New York: Viking Press, 1951; London: Bodley Head, 1961.

Crise, Stelio, *And Trieste Ah Trieste*. Milano: All'insegna del Pesce d'Oro, 1971.

———, *Epiphanies & Phadographs: James Joyce e Trieste*. Milano: All'insegna del Pesce d'Oro, 1967.

Croce, Benedetto, *The Philosophy of Giambattista Vico*. Translated by R.G. Collingwood. London: Macmillan, 1913.

Curran, Constantine P., 'When James Joyce Lived in Dublin', *Vogue*, vol.109, May 1947, pp.144–9.

———, *James Joyce Remembered*. London: Oxford University Press, 1968.

———, *Under the Receding Wave*. Dublin: Gill and Macmillan, 1970.

Curtayne, Alice, 'Portrait of the Artist as a Brother: an interview with James Joyce's sister.' *Critic*, vol.21, 1963, 43–47.

Dalton, Jack P. and Hart, Clive (eds), *Twelve and a Tilly*. London: Faber and Faber, 1966.

Davies, Stan Gébler, *James Joyce: A Portrait of the Artist*. London: Davis-Poynter, 1975.

Delaney, Frank, *James Joyce's Odyssey*. London: Hodder and Stoughton, 1982.

Devitt, Matthew, 'Clongowes Wood', *Co. Kildare Archaeological Society Journal*, vol.3, 1899–1902, pp.207–16, 493.

Duff, Charles, *James Joyce and the Plain Reader*. London, 1932.

———, *Ireland and the Irish*. London, 1951.

Dujardin, Edouard, *Les Lauriers sont coupés*. Paris: A. Messein, 1924.

———, *Le monologue intérieur: son apparition, ses origines, sa place dans l'oeuvre de James Joyce*. Paris, 1931.

Edel, Leon, 'James Joyce: The Last Journey', *Story*, XXXII, no.129. Summer 1948, pp.139–47; also New York: Gotham Book Mart, 1947.

Eglinton, John, *Irish Literary Portraits*. London: Macmillan, 1935.

Ellmann, Richard, *James Joyce*. London: Oxford University Press, 1959. (New edition, 1982.) The German edition (Zürich: Rhein-Verlag) contains an extensive bibliography in several languages compiled by Fritz Senn.

———, *Ulysses on the Liffey*. London: Faber and Faber, 1972.

———, *The Consciousness of Joyce*. London: Faber and Faber, 1977.

———, *James Joyce's Tower*. Dun Laoighaire: Eastern Regional Tourism Organisation, 1969.

Envoy (Dublin). James Joyce Special Number, edited by Brian O'Nolan (Flann O'Brien). Vol.5, no.17, April 1951.

Ernst, Morris L., *The Best is Yet*. New York: Harper and Brothers, 1945.

———, *The Censor Marches On*. New York: Random House, 1940.

Esterson, Aaron, *The Leaves of Spring – Schizophrenia, Family and Sacrifice*. London: Tavistock Press, 1970.

Fabricant, Nohan D., 'The Ocular History of James Joyce' in *Thirteen Famous Patients*. Philadelphia: Chilton Books, 1960.

Fagan, Patrick, *The Second City: Portrait of Dublin 1701–1760*. Dublin: Branar Books, 1986.

Fallon, W.G. *See* O'Connor, V.

Fanning, Michael (ed.), *France and Sherwood Anderson: Paris Notebook, 1921*. Baton Rouge: Louisiana State University Press, 1976.

Finnegan, John, *The Story of Monto*. Cork: Mercier Books, 1978.

Fitch, Noël Riley, *Sylvia Beach and the Lost Generation*. New York: W.W. Norton, 1985.

Fitzpatrick, Samuel A. Ossory, *Dublin: A Historical and Topographical Account of the City*. London, 1907.

Francini Bruni, Alessandro, *Joyce intimo spogliato in piazza*. Trieste: La Editoriale Libraria, 1922. Translation in Potts (1979).

Frank, Nino, 'Souvenirs sur James Joyce', *La Table Ronde* (Paris), 23 November 1947, pp.1671–93.

Freund, Gisèle, *Trois jours avec Joyce*. Paris: Denoël, 1982.

——— (with V.P. Carleton), *James Joyce in Paris – The Final Years*. New York: Harcourt, Brace, 1965; London: Cassell, 1965.

Furniss, Harry, *M.P.s in Session*, from *Mr Punch's Parliamentary Portrait Gallery*. London: Bradbury Agnew, 1889. [p.44: H.C.E. Childers, from *Punch*, 23 July 1889].

Galway Year Book and Directory. Galway: M'Donough and Brown, 1902.

Garvin, John, *James Joyce's Disunited Kingdom and the Irish Dimension*. Dublin: Gill and Macmillan, 1976. New York: Barnes & Noble, 1976.

Gheerbrandt, Bernard, *James Joyce – sa vie, son oeuvre, son rayonnment*. Paris: Librarie la Hune, 1949.

Giedion-Welcker, Carola, *In Memoriam James Joyce*. Zürich, 1941.

———, 'James Joyce in Zürich', *Horizon* (London), 1948.

Gifford, Don, *Joyce Annotated*. (Second edition.) Berkeley: University of California Press, 1982.

Gifford, Don (with Robert J. Seidman), *Ulysses Annotated*. Second edition (of *Notes for Joyce*). Berkeley: University of California Press, 1988.

Gilbert, Stuart, *James Joyce's Ulysses*. (Revised edition.) New York: Alfred A. Knopf, 1952.

———, 'The Latin Background of James Joyce's Art', *Horizon* (London), vol.10, 1944.

Gillet, Louis, *Claybook for James Joyce*. Translation and Introduction by Georges Markow-Totevy. London and New York: Abelard-Schuman, 1958.

Givens, Seon (ed.), *James Joyce: Two Decades of Criticism*. New York: Vanguard Press, 1948.

Glasheen, Adaline, *A Census of Finnegans Wake*. London: Faber and Faber, 1956.

———, *A Second Census of Finnegans Wake*. Evanston: Northwestern University Press, 1963.

Gogarty, Oliver St John, *As I Was Going Down Sackville Street*. London: Rich and Cowan, 1937.

———, *Tumbling in the Hay*. London: Constable, 1939.

———, 'The Joyce I Knew' [Obituary of Joyce], *Saturday Review of Literature*, vol, 23, 25 January 1941.

———, 'James Joyce: A Portrait of the Artist' in *Mourning Becomes Mrs Spendlove*. New York, 1948.

———, 'They think they know Joyce', *Saturday Review of Literature* (New York), vol.33, 18 March 1950, pp.8–9, 36–7.

———, *It Isn't This Time of Year at All*. London: MacGibbon and Kee, 1954.

Gogarty, Oliver, 'The Tower: Fact and Fiction', *Irish Times* (Dublin), 16 June 1962, p.11.

Goldberg, S.L., *The Classical Temper: a Study of James Joyce's 'Ulysses'*. London: Chatto and Windus, 1961.

Golding, Louis, *James Joyce*. London: Thornton Butterworth, 1933.

Gordon, John, *James Joyce's Metamorphoses*. Dublin: Gill and Macmillan, 1981.

Gorman, Herbert S., *James Joyce: His First Forty Years*. London: Geoffrey Bles, 1926.

———, *James Joyce: A definitive biography*. New York: Farrar & Rinehart, 1939; London: The Bodley Head, 1941.

Gross, John, *Joyce*. London: Collins/Fontana, 1971.

Gwynn, Stephen, *Experiences of a Literary Man*. London, Thornton Butterworth, 1926, pp.280–304; [Bodkin p.293.]

Hackett, Francis, *The Green Lion*. London: Nicholson and Watson, 1936.

Haliday, Charles, *The Scandinavian Kingdom of Dublin*. Dublin: Alex Thom, 1881.

Hall, J.B., *Random Records of a Reporter*. Dublin: Fodhla Printing Co., 1929.

Hare, Augustus J.C., *Days Near Paris*. Philadelphia: David McKay, n.d.

Harmon, Maurice (ed.), *The Celtic Master*. Dublin: The Dolmen Press, 1969.

Harrington, Timothy Charles, *The Maamtrasna Massacre*. Dublin: The Nation Office, 1884.

Hart, Clive, *A Concordance to Finnegans Wake*. Minneapolis: University of Minnesota Press, 1963.

——, *Structure and Motif in Finnegans Wake*. London: Faber and Faber, 1962.

Hart, Clive and Knuth, Leo, *A Topographical Guide to James Joyce's Ulysses*. Text and Maps. Colchester: A Wake Newslitter Press, 1975.

Harvey, John, *Dublin: A Study in Environment*. London: B.T. Batsford, 1949.

Hayman, David, *A First Draft Version of Finnegans Wake*. Austin: University of Texas Press, 1962.

Henchy, Deirdre, 'Dublin 80 Years Ago', *Dublin Historical Record*, vol.26, no.1, December 1972, pp.18–35.

Henry, Françoise (ed.), *The Book of Kells*. London: Thames and Hudson, 1974.

Herr, Cheryl, *Joyce's Anatomy of Culture*. Urbana and Chicago: University of Illinois Press, 1986.

Hill's Guide to Blackrock. Dublin, 1892; new edition, Blackrock, Carraig Books, 1976.

Hodgart, M.J.C. and Worthington, Mabel P., *Song in the Works of James Joyce*. New York: University of Columbia Press, 1959.

Hoek, Kees van, 'Mrs James Joyce', *The Irish Times* (Dublin), 12th November 1949.

Hone, Joseph M., 'A letter from Ireland', *London Mercury*, no.5, January 1923, pp.306–08.

Howarth, Herbert, *The Irish Writers 1880–1940. Literature under Parnell's Star*. London: Rockliff, 1958.

Huddleston, Sisley, *Bohemian Literary and Social Life in Paris: Salons, Cafés, Studios*. London: Harrap, 1928.

Hughes, Eileen Lanouette, 'The Mystery Lady of "Giacomo Joyce"', *Life* (New York), 19 February 1968, pp.54ff.

Hutchins, Patricia, *James Joyce's Dublin*. London: The Grey Walls Press, 1950.

——, *James Joyce's World*. London: Methuen, 1957.

Hyman, Louis, *The Jews in Ireland*. Shannon: Irish University Press, 1972.

Igoe, Vivien, *James Joyce's Dublin Houses & Nora Barnacle's Galway*. London: Mandarin, 1990.

James Joyce Quarterly (Tulsa) 'Joyce and Trieste Issue', vol.9, pp.307–49.

Jolas, Maria (ed.), *The James Joyce Yearbook*. Paris: Transition Press, 1949.

Jolly, W.P., *Jumbo*. London: Constable, 1976.

Journalist, A., *Two Weeks in Ireland in 1920*. London: Collins, 1920.

Joyce, Cecily, *Claddagh Ring Story*. Privately published, 1990.

Joyce, Giorgio, 'My father'. Interview by Maud Lennox, *Sunday Press* (Dublin), 18 June 1967.

Joyce, John Stanislaus, 'Interview with Mr John Stanislaus Joyce' in *A James Joyce Yearbook*, ed. Maria Jolas. Paris: Transition Press, 1949.

Joyce, Stanislaus, 'The Joyces', *New Yorker* (New York), 12 January 1935.

——, 'Early Memories of James Joyce', *The Listener* (London) vol.41, 26 May 1949, p.896.

——, 'James Joyce. A Memoir', *Hudson Review* (New York), 1949–50.

——, *Recollections of James Joyce, by His Brother*, 1941. New York: The James Joyce Society, 1950.

——, 'Joyce's Dublin', *Partisan Review* (New York), vol.19, Jan.–Feb. 1952, pp.103–9.

——, 'The Background to *Dubliners*', *The Listener* (London), vol.51, 25 March 1954, pp.526–7.

——, *My Brother's Keeper*. Edited with an introduction by Richard Ellmann. Preface by T.S. Eliot. London: Faber and Faber, 1958.

——, *The Complete Dublin Diary of Stanislaus Joyce*. Edited by George Healey. Ithaca: Cornell University Press, 1971.

Joyce, Patrick Weston, *The Origin and History of Irish Names of Places*. 3 vols. London: Longmans, 1898–1913.

Joyce, Weston St John, *The Neighbourhood of Dublin*. (Second edition (enlarged).) Dublin: M.H. Gill, 1921.

Kain, Richard M., *Fabulous Voyager: James Joyce's 'Ulysses'*. (New edition.) New York: The Viking Press, 1959.

——, *Dublin in the Age of William Butler Yeats and James Joyce*. (New edition.) Newton Abbott: David and Charles, 1972.

——, 'An interview with Carola Giedion-Welcker and Maria Jolas', *James Joyce Quarterly* (Tulsa), vol.11. no.2, Winter 1974, pp.94–122.

Kearney, Colbert, 'The Joycead', *Coping with Joyce*, edited by Morris Beja and Shari Benstock. Columbus: Ohio State University, 1989, pp.53–72.

Kee, Robert, *The Green Flag*. London: Chatto and Windus, 1956.

Kelly, William Patrick, *Schoolboys Three*. London: Downey, 1895.

Kenner, Hugh, *Dublin's Joyce*. London: Chatto and Windus, 1956.

Kettle, Thomas, [Review of *Chamber Music*] *Freeman's Journal*, 1 June 1907, p.5.

Krause, David, *Sean O'Casey – The Man and the Work*. London: Mac-Gibbon and Kee, 1960.

Laing, R.D., *The Divided Self*. London: Tavistock Publications, 1960.

——, *The Politics of the Family*. London: C.B.C. Publications, 1969.

——, *The Politics of Experience*. Harmondsworth: Penguin Books, 1969.

Lamb, Charles, *Adventures of Ulysses*. Edited, with introduction and notes, by John Cooke. Dublin: Browne and Nolan, [1892].

Larbaud, Valéry, 'James Joyce', *Nouvelle Revue Française* (Paris) April 1922.

——, 'A propos de James Joyce', *Nouvelle Revue Française* (Paris), January 1925.

Lennon, Michael J., 'James Joyce'. *Catholic World* (New York) vol.132, no.792, March 1931, pp.641–52.

Levenson, Leah, *With Wooden Sword. A Portrait of Francis Sheehy-Skeffington, Militant Pacifist*. Dublin: Gill and Macmillan, 1983.

Levenson, Samuel, *James Connolly: A Biography*. London: Martin, Brian & O'Keeffe, 1973.

Levin, Harry, *James Joyce, a critical introduction*. London: Faber and Faber, 1944; 1960.

Leslie, Sir Shane:, *Edward Tennyson Reed. A Memoir*. London: Heinemann, 1957.

Lewis, Sir George Cornewall, *Local Disturbances in Ireland*. London, 1836.

Lewis, Wyndham, 'An analysis of the mind of James Joyce', *Time and Western Man*. New York, 1928.

Lidderdale, Jane and Nicholson, Mary, *Dear Miss Weaver*. London: Faber and Faber, 1970.

Litz, Walton A., *The Art of James Joyce: Method and Design in 'Ulysses' and 'Finnegans Wake'*. London: Oxford University Press, 1964.

Lobner, Corinna del Greco, *James Joyce's Italian Connection*. Iowa City: University of Iowa Press, 1989.

Loyola, Ignatius, *Obras Completas de San Ignacio de Loyola*. (Edicion Manual.) Madrid: Biblioteca de Autores Cristianos, 1952.

Lyons, F.S.L., *The Irish Parliamentary Party*. London, 1951.

——, 'James Joyce's Dublin', *Twentieth Century Studies*, vol.4. November 1970, pp.6–25.

——, *Parnell*. London, 1978.

Lyons, J.B., *James Joyce and Medicine*. Dublin: The Dolmen Press, 1973.

——, *The Enigma of Tom Kettle*. Dublin: The Glendale Press, 1983.

——, *Thrust Syphilis Down to Hell*. Dublin: The Glendale Press, 1988.

Lyster, Thomas W.(ed.), *Select Poetry for Young Students*. Dublin: Browne and Nolan, 1893.

Macalister, R.A.S., *The Secret Languages of Ireland*. Cambridge: at the University Press, 1937.

McAlmon, Robert, (Revised and with supplementary chapters by Kay Boyle), *Being Geniuses Together, 1921–1930*. London: Hogarth Press, 1984.

McCarthy, Michael J., *Priests and People in Ireland*. Dublin: Hodges Figgis, 1902.

MacCarvill, Eileen, *Les années de formation de James Joyce à Dublin*. *Archives des lettres modernes*, no.12, Mai 1958.

——, 'James Joyce at University', *St Stephen's* (Dublin), Michaelmas 1960.

——, *Triv and Quad: James Joyce Examined*. Unpublished MSS, Dublin.

McCready, C.T., *Dublin Street Names Dated and Explained*. Dublin, 1892.

Mac Cóil, Liam, *The Book of Blackrock*. (Second edition.) Blackrock: Carraig Books, 1981.

MacDonagh, Donagh, 'The Lass of Aughrim, or the betrayal of James Joyce' in *The Celtic Master* (edited by Maurice Harmon). Dublin: The Dolmen Press, 1969.

McKenna, Lambert, *The Life and Works of the Rev. James Aloyius Cullen S.J.* London: Longmans, 1924.

McLuhan, Herbert Marshall, 'Joyce, Aquinas, and the Poetic Process', *Renascence* (Milwaukee), vol.IV, 1951.

McLuhan, Herbert Marshall, 'James Joyce; Trivial and Quadrivial', *Thought* (New York), 1953.

MacLysaght, Edward, *Irish Families*. Dublin, 1959.

McMillan, Dougald, *Transition: The History of a Literary Era 1927–1938*. London: Calder and Boyars, 1975.

MacNicholas, John, *James Joyce's 'Exiles': A Textual Companion*. New York: Garland, 1979.

Maddox, Brenda, *Nora. A Biography of Nora Joyce*. London: Hamish Hamilton, 1988. An American edition was published (Houghton, Mifflin) with the subtitle 'The Real Life of Molly Bloom'. Appeared in 1988.

Magalaner, Marvin, 'James Mangan and Joyce's Dedalus Family', *Philological Quarterly*, vol.31, Oct. 1952, pp.363–71.

——, *Time of Apprenticeship. The Fiction of the Young James Joyce*. London, New York and Toronto: Abelard-Schumann, 1959.

Magalaner, Marvin and Kain, Richard M., *Joyce: The Man, the Work, the Reputation*. New York: New York University Press, 1956; London: John Calder, 1957.

Mahony, Francis S., *The Works of Fr. Prout*. Edited with a biographical note by John Kent. London: Routledge, 1897.

Manganiello, Dominic, *Joyce's Politics*. London: Routledge & Kegan Paul, 1980.

Marcus, Steven, *The Other Victorians*. London: Weidenfeld and Nicolson, 1966.

Martyn, Edward, *The Dream Physician*. Dublin: The Talbot Press, 1915; London: Duckworth & Co., 1918.

Mayoux, Jean-Jacques, *James Joyce*. Paris: Gallimard, 1965.

Melchiori, Giorgio, *Joyce in Rome*. Roma: Bulzoni, 1984.

Mercanton, Jacques, *Les heures de James Joyce*. New edition. Arles: Actes Sud, 1988.

Mercier, Vivian, *The Irish Comic Tradition*. Oxford: Clarendon Press, 1962.

Mercure de France (Paris), Joyce Number with contributions by Sylvia Beach, Adrienne Monnier and Stuart Gilbert, no.1041, 1 May 1950.

Meyers, Jeffrey, 'James and Nora Joyce' in *Married to Genius*. New York: Barnes and Noble.

Mikhail, E.H., *James Joyce: Interviews and Recollections*. Foreword by Frank Delaney. London: Macmillan, 1990.

Mitchell, Flora, *Vanishing Dublin*. Dublin: Allen Figgis, 1966.

Mizener, Arthur, *The Cornell Joyce Collection, given to Cornell University by William G. Mennen*. Ithaca: Cornell University Press, 1958.

Mlakar, Stefan, *Ancient Pula*. Pula: Archaeological Museum of Istria, 1972.

Moore, George, *Vain Fortune*. London, 1895.

——, *The Untilled Field*. London: Fisher Unwin, 1903.

Morgan, Austen, *James Connolly. A political biography*. Manchester: Manchester U.P., 1988.

Morrisey, Thomas, *Towards a National University. William Delany S.J.* Dublin: Wolfhound Press, 1983.

Morse, J. Mitchell, *The Sympathetic Alien. James Joyce and Catholicism*. New York: New York University Press, 1959.

Morse, J. Mitchell, 'Molly Bloom revisited', in *A James Joyce Miscellany (Second series)*, edited by Marvin Magalaner. Carbondale: Southern Illinois University Press, 1958.

Murray, John (ed.), *A Handbook for Rome and Its Environs*. London: John Murray, 1881.

Myers, Frederic W.H., *Human Personality and Its Survival of Bodily Death*. London: Longmans, 1903.

Newman, John Henry, *Characteristics from the Writings of John Henry Newman*. Edited by W.S. Lilly. London: Kegan Paul and Co., 1874.

Nicolson, Harold, *The Desire to Please*. London: Constable, 1943.

Noël, Lucie, *James Joyce and Paul L. Léon: The Story of a Friendship*. New York: Gotham Book Mart, 1950.

Noon, William T., *Joyce and Aquinas*. New Haven: Yale University Press, 1957.

———, 'Joyce and Catholicism', *James Joyce Review* (New York), vol.1, no.4, 15 December 1957.

———, 'James Joyce: Unfacts, Fiction, and Facts', *Proceedings of the Modern Language Association* (New York) LXXVI, no.3, June 1961. Critical review of Ellmann's *James Joyce*.

O'Brien, Conor Cruise, *Parnell and His Party 1881–1890*. Oxford: Clarendon Press, 1957.

O'Brien, Darcy, *The Conscience of James Joyce*. Princeton: Princeton University Press, 1968.

———, 'Some determinants of Joyce's views on sex and love', in *New Light on Joyce from the Dublin Symposium* (ed. Fritz Senn). Bloomington: University of Indiana, 1972.

O'Brien, R. Barry, *The Life of Parnell*. London, 1898.

O'Connor, Frank, *The Lonely Voice*. London: Macmillan, 1963.

O'Connor, Ulick, *Oliver St. John Gogarty: A Poet and his Times*. London: Jonathan Cape, 1964.

———, *The Gresham Hotel 1865–1965*. Dublin: The Gresham Hotel, 1965.

———, (ed.), *The Joyce We Knew*. Cork: The Mercier Press, 1967.

———, (ed.), [Recollections of Joyce] in *The Joyce We Knew*. Cork: The Mercier Press, 1967.

O'Donnell, E.E., *The Annals of Dublin – Fair City*. Dublin: Wolfhound, 1987.

O'Duffy, R.J., *Historic Graves in Glasnevin Cemetary*. Dublin: James Duffy & Co., 1915.

O'Dwyer, Frederick, *Lost Dublin*. Gill and Macmillan, 1981.

O'Hart, John, *Irish Pedigrees; or, The Origin and Stem of the Irish Nation*. Dublin: M.H. Gill and Son, 1881.

O'Kelly, Seamus, *The Weaver's Grave*. Illustrated by Jack B. Yeats. Dublin: The Talbot Press, 1922.

O Laoi, Padraic, *Nora Barnacle Joyce*. Galway: Kenny's Bookshops, 1982.

O'Neill, M.I., 'The Joyces in the Holloway Diaries', in *A James Joyce Miscellany*, ed. Marvin Magalaner. Carbondale, Ill.: University of Southern Illinois Press, 1959.

Opler, Marvin K., 'Schizophrenia and Culture', *Scientific American* (New York), vol.197, August 1957, pp.103–112.

O'Shannon, Cathal, 'New Light on Joyce', *Evening Press* (Dublin), 27 April 1956. [Petronius Ryan]

———, 'Seed Cake for Tea', *Irish Independent* (Dublin), 12 February 1965, p.13.

Ovid, *The Metamorphoses*. Translated, and with an introduction, by Horace Gregory. New York: The Viking Press, 1958.

Paris, Jean, *Joyce par lui-même*. Paris: Éditions du Seuil, 1957.

Pearl, Cyril, *Dublin in Bloomtime: The City James Joyce Knew*. London: Angus and Robertson, 1969.

Perry, P.J. (ed.), *British Agriculture, 1875–1914*. London, 1973.

Pigott, Richard, *Personal Recollections of an Irish National Journalist*. Cork: Tower Books, 1979. (First edition 1882.)

Pinguentini, Gianni, *James Joyce in Italia*. Verona: Ghidini e Fiorini, 1966.

Pollack, Harry J., 'The girl Joyce did not marry', *James Joyce Quarterly*, vol.4, no.4, Summer 1967, pp.255–257.

Potts, Willard (ed.), *Portraits of the Artist in Exile*. Dublin: Wolfhound, 1979.

———, 'Joyce's Notes on the Gorman Biography', *Icarb*, vol.4. no.2, Spring–Summer 1981, pp.83–99.

Pound, Ezra, *Pound/Joyce: The Letters of Ezra Pound to James Joyce*. Edited by Forrest Read. London: Faber and Faber, 1967.

Power, Arthur, *From the Old Waterford House*. Waterford: The Carthage Press, 1940.

———, 'The James Joyce Exhibition in Paris', *Envoy* (Dublin), vol.1. no.3. February 1950, pp.49–56.

———, *Conversations with James Joyce* (edited by Clive Hart). London: Millington Books, 1974.

Radek, Karl, 'James Joyce or Socialist Realist?' in *Problems of Soviet Literature* (ed. A. Zhdanov and others). New York: International Publishers, 1935.

Raleigh, John Henry, *The Chronicles of Leopold and Molly Bloom*. Berkeley: University of California Press, 1977.

Reynolds, Mary T.,"Joyce and Nora – The Indispensable Countersign', *Sewanee Review*, LXXII, Winter 1964, pp.29–64.

———, *Joyce and Dante: The Shaping Imagination*. Princeton: Princeton University Press, 1981.

Richards, Grant, in 'Grant Richards to James Joyce' edited by Robert Scholes. *Studies in Bibliography*, (Charlottesville, Virginia) vol.16, 1963, pp.139–60.

Ridgeway, William, *The Early Age of Greece*. London, 1900.

Rogers, W.G., *Ladies Bountiful*. London: Gollancz, 1968.

Rogers, W.R., 'Joyce's Funeral', *Irish Times* (Dublin), 20 June 1964.

———(ed.), *Irish Literary Portraits*. London: British Broadcasting Corporation, 1972.

Ruskin, John, *Mornings in Florence*. Orpington: George Allen, 1875.

Russell, John and Vera, 'Death in Zürich', *Sunday Times* (London), 17 January 1965.

Ryan, John (ed.), *A Bash in the Tunnel: James Joyce by the Irish*. London and Brighton: Clifton Books, 1970.

——, (ed.) 'James Joyce – The Internationalist' in *A Bash in the Tunnel*. Brighton: London: Clifton Books, 1970.

Sacher-Masoch, Leopold von, (tr.)*Venus in Furs*. With an interpretation by Gilles Deleuze. London: Faber and Faber, 1972.

Saddlemeyer, Anne (ed.), *The Collected Letters of J. M. Synge*. Vol.I. London: Oxford University Press, 1982.

Scheper-Hughes, Nancy, *Saints, Scholars and Schizophrenics: Mental Illness in Rural Ireland*. Berkeley: University of California Press, 1979.

Schiff, Gert, 'Dublin and James Joyce', *Merian* (Hamburg), vol.12, no.4, 1959.

Scholes, Robert E., *The Cornell Joyce Collection: a Catalogue*. Ithaca, N. Y.: Cornell University Press, 1961.

Scholes, Robert E. and Kain, Richard M., *The Workshop of Daedalus*. Evanston, Ill.: Northwestern University Press, 1965.

Schwickerath, Robert, 'Ratio Studiorim' in *Catholic Encyclopedia*, 1911 edition, vol.12, pp.654–7.

Semple, Maurice, *Some Galway Memories*. Galway: Published by the author, 1969.

Shechner, Mark, *Joyce in Nighttown*. Berkeley: University of California Press, 1974.

Sheehy, Eugene, *May It Please the Court*. Dublin: C. J. Fallon, 1951.

Slater's Royal Directory of Ireland. Microfiche edition, 1848, 1880, 1894.

Somerville, Edith Œ. and Ross, Martin, *The Real Charlotte*. London: Ward and Downey, 1894.

Soupault, Philippe, *Souvenirs de James Joyce*. Paris: Charlot, 1945. (First edition: Algiers *c.* 1943.)

Staley, Thomas, 'James Joyce in Trieste', *The Georgia Review*, vol.16, October 1962, pp.446–49.

——, 'Composition of Place: Joyce and Trieste', *Modern British Literature*, vol.5, 1980, pp.3–9.

Stanford, W.B., 'The Mysticism that Pleased Him', *Envoy* (Dublin), April 1951, pp.62–69.

——, *The Ulysses Theme*. Oxford: Basil Blackwell, 1954.

——, *Ireland and the Classical Tradition*. Dublin: Allen Figgis, 1976.

Stark, Helmuth, 'Eine Begegnung aus dem Jahr 1915', *Akzente* (München), no.2, 1961.

Strong, L.A.G., *The Sacred River. An Approach to Joyce*. London: Methuen, 1949.

Sullivan, Donal, M. P., *The Story of Room 15*. Dublin: The National Press, 1891. (Reprinted from *The National Press*, Nov. 21 to Dec. 5 1891.)

Sullivan, Kevin, *Joyce Among the Jesuits*. New York: Columbia University Press, 1958.

Svevo, Italo, *James Joyce*. Translated by Stanislaus Joyce. (New edition.) San Francisco, City Lights Books, 1969.

Tierney, Mark, *Croke of Cashel. The Life of Archbishop Thomas William Croke 1832–1902*. Dublin: Gill & Macmillan, 1976, pp 28–29.

Thom's Official Dublin Directory. Dublin: Alex. Thom & Co., 1844–1966.

Thornton, Weldon, *Allusions in Ulysses*. Chapel Hill: University of North Carolina Press, 1968; New York: Simon and Schuster, 1969.

Tindall, William York, *James Joyce. His Way of Interpreting the Modern World*. New York: Scribner's, 1966.

———, *The Joyce Country*. Enlarged edition. New York: Schocken Books, 1966.

———, *A Reader's Guide to Finnegans Wake*. London: Thames and Hudson, 1969.

Tomkins, Calvin, *Living Well is the Best Revenge. Two Americans in Paris 1921–1923*. London: André Deutsch, 1972.

Torchiana, Donald, *Backgrounds to 'Dubliners'*. Boston: Allen and Unwin, 1986.

Touring Club of Italy, *Venezia Giulia e Friulia* (vol.21, *Attraverso d'Italia*). Milano, 1955; Trieste, pp.159–187.

Trilling, Lionel, 'James Joyce in his letters'. *Commentary* (New York), February 1968.

Troy, William, 'Stephen Dedalus and James Joyce', *The Nation* (New York), vol.138, 14 February 1934, pp.187–8.

Tuoni, Dario de, *Ricordo di Joyce a Trieste*. Milano: All'Insegna del Pesce d'Oro, 1966.

Tynan, Katharine, *Twenty-Five Years: Reminiscences*. London: Smith, Elder & Co., 1913.

Ussher, Arland, *The Face and Mind of Ireland*. London: Gollancz, 1949.

———, *Three Great Irishmen. Shaw, Yeats, Joyce*. London: Victor Gollancz, 1952.

Vance, Eileen, [Recollections quoted by Pollack], *James Joyce Quarterly* (Tulsa), vol.4. no.4, Summer 1967.

Wade, Allan (ed.), *The Letters of W.B. Yeats*. London: Rupert Hart-Davis, 1954.

Wall, Maureen, 'Catholics in Economic Life', in L.M. Cullen (ed.), *The Formation of the Irish Economy*. Cork: The Mercier Press, 1969.

Walsh, Louis J., 'With Joyce and Kettle at U.C.D.' *Irish Digest* (Dublin), vol.12, June 1942, pp.27–29.

West, Rebecca, *The Strange Necessity*. Garden City: Doubleday and Doran, 1928.

———, *Black Lamb and Grey Falcon*. New York: The Viking Press, 1941.

Weygandt, Cornelius, *Irish Plays and Playwrights*. Boston: Houghton, Mifflin, 1913, pp.121–122.

Wilson, Edmund, *Axel's Castle*. New York: Scribner's Sons, 1931.

———, 'The Dream of H.C. Earwicker' in *The Wound and the Bow*. Boston: Houghton Mifflin, 1941.

NOTES ON SOURCES

To keep these references to the minimum I have noted mainly manuscript, archival or obscure sources. It should be clear from the text what source in the bibliography has been used. Aside from the biographies and memoirs listed there, I have relied heavily throughout the book on the three volumes of Joyce's letters edited by Stuart Gilbert (*Ls* I) and by Richard Ellmann (*Ls* II and *Ls* III): in these James Joyce (with the able assistance of his editors) writes his own life better than any biographer could.

Other abbreviations: *DD* = *The Complete Dublin Diary* and *MBK* = *My Brother's Keeper*, both by Stanislaus Joyce; *SH* = *Stephen Hero*; *PSW* = *Poems and Shorter Writings*; *U* = *Ulysses*; *CW* = *Critical Writings*; *Sd Ls* = *Selected Letters*; *FJ* = *Freeman's Journal*; *DNB* = *Dictionary of National Biography*. The Registry of Deeds for Ireland = Reg. Deeds; the National Archives of Ireland (a unified collection in two repositories) = Nat. Arch; the National Library of Ireland = Nat. Lib.; RCPI = Royal College of Physicians of Ireland.

Preface – *p.1* Among the biographies of Joyce the very excellent book by J.B. Lyons, *James Joyce and Medicine* (1974), should also be noted, as his approach brings into perspective many facets of Joyce's life; *p.4* Candlemas is more properly the Feast of the Purification of the Virgin, marking the Presentation of Jesus in the Temple. It is not, as Ellmann thinks, the Feast of St Brigid.

Prologue – *p.5* described: *Ls* I, p.82; *p.9* Hella Elzholz: *James Joyce, The Lost Notebook*, ed. Danis Rose and John O'Hanlon, p.23; *p.9*

Anderson (1930), p.214; *p.10* contempt: see Rebecca West (1941); *p.11* revenge himself: Anderson (1930) p.214; *p.11* Lawrence: Bruce Arnold (1991), p.46; *p.12* Dublin sales: P.S. O'Hegarty mentions these imports in his Joyce bibliography; *p.12* censorship: Adams (1968), deals dispassionately with the actions of the Irish Censorship Board; *p.14* Sheehy Skeffington's visit is described by Andree Sheehy Skeffington in *Skeff* (Dublin, 1991), pp.62–63; *p.14* Anderson: op. cit., p.246ff; *p.15* an Irish writer: Clarke (1968), p.96; *p.16* John Joyce, *Joyce Yearbook* (1949), MacAlmon and Boyle (1975), Probate papers Estate of John Joyce 1932, Nat. Arch.; *p.18* ulcer: J. B. Lyons (1974) discusses in detail Joyce's health; *p.19* Hunter: death cert., and below, p.228.

Chapter One – *p.23* Flynn details from directories, Registrar General's records, parish records, *MBK*, and 'The Dead', and Fergus McNestry interview; *p.23* Catholic hands: Fagan (1986), p.4; *p.26* O'Connell: Father Edward O'Connell was related to a Father Charles O'Connell P.P. of the Dublin Diocese who died in 1871; *p.26* Balfe: Gilbert (1951 ed.) p.241; D'Arcy: Adams (1968), p.66; *p.26* Tallon: Census return 1901, 41 Aughrim Street; *p.27*: details of Leitrim provided by Michael Whelan; *p.27* literary talent: *Leitrim Advertiser* 23 May 1912, also see Hamell, *Maynooth Ordinations* (1984), *Catholic Directory 1912*, obits., Collins, *Blarney Magazine* (1951), *Ls* II, 196; *p.28* Eagle House: now Morris's, 107 Terenure Road North; *p.29* claimed: *SH*, p.138; *p.30* 'Garryowen': details in a letter from Sec. Irish Setter Club; *p.31* marriage: I am informed by a learned theologian, Father Tom O'Loughlin, that such a marriage was within Catholic Church law, though not Anglican custom; *p.31* Begge's: his career is outlined in his death notice in the *FJ* 15 March 1894; *p.32* Joyce: details in O'Hart; masons: Kearney, p.59; *p.33* land: Charles Chenevix Trench in lit.; *p.33* caste: *Ls II*, p.106; *p.34* sentenced to death: Broeker, pp.132–6, and Lewis on background; *p.34* Boreen: Kearney, op. cit.; *p.35* revisit: a postcard from Fermoy to James Joyce is in Cornell; *p.35*: White Street: Reg. Deeds 1830; *p.36*: lease and sale: Reg. Deeds 1843/18/40; *p.37* Winthrop Street address is given in period directories; *p.37* Presentation Convent: quoted by Kearney, op. cit. p.72, also Superior in lit.; *p.38* married: date in cert. supplied from parish records; *p.38* settlement: Reg. Deeds 1848/6/52; snout: *DD*, p.37; *p.39* sale of lands: Reg. Deeds 1852/31/130; *p.40* baptismal cert: of Charles Joyce, see below; *p.40* obedience: Tierney (1976), p.29; *p.41* pilot boats: this may have been while the family summered at Clifton Terrace, Glenbrook, Monkstown, where they were living in 1866; *p.41* fell ill: details from death cert.; *p.41* new directors: see list in Ulick O'Connor, *Gresham Hotel* (1962); *p.41* portraits: details of painters from W.G. Strickland *Dictionary of Irish Painters* (1913); *p.42* Queen's College: details supplied by Virginia Teahan, Archivist, UCC; *p.42* chancre: Walsh, *Irish Medical Times* 9 May 1975 p.22; *p.43* audience: *Cork Constitution* 12 March and 17 April 1869; *p.43* peers: J. Pope-Hennessy, *Veranda* (1964), p.19 on Cork youth; *p.44* Clerys: Costello and Farmar, *In the Heart of the City* (1992) on history of firm; *p.44* Cullen: Larkin passim; *p.45* Alleyn: Reg. Deeds 1874/3/180, 1874/23/190; *p.46* mortgage: Reg. Deeds 1876/12/125; *p.46* Master of the Rolls: *Irish Times* 2 Feb. 1878; *p.46* buried: death act from Mairie de Menton and Will Index 1878, Nat. Arch.; *p.46* distillery: details from Nicholas Morgan, company archivist, Distillers Co., Edinburgh, also William H. Ross, 'History of the Company: Purchase of Phoenix Park Distillery', *D.C.L. Gazette*, July 1923, pp.82ff.; *p.47* John Murray: marriage notice *FJ* 24 Nov. 1881; *p.47* office: *Thom's Directory* 1880; *p.47* election: John Joyce interview (1949); *p.47* franchise: Cannadine and his sources; *p.48* musical culture: Gilbert (1952 ed.) ch.11, p.240; *p.49* romances: *MBK*, p.58; *p.50*: child: named in death notice, *FJ* 2 Dec. 1880; *p.51* married life: *U*, p.162; *p.51* rent roll Reg. Deeds 1881/29/41; *p.52* nominating: CSORP 9806/1881, Nat. Arch.; *p.52* appointment: CSORP 17078, 24017, 24147/1881, Nat. Arch.; *p.53* Collector-General: Reg. Deeds 1881/43/214 [release 1883/38/192]; *p.53* baptism: cert. St Joseph's.

Chapter Two – *p.57* my life: *Ls* II p.22, *Ls* III p.212; *p.58*: control: Leslie (1957), p.39; *p.61* mortgage: for convenience those traced are listed here Reg. Deeds 1882/34/133, 1883/10/231 [release 1887/21/229], 1883/45/50 [release 1887/21/230], 1883/51/32 [release 1887/21/231], 1884/38/261 [release 1894], 1887/23/187 [release 1893], 1890/17/70; *p.62* will: Index to Wills 1862, Nat. Arch.; *p.63* Danby: details from Paula Hicks, National Gallery, also W.G. Strickland *Dictionary of Irish Artists* (1913); *p.64* Inchicore: information from Community; *p.65* godfather: baptismal cert. from Rathmines Parish; *p.66* country: Cannadine, p.39, p.169; *p.67* footman: detail from M.J. Lennon, who knew Joyce at college; *p.67* mortgage: Reg. Deeds 1887/23/187; *p.67* baptism: cert. Bray parish;

p.68 Blooms: details from records of Reg. General, Hyman (1972) pp.139, 167, 175 in part; *p.70* connection: see student lists in Corcoran (1932).

Chapter Three – based on Gorman, Corcoran, Costello, Sullivan, Bradley, and materials in Clongowes archives; *p.72* train: see Boyd-Barrett (1932); *p.75* Daly: information from Dr John and Mrs Marion Litton; *p.80* rector: *Ls* I 3 March 1890; *p.83* poems: T.W. Lyster (1894); *p.85* uneventful: Sullivan (1958), p.14.

Chapter Four – Family details largely from *MBK*; Igoe (1990) for some local details; *p.87* at Bray: Gorman, p.20; *p.87* Kelly: Valuation Office records; *p.89* weakling: *MBK*, p.39; *p.89* George: cert. Bray parish; *p.88* case of Mr Joyce: CSORP Index; *p.90* towel: *MBK* p.27; *p.91* servants: family details from *MBK* and certs.; *p.95* witnesses: Bray Parish records; *p.96* Bridgeman: Reg. Deeds 1890/17/185; *p.97* debates: Sullivan (1891) and *The Story of the Parnell Crisis* (1891); *p.99* Murray: death cert.

Chapter Five – See Chapter Three sources and *MBK*; *p.101* enrolled: Intermediate Board Papers 1891, Nat. Arch.; *p.104* Parnell's hand: see *FJ* 6 Oct. 1893; *p.103* convent: so Stanislaus claimed, but Sister Elizabeth Graham tells me no records survive; *p.104* Mrs Conway: death cert. and Index to Wills, Nat. Arch.; *p.104* Leoville: Hutchins, Igoe and visit: *p.105* Raynold: birth certs. and Census returns 1901 and 1911, Carysfort Avenue.

Chapter Six – *p.114* Fitzgibbon Street: see *Slater's Directory* 1894 for exact location; *p.115* moved: see *Thom's Directory* for these years; *p.116* trams: timetable of Dublin United Tram Co., National Library; *p.116* Dodd: Reg. Deeds 1892/55/70; *p.117* pensioned off: CSORP 1893/11865; *p.118* sloppy: Dublin Corporation Reports II 1894, p.717; *p.119* Christian Brothers: I am told no records survive; *p.119* Dodd: Reg. Deeds 1893/5/272.

Chapter Seven – For Joyce's education see Sullivan and Bradley passim; *p.123* Dodd: Reuben Dodd jnr. interview; *p.123* Youghal: *Ls* I p.74; *p.124* Chief See.: CSORP 1893 under Joyce; *p.124* Thornton: cert. from Parish records; *p.125* sales: Reg. Deeds, 1894/11/292, 1894/12/185, 1894/12/187, 1894/14/121, 1894/22/232;

p.125 Murray: death cert.; *p.128* Intermediate: details from Intermediate Calendars for respective years; *p.128* Dempsey: Gorman p.41–42; *p.129* Dr Redmond: information from Robert Mills, RCPI Lib.; *p.129* Morron: see *Thom's Directory* 1893; *p.132* Austin: see F.C. Benson, *As We Were,* and *DNB.*

Chapter Eight – *p.134* another Joyce: Index of Wills 1898, Nat. Arch., and *Burke's Peerage* under Mountmorres; *p.135* sexual experiences: compare Ellmann (1982 ed.) pp.48, 418; *p.136* Kelly: death cert. and obits. *Daily Independent* 14 and 19 April, *United Irishman* 18 April 1896; *p.137* Grogan: information City Archives and *City of Dublin Public Libraries – Catalogues 1884–1905* [A66 60993]; *p.140* Sheehy: Eugene Sheehy (1954), Sheehy Skeffington (1991) and Levenson (1983); *p.142* Kempis: comments from Father Tom O'Loughlin; *p.143* Harding: *MBK* p.61 *Ls* II, p.143; Horace: quoted in Gorman, p.45.

Chapter Nine – *p.149* writing: *Ls* II, p.79; *p.151 Sweet Brier*: see Allardyce Nicholl, *History of Nineteenth Century Drama* for details, and Holloway mss diary, Nat. Lib., under date for Dublin production; *p.152* Florence: Ruskin (1874), p.123; *p.153* soothed: *PSW*, p.212.

Chapter Ten – *p.157* Curran: Curran (1968), pp.4, 105ff; *p.158* university: see *A Page of Irish History* passim; *p.159* friends: Byrne (1953), for Kettle see Lyons (1983), for Skeffington Levenson (1983) and Sheehy Skeffington (1991), Clancy, family interviews; *p.159* courses: details from calendars of the Royal University 1898–1903; *p.160* L. and H.: Meenan ed. (1956) passim; *p.161* dissent: Holloway *Diary* ed. Hogan and O'Neill, p.6; *p.162 Disease of the Ox*: Byrne (1953), p.28; *p.163* Hughes: Census 1901 8 Royal Terrace 1, marriage cert. Robert Eugene Hughes 1898; *p.163* Bengal Terrace: *Evening Telegraph* 21 Oct. 1899, also *Evening Herald* 12 Nov. 1957, p.6; *p.251* Maria O'Donohoe: death cert.; *p.164* emulation: Sullivan (1958), p.198; *p.166* Gaelic League paper: *An Claidheamh Soluis* 2 June 1900, pp.181–183; *p.167* Mullingar: these visits and *SH* are discussed in Leo Daly (1975).

Chapter Eleven – *p.168* Archer: *Ls* II, p.7; *p.169* Flower: K. P. O'Rourke, *Dublin Historical Record*, vol. 31, no 3, 1977, pp.106–108;

p.172 Ibsen: text in *Ls* I, p.51; *p.174* publish them: *Ls* II p.9; *p.177* George's death: dates (which differ from Ellmann) from death cert.; *p.178* Russell: *Ls* II p.12, Holloway *Diary*, p.202, Gorman p.74, and A.E. intro, to J. O'Neill *Land Under England* (1935); *p.179* triduum: *DD* p.104; *p.179* mortgage: Reg. Deeds 1902/75/55, 1902/89/283, 1903/29/115 – see also p.321; *p.272* after death: Estate of John Joyce, Schedule of Assets 1932, Nat. Arch., with letter from Eagle Star Insurance; *p.180* Marsh's Library: *PSW*, p.214.

Chapter Twelve – Information on Mrs Meenan supplied by the late Prof. James Meenan, Mr Patrick Meenan and other members of the Meenan family; *p.185* remarkable piece of writing: *Ls* II, p.93; *p.185* after Christmas: *SH*, p.197ff; *p.186* Ellmann: *Ls* II, p.4, note 4; *p.187* women students: see *A Page of Irish History* for lists; *p.188* Mary Cleary; details from Royal University Calendars and records, NUI, birth and marriage certs. and Meenan family; *p.190* spoke Irish: see Census return 1901 8 Royal Terrace; *p.190* reviews: these appeared in the first issues of *The Loreto Magazine, Loreto Archives,* Rathfarnham; *p.191* Curran: Special Collections, UCD.

Chapter Thirteen – Largely based on Joyce's own letters, *Ls* II, pp.18–41, the letters of John Synge and Gorman, ch. 3; *p.198* faith like mine: *Ls* I p.53; *p.201* Clerkenwell: see also Montague Williams Q.C., *Leaves of a Life* (1899), ch. 27; *p.203* My dear Jim: *Ls* II p.22; *p.204* Kenington: *PSW* p.195; *p.206* *Men and Women*: British Library catalogue; *p.207* Chown was *Siamese* and not identical with the *Cambodian* Rita Rasi Joyce knew in the 1920s who took the name of René-Ulysse [compare Gorman, p.323 and Ellmann, pp.126, 663]; *p.208* loan from Douce: Gorman, p.108; *p.208* Gigantic mists: *PSW*, p.197.

Chapter Fourteen – *p.210* meeting: Byrne (1953), p.84; *p.212* Myers: Blake in W.R. Rogers (1972), p.29.

Chapter Fifteen – Largely *Ls* I, pp.54–57, *Ls* II, pp.41–59; *p.214* iron bed: Gorman, p.113; *p.214* Bleak House: *DD* p.39; *p.214* Hardwicke St: this address though listed by Stanislaus for Ellmann is not among the homes Joyce himself lists in *FW*, and there is no documentary evidence in support of it; *p.214* not an artist: *DD*, p.2 note; *p.215* IRSP: the history is discussed in the several biographies of Connolly, all of which draw upon the papers of William O'Brien, Nat. Lib.; *p.215* socialism: see Gorman p.183ff; *p.216* reviews: in *CW*; *p.216* Dempsey: the postcard is in Cornell; *p.217* Browne: Stanford (1976), p.65ff provides a general account of his place in classical studies, but does not see the Joyce connection; Walter Leaf: *The Lost Notebook*, p.xxviiiff; *p.218* anti-semitism: for a general account see Hyman (1972), pp.212–217, 374, also CSORP Index 1903 and 1904 for papers on Jews in Ireland and CSORP 14788/1904; *p.219* 'A Portrait': reprinted in *PSW*; *p.219* lying auto-biography: *DD*, p.20; *p.221* literati: see L.M. Cullen, *Eason & Sons A History* (1989), pp.5–11 for details of rise in sales and background; *p.222* mortgage: Reg. Deeds 1903/74/178, sale of house 1905/48/142; *p.224* Holloway: *Diary*, p.40; *p.226* courtship: can best be followed in *Ls* II; *p.226* fight: Ellmann suggests this was the occasion on which he met Hunter, which seems impossible (see below *p.231*); *p.228* funeral: not mentioned in Ellmann, but see Adams (1962) p.62ff and *FJ* 14 July p.2; *p.229* Martello Tower: Ellmann (1969) gives a concise account of the tower's history; *p.230* Costello: after working in the Far East he died in Dublin in 1948, the *Medical Register* provides a résumé of his career; *p.230* Monto: details from Census returns for Tyrone St 1901 and 1911; *p.231ff* see *Ls* II and Gorman, Ch. four.

Chapter Sixteen – The research for this chapter was done in 1975–76 and draws on inquiries and interviews made in Galway and Dublin at this time. For some other details I have also drawn upon information from Maurice Semple, Padraic O Laoi (1982) and Brenda Maddox (1989); *p.239* convents and churches: M.J. McCarthy, *Priests and People in Ireland* (1902), p.265ff; *p.241* memories: notes to *Exiles*; *p.244* I am grateful to Violet Cunningham, Leo's daughter, for information about the Bodkin family; *p.246* Father Moran: details from *Ls* II, p.72, *Catholic Directories* for period and obit. in *Connaught Tribune*, 9 July 1923; *p.250* Holohan: mentioned by Joyce in a letter 7 Aug. 1909, *Sd Ls* p.158.

Chapter Seventeen – Based largely on *Ls* I, pp.59–63, *Ls* II, pp.66–144, Gorman and Ellmann; *p.259* polished looking glass: *Ls* I p.64.

Chapter Eighteen – based largely *Ls* II, pp.144–220; Murray's *Guide to Rome* and Baedeker for contemporary topographical details;

p.266 Socialist Conference: *The Times* (London) 9, 10, 11, 19 Oct. 1906; *p.267* Bombs: Joyce's own letters, *The Times* (London), 15 Oct., *Illustrated London News*, 24 Oct. 1906, and Gorman, p.184.

Chapter Nineteen – Largely *L* I, pp.65–67, *L* II, pp.220–228; Joyce's articles are all collected in *CW*, for the original versions see *Scritti Italiani*; *p.275* clarifying it: Gorman, p.196.

Chapter Twenty – *Ls* I, pp.68–69, Ls II, 228–296; *p.277*: articles in *CW* and in *Scritti Italiani*; *p.278* Hone: his recollections were written in 1951 for *Envoy*, his critical article is from 1923; *p.281* I have been frank: context in *Ls* II, pp.230–252, texts in *Sd Ls* pp.156–172; *p.284* Cosgrave: reports of death and inquest appeared in *Reynold's News* and several London and Dublin papers on 5 and 6 September 1926; *p.284* professorship: the NUI commenced in October 1909, under an act of 1908 – Kettle became Professor of National Economics; *p.286* Mr darling: *Ls* II, p.235; *p.287* My dear little Nora: *Ls* II, pp.236–7; *p.287* Holloway: *Diary*, p.130; *p.288* O'Donoghue: Joyce's letter LA 15/915 UCD Archives Department; *p.288* devoted to business: details of the *Volta* from a file in Liam O'Leary Irish Film Archive, Nat. Lib. and Liam O'Leary conversations; *p.290* Collinge: various interviews in Film Archive *Volta* file; *p.291* 'Opera' films: this was Patricia Hutchins's idea; *p.293* Charles Duff: in *Ireland and the Irish* (1952), pp.169–71.

Chapter Twenty-One – *Ls* II, pp.296–320; *p.298* grave of Shelley: notes to *Exiles*; *p.301* John Lane: see the introduction to his edition of Hermann Sudermann's novel, *The Song of Songs* (London, 1913).

Chapter Twenty-Two – *Ls* I, pp.72–82, *Ls* II, pp.320–341 and Gorman; *p.305* This lovely land: *CW*, p.242; *p.306* first edition: *Ls* I, p.71; *p.307* syphilis: for contemporary views on the disease see C.F. Marshall, M.D., *Syphilology and Venereal Disease* (London, 1914), pp.214–219, and its imitation of chronic alcoholism (p.219); *p.309* Dublin 1913: Arnold Wright (1914); *p.311* fond of Eileen: *Ls* II, p.331; *p.312* Brown, *Ireland in Fiction* (1919), p.149; *p.312* Martyn, *The Dream Physician* (1918), p.67; *p.314* generosity: Gorman, p.226; *p.316* Prince Hohenlohe: Bruni in Potts (1979), p.43; *p.316* Trieste: for this date see *Ls* I, p.82 compared with Gorman, p.229 and Ellmann (1982), p.386.

Appendix I – *p.318* theology: Lord Raglan, *Jocasta's Crime* (London, 1940), p.vii; *p.318* six in the morning: information from his daughter Eva Joyce, quoted in Ellmann (1982), p.642.

Family Trees – Dr Halliday Sutherland, quoted in D.B. Wyndham Lewis, *The Hooded Hawk or The Case of Mr Boswell* (London, 1946), pp.278–279; see also the general account in J.A. Fraser Roberts, *An Introduction to Medical Genetics*, Second Edition (London, 1959). Samuel Butler, too, has many things to say in *Life and Habit* [1878] and *Unconscious Memory* [1880] on 'Life as Memory' and the origins of personality, relevant to a study of Joyce.

ACKNOWLEDGEMENTS

I am grateful for their help and advice to the following people in Dublin and elsewhere: The Society of Authors as representatives of the Estate of James Joyce, for the use of materials still in copyright; Faber & Faber and the Viking Press for the use of materials from *The Letters of James Joyce* and *My Brother's Keeper* by Prof. Stanislaus Joyce; John Wyse Jackson and Bernard McGinley, who have laboured long to prevent me from committing too many outrageous solecisms; Kyle Cathie, my publisher, for her exemplary patience with a writer who prefered research to writing; and Jean Maund, for her heroic editing of my typescript; and to all the following (in alphabetical order):

Robert Allen, Dublin; Sister M. Angela Bolster, Diocesan Archivist, Cork; Bruce Bradley S.J., Belvedere College; Niall Bruncardi, Fermoy; Sister Mary Burke, Loretto Convent, Rathfarnham; Dr Frank Callanan; Mary Clarke, Dublin City Archives; Rory Costello, New York City; Mrs. Violet Cunningham, Galway; Dr Patricia Donlon, Director National Library of Ireland and her staff; Nodlaigh Hardiman, Dublin City Public Libraries; Mrs M. Harding, National Army Museum, London; Vivien Igoe, Dublin; Miss Norma Jessup, U.C.D.; Colbert Kearney, University College Cork; Dr J.B. Lyons, Hon. Librarian, Royal College of Surgeons, Dublin; C.J.F. McCarthy, Cork City; Rex Mackie, S.C., Dublin; Richard Mangan, Mander and Mitchenson Theatre Collection; Prof. T.A. Martin, University College Dublin; Robert Mills, Librarian Royal College of Physicians in Ireland; the late Prof. James Meenan and other members of his family; John Mullins, Reference Librarian, Cork City Library; Robert Nicholson, former curator James Joyce

ACKNOWLEDGEMENTS

Tower; the Director and staff, National Archives of Ireland, for access to and use of materials in their charge; Donal O'Donovan, Bray; Liam O'Leary, Irish Film Archive; Father Tom O'Loughlin, Arundel Diocese; Kevin O'Sullivan, Dublin; Father Stephen Redmond S.J., Provincial Assistant Archivist; Father Roland Burke Savage S.J., Clongowes Wood College; Dr Eamonn Sheehan, Kerry; Maurice Semple, Galway; Mrs Elizabeth Solterer, Washington, D.C., the heir of C.P. Curran, for the use of her father's papers (V.C.D.); Dr Peter van de Kamp, University College Dublin; Michael Whelan N.T., Aughavas, Leitrim; and many others, including the authors listed in the bibliography above, all of whom have my grateful thanks. I apologise to any copyright holders whom I have inadvertently overlooked, or failed to trace.

INDEX